THE NEWLY INDUSTRIALISING ECONOMIES OF EAST ASIA

The spectacular success of the NIEs of Korea, Taiwan, Hong Kong and Singapore has prompted debate on whether there is an East Asian growth model. This success has been the subject of much discussion and the already voluminous literature continues to grow at a rapid rate.

The Newly Industrialising Economies of East Asia is one of the first texts to synthesise work on the region. The authors discuss how much the countries do, in fact, have in common and analyse crucial issues such as the role of new technology, labour relations and industrial policy. In the course of this discussion, two competing paradigms become clear: the neoclassical approach which interprets the East Asian economic miracle as the predictable outcome of 'good' economic policies, and the statist perspective which draws attention to the central role of government in guiding East Asian economic development. The conclusions of this survey suggest that the available evidence does not vindicate extremes of either case. The distinctive feature of the book is that it seeks to highlight literature which has advanced our knowledge of the process of development in East Asia as well as identifying areas where current knowledge is lacking. From this evidence it appears that considerable uncertainties afflict such topical areas as trade liberalisation, financial liberalisation, the appropriate role of the state in 'late industrialisation', and the future evolution of the East Asian NIEs in an era of democratisation. Throughout the book the authors make a consistent effort to mix country-specific experiences with broader trends and fundamental themes.

Anis Chowdhury is Senior Lecturer in Economics at the University of Western Sydney, Australia. **Iyanatul Islam** is Senior Lecturer in Economics at Griffith University, Queensland, Australia. Both have taught and undertaken research at the National University of Singapore and therefore had the opportunity of witnessing at close quarters the unfolding of the East Asian economic miracle.

THE NEWLY
INDUSTRIALISING
ECONOMIES OF
EAST ASIA

Anis Chowdhury and Iyanatul Islam

London and New York

First published 1993
by Routledge
11 New Fetter Lane, London EC4P 4EE

Simultaneously published in the USA and Canada
by Routledge
29 West 35th Street, New York, NY 10001

Reprinted 1995

Typeset in Scantext September
by Leaper and Gard Ltd, Bristol
Printed and bound in Great Britain by
Mackays of Chatham PLC, Chatham, Kent

British Library Cataloguing in Publication Data
A catalogue record for this book is available from the British Library

Library of Congress Cataloging in Publication Data
has been applied for

ISBN 0–415–06876–2
ISBN 0–415–09749–5 (pbk)

CONTENTS

CONTENTS

FIGURES

TABLES

PREFACE

The success of the East Asian Newly Industrialising Economies (NIEs) of Korea, Taiwan, Hong Kong and Singapore is by now well known. Although it took nearly a decade for the development studies profession to recognise this phenomenon, the literature on the East Asian NIEs is voluminous and continues to grow at a rapid rate. This textbook survey attempts to take a fresh look at the relevant literature. One can discern two competing paradigms: the neoclassical approach, which interprets the East Asian economic miracle as the predictable outcome of 'good' economic policies; and the statist perspective which draws attention to the central role of the government in guiding East Asian economic development. The approach taken by this survey is eclectic, suggesting that the available evidence does not vindicate either of the extreme neoclassical and statist positions.

The distinctive feature of the book is that it seeks to highlight literature which has advanced our knowledge of the process of development in East Asia as well as identifying areas where current knowledge is lacking. Notwithstanding the confidence of some commentators, it seems that considerable uncertainties afflict such topical areas as trade liberalisation, financial liberalisation, the appropriate role of the state in 'late industrialisation' and the future evolution of the East Asian NIEs in an era of democratisation. Thus the present study can be seen as an attempt to blend country-specific experiences with fundamental themes in development studies.

Both of us had the rare opportunity to witness the unfolding of the East Asian economic miracle when we taught and undertook research at the National University of Singapore. The book has grown out of these experiences. It is primarily intended for the use of advanced undergraduates and graduate students in development studies. However, we believe that the book is sufficiently topical to appeal to academic practitioners interested in the region as well as policy makers seeking deeper insights into replicable models of successful development.

In writing this book, we have incurred an intellectual debt to many individuals – friends and colleagues with whom we shared our ideas in order to sharpen them. We wish to thank especially Professor H.W. Arndt of the Australian National University, Professor C.H. Kirkpatrick of the University of Bradford, Professor M.L. Treadgold and Mr G.T. Harris of the University of New England, each of whom has kindly read various chapters of the book. Their comments have been immensely useful in improving the quality of this book. The standard disclaimer applies: any remaining errors are the sole responsibility of the authors.

A substantial part of this book was written while one of the authors (A. Chowdhury) spent a period of study leave at the Development and Project Planning Centre (DPPC), University of Bradford, and thanks are due to both the University of New England for granting study leave and the DPPC for offering a visiting fellowship. We also wish to thank Routledge for accepting this book for publication.

Perhaps no acknowledgement is complete without a few words of appreciation for our families. We are indeed grateful to our wives and children for quietly enduring the loneliness during the arduous and seemingly endless hours we spent on this book. They have been understanding and loving. We dedicate this book to our loving families and to our wonderful parents who have been most kind and caring.

1

THE RISE OF THE EAST ASIAN NEWLY INDUSTRIALISING ECONOMIES

An overview

The spectacular economic performance of the four East Asian economies – Hong Kong, Korea, Singapore and Taiwan – since the 1960s is by now well known. Success always attracts attention. As Krause (1985: 3) notes, '[t]here would clearly be much less interest in the four Asian Newly Industrializing Countries (NICs) if they had not been so remarkably successful. They led the world and in recent years they have grown twice as fast as Japan, the most successful industrial country in the post-war era.' Several epithets have been used to dramatise this success. Woronoff (1986), for example, uses the term 'miracle economies'. Other popular labels include 'gang of four' or 'four little tigers'. A more neutral or generic term is 'newly industrialising economies' (NIEs) or 'newly industrialising countries (NICs).

Ironically, it took nearly a decade for the development economics profession to become aware of the East Asian ascendency. The pioneers of the profession, such as Chenery, Higgins and Rosenstein-Rodan, writing in the 1960s, did not include the four little tigers as part of their list of economies most likely to succeed (Hicks, 1989). Perhaps Hughes (1971) and Myint (1969) were among the first few economists who took note of the phenomenon of East Asian success and drew attention to Singapore and Hong Kong. One could argue that a paradigm shift took place around the late 1960s and 1970 with such publications as Balassa (1968), Keesing (1967) and Little *et al.* (1970) – see Arndt (1987b). This framework was subsequently applied to explain the economic performance of East Asian NIEs in the latter part of 1970s (e.g. Little, 1979; Chen, 1979; Balassa, 1980, 1981).

It would be fair to maintain that since the late 1970s the success stories of Hong Kong, Korea, Singapore and Taiwan have become entrenched as part of the folklore of development economics. This book takes a fresh look at the voluminous literature on the East Asian NIEs and attempts to sift rhetoric from reality. A consistent effort is made to blend the country-specific experiences with broader themes in development economics. Within this broad objective, the specific purpose of this chapter is to provide an empirical overview of the rise of

1

the East Asian NIEs. A useful way to start is to focus on the definition of the term NIE.

WHAT IS AN NIE?

There is no official definition or list of newly industrialising economies (Grimwade, 1989: 312). However, one can identify two broad aspects in the way the term is being used. The first, a comparative–static view, sees such economies occurring as an event in historical time and demarcates the phenomenon of industrialisation between pre and post Second World War. In that sense, countries which have been able to transform themselves in the post-war era into industrial economies where manufacturing plays an important role qualify as NIEs. Thus, Japan can be regarded as being the first of the post-war NIEs. They are 'new' in comparison with the 'old' industrialised countries of pre-war era. According to this view, industrialisation is a phenomenon, unique to specific conditions obtaining in particular countries at a particular point in time.

The second is a more dynamic and global definition and sees the emergence of the NIEs as an outcome of a changing world production structure corresponding to shifts in the international division of labour. To quote a leading author on the subject,

> These changes occur as a result of a generalized historical movement in which industrialized countries vacate intermediate sectors in industrial production in which advanced developing countries are currently more competitive and advanced developing countries, in turn, vacate more basic industrial sectors in which the next tier of developing countries have a relative advantage. This view, then, sees the process of industrialization as one of historical spread in which the number of NICs will continue to increase.
>
> (Bradford, 1982: 11)

How does one operationalise the definition of NIEs? Are there any *quantitative* criteria by which to classify economies at a particular point in time as NIEs? While there is some element of arbitrariness, the choice of criteria depends very much on the views one takes on development. For example, Turner (1982), working for the Royal Institute of International Affairs (RIIA) has used the sole criterion of shares in world trade in manufacturing and reduced the list of NIEs to eight core countries: South Korea, Taiwan, Hong Kong, Singapore, Brazil, Mexico, Argentina and India. Although trade may unleash forces of dynamism, this view is a static one as is evident from the following quote:

> To call such nations (Hong Kong's status is still colonial) 'NICs' is to pass no judgement about how dynamic their economies currently are. Instead, we reflect the fact that these are the eight largest exporters of manufactures in the non-European developing world.
>
> (Turner, 1982: 6)

2

Balassa (1980), working under the auspices of the World Bank, defines the newly industrialising countries (NICs) as developing countries that had per capita incomes in excess of $1,100 in 1978 and where the share of the manufacturing sector in the gross domestic product (GDP) was 20 per cent or higher in 1977. According to these criteria the NICs overlap with the upper ranges of the group of middle-income countries as defined in the *World Development Report*.

The Organisation for Economic Cooperation and Development (OECD, 1979) adopted a three-fold criterion to define a developing country as an NIE. Namely:

1 Fast growth in both the absolute level of industrial employment and the share of industrial employment in total employment.
2 A rising share of world exports of manufactures.
3 Fast growth in real per capita GDP such that the country was successful in narrowing the gap with the advanced industrialised countries.

Thus, the OECD (op. cit.) listed Spain, Portugal, Greece, Yugoslavia, Brazil, Mexico, Hong Kong, South Korea, Singapore and Taiwan as NICs. Britain's Foreign and Commonwealth Office (FCO) works with a wider definition and also includes Israel, Malta, Iran, Malaysia, Pakistan, the Philippines and Thailand in the list of NIEs. The FCO also suggests to include Poland, Rumania and Hungary in the list of NIEs. Others even include India and Argentina.

While Balassa, the OECD and the FCO see the emergence of NIEs as a dynamic phenomenon, none emphasises the *quality* of their development. This stems from a narrow view of development, taken to be largely synonymous with economic growth. In contrast, a wider view of development is taken here and the emphasis is on *qualitative* aspects of growth. In other words, an NIE is defined by asking the question, 'has the economic growth been associated with an enlargement of people's choices?' Thus, those developing countries are regarded as NIEs which have been able to break loose from the 'vicious circle of poverty' and 'take-off' from a 'low level equilibrium' to a path of continuous growth in living standard of their people. Therefore, a country must satisfy at least two conditions in order to be considered an NIE. First, it must take-off to a self-sustaining growth path. Second, there must be a sustained reduction in poverty and inequality and a continuing improvement in the standard of living. In short, these economies must achieve a certain level of 'human development' in the sense of 'enlarged choices' for their people.

The United Nations Development Program (UNDP) (1990) has developed an index, known as the Human Development Index (HDI), to measure relative deprivation. It combines purchasing power, life expectancy and literacy for each of 130 countries and measures the relative position of each country with respect to the minimum and desirable values for the three. The index varies from zero to one in ascending order. Therefore, an HDI of 0.75 implies an above average human development in the sense of enlarged choices for the people.

According to the Nobel Laureate development economist W.A. Lewis (Lewis,

3

1965), a country reaches the take-off point once it converts itself from being a 4 or 5 per cent to a 12 or 15 per cent saver (investor). Tsiang and Wu (1985) have provided a theoretical basis for Lewis' claim and, according to them, for a country to take-off, the savings ratio must exceed the capital/output ratio times the rate of population growth. Therefore, assuming an average capital/output ratio of 5 and a 3 per cent rate of population growth for developing countries, a country must achieve a savings/output ratio of 15 per cent or more to be able to graduate to an NIE.

There is a strong positive relationship between rate of savings and income per capita. A high domestic savings ratio can only be maintained if income per capita continues to rise. On the other hand, high savings and investment are essential for sustained income growth. Thus, once a country takes-off, the 'law of cumulative causation' implies that it should be able to transform the 'vicious circle of poverty' into a 'virtuous circle of prosperity'.

Of course to be termed an industrialising country, manufacturing must play an important role. As a matter of fact, industrialisation has been vital for economic growth in most countries, except for those with small population and high concentration of natural resources. The patterns of structural change observed in developed and developing countries suggest that changes in the composition of GDP are extensive once the country has reached an intermediate income range ($300–$1,000 per capita). The expansion of manufacturing becomes very rapid in this phase and provides the impetus for structural change. In the emergent structure, the share of manufacturing in both GDP and employment will continue to grow, albeit at a slower pace once the country reaches an advanced stage (Ballance and Sinclair, 1983: 60). The share of manufacturing sector is found to rise rapidly once it reaches a critical level of 18–20 per cent (United Nations Industrial Development Organization (UNIDO), 1979a).

While the borderline between categories is bound to be arbitrary, the above discussion enables us to lay down a four-fold criterion to statistically define an NIE. To be regarded as an NIE, an economy must have *at least* the following:

1   a savings ratio equal to 15 per cent;
2   a real GDP per capita equal to US$1,000;
3   a share of manufacturing in GDP and employment equal to 20 per cent;
4   an HDI equal to 0.75.

Using the above four-fold criterion, one can list twenty-two countries as NIEs (Table 1.1). The list is a snap shot at a particular point in time. In a dynamic context, the savings ratio, income per capita and the share of manufacturing in GDP must continue to rise and there must be a sustained improvement in human condition, measured by HDI. Failing to do so, a country will slip down the ladder and, at the same time, other developing countries may succeed in taking-off and join the group of NIEs. Over time, the successful NIEs will graduate to becoming fully fledged industrialised countries in their own right. Thus, 'countries form a dynamic continuum in the development process. ... [T]he borderline between

Table 1.1 Newly industrialising economies

Economy	Gross domestic savings ratio (%) 1988	GNP per capita ($) 1988	Share of manufacturing (%) 1988	Human development index 1989
Thailand	34	1,000	24	0.783
Jamaica	19	1,070	21	0.824
Ecuador	21	1,120	21	0.758
Columbia	22	1,180	20	0.801
Turkey	26	1,280	26	0.753
Peru	24	1,300	24	0.753
Chile	24	1,510	21[a]	0.931
Costa Rica	26	1,680	20[a]	0.916
Mexico	23	1,760	26	0.876
Mauritius	25	1,800	25	0.788
Malaysia	36	1,940	23[a]	0.800
Brazil	28	2,160	29	0.784
South Africa	25	2,290	25	0.731
Uruguay	14	2,470	24	0.916
Argentina	18	2,520	31	0.910
Yugoslavia	40	2,520	30[a]	0.913
Venezuela	25	3,250	22	0.861
South Korea	38	3,600	32	0.903
Portugal	21	3,650	36[a]	0.899
Taiwan[b]	33	4,960	39	0.920[c]
Singapore	41	9,070	30	0.899
Hong Kong	33	9,200	22	0.936

Potential newly industrialising economies

Economy	Gross domestic savings ratio (%) 1988	GNP per capita ($) 1988	Share of manufacturing (%) 1988	Human development index 1989
Israel	10	8,650	24[a]	0.957
Nigeria	15	290	18	0.322
Zambia	14	290	25	0.481
China	37	330	33	0.716
India	21	340	19	0.430
Pakistan	13	350	17	0.423
Indonesia	25	440	19	0.591
Philippines	18	630	25	0.714
Zimbabwe	24	650	31	0.576
Morocco	23	830	18	0.489

Sources: World Bank, *World Development Report* (various issues); UNDP (1990).
Notes: a 1980 figures.
  b Asian Development Bank, *Key Indicators*.
  c Own calculations, using the UNDP methodology.

advanced industrial countries and the NICs on one hand, and between the NICs and other developing countries on the other, is moving all the time and will always be a matter on which views may differ' (OECD, op. cit.: 6).

5

There is considerable debate regarding the role of manufactured exports in industrialisation. This is because the nature of the relationship between the emergence of manufactured exports and patterns of development remains unclear. It is argued that a country can become reasonably industrialised without engaging significantly in manufactured exports if the domestic market is large enough. As Chenery (1979: 130) concludes:

> The small, manufacturing oriented countries resemble other small countries in their dependence on trade but are closer to the large countries in the overall composition of their exports. ... The result is a unique development pattern whose properties are less easily predictable from general economic reasoning than are those of the other two patterns (large countries and small primary product oriented countries).

Some, for example Riedel (1984), go even further and argue that, instead of trade determining the rate of growth of output in developing countries, it is rather the growth of output that determines their trade. In other words, the rapid structural change in exports should be expected to follow from rapid structural change *internally* and not vice versa.

On the other hand, the success of the Asian NIEs in achieving dynamic export expansion and fast economic growth has been used as evidence of the importance of trade. It is argued that even for large economies such as India and Brazil, the domestic market may become saturated and export expansion should play a vital role at a later stage. More importantly, a liberal trade regime is likely to impose discipline on the domestic producers by unleashing the forces of competition. The outward-oriented countries are said to have less distortions in such key price variables as real interest rates and exchange rates. The lower degree of price distortions in outward-oriented economies is believed to be responsible for their high savings/investment ratios and above average GDP growth rates (Agarwala, 1983; Balassa, 1983; Bhagwati and Srinivasan, 1975; Krueger, 1978).

However, this view, too, is challenged. Bradford (1987a, b) concludes that there is no general association between the degree of price distortion and trade orientation. Inward-oriented India, the Philippines and Brazil have roughly the same order of price distortions as outward-oriented Korea and Thailand. According to Bradford (ibid.), there is almost no difference in the average GDP growth and savings ratios of the outward- and inward-oriented developing countries, and savings ratios are actually slightly higher in the inward-oriented countries.

Notwithstanding the debate concerning the role of trade, in particular of manufactured exports, it remains a fact that there is a close association between manufactured goods exports and economic growth in the small economies of Hong Kong, Korea, Singapore and Taiwan. The outward orientation of these economies is a necessity arising from the smallness of their domestic market and the lack of natural resources (Little, op. cit.). What is, however, more interesting

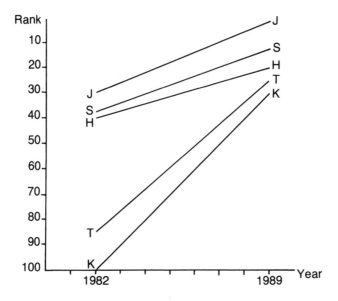

Figure 1.1 Per capita income rank, 1982–9 (in descending order: JJ, Japan;
SS, Singapore; HH, Hong Kong; TT, Taiwan; KK, Korea)

Sources: Wade (1990: 35); Wu (1992: 53)

is their ability to penetrate the world trade in manufacturing.

Despite differences as to what it means to be an NIE, the four East Asian economies undoubtedly qualify as NIEs according to almost all classifications. Among the NIEs, the four East Asian economies performed most brilliantly in terms of both their absolute achievements and the rate of progress. In only two decades, they have been able to raise their savings ratios from below 10 per cent to above 30 per cent. Income per capita has grown at an average annual rate of around 7 per cent since their take-off in the mid-1960s. During the same period (1965–85), gross national product (GNP) per capita grew on average at only 3.3 per cent in the upper middle-income countries and the industrial countries could manage only 2.4 per cent. The exceptionally high growth rate has enabled the East Asian NIEs to double their per capita income in about 10 years. A graphic description of this transformation can be seen in Figure 1.1. It shows how these economies have changed their income ranks (measured in US$) between 1962 and 1989. The magnitude of the change is such that the per capita GNP of the two city states – Hong Kong and Singapore – is now close to that of West European developed countries (Table 1.2a). Korea and Taiwan's per capita GNP is three to four times the average GNP of the group of upper middle-income developing countries to which they are allocated in the *World Development Report* classification. Korea has been able to increase its share of world GDP

Table 1.2a Indices of success: an economic perspective

Economy	Area (km², 1000)	Population 1989 (million)	Per capita GNP 1988 (US$)	Average annual per capita income growth 1965–89 (%)	Average annual inflation rate 1965–89 (%)	Average annual unemployment rate 1971–89 (%)	Average resource balance[a]/GNP 1971–89 (%)	Share in world GDP 1986/1965[b]*	Share in world MVA 1986/1965*
Hong Kong	1	5.8	9,230	6.3	7.6	3.4	0.02[b]	2.07	1.89
Korea	98	42.4	3,530	7.0	11.7	3.9	−0.02	4.45	3.59
Singapore	1	2.7	9,100	7.0	3.3	3.9	−0.06	2.22	2.83
Taiwan	36	20.0	4,960	7.0[c]	6.8[c]	1.8	0.06	3.63	6.79

Sources Asian Development Bank (various issues); *Dahlman (1989: Tables 2.2, 2.3); World Bank (various issues).
Notes: a Resource balance = exports − imports of goods and services.
b % of GDP.
c 1965–86.

four-fold during 1965–86. Taiwan's share in world GDP has increased more than three times and that of Hong Kong and Singapore has doubled during the same period. The transformation of these economies has been so extensive that their share in world manufacturing value added (MVA) has more than doubled during 1965–86, and in the case of Taiwan it has risen nearly seven times.

The change in the structure of production has also been quite extensive. Except for Hong Kong, which had substantial industrial activities in the early days, the share of manufacturing in GDP has been more than doubled and manufacturing now contributes 30 per cent or more to their GDP. There has been a parallel development in employment and manufacturing now accounts for 30 per cent or more of total employment as opposed to less than 20 per cent in 1960.

What is more remarkable about this spectacular growth and transformation is its quality. Except in Korea, the phenomenal growth has been achieved with remarkable price stability. While most countries were confronting double digit inflation in the aftermath of two oil price shocks, the East Asian NIEs' average annual inflation rate during 1971–89 remained below 10 per cent. The inflation performance is more impressive in recent years (1986–9). Korea has been successful in bringing average annual inflation rate down to 4.6 per cent. The average annual inflation rate of Hong Kong, Singapore and Taiwan has been 6.5, 0.9 and 1.8 per cent respectively during 1986–9. Their internal and external balance record is equally impressive. The average annual unemployment rate has been well below what has been experienced by most developed and developing countries. These economies operated at near full employment during most of 1971–89 except for a few short periods. For most of the 1970s and 1980s, these four economies have lived within their means; the average resource balance (= GDP − domestic demand = exports − imports of goods and services) has been less than 1 per cent of GDP during 1971–89.

Table 1.2b Social indicators of development

Economy	Infant mortality 1989 (per 1,000)	Adult literacy 1989 (%)	Life expectancy at birth 1989 (years)	HDI[a,*] 1989	Income distribution and per capita growth rank[b,†]
Hong Kong	7	88	77	0.936	4
Korea	24	93[c]	70	0.903	3
Singapore	7	87	74	0.899	2
Taiwan	5	91	74	0.920[d]	1

Sources: World Bank, *World Development Report* (various issues); Asian Development Bank (various issues); *UNDP (1990); †Riedel (1988: Table 1.8).
Notes: a Human Development Index.
  b Rank among 34 developing countries.
  c 1984.
  d Authors' own calculation.

The growth in income has also been accompanied by a sustained reduction in poverty and inequality (Table 1.2b). In terms of degree of equality of income distribution and per capita growth ranking, the East Asian NIEs occupy the first four positions among a sample of thirty-four developing countries (Riedel, 1988: 19). In terms of infant mortality, life expectancy at birth and adult literacy rate, all four East Asian NIEs are very close to the developed world. High growth in income per capita, more equitable distribution of income and low inflation have meant a rise in the purchasing power of their populations. This together with high adult literacy rate and life expectancy has been responsible in reducing the relative deprivation of their people. The index of relative deprivation, HDI, too, shows that the 'range of choices opened to their people has enlarged' in the East Asian NIEs. It ranges from 0.899 (Singapore) to 0.936 (Hong Kong) compared with Japan (0.996) which tops the list.

These impressive achievements have led one prominent observer to label them as 'leaders in social development' (Hughes, 1989). However, as will be shown in the subsequent chapters, the East Asian NIEs suffered from episodic distresses. What is noteworthy though is their ability to overcome these difficulties reasonably quickly. One may ask what are the reasons for their relative success. The main objective of this volume is to provide a balanced view of issues and debates pertaining to East Asian success.

THE EMERGENCE OF EAST ASIAN NIEs: THE SALIENT FEATURES

The outstanding performance of the four East Asian economies has naturally attracted a lot of attention and many attempts have been made to understand the process of their development. This section will try to trace their graduation into NIEs and highlight the similarities and differences among them.

The take-off

To pin-point the year of take-off one can follow Tsiang and Wu (op. cit.). The basic condition for take-off, it may be recalled, is that savings per capita must be more than sufficient to maintain the capital/labour ratio. In simple terms, if population is growing then capital stock must also grow, at least at the same rate, in order to maintain a constant capital/labour ratio. Otherwise, diminishing returns to labour will retard output growth. In quantitative terms, the savings/output ratio must exceed capital/output ratio times the rate of population growth. In that case, the supply of savings needed for investment and capital formation will be sufficient to maintain a constant capital/labour ratio in the face of continuous population growth.

Therefore, the three crucial factors in the successful take-off of an economy are the savings ratio, the capital/output ratio and the population growth rate. A country can achieve the take-off threshold by either raising the savings ratio, or

Table 1.3 Estimation of the approximate take-off year

Year	Hong Kong				Korea				Singapore				Taiwan			
	a	b	c	$a-bc$	a	b	c	$a-bc$	a	b	c	$a-bc$	a	b	c	$a-bc$
1961	-5.2	1.4	3.0	-9.4	-2.3	2.3	2.9	-9.0	-15.0	1.5	3.7	-20.6	8.0	3.6	3.3	-3.9
1963	2.5	1.4	3.5	-2.4	3.9	2.2	2.8	-2.3	-8.6	1.3	2.9	-12.4	13.4	3.2	3.2	3.2
1965	7.2	1.4	2.7	3.4	1.9	2.0	2.6	-3.3	-0.1	1.4	2.7	-3.9	16.5	2.7	3.0	8.4
1966	–	–	–	–	7.0	1.9	2.5	2.2	4.1	1.3	2.1	1.4	–	–	–	–
1967	10.2	1.5	2.6	6.1	6.2	1.9	2.3	1.8	4.2	1.3	2.6	0.8	20.1	2.5	2.3	14.4
1969	12.8	1.3	1.6	10.7	14.8	1.9	2.3	10.4	9.0	1.3	1.5	7.0	22.1	2.3	2.5	16.4

Source: Tsiang and Wu (1985: Tables 7.4–7.7).
Notes: a Savings ratio.
      b Capital/output ratio.
      c Population growth rate.

by lowering both the capital/output ratio and the population growth rate or by some combination of them. While raising the savings ratio entails a sacrifice of current consumption, the capital/output ratio can be lowered by improving the efficiency with which capital is employed.

Table 1.3 shows that the four East Asian NIEs achieved successful take-off by raising their savings ratios and simultaneously lowering population growth and improving the efficiency of capital. Even though they took-off within a few years of each other, their initial conditions differed significantly. Taiwan had achieved a significant positive savings ratio in the early 1960s, whereas Singapore had a negative savings ratio until 1965, the year before it took-off. Both Hong Kong and Korea had a negative savings ratio until 1961.

The East Asian NIEs, particularly Taiwan and Korea, carried out substantial reforms in their financial sectors in the early and mid-1960s. There are considerable debates regarding the impact of financial reforms on their saving rates and capital/output ratios. Chapter 8 reflects on the effects of interest rates on East Asian NIEs' savings and investment efficiency.

The uncertainty about the impact of interest rates on savings led observers to look at other determinants of savings. According to Kuznets (1988), the incorporation of bonuses into the wage structure provided transitory income (which is likely to have been saved) and may have contributed to the rise in household savings. The growth in export-led income and self-employment may also have contributed to their improved savings performance. The rapid growth and spread of financial institutions helped tap increased household savings. In addition, specific schemes were designed to generate voluntary and/or forced savings. Korea, for example, introduced various incentive measures for different types of savers and Singapore adopted a compulsory savings scheme. By 1970, the government budget was also making its own contribution to domestic savings in all of the NIEs.

Their initial conditions also differed with respect to the capital/output ratio. Taiwan had the highest capital/output ratio among the NIEs in the 1960s, implying inefficiency of capital use. Hong Kong and Singapore had the most favourable capital/output ratio, perhaps due to the differences in their industrial and trade policies in the early days. In the post-war period until about the early 1960s, Taiwan and Korea followed a capital-intensive import substitution industrialisation (ISI) policy, resulting in a high capital/output ratio. On the other hand, Hong Kong never followed ISI and Singapore's experience with ISI was very brief. Export-oriented industrialisation (EOI) is subject to international competition and is likely to force efficient uses of capital. However, research on the impact of trade orientation on productivity or capital/output ratio has so far failed to produce conclusive results. Chapter 5 looks at some of the issues pertaining to the trade policy–productivity link in the light of East Asian experience.

Industrialisation and structural change

The superlative growth of the four East Asian NIEs has been accompanied by extensive changes in the structure of their production. By 1986 Korea, Singapore and Taiwan had a greater share of production in industry than the average for the matured industrial market economies. The rapid structural transformation created adjustment problems for the declining sectors, namely agriculture in Taiwan and South Korea. So far, the policy makers have tried to cope with adjustment difficulties in agriculture with protective tariffs. The issues and problems of adjustment in agriculture are discussed in Chapter 4.

Once the East Asian NIEs reached an intermediate income range of $300–1,000 per capita, manufacturing started to expand quite rapidly. As can be seen from Table 1.4, the manufacturing sector has grown at phenomenal rates in all East Asian NIEs, except Hong Kong which had the highest share of production in manufacturing among the four economies in 1960.

The rapid growth in manufacturing provided the impetus for structural change. The shares of manufacturing in both GDP and employment (Tables 1.5 and 1.6) have risen in all except Hong Kong. The extent of structural change, however, varies depending on the base and initial conditions. Korea and Taiwan started from a very low income level with a smaller industrial base. Consequently, they have experienced the greatest absolute changes of more than 50 percentage points in the distribution of production among agriculture, industry and services between 1960 and 1989. On the other hand, Hong Kong and Singapore, which had a very small agricultural sector to begin with, experienced a lower growth of manufacturing and smaller absolute changes.

The process of industrialisation observed in the matured industrial economies suggests that the manufacturing sector follows an S-shaped curve (UNIDO, op. cit.). According to this hypothesis, the growth in the share of manufacturing in GDP declines after GDP per capita reaches a certain level. As a result, the share of income derived from manufacturing (or industry in general) begins to fall. While Hong Kong is definitely exhibiting the trend, it appears that the pattern of structural transformation in other three East Asian NIEs is also following the S-shaped logistic curve. This means that the dynamic role of the manufacturing sector is waning. This stylised growth pattern has important implications for industrial policy and interest group behaviour. Ballance and Sinclair (op. cit.) note that the manufacturing sector can try to maintain its influence and role either by a defensive policy of protectionism or by restructuring and technological development. The latter is aimed at shifting the logistic curve outward. In contrast to the matured industrial economies, Korea, Singapore and Taiwan have chosen to follow the latter course of upgrading and restructuring. However, Hong Kong's case is not clear, probably due to political uncertainty.

The restructuring of the manufacturing sector entails changing the type of manufacturing activities themselves. In their attempt at restructuring, the NIEs followed the dictates of comparative advantage. They were very prompt in

Table 1.4 Growth of production (average annual growth rate, %)

Economy	GDP			Agriculture			Manufacturing			Services		
	1960–70	1971–80	1981–9	1960–70	1971–80	1981–9	1960–70	1971–80	1981–9	1960–70	1971–80	1981–9
Hong Kong[a]	10.0	9.5	8.9	–	–0.2	–	–	5.6	–	–	10.1	–
Korea	8.5	8.7	9.2	4.5	1.4	4.2	17.2	14.2	11.5	8.4	7.8	8.7
Singapore	8.8	9.0	6.9	5.0	2.2	–4.7	13.0	9.8	6.4	7.7	8.8	7.5
Taiwan	9.2	9.7	8.0	3.4	1.8	1.3	17.3	12.8	8.1	7.8	9.0	7.8

Sources: World Bank, *World Development Report* (various issues); Asian Development Bank (various issues).
Note: a Sectoral growth rates are for 1970–8.

Table 1.5 Share of major sectors in GDP (%)

Economy	Agriculture				All industry				Manufacturing				Services			
	1960	1970	1980	1989	1960	1970	1980	1989	1960	1970	1980	1989	1960	1970	1980	1989
Hong Kong[a]	4.0	2.0	0.9	0.4	39.0	37.0	32.0	28.8	26.0	30.0	23.8	21.4	57.0	61.0	67.1	70.9
Korea	37.0	28.9	14.2	9.0	20.0	24.4	37.8	45.2	14.0	14.3	26.7	34.4	43.0	46.7	48.0	45.8
Singapore	4.0	2.3	1.1	0.4	18.0	29.8	38.8	36.6	12.0	20.5	29.5	28.6	79.0	67.9	60.1	63.0
Taiwan	33.0	17.7	7.9	4.4	25.0	40.9	46.0	45.4	17.0	33.0	36.3	37.5	42.0	41.4	46.1	50.1

Sources: Asian Development Bank (various issues).
Note: a Computed on the basis of current price data.

Table 1.6 Distribution of employment (%)

Economy	Agriculture				Manufacturing				Services			
	1960[a]	1970	1980	1989	1960[b]	1970	1980	1989	1960[a]	1970	1980	1989
Hong Kong	8.0	2.0	1.3	1.1	52	35.0	42.2	29.8	40	63[c]	56.5	69.1
Korea	66.0	50.0	34.0	19.5	9	13.0	21.6	27.6	25	36	43.5	52.3
Singapore	8.0	3.0	1.6	0.5	23	22.0	30.1	29.0	69	74	68.2	70.5
Taiwan	56.0	35.0	19.5	12.5	11	20.0	32.7	33.9	33	43	47.0	52.9

Sources: World Bank, World Development Report (various issues).
Notes: a 1960 figures are percentage of labour force.
b Percentage of labour force in industry.
c 1971.

Table 1.7 Structure of manufacturing 1970 and 1988: percentage distribution of MVA

Economy	Food, beverages, tobacco		Textiles and clothing		Machinery and transport equipment		Chemicals		Others	
	1970	1988	1970	1988	1970	1988	1970	1988	1970	1988
Hong Kong	4	6	41	38	16	22	2	2	36	33
Korea	26	11	17	15	11	32	11	9	35	33
Singapore	12	5	5	4	28	52	4	12	51	27
Taiwan[a]	–	14	–	15	–	17	–	10	–	44

Sources: World Development Report (various issues); for Taiwan, Dahlman (1989: Table 2.5).
Note: a 1985.

reorienting their industries from import substitution to exports. As labour cost rose and the stock and quality of human and physical capital improved, they moved gradually from low-technology, labour-intensive activities to capital- and skill-intensive branches. Table 1.7 shows that the share of such capital- and skill-intensive branches as machinery and transport equipment in MVA rose significantly in all four East Asian NIEs. It will be interesting to see whether they can sustain their comparative advantage during this phase of industrialisation. Among others this depends very much on their indigenous technological capabilities. Although direct foreign investment (DFI) played a significant role in acquiring technology in their early phase of industrialisation, DFI may not serve the purpose during the phase of 'innovation-driven' industrialisation. The issues pertaining to DFI and technological capabilities are discussed in Chapter 7.

Although structural changes in the East Asian NIEs followed very much the dictates of international division of labour, it is well known that, except perhaps in Hong Kong, the government played a significant role. While government interventions can change the industrial structure the ability of the government to 'pick winners' is a contentious issue. The theme of Chapter 6 is to what extent the industrialisation process in East Asian NIEs is the result of industry-specific government interventions or pro-market policies. In other words, it reflects on the question, 'can the government pick a "winning" industrial structure?'.

Export expansion and diversification

Export expansion has been a necessity for all four East Asian NIEs because of the smallness of their domestic market. The earlier phase of ISI was short-lived and was abandoned as the inefficiency of ISI became evident due to the limitation of the domestic market. Hong Kong and Singapore had been entrepôts for exports to the neighbouring countries and had a high export/GDP ratio. Korea has been most successful in raising its export/GDP ratio, followed by Taiwan (Table 1.8).

Their export growth has been much faster than their growth in GDP. As a result, the four East Asian NIEs have been able to increase their shares of world exports more quickly than they could increase their shares of either world GDP or MVA. By 1986, their shares of world exports exceeded their shares of world GDP. What is more noteworthy is that their exports are dominated by manufactured goods. In 1982, about 90 per cent or more of these economies' exports, except Singapore's, were manufactured goods (Table 1.8). Manufactured exports from Korea, Singapore and Taiwan grew at more than twice the growth rate of world exports (13.9 per cent) in manufactured goods during 1970–85.

The export structure has also undergone significant changes. The share of more capital-intensive products like machinery and transport equipment in merchandise exports has gone up in all four NIEs quite significantly (Table 1.9). At the same time they (except Singapore which has a large oil-refining sector) have reduced their shares of fuels, minerals and other primary products to 9 per cent or less. Hong Kong has been left behind in the changes in its trade structure

Table 1.8 Export expansion

Economy	Exports (% GDP) 1950–60*	Exports (% GDP) 1989†	Share of world total† 1989	Share of manufacturers in merchandise exports‡ 1960	Share of manufacturers in merchandise exports‡ 1982	Growth of manufactured exports¶ 1970–85
Hong Kong	109	121	2.6	80.0	97.0	15.0
Korea	3	29.6	2.1	14.0	90.0	28.0
Singapore	163	162.0	1.5	26.0	56.0	24.8
Taiwan	10	45.7	2.3	79.4 (1975)	89.0	26.4

Sources: *Hughes (1989); †Asian Development Bank (various issues); ‡Barrett and Chin (1987: Table 5); ¶James *et al.* (1989: Table 2.3).

(the absolute change between 1965 and 1986 was only 30 percentage points). This is mainly because, as far back as 1965, 92 per cent of its merchandise exports were already manufactured exports. Given such changes, the structure of East Asian NIEs' merchandise exports by the mid-1980s looked more similar to that of industrial market economies than that of middle-income economies. Further details on these issues are covered in Chapter 5.

Labour market performance and human resource development

The process of industrialisation and labour market development are closely related. Table 1.10 shows that, with the rise in manufacturing activities, employment in that sector grew throughout the period since the early 1960s. In particular, the increase in manufacturing employment has occurred in an environment of rapid growth in labour-intensive manufacturing exports.

Increases in manufacturing employment are important for at least two reasons. First, labour productivity is higher and increases more rapidly in manufacturing than in other sectors. This helps maintain a high GDP growth rate. Second, the growth in manufacturing employment reduces the incidence of underemployment and/or disguised unemployment and problems associated with rural–urban migration as is observed in many developing countries. Issues related to labour market performance and human resource development form the subject matter of Chapter 9.

Table 1.10 also reveals that the four East Asian NIEs have done quite well in terms of creating overall employment opportunities. The unemployment rate has been remarkably low in all four economies. The performance of Taiwan is most impressive. The open unemployment rate in Taiwan has been below 2 per cent since 1960. The other three have been able to improve their labour utilisation rates and brought down the unemployment rate to the neighbourhood of 2 per

17

Table 1.9 Structure of merchandise exports (% share)

Economy	Fuels, minerals, metals		Other primary commodities		Machinery and transport equipment		Other manufactures		Textiles and clothing[b]	
	1965	1989	1965	1989	1965	1989	1965	1989	1965	1989
Hong Kong	1	1	5	2	7	23	87	73	52	39
Korea	15	2	25	5	3	38	56	55	27	23
Singapore	21	18	44	9	10	47	24	26	6	5
Taiwan[a,*]	2	2	57	7	4	29	37	62	–	–
Middle-income economies	27	26	46	21	14	20	13	33	3	11
Industrial market economies	9	7	21	12	31	41	39	40	7	4

Sources: World Bank, *World Development Report* (various issues); *Dahlman (op cit: Table 2.9).
Notes: a 1965 and 1986.
      b 'Textiles and clothing' is a subgroup of 'Other manufactures'.

Table 1.10 Indicators of labour market development

Economy	Economically active population (%)*		Growth of real wages		Open unemployment		Growth of manufacturing employment	
	Period	Rate	Period	Rate	Period	Rate	Period	Rate
Hong Kong	1970	41.7	1960–70	4.7	1960–70	4.2	1961–71	4.7
	1985	51.6	1970–80	4.2	1970–80	4.5	1971–84	4.3
					1989	1.1		
Korea	1970	35.7	1963–73	5.4	1965–73	5.3	1963–73	11.2
	1985	41.3	1973–83	9.5	1973–83	4.2	1973–83	6.3
					1989	2.6		
Singapore	1970	35.0	1965–73	0.6	1967–73	6.0	–	–
	1985	47.9	1973–83	5.4	1973–83	3.7	1973–83	5.5
					1989	2.1		
Taiwan	1970	31.7	1960–73	7.7	1960–73	1.6	1960–73	8.1
	1980	45.0	1973–83	6.5	1973–83	1.0	1973–83	4.8
					1989	1.6		

Sources: Riedel (1988: Table 1.7); * Asian Development Bank (various issues).

cent by the late 1980s. What is more remarkable is that this has been achieved in the face of a rise in economically active population.

The quality of development is also reflected in the movement of real wages. Except in Singapore, real wages have risen significantly in the other three economies. This, together with the rise in employment, may have gone a long way in improving income distribution (Fields, 1984; Islam and Kirkpatrick, 1986a, b). Real wages began to rise in Singapore only after 1978 as a consequence of a deliberate policy associated with restructuring manufacturing away from unskilled labour-intensive areas to high value added, capital-intensive activities, involving higher labour skills.

As mentioned earlier, attempts at restructuring industrial activities have been going on in Korea and Taiwan and possibly in Hong Kong as well. This has important consequences for human resource development. A comparative advantage in skill-intensive activities can only be 'created' if the stock and quality of human resources improves. Therefore, in line with their objective of shifting the industrial structure towards more skill- and technology-intensive activities, the East Asian NIEs invested massively in education. The enrollment ratios increased in all categories (Table 1.11). With respect to secondary education, the NIEs' enrollment ratio is much above that of the middle-income countries and close to that of industrial market economies. There has also been great emphasis

THE NEWLY INDUSTRIALISING ECONOMIES OF EAST ASIA

Table 1.11 Human resource development

Economy	Number enrolled (% of age group)					
	Primary		Secondary		Tertiary	
	1965	1988	1965	1988	1965	1988
Hong Kong	65	88	29	74	5	13[a]
Korea	103	106	35	87	6	37
Singapore	101	104	45	69	10	12[a]
Taiwan*	–	–	–	–	8	21[a]
Middle-income	92	104	26	55	7	17
Industrial market	104	103	63	95	21	41

Sources: World Bank, *World Development Report* (various issues); *Dahlman (1989: Table 2.14).
Note: a 1985.

on engineering and technical education. Generally, in Korea, Singapore and Taiwan, admissions to higher education are adjusted by government fiat to produce the skills that are deemed to be needed (Amjad, 1987). In the words of Papanek (1988: 67), 'the [education] system in East Asia was more appropriate to the needs of the economy as a whole'.

Domestic financial development

A crude measure of financial development or 'deepening' is the ratio of broad money M_2 to GDP. This ratio has risen in all four East Asian NIEs since 1961 (Table 1.12). Financial deepening has been most rapid in Taiwan and only Korea has lagged behind the others. In order to encourage investment, Korea followed a low interest rate policy until the mid-1960s. Together with high inflation (Table 1.13), this resulted in a very low real deposit rate of interest. Since demand for money is influenced by real deposit rate of interest, the 'repression' of interest rate may have produced a low M_2/GDP ratio in Korea.

Both Hong Kong and Singapore have become leading financial centres and the stock exchange dominates the capital market. Hong Kong's securities/GDP ratio has been close to 200 in 1980 and that of Singapore has been 130. The M_2/GDP ratios for Hong Kong and Singapore are comparable with those of most industrial economies.

The rapid financial deepening of these economies is also evident from the rise in the number and types of financial institutions. For example, Korea's population per depository institution branches dropped from 63,400 in 1961 to 10,100 in 1982. During the same period the comparable figures for Taiwan were 15,000 and 9,200.

20

Table 1.12 Financial deepening

	Average M$_2$/GDP (%)			Securities/ GDP 1980[‡]	Average real deposit rate (%) 1961–81[*]
	1961–70[*]	1971–80[*]	1981–90[†]		
Hong Kong	89.3	85.7	155.0	192	1.8
Korea	19.0	33.7	36.8	14	1.0
Singapore	59.8	61.7	78.8	130	2.8
Taiwan	34.1	58.1	110.2	17	4.1

Sources: [*]James *et al.* (1989: Table 3.3); [†]Asian Development Bank (various issues); [‡]Riedel (1988: Table 1.6).

There is a high correlation between real economic growth and financial development. This has led to some debates on the direction of causality which are covered in Chapter 8.

Macroeconomic management and external shocks

The East Asian NIEs are generally hailed for their prudent macroeconomic management. They have used a wide variety of instruments (fiscal, monetary, exchange rate and wages policies) to attain and maintain internal and external balance. They have been able to maintain high growth rates with relatively low inflation (Table 1.13). Nonetheless, it should be noted that their inflation performance shows some variations. Singapore has the best record, whereas Korea has been prone to high inflation. However, in the 1980s, Korea has been able to bring its average annual inflation rate down to one digit levels. Despite a good overall record of macroeconomic management, the East Asian NIEs have had episodes of policy failures. These episodes are highlighted as part of the broader discussion of macroeconomic management in Chapter 10.

A standard macroeconomic identity is that, if aggregate investment exceeds domestic savings, then this imbalance is reflected in a current account deficit. The counterpart of a current account deficit is external resource flows. As can be seen from Table 1.13, the investment ratio exceeded the savings ratio until 1980; the shortfall was met by foreign capital inflow. Only very recently (in 1989) did all four become net exporters of capital. However, since 1991 the trend seems to have reversed in Korea.

Korea has been most heavily dependent on external resources, followed by Singapore. This is also reflected in the debt/GNP ratio (Table 1.14). While Korea always had a high debt/GNP ratio, Singapore's debt/GNP ratio exceeded that of Korea in the latter half of the 1980s. In addition to a high debt ratio, Korea is also unique in terms of a high debt service/exports (debt service) ratio. Its debt service ratio has been above that of Singapore in the latter half of the 1980s

Table 1.13 Macroeconomic performance

Economy	Average annual growth rate			Average annual inflation			Average annual resource gap[a] (% of GDP)		Overall budget surplus/deficit (% of GDP)		
	1960–70	1971–80	1981–90	1960–70	1971–80	1981–90	1971–80	1981–90	1971	1981	1990
Hong Kong	10.0	9.5	8.7	2.3	8.5	8.2	−1.0[b]	−1.6[b]	2.9	4.0	0.1
Korea	8.6	8.7	7.1	17.5	16.4	6.5	6.6	−1.3[b]	−1.6[b]	−3.3[b]	−0.7[b]
Singapore	8.8	9.0	9.9	1.1	6.7	2.3	11.1	−0.3[b]	1.2	−1.0[b]	2.9
Taiwan	7.6	9.7	8.5	4.1	11.1	3.1	−1.6[b]	−10.3[b]	0.5	−0.7[b]	1.6

Sources: Asian Development Bank (various issues).
Notes: a Resouce gap = gross domestic investment − gross domestic savings.
         b Minus indicates net capital exporter.

Table 1.14 External indebtedness

	Hong Kong	Korea	Singapore	Taiwan
Total external debt/DDP				
1975	0.36[a]	29.4	9.7	10.6[a]
1980	2.30[a] (1979)	48.7	18.3	10.0
1988	18.3 (1987)	22.0	24.9	19.2 (1987)
Total external debt/exports				
1975	—	103.7	6.6	—
1980	—	130.6	8.2	—
1988	—	52.4	13.7 (1987)	32.3 (1987)
Total debt service/exports				
1975	0.04[b]	12.7	1.6	3.8
1980	0.1[b] (1979)	14.1	21.0	4.3 (1979)
1988	2.9 (1986)	11.5	2.3 (1987)	3.2 (1987)

Sources: Asian Development Bank (various issues).
Notes: a External public debt/GDP.
          b Service payments/merchandise exports.

(when Singapore had a higher debt/GNP ratio) largely due to the nature of external resource inflow. Korea depended mostly on borrowing while Singapore preferred DFI – see Chapter 7.

Being highly dependent on trade and net importers of oil, all four East Asian NIEs suffered in varying degrees from the two oil price shocks of the 1970s and the consequent world recessions. The oil price rises, referred to as 'terms of trade shocks', meant increases in the import bill. Economies can adjust to the resource gap caused by adverse external shocks by reducing domestic demand, increasing exports and/or reducing imports, but the slow-down of world economy affected exports from the NIEs and aggravated the 'external shock'.

Singapore has been the worst hit NIE followed by Hong Kong. The larger economies, Korea and Taiwan, have been able to better absorb the shocks. The ratio of additional resource gap (increase in current account deficits) due to the shocks to GNP between 1974 and 1982 has been estimated at −46.3 per cent for Singapore as opposed to about −13 per cent for Korea and Taiwan. The ratio for Hong Kong has been −26.7. Singapore has been unable to offset the external

Table 1.15 The role of government in the East Asian NIEs in 1984 (current prices, %)

Classification	Hong Kong	Singapore	Korea	Taiwan
1 Government revenue plus current surpluses of government enterprises/ GNP	–	43.5[a]	18.4	22.9
2 Government revenue/GNP	15.5	29.4	17.1	18.0
3 Government expenditure/GNP	14.5	20.8	17.3[b]	22.7
4 Current government expenditures/ GNP	10.5	15.2	10.0	16.6
5 Government development expenditure/ GNP	4.1	5.6	7.3	6.1
6 Public sector gross saving/gross national saving	–	64.0[c]	28.8	12.7
7 Public gross domestic fixed capital formation/total gross domestic fixed capital formation	21.9	33.4[d]	17.6	42.7
8 Government consumption/total consumption	10.3	19.9	14.8	24.4

Sources: Singapore, Korea and Taiwan: Rieger and Veit (1991: Table 1). Hong Kong: Asian Development Bank (various issues).
Notes: a Government revenues plus current surpluses of seven major statutory boards, but excludes undistributed profits of public enterprises.
  b Excludes other special accounts separately funded, which amounted to 3.7% of GNP in 1984.
  c Current surplus of government plus current surpluses of seven major statutory boards, but excludes undistributed profits of public enterprises.
  d If measured in 1968 prices it would be 22.6%.

shocks completely by export expansion and had to fill the resource gap with additional borrowing. This perhaps explains the sudden rise in its debt/GNP ratio in 1980, immediately after the second oil price shock. Korea also had to resort to additional borrowing. But both Korea and Taiwan have been successful in expanding exports and substitute imports which more than offset the external shocks. Despite the fact that the NIEs have been most vulnerable to external shocks, they have, in general, adjusted more quickly and outperformed all other countries. The adjustment experience of the East Asian NIEs is discussed in Chapter 11.

The size of government

Governments play a pervasive role in many developing countries. There is a general consensus among the observers of NIEs that the governments of the NIEs (except in Hong Kong) are interventionist. The role of the government in economic development is a recurring theme throughout this book while the main issues are examined in Chapter 3.

Table 1.16 Income distribution and quality of life

	Gini coefficient*	Percentage share of household income[†]		Income distribution rank out of 34 countries[‡]	Physical Quality of Life Index (PQLI)[†]	Human Development Index (HDI)[¶] (Rank)[a] 1989
		Lowest 20%	Highest 20%			
Hong Kong	0.462 (1963)	5.3	57.7 (1965)	11	76 (1960)	108
	0.453 (1981)	5.4	47.0 (1980)		86 (1970)	
Korea	0.334 (1965)	9.4	35.8 (1965)	8	76 (1965)	97
	0.36 (1984)[§]	5.7	45.3 (1975)		82 (1970)	
Singapore	0.498 (1966)			5	—	96
	0.474 (1984)				83 (1980)	
Taiwan	0.440 (1961)	5.6	50.9 (1960)	1	77 (1960)	105[b]
	0.317 (1985)	8.8	36.8 (1980)		90 (1975)	

Sources: *Rao (1988: 28); [†]Morris (1979: Table 1, Appendix B–C); [‡]Riedel (1988: Table 1.8); [¶]UNDP (1990); [§]Nam (1988: Table 6).

Notes: a Rank in ascending order from 1 to 130.

b Based on 1980 purchasing power parity (own calculation using the UNDP formula).

Table 1.15 presents some indicators of the size of the government in the East Asian NIEs. Although the data pertain to only 1 year, they show that governments in Korea, Singapore and Taiwan have a significant command over national income and expenditure. The contribution of public investment to gross capital formation in these economies is quite significant. Even the laissez-faire Hong Kong does not look very different from others. However, what is more interesting is that by running a budget surplus they (Korea excepted) contribute significantly to national savings. An estimate shows that government savings have ranged from 3 per cent (in Hong Kong) to 11 per cent (in Singapore) during 1980–5 (James *et al.*, 1989: 86).

Income distribution and basic needs

The broader issues of income distribution and poverty form the subject matter of Chapter 12. This section highlights the performance of the four East Asian NIEs with respect to income distribution, physical quality of life and human development. As can be seen from Table 1.16, Taiwan has outperformed the other three in reducing income inequality. In fact, the decline of Taiwan's Gini coefficient from 0.44 to 0.32 in only two decades is probably the largest decline in any non-socialist nation since 1900 (Deyo, 1987: 29). Korea's Gini coefficient, which showed a rising trend until 1981, had fallen in 1984 to 0.357, a level observed in 1965. However, both Hong Kong and and Singapore are less successful in reducing income inequality and their Gini coefficient remains high after an initial decline in the early 1970s.

A measure of income inequality which is also linked to poverty is the shares of various income groups in national income. Consistent with the remarkable decline in its Gini coefficient, the share of the poorest 20 per cent in Taiwan's national income rose from 5.6 in 1960 to 8.8 per cent in 1980. The percentage share of the poorest 20 per cent dropped in Korea and that of the richest 20 per cent increased. From a relatively stable share of the poorest 20 per cent and a drop in the share of the richest 20 per cent, it seems that the income share of the middle class has risen in Hong Kong.

Riedel (1988) has provided income distribution ranks of the East Asian NIEs by ranking countries according to their household income shares of successive cumulative quintile aggregates (i.e. the share of the bottom 20 per cent, bottom 40 per cent, bottom 80 per cent and so on, respectively). The ranks of the four East Asian NIEs among thirty-four developing countries are consistent with their Gini coefficients and Taiwan tops the list.

The basic needs approach to poverty emphasises such social indicators as life expectancy, infant mortality and adult literacy. Morris (1979) has developed a composite index, known as the Physical Quality of Life Index (PQLI), of these indicators. The PQLI shows that the quality of life in all four countries is very close to those observed in developed countries. In Streeten's (1979) view, the investment in basic human needs and the development of human capital in Korea and Taiwan laid 'the runway for future take-off into self-sustained growth'.

'The link between economic growth and human progress is not automatic' and 'although GNP growth is absolutely necessary to meet all essential human objectives, countries differ in the way that they translate growth into human development' (UNDP, op. cit.). However, the four East Asian NIEs have done remarkably well in translating their economic growth into human development within a very short span of time. Despite Singapore being three places lower than Argentina, the four Asian NIEs rank within the first twenty-two among 130 countries in terms of their HDI. This indicates that the Asian NIEs have been spectacularly successful in reducing the 'relative deprivation' of their people. The range of choices open to their people is not far behind the top most country,

Japan. The performance is more impressive when one sees that this quality of life has been achieved in little over two decades.

LOOKING AHEAD: CONCLUDING REMARKS

The preceding discussion has demonstrated the remarkable achievements of East Asian NIEs. How can one explain their successes? What are the lessons to be learned? The subsequent chapters attempt at providing a comprehensive survey of literature on the East Asian NIEs with a view to finding answers to these questions. The survey shows that a combination of internal (endogenous) and external (exogenous) factors played a role in the graduation of Hong Kong, Singapore, Korea and Taiwan into NIEs. While the exogenous factors (history, culture and geopolitics) have provided circumstances for the emergence of states relatively free from interest group pressure, which, in turn, created a favourable policy environment (endogenous factors), the relative contributions of each of these factors are not fully clear. Thus, the lesson is for a cautious approach and to avoid ready generalisations.

A more fundamental question is whether the East Asian NIEs can continue to prosper in the future. This depends on how they adjust to their success. In other words, it depends on their ability to restructure the economy towards the one which is driven by innovation. The book argues that the institutional structure which was conducive for their initial successes may not help the politics of policy making at this juncture. The current political unrests in Korea and Taiwan are indications of likely frictions arising from the problems of adjusting to success. Thus, whether or not the East Asian NIEs can graduate to an 'innovation-driven' stage of development depends on the success of the democratisation movements in creating an institutional environment which encourages diversity and creativity.

2

HISTORICAL ANTECEDENTS AND THE IMPACT OF GEOPOLITICAL REALITIES

The origins of modern economic growth in East Asia have deep historical roots. Despite the impression that one gets from some popular writings (e.g. Galenson, 1982; Myint, 1982), the East Asian NIEs did not suddenly spring to life in the 1960s. As Cumings (1987: 46) notes, 'if there has been an economic miracle in East Asia, it has not occurred just since 1960; it would be profoundly ahistorical to think that it did'. In taking such a historical perspective, one has to distinguish between two strands of thought. One maintains that the East Asia NIEs are special cases, to the extent that their rapid economic growth is the product of fortuitous historical circumstances, strategic links to the USA, and culturally specific factors. The alternative view is that, while favourable exogenous factors were important, subsequent political and policy developments converted such favourable conditions into a process of rapid, self-sustaining growth. This chapter is sympathetic to the latter view. The relevant arguments in this debate are articulated by focusing on a number of issues: the role of a historical constant in the form of the Confucian heritage, the impact of colonisation on post-war economic growth and the geopolitical realities of the 1950s and 1960s (as manifested, for example, in the particular form of US aid and the Vietnam War). As a prelude to an examination of these issues, it would be useful to provide brief political histories of the East Asian NIEs.

THE EAST ASIAN NIEs:
SYNOPTIC POLITICAL HISTORIES

Korea and Taiwan

This account draws upon a number of sources: Far Eastern Economic Review (1990), Wade (1990), Ho (1984), Cho and Kim (1991), Song (1990). The fourteenth century saw the entrenchment of strong, centralised and durable states in China and Korea. In the latter, the Yi dynasty lasted until 1910. In that year, Korea was formally annexed by Japan. The era of Japanese colonisation lasted for 35 years and ended after the Second World War. At that point, the country was divided, the Americans holding the South and the then Soviets the North.

The Republic of Korea   More popularly known as South Korea, the Republic of Korea was proclaimed in the South on 15 August 1948. Syngman Rhee became the first President of independent Korea. In June 1950 war broke out between North and South. Rhee's government successfully defended South Korea, with the aid of UN forces, but this defence was achieved at a terrible cost. The Korean war lasted 3 years, decimated approximately 25 per cent of the country's wealth and entailed the loss of over a million lives.

The Rhee government was toppled by student riots in April 1960. At this juncture, the nation changed its form of government from a presidential to a cabinet system electing Chang Myon in 1960. This was the first, fleeting appearance of democracy in Korea. The Myon government (the Second Republic) was abruptly terminated in May 1961 through a military coup.

The military coup of 1961 was led by General Park Chung Hee and marked the beginning of the political involvement of the military in Korean society for the next 27 years. Park presided over two republics (1963–79) and is generally credited with paving the way for the Korean economic miracle. The early part of the Third Republic (1963–72) did not put much emphasis on centralisation of political control, but this changed conspicuously with the onset of the Fourth Republic (1972–80). In October 1972 Park proclaimed a national emergency in the light of changing geopolitical realities. Under the umbrella of the Yushin constitution, the national assembly was weakened and the bureaucracy strengthened. Stringent limits were placed on civil and political liberties. Most importantly, the Yushin constitution allowed for the virtual elimination of all constraints on Park's future re-election.

Park was assassinated by the head of the Korean Intelligence Agency in October 1979. President Park's Prime Minister, Choi Kyu Hah, was sworn in as interim President. Choi's regime lasted for a very short period, amidst promises for political reform. In December 1979 a power struggle with the military led to the assumption of power by General Chun Doo Hwan in August 1980. This period of transition is marred by the infamous Kwangju incident in which a popular protest movement was brutally suppressed. Chun's regime (the Fifth Republic, 1980–7) tended to perpetuate the authoritarian features of the Park regime. The Chun government succumbed to massive protests in June 1987. This represents a watershed year in Korean political history. At this juncture, a comprehensive plan for political democratisation was announced by Roh Tae Woo, head of the Democratic Justice Party, presidential candidate, fellow classmate and a subordinate of Chun. Roh registered a massive victory in the presidential election. Korea thus continues its hazardous transition to a full-scale democratic form of government.

Taiwan   Located 150 kilometres off the Chinese mainland, Taiwan existed as a peripheral part of the Chinese empire. It was ceded to Japan after the Sino-Japanese war in 1895 and it remained a Japanese colony until 1945. Thus, compared with Korea, Taiwan experienced a longer period of colonisation.

With Japan's defeat in the Second World War, Taiwan reverted to China under rather turbulent circumstances. The Nationalist Party (Kuomingtang, or KMT) was engaged in a protracted civil war with the Chinese Communist Party and its army. In December 1949, the KMT moved to Taiwan after being over-whelmed by the military forces of the Communist Party. Between 1 and 2 million soldiers and civilians arrived at about the same time to swell an indigenous popu-lation of 6 million.

The strategic intervention of the USA began to play an important role in the political development of Taiwan after the outbreak of the Korean War. Taiwan was perceived as a frontline state against the communist tide. The then US President, Harry Truman, ordered the US navy to repel any attack on the island from mainland China.

The security net offered by the USA allowed Chiang Kai-shek to consolidate his position in the island state. Taiwan was placed under martial law which was only withdrawn in 1987. Chiang Kai-shek had led the KMT since 1926 and had been President almost continuously since 1948. He died in April 1975 after being dogged by ill-health since 1972. His son Chiang Ching-kuo effectively took over leadership of the KMT. He formally took over the presidency in 1978 and incorporated two native Taiwanese as senior members (Vice-President and Prime Minister) of the government. Chiang Ching-kuo died in May 1988 thus bringing to an end six decades of Chiang family rule. When Vice-President Lee Teng-hui succeeded to the presidency, he earned the dubious distinction of being the first native-born Taiwanese to become head of state and head of the KMT.

Internal political developments in Taiwan have to be set against the broader international political environment. Taiwan's legitimacy as an independent political entity continued to be threatened by the shifting contours of inter-national diplomacy. The first major debacle occurred in November 1971 when the UN General Assembly voted to expel Taiwan and seat the People's Republic of China. This was compounded by the event of January 1979 when the USA formally recognised mainland China. In addition, the Shanghai communiqué of August 1982 entailed the promise by the USA to reduce arms sales to Taiwan. These diplomatic blows were, however, counterbalanced by the Taiwan Relations Act of April 1979 which provides for Taiwan's security.

Hong Kong and Singapore

This account draws upon Far Eastern Economic Review (op. cit.), Steinberg (1987), Geiger and Geiger (1973), Osborne (1987), Youngson (1982), Miners (1981), Quah et al. (1985), Chee (1971). Both Hong Kong and Singapore have historically developed as entrepôts.

Hong Kong   Hong Kong was acquired by the British from China in several stages. The Treaty of Nanking led to the acquisition of Hong Kong island, while the Kowloon peninsula was acquired under the Convention of Peking in 1860.

The Second Convention of Peking in 1898 led to the drawing up of a 99-year lease on the New Territories (Kowloon and more than 200 adjacent islands).

For nearly 100 years (1840s–1940s) Hong Kong operated virtually as an autonomous entrepôt serving the trade between China and the Western world. There was a brief interruption to this role as a result of Japanese occupation over the 1942–5 period. Hong Kong was in dire straits when the Japanese surrendered in 1945. The post-war period witnessed periodic 'entrepôt crises'. Thus the Chinese Revolution temporarily terminated the lucrative entrepôt trade. This was counterbalanced by the influx of entrepreneurs and workers from the mainland. A similar reduction in entrepôt occurred during the Korean war when the UN placed an embargo on the export of strategic goods to China. These events eventually proved to be a blessing in disguise as it forced Hong Kong to engage in export-oriented manufacturing and, later, to specialise in financial services.

Political developments in Hong Kong are dominated by the fact that it is due to revert to Chinese rule in 1997. This was the outcome of protracted Sino-British negotiations which began in 1982. A joint declaration was made in December 1984 and later ratified in May 1985 that Hong Kong would be restored to China on 1 July 1997.

Singapore   Singapore shares a fundamental similarity with Hong Kong in the sense that it too developed as an entrepôt. The story of modern Singapore starts in 1819 when it was founded by Stamford Raffles on behalf of the British Crown. At that point it was a sparsely populated haven of fishermen and pirates from the adjoining Malay world. Raffles' primary objective was to develop the island into a centre of international trade in Southern Asia. This had dramatic consequences. The population grew very rapidly within a very short period of time mainly as a result of the influx of migrant workers and entrepreneurs. More importantly, the demographic balance changed dramatically. Within 25 years of Singapore's foundation, the Chinese accounted for 61 per cent of the population where previously there were no Chinese settlers at all.

Singapore was ruled as a British colony as part of the Straits Settlement in association with Penang and Malacca. It soon became one of the richest spots in Asia. As in the case of Hong Kong, there was a Japanese interregnum (1942–5). The Second World War inflicted heavy casualties on the local population. As in the case of Hong Kong, Singapore experienced a phase of 'entrepôt crisis', particularly from 1953 to 1962 as a result of the emergency with Malaya and the confrontation with Indonesia.

Singapore became self-governing in 1959. There was a brief period of association (1963–5) with Malaysia which was eventually abandoned for political reasons. Singapore became fully independent on 9 August 1965, and on 22 December 1965 it became a republic. This is often regarded as the turning point in the city state's economic development when policy makers vigorously embarked on export-oriented, foreign investment-driven industrialisation. Since 1959 it has been ruled by the People's Action Party. The political scene has been dominated by Lee Kuan Yew as Prime Minister. The current Prime Minister is Goh Chok Tong, but the general expectation is that Lee's son (Lee Hsien Loong) will assume the mantle of Prime Minister in due course.

CONFUCIANISM AND EAST ASIAN ECONOMIC DEVELOPMENT

The synoptic political histories of the East Asian NIEs provide the necessary context within which one can examine the particular historical antecedents of the economic miracle in East Asia. One could argue that cultural and social values represent fundamental historical parameters that need to be appreciated as part of understanding the dynamics of development. Obviously, the NIEs have cultural affinities. Taiwan, Hong Kong and Singapore are predominantly Chinese and are influenced by Confucian values. Korea has historically been strongly influenced by the Chinese and Confucian values. There is little doubt that political leaders in these countries (with the possible exception of Hong Kong) have periodically invoked Confucianism as a means of political and social mobilisation. A typical example is offered by Cho and Kim (op. cit.: 29) on Korea. They note, 'Park made explicit efforts to inculcate in the Korean populace the Confucian value of "chung hyo" (loyalty to the state, filial piety, and harmony)'.

Given the cultural similarities of the East Asian NIEs, and given the evidence of the government in these economies making use of Confucian values for the purpose of political and social mobilisation, it is tempting to make a connection between Confucianism and economic success. Certainly, there is an enduring perception among many scholars that such a connection exists (e.g. Berger, 1988; Pye, 1988; O'Malley, 1988; Hofheinz and Calder, 1982; Kahn, 1979). What is Confucianism and how does it promote growth? The discussion that follows draws upon O'Malley (ibid.) and Pye (ibid.).

Confucianism has gone through a lot of transformations over the course of two and a half millennia. Despite such a metamorphosis, key elements of it have endured the passage of time to the extent that one can suggest a recognisable post-Confucian culture. Confucianism, as practised today, is not a 'religion stressing an afterlife; it is a code of ethics meant to guide the relationships between human beings' (O'Malley, ibid.: 332). The most important relationships are hierarchical encompassing relationships between generations, within families, between the ruler and ruled. The duty of the subordinate in these relationships is to show respect and loyalty, while the duty of the superior is to lead by setting the highest moral and intellectual standards. More importantly, 'within these relationships, a common understanding obviates the need for much forthright communication' (O'Malley, ibid.: 332).

The Confucian value system generates particular institutional outcomes that are reflected at the level of the political system, in the arena of industrial organisation, and the interaction between the government and the private sector. First, it imparts a 'strong ethical–moral basis of government ... that both sets the limits

32

on the pragmatic uses of power and requires that authority act with compassion for the people' (Pye, ibid.: 86). Second, it justifies the existence of hierarchical political systems. More specifically, given its emphasis on leadership based on the highest standards, it suggests the need for a centralised, meritocratic bureaucracy that operates within an authoritarian political tradition. Third, the stress on respect and loyalty to superiors gets translated into a demand for consensus and conformity. This in turn implies that 'Confucian political cultures places obstacles on ... challengers of the status quo' (Pye, ibid.: 86). Fourth, it breeds a particular type of industrial organisation in which

> companies ... are organised in community-like, almost family-like ways, with a strong emphasis on team spirit and mutual respect. In the larger and more successful firms, employees ... are almost guaranteed life-long employment and predictable advances in rank and salary. ... The result ... is a highly developed sense of loyalty ... for the good of the collective effort which is the company.
>
> (O'Malley, ibid.: 341)

Finally, the Confucian value system leads to the evolution of a cooperative relationship between the government and corporate interests.

Apart from encouraging the development of particular institutional outcomes, the Confucian value system encourages hard work, diligence and a reverential attitude towards education, given that such traits are widely perceived to be the most acceptable means of career progression in a hierarchical system. This in turn implies that Confucianism encourages rapid human capital formation.

The O'Malley–Pye framework of interpreting the impact of Confucianism on economic development is very much in line with more standard interpretations of East Asian economic success. In Chapter 3, it will be noted that there is a well-entrenched body of scholarship which maintains that the fundamental source of East Asian economic success is a set of particular institutional arrangements – centralised, meritocratic bureaucracy, 'insulated' political systems that are able to withstand the pressures of sectional interests, close government–business inter-actions – which facilitated the implementation of coherent economic policies. In addition, Chapter 9 will note that the East Asian economic miracle has also been characterised by a rapid rate of human capital formation. What the O'Malley–Pye framework has done is to extend this analysis by suggesting that East Asian-style institutional arrangements have culturally specific, Confucian origins. Despite this, the framework has important analytical flaws.

First, the evolution of growth-promoting institutions in East Asia can be explained in terms of general economic principles (see Chapter 3). One need not invoke culturally specific factors.

Second, it is factually incorrect to suggest, as O'Malley (op. cit.) does, that the East Asian NIEs have a common industrial organisation of family-oriented firms with long-term employer–employee relationships. High labour turnover is rampant in such economies (see, e.g., Lansbury and Zappala, 1990). The industrial organisation of Korea is quite different from that of Taiwan (Whitley, 1990). In the case of Singapore, the process of industrialisation has been led by multinational companies (MNCs) rather than local, family-based firms. Presumably, MNCs do not subscribe to, nor are they circumscribed by, Confucian conventions!

Third, it is by no means obvious that a meritocratic bureaucracy in a centralised system is a key to rapid economic development. Sah offers the following counterargument to this proposition:

> A system of merit-based selection of (policy makers) is obviously better than one based on bribery and nepotism. However, there are several reasons ... that limit the extent to which it can improve the performance of centralised societies. Once a system has been in place for some time, and this is well understood, a larger proportion of those who qualify are likely to do so less because of their intrinsic abilities and more because of the resources they spent on the coaching they needed to master the techniques necessary to qualify. More important, selection systems do not change as rapidly as does the mix of the characteristics of (policy makers) that is most useful to society.
>
> (Sah, 1991: 72)

Sah's observations represent a specific expression of the more general point that hierarchical systems can paradoxically inculcate traits that can turn out to be counterproductive in the long run – a theme which is taken up with considerable vigour in Chapter 13.

Fourth, Confucian-based political systems are always vulnerable to legitimacy crises. Pye is acutely aware of the

> troublesome fact that the failure of the East Asian countries to keep pace politically with their economic achievements has left all ... with some legitimacy problems. The root of the difficulties has been the need to find another basis for legitimacy to replace the traditional Confucian ideal of rule by ... superior men.
>
> (Pye, op. cit.: 92)

Fifth, the Confucian model always finds it difficult to cope with the critique that, while Confucianism has been around for centuries, East Asian success is of 1960s vintage (Pang, 1988; Papanek, 1988). Neoclassical economists (e.g. Little, 1979, 1981) resolve this puzzle by offering a simple, but effective, interpretation of East Asian success. They emphasise that the 1960s represent a turning point in the economic development of the East Asian NIEs because at that juncture the NIEs managed to implement a set of broad-based policy reforms (see subsequent chapters for further details). Pye obliquely admits this to be the case:

> [T]he Confucian tradition had to be coupled with advances in economics as an intellectual discipline in order to produce the economic miracles of

East Asia. The new mandarins had to be schooled in the wisdom of Western economic theories and practices.

(Pye, op. cit.: 86))

Given such analytical limitations of the Confucian model of economic development, can one draw any firm conclusions concerning its relevance to East Asia? Perhaps the most appropriate position to take is the one suggested by Little (1979: 463). He notes, 'cultural factors cannot be more than contributory factors, which may play their part, but only when other conditions are favourable'.

THE COLONIAL EXPERIENCE AND ITS RELEVANCE TO MODERN ECONOMIC GROWTH

It is an undeniable fact that Hong Kong and Singapore prospered as entrepôts long before their era of export-oriented manufacturing. It is also an undeniable fact that the evolution of the city states as entrepôts is really the product of British colonial rule. More generally, the British brought to these economies the notion and practice of modern capitalism, with all its paraphernalia of a well-functioning system of property rights, an efficient legal system and so forth. Haggard (1986) has suggested that the transmission of available ideas about the development process (in the sense of access to the stock of knowledge on efficient development policies) in the city states has also been strongly influenced by the British. Thus, he notes, 'Hong Kong's economic orientation has been institutionally entrenched by a succession of powerful, laissez-faire British Financial Secretaries' (Haggard, ibid.: 369).

It appears that, if one takes a historical perspective, one could suggest that Hong Kong and Singapore have prospered because of their favourable historical experiences. The trouble with this interpretation is that it is static in nature, failing to explain how a set of initial favourable conditions were converted into a phase of sustained success. Certainly, the city states were subjected to periodic entrepôt crises and by the 1950s were facing insurmountable limits to maintaining rapid growth by relying on the traditional economic structure. The turning point in their economic development really came when policy makers in Hong Kong and Singapore made a deliberate transition to export-oriented manufacturing.

Korea and Taiwan need to be discussed separately as they bear the imprint of Japanese, rather than British, colonial rule. Myers and Petrie (1984) have suggested that Japanese colonial development has distinctive features that set it apart from colonial development elsewhere. This theme is also evident in the work of Cumings (op. cit.). On the whole, the prevailing wisdom seems to be that modern economic growth in former Japanese colonies owes much to the era of Japanese imperialism. This thesis apparently finds much support in the experiences of Taiwan and Korea. The subsequent discussion focuses critically on this point.

As is well known, Korea was a Japanese colony from 1910 to 1945, while Taiwan was a Japanese colony from 1895 to 1945. Cumings (ibid.) is perhaps the strongest advocate of the view that one cannot really understand post-war growth in Korea and Taiwan without appreciating their development as colonial economies. He suggests, based on the work of Allen (1980), Okhawa and Rosovsky (1973) and Umemura and Mizoguchi (1981), that 'both Korea and Taiwan experienced higher GDP growth rates than Japan between 1911 and 1939 (Japan, 3.36%; Korea, 3.57%; Taiwan, 3.85%)' (Cumings, ibid.: 45). Elsewhere he notes, '[t]he period from 1935 to 1945 was when Korea's industrial revolution began' (Cumings, ibid.: 57). He goes on to suggest that Korea and Taiwan inherited their state-directed development from the Japanese colonial state. Thus, '[t]he colonial state replaced an old weak state, holding society at bay, so to speak; this experience goes a long way towards explaining ... subsequent ... state-directed development in (Taiwan and Korea)' (Cumings, ibid.: 54).

Wade also offers a rather favourable interpretation of the Japanese colonial period. This is evident in the following remarks on Taiwan: 'some evidence suggests that the welfare of the Taiwanese peasant in the first half of the twentieth century may have exceeded that of the Japanese peasant' (Wade, ibid.: 74).

Two points need to be clarified in the wake of the above observations. First, is the evidence really so favourable? Second, if it is, how can one explain the evidence? It appears that Ho (1968, 1978, 1984) is the definitive account of Korea and Taiwan as Japanese colonies. His analysis provides a more balanced perspective on this sensitive issue and the discussion that follows largely draws upon this key source. One should note that good accounts of the colonial experience can also be found in Gold (1986), Song (op. cit.), Cho and Kim (op. cit.), Ranis (1979), Barclay (1954), Lin (1973) and Myers and Ching (1964).

To start with, it is necessary to emphasise that estimates of economic growth during the colonial period vary quite significantly, so that it is not really possible to make the confident assertions that Cumings does (see above). For instance, one estimate in Taiwan suggests growth of GDP to be 4.3 per cent in the 1927–37 period, while another estimate suggests a growth rate of only 1.4 per cent over the same period (Ho, 1984: Table 1). Subject to this significant reservation, the data seem to suggest that total product grew between 3.6 per cent and 2.7 per cent in Korea over the 1912–37 period and between 4.3 per cent and 3.9 per cent over the same period in Taiwan. In per capita terms, the growth rates were more modest, probably no higher than 1.5 per cent.

Second, one has to take account of the changing pattern of colonial development. Initially, Korea and Taiwan grew as 'agricultural appendages' of Japan, but the growth of agriculture was more rapid and sustained in the latter than in the former. More importantly, in both economies there were periods of slow growth juxtaposed with periods of rapid growth. Thus, in Korea, agricultural value added grew only at 1.3 per cent in the 1927–37 period, but at 1.9 per cent in the 1912–27 period (Ho, ibid.: Table 1). In Taiwan the comparable figures are 3.0 per cent (1927–37) and 2.0 per cent (1912–27). Furthermore, Japanese policy towards its colonies changed during the 1930s, and it is over this period that major efforts towards industrialisation took place. The outcomes were divergent, being more evident in Korea than in Taiwan (in the sense that Korea experienced more rapid growth in manufacturing than Taiwan did).

The Japanese colonial state did not limit its efforts to agriculture and industry. Most observers maintain that the Japanese made substantial investments in infrastructure, health and primary education in Taiwan and Korea. For instance, in 1900 Taiwan had very few roads or railroads, but, by 1920, it had more than 600 kilometres of public railways, 3,553 kilometres of roads and significant harbour facilities. A similar pattern can be observed in Korea (Ho, ibid.: fn. 5). Although the Japanese colonial state apparently made a modest allocation of its expenditure to health and medical services, its heavy reliance on preventive measures against infectious disease led to significant drops in mortality. In Taiwan, the death rate declined from 33 to 19 deaths per thousand between 1906 and 1940 (Ho, 1978: Table A11). In Korea, the death rate fell from 35 to 23 deaths per thousand between 1910 and 1935–40 (Kwan, 1975: Table 11.4).

In the sphere of education, one can observe impressive advances. Primary school enrollment increased from 20,000 in 1910 in Korea to 901,100 in 1937 (Grajdanzev, 1944: 261). In Taiwan, the improvement was even more impressive. By the end of the colonial rule, the primary school enrollment ratio stood at 71 per cent (Ho, 1984: 353).

Despite these impressive achievements, one should be cautious about exaggerating the contributions of Japanese colonial rule to the economic development of Taiwan and Korea. It has already been noted that the estimates on growth performance in the two ex-Japanese colonies are subject to wide variations. The growth performance was also uneven, being more sluggish in some periods and sectors than others. More importantly, the Japanese state developed the colonies to meet the short-term needs of its economy. In some cases, as in health and infrastructure, this strategy produced tangible benefits. In other cases, the results were inefficient and inequitable. This point can be illustrated by focusing on education, the pattern of industrialisation and indicators of welfare. Ho notes:

> [T]he contribution of formal schooling to the development of the Japanese colonies should not be over-exaggerated ... the colonial system was devised and administered to discriminate against the colonial populations, and this effectively reduced the positive effects of schooling on the productivity of the colonial populations.
>
> (Ho, ibid.: 354)

The efforts of the Japanese colonial state to industrialise Korea and Taiwan primarily developed as a result of the objective to build up heavy industry in order to achieve self-sufficiency. The consequence was that:

[i]ndustrialisation was not broadly based. Growth was selective, occurring only in the government-promoted industries. ... By world standards the Japanese colonies were not low cost producers. ... The colonial sectors had developed not according to their comparative advantages but rather to meet specific Japanese needs.

(Ho, ibid.: 368–9)

The clear implication is that the Japanese left behind an industrial structure which was inefficient and thus not the basis upon which one could build the export-oriented manufacturing revolution of the 1960s. In any case, the industrial base of the Japanese period hardly remained intact, given the destruction of the Second World War, the splitting up of Korea and the calamities of the Korean War. Indeed the post-war dislocation was so severe in the case of Taiwan that 'total domestic product ... on a per capita basis had not recovered to the 1937 level until 1953' (Little, 1979: 454). In the case of Korea, the partition meant that at one stroke South Korea lost the bulk of her heavy industry and electricity generation to the North. This was not surprising given the regional concentration of industry during the colonial era. Thus, 85 per cent of the hydroelectric power, 95 per cent of iron and steel, 80 per cent of the coal industry and 85 per cent of the chemicals industry were located in the North (Woo, 1991: 41).

The ultimate test of development is the extent to which it leads to an improvement in the welfare of the population. The available indicators of welfare suggest a rather uncertain picture in the colonial era in Korea and Taiwan. If one looks at daily per capita food availability in Korea, it fell from 2,133 in the 1910–14 period to 1,812 in 1930–4 period (Ho, 1984: Table 5). Data on real wages in Taiwan show that they remained constant between 1910 and 1919, rose between 1920 and 1934 but fell significantly after that. In other words, while Korea and Taiwan certainly did not stagnate during the colonial era, indicators on welfare suggest a possible paradox of growth without development.

GEOPOLITICAL REALITIES: THE IMPACT OF US AID AND THE VIETNAM WAR

There is an enduring belief that the East Asian NIEs benefited from the US perception of the region and that the USA used its aid leverage to reinforce the position of pro-American elites and to cement strategic ties with economic ties. It is alleged that these geopolitical realities go a long way towards an understanding of the dynamism of the region. Haggard offers a clear expression of this view:

[I]nternational political conditions ... have had an important bearing on East Asia's economic development. Japan's defeat in the Second World War made the United States the pre-eminent political power in the region. The outbreak of conflict on the Korean peninsula extended the Cold War to Asia, altering the United States' strategic perception of the region and creating expanded political and economic commitments to the Republic of

Korea and Taiwan. The growth of a regional economy in the Pacific Basin cannot be understood without reference to this underlying strategic context.

(Haggard, 1988: 265)

The immediate outcome of this 'strategic context' was the massive influx of US aid to Korea and Taiwan during the 1950s and 1960s. Woo highlights the magnitude of this aid inflow in the following manner:

From 1946 to 1976, the United States provided $12.6 billion in American economic and military aid to Korea (for Taiwan, it was $5.6 billion). ... No other country in the world received such large sums ... with the exception of Israel and South Vietnam. The Korean total of $6 billion in US economic grants and loans, 1946–78, compares to $6.89 billion for all Africa, and $14.89 billion for all Latin America. US military deliveries to Taiwan and Korea in 1955–78 ... totalled $9.05 billion, whereas Latin America combined received $3.2 billion.

(Woo, op. cit.: 45)

Little (op. cit.: 456) recognises the importance of the aid inflow to Taiwan (based on figures compiled by Jacoby, 1966) and Korea, but notes that they tapered off by the early 1960s, at which point other countries were more significant aid recipients. The shifting importance of US military and economic assistance can be gauged from the fact that in Taiwan aid as a proportion of GNP was 6–7 per cent in the 1958–61 period but became negligible by 1968 (Little, ibid.: fn. 31: 458). In the case of Korea, US military assistance fell from well over 10 per cent of GNP in the late 1950s to under 5 per cent in the second half of the 1960s (Little, ibid.: 459).

Wade (1990: 83) emphasises that the aid inflow assisted Taiwan in several important ways. His arguments are general and broadly apply to Korea as well. Thus:

1 The aid inflow met the immediate need of stabilising the economies in the wake of post-war dislocation.
2 It gave local and foreign investors confidence in the viability of the regime.
3 It helped finance land reform, dampen inflation and act as an important channel of technology transfer.
4 It allowed the economies to maintain large military establishments without becoming a major drain on resources.
5 American aid advisers played a role in the shift towards export-oriented industrialisation – a point which is also emphasised by Haggard (op. cit.).

Despite these important contributions which US aid made to the economies, Wade (op. cit.) recognises that aid cannot really be taken as a sufficient condition for superior economic performance of East Asia. Little (op. cit.: 457) also emphasises this point by observing that '[h]eavy aid coincided roughly with their

[Korea and Taiwan] period of slow growth, and they became miracle economies when aid dwindled away'. Riedel (1988: 25) makes a similar point and emphasises that 'Hong Kong did not receive much aid. . . . Singapore borrowed heavily in the early 1960s from the World Bank and the Asian Development Bank, but on relatively hard terms'.

It thus appears that one can easily exaggerate the importance of US aid to the East Asian NIEs. Ultimately, the impact of aid inflows depends on the absorptive capacity of recipients. Aid dependency is a well-known sydrome. The East Asian NIEs escaped from this syndrome because of their capacity to utilise the aid inflow in a productive manner.

Several authors have also emphasised the importance of the Vietnam War to the development of the East Asian NIEs. Cole and Lyman (1971: 135) have called it 'Korea's El Dorado'. Naya (1971) is one of the few studies which has attempted to analyse the impact of the Vietnam War on various economies. His methodology entailed the idea of interpreting the rapid increase in US military expenditures after 1964 as a result of the Vietnam War and dividing that magnitude by the GDP of the Asian countries under review. According to this indicator, Singapore appears to have the greatest impact followed by Korea and Taiwan.

Woo (op. cit.) offers an in-depth analysis on the impact of the Vietnam War on Korea. Her point is that the Vietnam War acted 'as an incubator of new industries before testing the fires of international competition' (Woo, ibid.: 97). These industries (steel, transport equipment, etc.) subsequently became the leader of the 1970s and 1980s. In addition, the Vietnam War offered an avenue for large Korean firms to gain experience in international construction projects by undertaking large-scale construction work in South Vietnam.

The Vietnam War was, in retrospect, a fortuitous event for the East Asian NIEs (in particular Korea). However, its implications have to be set in a broader perspective. A lucky event can only become a launching pad for sustained industrialisation if the country or countries in question have the initiative and enterprise to exploit the event to its advantage. The East Asian NIEs demonstrated that they could do so. Otherwise one would have seen a deceleration of growth after the termination of the Vietnam War.

CONCLUDING OBSERVATIONS

This chapter has examined the view that the miracle economies of East Asia are largely the product of fortuitous historical events. They were aided and buttressed by the USA, particularly in their critical post-war years, because of strategic and political considerations. The implication of this view is that the East Asian NIEs are special cases. This in turn entails the profoundly pessimistic message that these economies do not carry replicable policy lessons for the other developing countries. The chapter – and hence the book – rejects these implications on several grounds. It is difficult to establish convincingly that the East

Asian NIEs' superior economic performance can be traced to the historically entrenched Confucian value system. The evidence, as well as the dynamics, does not allow one to assert that these countries benefited enormously from a favourable colonial experience. Admittedly, they were major recipients of US aid (although this proposition does not extend to the city states) and generally gained from being strategic allies of the USA. However, to highlight the strategic context of East Asian growth at the expense of all other factors is to take a rather partial view of the development process. Development is typically a combination of exogenous (in the sense of initial conditions and external circumstances) and endogenous (in the form of internal political and policy circumstances) factors. Appropriate theories must also be dynamic and forward-looking, attempting to explain how favourable exogenous circumstances can be exploited into a phase of sustained success. The next chapter reviews such views.

3

EXPLAINING EAST ASIAN SUCCESS

Between the state and the market

Chapter 1 provided an empirical sketch of the phenomenal success of the East Asian newly industrialising economies, while Chapter 2 set the broad historical and strategic context of this ascendency. The purpose of this chapter is to focus on explanations which emphasise the role of internal policy and political factors in the rise of East Asian NIEs. There are two competing paradigms. A well-entrenched view maintains that East Asian success provides a clear demonstration of vigorous market competition and free trade as the twin 'engines of growth'. The alternative interpretation is that the state in East Asia represents the 'engine of growth'. The market-oriented explanation is often closely identified with neoclassical economics and, more recently, with neoclassical political economy. The statist interpretation of East Asian success belongs to the genre of new political economy. The dividing line between the two contending paradigms is, however, not always clear cut. There is a significant degree of overlap between the state and the market, suggesting that a broad-based, eclectic approach is more useful in understanding the nature of East Asian economic development. This represents the key message of this chapter and its exposition draws on Islam (1992a, b).

ORIGINS OF THE DEBATE

It is important to adopt an evolutionary perspective on the current debate on East Asian development. Its roots can in fact be traced to the paradigmatic evolution of development economics as an intellectual discipline. The pioneers of development economics (e.g. Rosentein-Rodan, 1943; Nurkse, 1953) regarded underdevelopment as a case of endemic 'market failure'. In other words, the private sector (the market) systematically undercommitted resources to growth-promoting activities. Rosentein-Rodan (op. cit.), for example, analysed the development problem as one in which decentralised entrepreneurs failed to invest since none of them in isolation had the guarantee that concurrent investment by others would occur in order to create a demand for one's output. Thus came Rosentein-Rodan's celebrated prescription for 'balanced growth' – a coordinated plan of investments by the government in strategic sectors of the economy.

This view firmly established the intellectual rationale for planning in the development literature – the so-called dirigisme syndrome.

Closely linked to the notion of endemic market failure in developing countries was a pervasive mood of 'export pessimism' that prevailed among the pioneers of development economics. Bhagwati has noted how this export pessimism is explicit and implicit in the writings of Nurkse (1953, 1959), Rosenstein-Rodan (op. cit.), Hirschman (1958), Prebisch (1959) and others:

> Astonishingly, many major development economists were pessimistic about foreign trade opportunities. Either they argued ... that the era of export-led growth was over and that trade could not be expected to be an engine of growth; or they argued, in varying ways, that trade opportunities became so restricted that development strategies would have to turn increasingly inward-looking, import substituting and the like.
>
> (Bhagwati, 1984: 28–9)

A particular version of the export pessimism thesis which became famous (or notorious depending on one's view!) pertains to the writings of Prebisch (op. cit.) who advocated import substituting industrialisation (ISI) in Latin America on the ground that the terms of trade for primary exports – historically the key export products of poor economies – were experiencing a secular decline. The Prebisch thesis launched a protracted period of ISI and critics have maintained ever since that this represented the key failure of traditional development economics. There is now a substantial body of theory and evidence which has comprehensively demonstrated that the costs of ISI have significantly outweighed its benefits (see, e.g., Little et al., 1970; Donges, 1976; Balassa, 1977a; Bhagwati and Srinivasan, 1975; Krueger, 1978). This literature is of such importance in tracing the debate on East Asian development that an overview is necessary.

In the initial phase, which usually covered non-durable consumer goods industries, ISI appeared to generate promising results. This was reflected in relatively rapid growth of the manufacturing sector. However, after the satisfaction of market demand for these goods, industrial growth typically slowed down to the rate of growth of domestic demand. Attempts to move on to the more mature phase of ISI, namely production of intermediate and capital goods, often did not yield much success.

The faltering pace of ISI in its mature phase was really a reflection of microeconomic inefficiencies which became entrenched in the manufacturing sector. These inefficiencies, in turn, typically represented wide-ranging direct interventions by the government: minimum wage laws, interest rate controls, tariff concessions on imported capital inputs, artificially high and multiple exchange rates, and tax concessions on investment and capital equipment. These microeconomic inefficiencies led to predictable effects: rather low labour absorption as the use of (scarce) physical capital was artificially encouraged at the expense of (abundant) semi-skilled labour; discrimination against export-oriented and agricultural activities; and, more ominously, it entrenches special interest groups interested in retaining monopoly privileges rather than in raising productive efficiency. On top of these microeconomic inefficiencies one must emphasise some adverse macroeconomic consequences. The spending programmes of governments intent on pursuing ISI often were not matched by increased tax revenues. This gave rise to progressively large fiscal deficits which were financed primarily by accelerating inflation and rising external indebtedness (Fishlow, 1990).

The policy regime that offers an alternative to ISI is often referred to as export-oriented industrialisation (EOI). Throughout this discussion, EOI will be defined to mean a set of trade and industrial policies which do not discriminate between production for the domestic market and exports, or between the purchases of domestic goods and foreign goods. Advocates of EOI argue that such a strategy yields substantial benefits to society. The primary advantage of EOI, according to its supporters, is that it promotes both allocative and dynamic efficiency. Resources are allocated according to the principle of comparative advantage so that one attains maximum production from a given stock of resources and a given state of technology. Perhaps more crucial are the additional benefits that are supposed to flow from the implementation of export-oriented policies: exploitation of economies of scale in the wider export market and enlarged technological and social capabilities as a result of the exposure to foreign know-how. In addition to allocative efficiency gains, advocates of EOI also claim that the strategy generates higher savings which in turn provides an additional boost to economic growth. The higher savings take place through several channels: higher household income generated by increased exports, a less distorted capital market compared to ISI in the sense that interest rates at least keep pace with the rate of inflation, and the greater inflow of foreign capital that seems to be associated with EOI. (See Chapters 5 and 8 for discussions on related issues.)

It has also been suggested (World Bank, 1987b) that EOI provides for self-correcting mechanisms for efficient macroeconomic management. The argument seems to be that misaligned macroeconomic variables, such as overvalued exchange rates and persistently high inflation rates, become quickly obvious because of their direct influence on a key performance target, the current account of the balance of payments.

Finally, advocates of EOI argue that it promotes equitable growth (Little, 1979; Papanek, 1988). This argument depends on the link between employment growth and EOI. The strategy by its very nature focuses on the growth of labour-intensive exports. This increases the demand for semi-skilled labour and thus allows the poorer sections of society to participate in the growth process. (See Chapters 9 and 12.)

The East Asian success stories, in fact, first came into the limelight through this protracted debate on the relationship between trade regimes and economic development. Supporters of the EOI strategy felt that the experience of East Asia vindicated their position. The following observations are typical:

The evidence is quite conclusive: countries applying outward-oriented development strategies had a superior performance in terms of exports, economic growth, and employment whereas countries with continued inward orientation encountered increasing economic difficulties.

(Balassa, 1981: 16–17)

It seems to be as firm a stylized fact as any in the economics of developing countries: a sustained movement to an outward-oriented trade regime leads to faster growth of both exports and income.

(Lal and Rajapatirana, 1987: 208)

Experience has been that growth performance has been more satisfactory under export promotion strategies ... than under import substitution strategies. ... There is little doubt the link between export performance and growth rates.

(Krueger, 1980: 288–9)

NEOCLASSICAL POLITICAL ECONOMY AND EAST ASIA

It thus appears that the notion that the state should play the role of an 'engine of growth' in the process of development came under relentless attack from the supporters of the EOI strategy. Indeed, Little (1982) regards this phenomenon as the 'resurgence of neoclassical economics' in development economics. As applied to the role of the state in economic development, neoclassical economics manifests itself in the specific form of 'neoclassical political economy' (Srinivasan, 1985).

The essence of neoclassical political economy can perhaps be best exemplified by focusing on a particular example. Suppose that the central policy makers of a hypothetical low-income country are able to establish that there is underinvestment by the private sector in a 'socially desirable' industry (e.g. a 'high-tech' industry). It then decides to 'target' this industry as a priority investment area and tries to achieve this aim through a complex array of policy instruments. Thus, it offers subsidised credit, restrains competing imports through a combination of tariffs and quotas, regulates entry to the industry by issuing licences to a limited number of firms and provides a captive market for the products of the industry through its procurement policies. The net effect of these policy interventions is to create monopoly rents or scarcity premiums. The presence of such rents can induce responses among private sector participants that go beyond the 'public interest' objectives of the policy makers. Thus the private sector could form 'distributional coalitions' (Olson, 1982) and engage in lobbying activities designed to capture the rents. These rent-seeking activities – which can range from lobbying within legal limits to outright bribery and corruption – are unproductive in the sense that they yield income or profits to private interests but do not produce goods or services that add to societal output. Even worse, a vicious circle may set in: an initial policy intervention creates monopoly elements which then become entrenched and oppose change and reform and in fact induce further policy interventions that create cumulative monopoly rents. State activism thus engenders cumulative inefficiencies that retard economic development. Some crude estimates suggest that policy-induced rent-seeking costs may be as high as 15 per cent of GNP (World Bank, op. cit.: 76).

Given the gory neoclassical account of the regressive role of the state in economic development, neoclassical political economy adherents suggest that the state in developing economies should operate within carefully prescribed limits. Thus:

1   The state should primarily rely on market-based, private-sector-driven initiatives in the mobilisation and allocation of resources to growth-promoting activities.
2   The state should intervene only in cases of clearly established 'market failure' (i.e. in cases where private sector operations do not correspond to societal interests).
3   Even in cases of proven market failure, the appropriate policy responses should be parametric measures (such as lump-sum taxes and subsidies) as well as incentives that establish a private market (such as a venture capital market).
4   The state should provide 'pure public goods' (law and order, national defence, public infrastructure) including the proper assignment and enforcement of property rights.
5   The state should provide a stable and predictable macroeconomic environment through appropriate coordination of fiscal, monetary and exchange rate policies.
6   The state should adopt a free trade (or almost free trade) regime as a core component of a neutral policy regime.

The areas designated by (1)–(6) are areas in which the state has a distinct comparative advantage over the private sector. If the state progressively exceeds the limits set by the aforementioned prescriptions, then eventually 'government failure' will occur which will more than offset the alleged inadequacies of the private sector.

In applying these ideas to the East Asian NIEs, the adherents of neoclassical political economy would argue that by relying on the private sector and free trade, these countries have been able to minimise government failure so common in other developing countries. Hence, the secret behind their dynamic economic growth is not really a secret.

NEW POLITICAL ECONOMY AND EAST ASIA

Neoclassical political economy has undoubtedly established itself as a dominant paradigm in development economics. However, a growing body of research on the role of the state in economic development has begun to question the tenets of neoclassical political economy. This literature is largely a phenomenon of the 1980s and is still in search of a coherent identity. One may attach the label of 'new political economy' to this literature for ease of reference. It may, in fact, be seen as an attempt to revive the notion of the state as an engine of growth.

The starting point of new political economy is that 'the rent-seeking literature is better at explaining failures ... rather than success stories, particularly of state-led industrialisation, and there have been some dramatic cases of the latter ...' (Bardhan, 1990: 5). Like neoclassical political economy, new political economy draws its inspiration from East Asia. It also draws its inspiration from the parallel literature on Japanese economic success. It contends that at the core of East Asian success lies enlightened policy activism of national governments. This interpretation of the East Asian case is, of course, in sharp contrast to the neo-classical view: 'Every successful country (Taiwan, South Korea, Singapore, Hong Kong, Japan) has relied primarily on private enterprise and free markets to achieve economic development. Every country in trouble has relied primarily on government to guide and direct its economic development' (Friedman, as quoted in Sachs, 1985).

Advocates of new political economy are keen to point out that the East Asian NIEs have been as interventionist as some of the less successful developing countries. Thus, for example, the weight of the government in the economy measured in terms of the share of GDP in state enterprise is apparently greater in Taiwan and South Korea than in many Latin American countries. A more searching analysis of regulatory mechanisms in East Asia (e.g. the regulation of the financial sector) suggests an equally pervasive presence of the state (Wade, 1988, 1990). This has led to the growing realisation that what matters to the process of economic development is not the extent of intervention but the quality of such intervention (Bardhan, op. cit.; Sen, 1983; Sachs, op. cit.).

According to new political economy, it is necessary to distinguish between different types of state as a means of analysing the circumstances in which policy activism will yield social benefits. As a first approximation, one may distinguish two generic types: the 'weak' and the 'strong' state. The former is captive to a wide array of distributional coalitions and thus exposed to the ravages of rent-seeking activities. The latter, on the other hand, is able to develop a considerable degree of insulation (or relative autonomy) from the ravages of rent-seeking groups (Haggard, 1988, 1990). The emphasis on 'relative autonomy' is important: no state operates in a vacuum. The ideal-type strong state may in fact develop durable links with some modernising interests but exclude or restrict the access of more narrowly based and fractious groups to the policy-making process. Given these distinctive features, the 'strong' state is able, on average, to formulate and implement policies that are broadly in line with societal interests. Thus, for example, the strong state is more likely to resist protectionist measures and adopt policies that facilitate export-oriented industrialisation.

What are the institutional mechanisms that allow a state to develop 'relative autonomy'? Initial work in this area was influenced by the Japanese experience in the post-war period. Hailed by many as a shining example of state-led industrialisation, the characteristic features of the Japanese policy-making process is seen as providing the archetypical institutional mechanisms of the 'strong, developmental state' (Vogel, 1979; Dore, 1986; Johnson, 1982). These ideas have also been used to analyse the nature of the policy-making regime of the East Asian NIEs (Wade, op. cit.; Lee and Naya, 1988; C.H. Lee, 1992; Johnson, 1987; White, 1988; Gereffi and Wyman, 1990; Onis, 1991; Jones and Sakong, 1980; Rodan, 1989). The East Asian state is supposedly characterised by:

1 an elite bureaucracy staffed by the best managerial talent in the system;
2 an authoritarian political system in which the bureaucracy is given sufficient scope to take policy initiatives;
3 close government–big business cooperation in the policy-making process.

Some observers (C.H. Lee, op. cit.; Lee and Naya, op. cit.) regard (3) as being the most important element of the East Asian State. According to this view, the close government–big business cooperation converts the state into a 'quasi-internal organisation' (QIO).

How is the QIO supposed to operate? It can do so in two forms:

1 As an 'internal capital market' (Zysman, 1983; Wade, 1988; C.H. Lee, op. cit.).
2 As a subtle network of long-term ties with the corporate sector (Okimoto, 1989; Lee and Naya, op. cit.).

The QIO as 'internal capital market' can be related to the ideas of Williamson's (1975, 1985) theory of the firm. Williamson argued that in the presence of high business transaction costs and imperfect capital markets, the firm would tend to use its internal funds to finance its operations. Thus, the firm would act as an 'internal capital market'. Similarly, in the presence of under-developed capital markets, as is typically the case in developing economies, the state can control and regulate the financial system in order to finance development activities. Hence, under these circumstances, the state can operate as a vast 'internal capital market'. This, in turn, provides the state with considerable leverage over the private corporate sector, as it can exercise discretion in channelling credit to various sectors and industries. Thus, in terms of this framework, the state acts as a QIO through its control and regulation of the financial system.

The notion of the QIO as a subtle network of long-term ties with the corporate sector derives from the notion that, in East Asia, the ruling élite (consisting of key members of the ruling political party, centralised bureaucrats and managers of large private enterprises) share a common background (in terms of coming from the same school and university). This provides the basis for developing informal, but binding, ties between key representatives of the state and key representatives of the private sector. In many cases, these informal ties are reinforced through a variety of institutional arrangements. Thus, for example, 'discussion councils' provide a forum for private and public sector personnel to exchange views and opinions on the future course of the economy and society. One may also mention the practice of 'amakaduri' in Japan, whereby senior civil servants move into the boardrooms of large private organisations after retirement (Whitehill, 1990).

The two forms in which the East Asian QIO is supposed to operate are summarised in Figure 3.1 for ease of reference. As can be seen, where the state acts as an internal capital market, the emphasis is on the way the policy makers exercise influence over the private sector through the financial system. In the case where the QIO operates as a 'network' state, the emphasis is on a variety of informal and formal institutional arrangements of cooperation between the private and public sectors.

QIO AS AN 'INTERNAL CAPITAL MARKET'

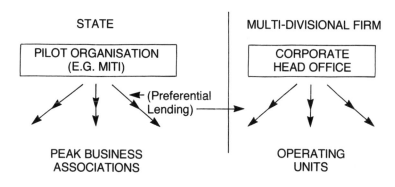

QIO AS A "NETWORK" STATE

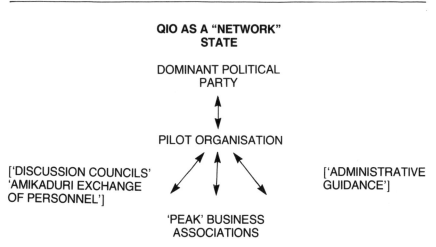

Figure 3.1 Schematic presentation of QIO

49

Proponents of the QIO paradigm are keen to show that as an institutional arrangement it is optimal in terms of economic policy making. Once this hypothesis can be established, it is possible to argue that, given that the East Asian state is organised as a QIO, it will generate more efficient economic policies – and correspondingly superior economic performance – compared with non-QIO regimes in other developing countries.

Why is the QIO so efficient in terms of economic policy making? There are several ways of justifying this notion:

1   The theorem of collective action derived from Olson (op. cit.).
2   The game theoretic rationale based on the work of Axelrod (1984).
3   Transaction costs economics as developed by Williamson (op. cit.).

The Olsonian approach would concede that 'distributional coalitions' and rent-seeking activities are common in any society. However, it would provide a more subtle interpretation of rent-seeking activity. The Olsonian approach, which prefers to use the more neutral term of 'collective action' as a synonym for rent-seeking activities, argues that not all distributional coalitions are counterproductive. If distributional coalitions are organised as broad-based or encompassing organisations, then they are likely to align societal interests with private interests compared with more narrowly based distributional coalitions. This is the fundamental logic of collective action. Narrowly based distributional coalitions have an incentive to engage in 'zero sum' activities: their gain is another group's loss. Encompassing organisations, on the other hand, do not have a similar incentive to engage in 'zero sum' activities. Given their very weight in the economy, the larger the societal output the greater is the gain for an encompassing organisation. Hence, there is an incentive to attach primacy to societal interests at the expense of competing private interests. The QIO is a classic example of an encompassing organisation. The logic of the Olsonian approach would thus suggest that the QIO is likely to adopt policies which are aligned with societal interests. It is for this reason that the East Asian state is able to resist the ravages of rent-seeking behaviour.

The second approach entails an application of the basic principles of game theory to the East Asian context. A fundamental tenet of game theory is that when 'players' (the appropriate analogue in this case being distributional coalitions) compete with each other, the individual outcome is paradoxically less profitable than an outcome in which 'players' are able to cooperate with each other. A way out of this paradox – often called the 'prisoner's dilemma' – has been suggested by Axelrod (op. cit.). His point is that if dominant players engaged in a game of repeated interaction then this could induce cooperative behaviour to emerge. These game theoretic ideas have obvious implications for the QIO. The representatives of the QIO are at the same time dominant players of society. Repeated interaction among such dominant players induces an atmosphere of trust and cooperation to emerge. This in turn allows a substantial agreement on an agenda of economic development to emerge. At the same time, it allows the QIO to fend off or modulate pressures from other elements of society when it is perceived that these pressures might deter or impair the critical elements of the economic development agenda.

The final approach, which has received considerable prominence in the writings of Lee and Naya (op. cit.) and C.H.Lee (op. cit.), derives its intellectual inspiration from transaction costs economics, at the core of which are the contributions of Williamson (op. cit.). Williamson considers *internal organisations*, of which the private firm is a prime example, and the *market* as alternative institutional modes for organising the exchange of goods and services (including such intangibles as knowledge and technology). He identifies a generic class of 'market failure' (i.e. the market will not be efficient in organising transactions) which is conceptually distinct from the familiar ones of externalities and monopoly imperfections. All transactions are characterised by either implicit or explicit contractual arrangements. There are both ex-ante and ex-post costs of negotiating, implementing and enforcing contracts. These 'transaction costs' – which can be particularly acute for complex exchange, such as transfer of technology – stem from *bounded rationality* and *opportunistic behaviour*. The former pertains to the notion that individual economic agents have a limited capacity to comprehend and foresee all possible contingencies. The latter relates to the notion that parties to a contract tend to exploit asymmetric information to their advantage.

In the presence of pervasive transactions costs, 'market failure' is common. The internal organisation – such as a firm – may be seen as a response to 'market failure'. Thus, 'profit seeking firms internalise transactions when by doing so the costs of organising and transacting business will thereby be lowered' (Teece, 1986: 23). It is in this sense that internal organisations like firms are more efficient than the market.

It is important to note that not all internal organisations will be equally efficient. Thus, as firms become large through progressive internalisation of transactions, owners necessarily have to delegate control to professional managers. This creates conditions for 'organisational failures', as managers engage in opportunistic behaviour to pursue goals that do not necessarily maximise profits. Williamson argued that the firm itself will respond to organisational failure by changing its internal organisational design into an M-form (multi-divisional) structure. A stylised characterisation of the M-form firm may be provided as follows:

1   It has a corporate head office which oversees a set of quasi-autonomous operating divisions.
2   The head office is principally concerned with strategic decisions involving planning, appraisal and control, while operating decisions fall within the domain of the divisions.
3   In carrying out its functions, the head office performs the role of an 'internal

capital market' in the sense that funds are allocated to competing divisions on the basis of high-yield use.

4   The internal capital market role of the head office is supported by *control* and *incentive* machinery. Control mechanisms include such measures as regular internal audit to identify below-average performance, while incentives such as salaries, bonuses, etc., may be used to reward performance consistent with corporate goals.

5   The efficacy of the internal capital market function of the head office is greatly assisted by the fact that, given the quasi-autonomous standing of the divisions, the contribution of each division to corporate-level profit can be easily observed and measured. As a result, top executives can measure performance on the basis of profit criteria.

6   Finally, the separation of operating and head office functions provides executives with a psychological commitment to overall performance of the organisation.

The detailed depiction of Williamson's M-form hypothesis leads to a fundamental point: the M-form firm is more efficient than both the *market* (which is afflicted by transaction costs-related market failure) and *firms not organised along M-form lines* (they are afflicted by organisational failure).

The QIO paradigm (as developed by Lee and Naya (op. cit.) and C.H. Lee (op. cit.)) attempts to apply the Williamsonian theory of the firm to the East Asian state and to draw equivalent normative implications. Thus, when the state is organised as a QIO, the role of the centralised policy maker becomes equivalent to the role of the head office, while the role of the business groups become equivalent to the divisions (see Figure 3.1).

How do policy makers maintain control over the corporate sector and ensure that it adheres to state-articulated goals? Once again the control and incentive machinery are rather similar to the M-form firm. Thus, for example, policy makers would perform internal audits on the corporate sector through tax audits. More importantly, the government would operate as a vast internal capital market by allocating funds to key corporate clients. These funds are in effect subsidised credit provided to 'targeted' business groups. In order to ensure efficiency, the state would need to impose performance standards on subsidy recipients. This suggests the use of performance targets which can be functionally related in a direct, observable manner to central development goals. If, as in East Asia, the centralised policy makers are committed to economic growth via export growth, the use of export targets closely tied to the allocation of subsidised credit appears to be a logical choice.

Having established the similarity between the QIO and the M-form enterprise, the proponents of this paradigm note: 'given [that] the modern multi-unit enterprise is an efficient institution ... it follows that the quasi-internal organization can be efficient in achieving its objectives, (C.H. Lee, op. cit.: 13).

WHICH WAY NOW?

The debate on the East Asian success stories has so far been depicted as a case of choosing two alternative explanatory variables: the state vs the market. The purpose of this section is to convey the important message that there is an overlap between the two. The market needs the state as much as the state needs the market. This point is established by summarising the contributions and limitations of both neoclassical political economy and new political economy, particularly in terms of their implications for East Asia.

Neoclassical political economy has made an important contribution to the development literature by popularising the notion of 'government failure'. There has been an unfortunate tendency among many observers working in this tradition to make the unwarranted inference that 'government failure' is common, while 'market failure' is rare and exceptional. Thus, any attempt to interfere with the market would retard economic development (Lal, 1983; Bauer 1972, 1984). Shapiro and Taylor (1990) have, with some justification, referred to this phenomenon as the reification of the market. On the other hand, some serious scholars steeped in the neoclassical tradition tend to argue that both 'government failure' and 'market failure' are common, so that the fundamental development challenge is to devise institutional arrangements which minimise 'government failure' while at the same time preserving the benefits that flow from the rectification of 'market failure' (Stiglitz, 1990). This suggests that the state has a fundamental role to play in economic development. This does not necessarily mean that the state then becomes an 'engine of growth', as suggested by the pioneers of development economics and as argued by the new political economy of East Asia. Perhaps a more appropriate characterisation is to regard the state as a 'handmaiden of growth'. This suggests a regime where policy makers limit their functions to areas where they have a comparative advantage over the private sector (macroeconomic management, provision of public goods, including enforcement and clear assignment of property rights), where they use parametric measures to cope with proven cases of market failure, and where they show a firm commitment to free trade.

The attractiveness of the neoclassical political economy – but only in terms of its more eclectic versions – is that it suggests a relatively simple institutional arrangement for minimising 'government failure'. Thus, the archetypical neoclassical state would minimise the opportunity and incentive for rent-seeking behaviour, economise on the information burden on policy makers and economise on scarce managerial and administrative talent in the public sector. The archetypical neoclassical state is also compatible with both an authoritarian political structure and democratic institutions.

The new political economy of East Asia has also made a significant contribution to the greater understanding of the policy process and politics that underpin any successful development strategy. In making such a contribution, it has exposed the misleading nature of the more strident and uncritical neoclassical interpretations of East Asian economic success. Yet, in many respects, recent versions of the new political economy in the context of East Asia overstate their case. This point is established by highlighting several analytical deficiencies of new political economy.

First, one has to note that the QIO as a 'network state' is a nebulous concept. Its propositions are difficult to falsify. This is because the dense organisational network which is supposed to exist between the policy makers and the private sector is primarily of a subtle and informal nature and hence not readily observable.

Second, while the QIO as an internal capital market is an empirically tractable notion, it does not really apply to all the East Asian economies. In terms of accuracy of institutional details, the QIO as an internal capital market is far more relevant to South Korea than to the rest of East Asia. The Hong Kong and Singapore cases would probably be readily acknowledged by the QIO proponents. The Taiwan case is more debatable, with Wade (1988, 1990) arguing in favour of the hypothesis, but Park (1990) suggesting otherwise. Even within South Korea, the internal capital market model is historically specific, being more applicable to certain periods than to others. Certainly, as subsequent chapters of this book will show, South Korean policy makers tried to use its control of the financial system to allocate credit to priority sectors during the 1970s. However, the government has tried to reduce its role as an internal capital market during the 1980s by attempting to deregulate the financial sector.

Third, the efficiency of the QIO as an internal capital market is typically justified by appealing to transaction costs economics as articulated by Williamson. However, Hill (1985, 1988) has shown that Williamson's central propositions are not empirically robust. In other words, there is no clear evidence that the large, diversified firm – the so-called M-form firm – generates consistently superior economic performance compared with other organisational modes when it operates as an internal capital market. If this is the case, the lack of empirical credibility of Williamson's M-form hypothesis simultaneously affects the credibility of the QIO paradigm.

Fourth, there is a tendency in this approach to treat the policy-making process in a mechanical fashion, with the private sector responding passively to bureaucratic initiative and guidance. A better characterisation of the complex dynamics of the policy-making process in East Asia is the 'politics of reciprocal consent' (Samuels, 1987), where a fragmented state authority (caused, for example, by inter- and intra-bureaucratic rivalry) negotiates with a powerful private sector. This portrait of the policy-making process strongly implies that consensus building is often a matter of negotiation and compromise, carrying with it the risk that state preferences may not necessarily prevail over private preferences even in the case of a QIO.

Fifth, the validity of the new political economy approach to economic development cannot be separated from the role of foreign trade and the way it shapes state autonomy. In their eagerness to construct the hypothesis of the state as an engine of growth, new political economy theorists sometimes imply that foreign trade – in the specific form of export-oriented policies – plays a superficial role in economic development. Yet they also argue that the reason why policy makers in East Asia managed to maintain efficient policies had to do with the foreign trade dependence of their economies. In other words, once policy makers became aware that domestic economic fortunes were closely linked to export growth, they were constrained from making persistent policy mistakes. If this is the case, then export orientation plays a primary role in East Asian economic development, with state activism playing a supplementary role – an implication that runs contrary to the central arguments of new political economy!

Sixth, new political economy pays insufficient attention to the fact that there is a range of institutional arrangements for achieving relative state autonomy (Ragowski, 1987; Haggard and Moon, 1990). The QIO is one possible arrangement, the neoclassical state is yet another. Failure to emphasise the functional equivalence of institutional arrangements for achieving state autonomy leads new political economy into the trap of implying that authoritarianism is necessary for economic growth. This provides an easy target for those who are keen to tell sordid stories of labour repression 'beneath the economic miracle' of East Asia (Deyo, 1989).

Finally, it is worth emphasising that advocates of QIO are aware that the state, even when organised as a QIO within an export-oriented regime, can make episodic, but significant, policy mistakes. This is evident in the following observations :

> It is important to point out here that the quasi-internal organization is not relatively efficient under all circumstances. As the economy grows and as the number of enterprises increases within the organization, it will run into more of 'internal organizational failures', increasing the cost of policy implementation. Moreover, as the economy graduates from producing simple labour-intensive products, choosing right industries to promote will become more difficult. Consequently, the quasi-internal organization is more likely to make mistakes of choosing wrong policies than before.
>
> (Lee and Naya, op. cit.: S147)

Given the above observations, is it possible to draw firm conclusions about the role of the state in East Asian economic development? It is tempting to suggest that the issue should be resolved by making use of the available evidence. The problem is that the evidence – which is covered in detail at various stages in the rest of the book – is equivocal, supporting elements of both the statist and neoclassical interpretations (Wade, 1990). This is perhaps to be expected. The extreme versions of the statist as well as the neoclassical models of East Asian success lack analytical and empirical credibility. One must move away from the idea that the 'strong, developmental state' in East Asia produced error-free policies. Equally, one must move away from the naive notion that East Asian success vindicates the efficacy of 'laissez-faire' policies. The truth probably lies in a synergistic interaction between the state and the market. More importantly, while the state in East Asia may not have played the role of an 'engine of growth', it has certainly played the role of a 'handmaiden of growth'. Policy makers in such countries fulfilled an important developmental function by carrying out necessary policy reforms which created and maintained an environment conducive to rapid economic growth. They have also fulfilled an important task by making necessary investments in essential infrastructure. In cases where policy makers moved to the much more ambitious and risky realm of industry-specific interventions, the limits to their potency became evident. This is the fundamental lesson to be learnt from the political economy of East Asian economic development.

4

AGRICULTURE AND RURAL DEVELOPMENT

The fundamental importance of agriculture to economic development was first expounded by Johnston and Mellor (1961). They argued that agriculture provided five vital contributions to the development process: (1) meeting the demand for food for a growing population, as long as this was consistent with comparative advantage; (2) providing a source of foreign savings or earnings; (3) providing a source of savings for investment in development of other sectors, mainly industry; (4) providing human resources and raw materials for other sectors; (5) providing an internal market for the goods and services of other sectors (industry and services). Despite the vital role that agriculture can play in the development process, both the theory and practice of development economics in the 1950s and 1960s tended to neglect the agricultural sector (Mellor, 1986; Little, 1982), regarding the latter as peripheral to the fundamental task of industrialisation.

Several factors lie behind the relative neglect of the agricultural sector during the 1950s and the 1960s. To start with, the development models of the time emphasised capital accumulation and the latter was seen as synonymous with industrialisation. Second, there was an enduring perception that the agricultural sector provided a source of 'surplus' labour which could be costlessly transferred to the urban industrial sector (Lewis, 1954). Finally, farmers were considered irrational peasants who did not respond to price incentives. These views, however, came to be increasingly challenged, starting with the pioneering work of Schultz (1964). There was the growing realisation that a sluggish agricultural sector held back the growth of the overall economy and perpetuated rural poverty. Increasingly, the emphasis was on an appropriate policy mix which entailed broad-based investment in rural infrastructure (adequate provision of infrastructure in the form of roads, electrification, irrigation systems, etc.), price incentives for farmers, and education and training to enhance the capacity of farmers to adopt innovations, particularly in the light of the 'green revolution' (or the spread of technological progress in the agricultural sector). Several commentators also emphasised that policies towards agriculture and rural development must move beyond microlevel and sector-specific concerns and ensure that the overall macropolicy environment is conducive to the growth of the agricultural sector (e.g. Johnston and Kilby, 1975). This meant ensuring that trade policy was not biased in favour of capital-intensive import substituting industries, that exchange rates were maintained at realistic levels and that factor markets were broadly in equilibrium.

How does the experience of the NIEs with respect to the agricultural sector fare in light of the changing perceptions on the role of agriculture and rural development in overall development? This issue represents the subject matter of this chapter. The popular perception is that the NIEs prospered because, unlike other developing countries, they did not neglect the agricultural sector. Relatively rapid agricultural growth preceded rapid industrial growth. In arriving at this happy outcome they were assisted by conducive macroeconomic policies, appropriate sector-specific policies and favourable initial conditions (particularly in the form of land reform). The chapter suggests that such a broad generalisation hides some unpalatable facts and overlooks divergent experiences. Moreover, as the NIEs approach industrial maturity, the agricultural sector is increasingly emerging as the 'problem sector'. These key points are developed by focusing on several areas: the contemporary relevance of land reform to the performance of the agricultural sector, the diversification of farm household incomes through the provision of off-farm employment opportunities (a phenomenon referred to as 'rural industrialisation') and the evolution of agricultural protection.

In developing the key arguments in this chapter, the focus will be on Korea and Taiwan. The city states of Hong Kong and Singapore historically have had a peripheral agricultural sector and it continues to play a minor role. It is also important to note that the perception of the agriculture sector as a 'problem sector' is particularly valid for Korea.

EAST ASIAN AGRICULTURE IN TRANSITION: HISTORICAL OVERVIEW

Before delving into specific issues, it would be useful to provide a broad empirical context. Accordingly, Table 4.1 presents some basic indicators as a means of capturing the changing importance of agriculture in Korea and Taiwan. As can be seen, the share of agriculture in GDP has declined from 37.0 per cent in 1960 to 9.0 per cent by 1989 in Korea, and from 33.0 per cent to 4.4 per cent over the same period in Taiwan – reflecting the emergence of these economies as relatively industrialised societies. The sectoral reallocation of employment has been less rapid. Even in 1989, the agricultural sector employed nearly 20 per cent of the work force in Korea and about 13 per cent of the labour force in Taiwan.

The growth performance of the agricultural sector is shown in Table 4.2. Korea and Taiwan represent interesting contrasts. In the case of Korea, the growth of the agricultural sector decelerated sharply, when one compares the 1960s to the 1970s, with agricultural growth falling from 4.5 per cent in the 1960–70 period to 1.4 per cent in the 1971–80 period. Buoyant growth (4.5 per cent) resumes in the 1980s. In Taiwan, the sharp deceleration in agricultural

Table 4.1 Sectoral distribution of GDP and employment

Economy and year	GDP (%)			Employment (%)		
	Agriculture	Manufacturing*	Services	Agriculture	Manufacturing	Services
Korea						
1960	37.0	20.0	43.0	66.0	9.0	25.0
1970	28.9	29.4	46.7	50.0	13.0	36.0
1980	14.2	37.8	48.0	34.0	21.6	43.5
1989	9.0	45.2	45.8	19.5	27.6	52.3
Taiwan						
1960	33.0	25.0	42.0	56.0	11.0	33.0
1970	17.9	40.9	41.4	35.0	20.0	43.0
1980	7.9	46.0	46.1	19.5	32.7	47.0
1989	4.4	45.4	50.1	12.5	33.9	52.9

Sources: See Tables 1.5 and 1.6.
* Pertains to the industrial sector as a whole.

growth continues unabated, falling from 3.4 per cent in the 1960–70 period to 1.3 per cent in the 1981–9 period.

The intertemporal growth patterns in agriculture raise some important implications. The standard position taken by many development economists is that a sluggish agricultural sector can act as a major constraint on overall growth. This point is of course valid for a largely agrarian economy. By the end of the 1960s, however, the process of industrialisation had consolidated itself in Taiwan and Korea, so that buoyant growth in the non-agricultural sector (especially manufacturing) more than offset the sluggish growth of the agricultural sector. This implies that one should look to periods preceding the 1960s in order the obtain a fuller understanding of the historical role of agriculture in the economic development of the NIEs.

Some estimates suggest that agricultural growth was highest in the 1950s, averaging around 5 per cent in Taiwan (Economist Intelligence Unit, 1991: 19). This rapid growth, however, cannot be attributed to a conducive macroeconomic policy environment. As is well known, the period of the 1950s is dominated by import substituting industrialisation (ISI) and ISI imparts a systematic bias against the agricultural sector. This means that one has to look at a broader framework in assessing the impact of agriculture on economic development. T.H. Lee (1971), among others, has investigated the contribution of the agricultural sector to Taiwanese economic growth within a Johnston–Mellor framework over the 1895–1960 period. Thus, he contends that rising agricultural productivity fuelled the growth in farmers' incomes. This in turn assisted in widening the domestic market for manufactures and services, particularly in labour-intensive activities. In addition, agricultural exports which were dominant in the 1950s and the early

Table 4.2   Growth of production (average annual growth rate, %)

Economy and year	Agriculture	Manufacturing	Services
Korea			
1960–70	4.5	17.2	8.4
1971–80	1.4	14.2	7.8
1981–9	4.2	11.5	8.7
Taiwan			
1960–70	3.4	17.3	7.8
1971–80	1.8	12.8	9.0
1981–9	1.3	8.1	7.8

Sources: World Bank, *Work Development Report* (various issues); Asian Development Bank, *Key Indicators* (various issues).

1960s released the constraints on farm earnings from domestic sales alone (Fei *et al.*, 1979).

Taiwan, in the 1950s, relied on the policy instrument of shifting the terms of trade against agriculture in order to aid industrial growth. It led to a sizeable outflow of surplus and financed approximately 75 per cent of capital formation in the 1951–5 period (T.H. Lee, op. cit.: 29). Other analysts have supported a similar view (Dorner, 1969; Koo, 1968). Christensen (1968) has emphasised that the increase in farm productivity over this period was sufficiently rapid to permit these intersectoral transfers and still allow an increase in living standards of the rural population.

Korea in the 1950s also placed considerable emphasis in shifting the terms of trade against agriculture in order to aid industrial growth (Moon, 1991). This was achieved by maintaining low prices for staple food grains and preventing wide seasonal price fluctuations. Unlike Taiwan, the results were unsatisfactory. Moon (ibid.: 373–4) offers a critique in the following manner:

> [l]ow food prices primarily served to increase industrial profits and capital formation at the expense of farm producers. The adverse terms of trade ... impoverished the ... rural economy. It also hindered efforts to increase food production. ... Against this background, the government began in the late 1960s to improve the terms of trade for agricultural products ... the level of government investment in the agricultural sector was also substantially increased.

Moon (ibid.: 373) also emphasises that there is little evidence to support the view that the agricultural sector 'provided sizeable financial resources for investment in the non-agricultural sectors during the 1950s and 1960s'. One is thus left with the impression that the process of agricultural growth followed apparently divergent patterns in Taiwan and Korea. This, as will be seen at subsequent stages, is a recurring theme of this chapter.

LAND REFORM AND AGRICULTURAL DEVELOPMENT

It is widely acknowledged that land reform played a key role in the agricultural development of Korea and Taiwan. The purpose of this section is to trace this relationship and focus on its contemporary relevance.

When Taiwan was under Japanese occupation, Japanese landlords controlled a substantial part of the land. Land reform in Taiwan was carried out in three distinct phases: rent reduction, sale of public land and the land-to-the-tiller programme (Dorner and Thiesenhusen, 1990, based on Yager, 1988; Parsons *et al.*, 1956; Christensen, op. cit.). The rent reduction rule (whereby rents dropped from 50–70 per cent of the annual yield of the main crop to 37.5 per cent) was implemented in April 1949. Initially, problems of non-compliance were widespread. The government responded with a massive inspection and supervision programme which eventually led to a relatively effective implementation of the legislation.

The second phase of the land reform began with the sale of farmland that had belonged to Japanese government agencies and private Japanese citizens. Such 'public' land amounted to 20 per cent of arable land. By December 1953, when these sales were completed, 35 per cent of these public lands were sold to cultivators, 24 per cent continued under lease to private cultivators and 41 per cent was retained by public enterprises and government agencies for their own use (Yager, op. cit.).

The land-to-the-tiller programme, which was the final phase of the land reform programme in Taiwan was carried out between 1953 and 1954. Its key feature was that tenanted land would be purchased by the government and sold to current cultivators. These purchases were financed by sales of stocks and bonds. By the time this component of the reform was completed, the tenancy rate fell to 15 per cent compared with the pre-reform period of 38 per cent (Yager, ibid.).

Commentators on the Taiwanese experience with land reform generally agree that the reform programme had many beneficial consequences (Dorner and Thiesenhusen, op. cit.). Farm operators became substantially better off, through a combination of rent reduction and acquisition of ownership. They also became a progressive force in farmers' associations. These associations were instrumental in the promotion of research and technology for agriculture, extension services, provision of various inputs to the farming sector and so on. Land reform also played a key role in improving the distribution of income (see Chapter 12 for details). Finally, land reform provided the basis for the rapid growth of the agricultural sector in the 1950s.

It is easy, however, to exaggerate the beneficial effects of land reform. For instance, Yager (op. cit.: 51) notes that agricultural output increased by 10 per cent annually from 1946 to 1951. It is misleading to attribute this increase to land reform for two reasons. First, the rather impressive growth rate of the agricultural sector is biased by the fact that output started from a very low base (given the destruction of the Second World War). Second, the land reform programme was substantially incomplete even by 1951. It must also be emphasised that the much-praised farmers' associations were a legacy of Japanese colonial rule and were not the product of the land reform (Dorner and Thiesenhusen, op. cit.: 76). More generally, the entrepreneurial and managerial capacity of farmers did not suddenly blossom after the land reform. These are durable traits that existed prior to the reform period. The substantial outflow from agriculture that financed incipient industrialisation in Taiwan cannot also be directly linked to land reform. The intersectoral resource flow occurred largely via the mechanism of shifting the terms of trade against agriculture (see previous discussion). Land reform played a more indirect role in the sense that, by boosting real incomes of farmers, it permitted the intersectoral resource flows to take place. Finally, while land reform was a key factor in improving income distribution in Taiwan, it was not the only factor (see Chapter 12).

Consider now the experience of Korean land reform. Under Japanese colonial rule, land ownership was extremely skewed. In the mid-1940s, for example, 3 per cent of owners held 64 per cent of the land (Ahmed, 1975). More importantly, the majority of the landlords were Japanese. When the Second World War liberated Korea from Japan, the political and social situation was ripe for agrarian reforms. As in the case of Taiwan, land reform was initiated by outside influences – in the specific form of US military rulers. Dorner and Thiesenhusen have emphasised that the motives were primarily political rather than economic:

> The central idea was not that land reform would necessarily increase agricultural productivity . . . they viewed the purpose of this agrarian reform as pacifying a dissatisfied peasantry . . . (another) goal of agrarian reform was to dissuade the south from becoming enamoured with the prevailing Marxist ideology of the north.
>
> (Dorner and Thiesenhusen, op. cit.: 78–9)

Land reform in Korea occurred in two phases (Dorner and Thiesenhusen, op. cit., based on Ahmed, op. cit., King, 1977; Powelson and Stock, 1987). In the first phase, which lasted between 1948 and 1950, the government – under the direction of the US military rulers – acquired formerly Japanese-held land. Such land amounted to 13–15 per cent of arable hectares. When they were eventually distributed, they benefited 35 per cent of all families. In the second phase, which began in 1950, legislation was enacted which empowered the government to purchase farmland in the following circumstances: absentee landlords, farm property exceeding 3 hectares, and farmland not owner cultivated. When this phase was eventually completed by 1964, Korea was turned into a nation of smallholders. In 1947, 16.5 per cent of farm households were owned. The corresponding figure was 71.6 per cent in 1964. At the same time, the tenancy rate dropped from 42.1 per cent to 7 per cent over the 1947–64 period (Wang, 1988).

It must be emphasised that the passage of land reform was not as smooth and as effective as in Taiwan. To start with, it was a much more protracted affair, taking approximately 20 years to accomplish. The early years of reform were also afflicted by the disruption of the Korean war, the heavy burden of mortgage payments on beneficiaries, adverse environmental conditions leading to damage to crops and drought (Dorner and Thiesenhusen, op. cit.: 81). Commentators are also rather ambivalent about the beneficial effects of land reform. Ahmed (op. cit.) has tried to link the dramatic increases in land productivity for rice, wheat, and barley after 1950 to land reform, but his results are biased by the incidence of the Korean war and the fact that he does not distinguish between reform and non-reform areas.

The popular view that land reform substantially improved rural income distribution in Korea can also be questioned. While one does not doubt the salutary once-and-for-all effect on asset distribution, some observers have argued that by the late 1960s these salutary effects were reversed. Farm-size distribution apparently approached the pre-reform norm (King, op. cit.). Others have argued that the land reform programmes were not as radical as they are usually supposed, given that they merely transferred land to those who were operating it (Douglass, 1983).

Perhaps the most serious doubts on the effects of land reform in Korea have been raised by those who maintain that land reform legislation of the 1940s and 1950s has now become increasingly anachronistic and is acting as an impediment to rural development. The Land Reform Law of 1940–50, which is still in effect, puts a three hectare limit on landholdings. The notion of creating employment through small farmholdings may have been appropriate in the labour surplus conditions of the 1950s, but makes very little economic sense in the tight labour-scarce situation of contemporary times. It thus seems that consolidation of landholdings in order to enhance productive efficiency should be allowed through prudent revisions to the Land Reform Law.

Some observers (Song, 1990; Pak, 1983) have noted that the contemporary issue of land reform is tied up with the more fundamental issue of land management. Given the emphasis of the government on maintaining an agricultural sector for strategic reasons (in order to achieve self-sufficiency in rice production), it is very difficult to reallocate arable land to industrial and urban use. This compounds the existing scarcity of land in Korea, fuels land prices in urban and industrial areas and poses a threat to industrial expansion.

In sum, the enduring perception that land reform in Korea and Taiwan is an unmitigated success story abstracts from some unpalatable truths. This perception is more valid in the case of Taiwan than in the case of Korea. Even so, in the latter, the unchanged character of the 1949–50 Land Reform Law may well be interfering with efficient rural development and overall land management.

RURAL DEVELOPMENT THROUGH RURAL INDUSTRIALISATION

Farm households can derive income from both agricultural and non-agricultural sources. One way of boosting non-agricultural sources of income – and hence living standards of farm households – is to provide employment opportunities in the off-farm sector via rural industrialisation. The experiences of Taiwan and Korea in the successful implementation of rural industrialisation are quite different. Taiwan is held up as a model of success, Korea as a case of relative failure (Scitovsky, 1990; Saith, 1987). As will be shown in Chapter 12, the ability of the Taiwanese government to implement rural-based, decentralised industrial location policy played an important role in contributing to the relatively equitable distribution of income.

Taiwan's efforts to engage in rural industrialisation go back to the late 1950s and early 1960s, when the government emphasised export-oriented industrialisation. Export industries were encouraged to locate in rural areas in order to tap the labour-surplus conditions in such areas. In many cases, small rural firms acted as subcontractors through a network organised by urban-based international and domestic trading houses (Amsden, 1979). Rural industrialisation was also facilitated by public policy that managed to ensure that the necessary infrastructure and services to attract establishments and labour to designated rural areas were available (Ranis, 1979).

The divergent patterns of rural industrialisation in Taiwan and Korea can be gauged in a number of ways. One indicator is the rural–urban distribution of

Table 4.3 Composition of farm household income (%)

Economy and year	Agricultural income	Non-agricultural income
Korea		
1962	79.6	20.4
1965	79.2	20.8
1970	75.9	24.1
1975	81.9	18.1
1980	65.2	34.8
1985	64.5	35.5
1987	61.4	38.5
Taiwan		
1966	66.0	34.0
1970	48.7	51.3
1974	48.1	51.9
1980	26.4	73.6
1985	24.8	75.2
1989	22.0	78.0

Source: Kim (1991: Tables I, II).

industrial concentration. While the spread of industries between rural and urban areas in Taiwan remained relatively even, the proportion of manufacturing firms located in urban areas in Korea rose from 55.4 per cent in 1971 to 75.6 per cent in 1988 (J.G. Kim, 1991: 3). Another indicator is the composition of Korean farm household income vis-à-vis the same composition in Taiwan. The rationale behind this indicator is that a greater proportion of non-farm income reflects the success of rural industrialisation in providing off-farm employment opportunities. Table 4.3 throws some light on this issue. The proportion of non-farm income ranged between 38 and 35 per cent in the 1980s in Korea, while in Taiwan it ranged between 78 per cent and 74 per cent over the same period.

What factors lie behind Korea's relative failure to achieve rural development via rural industrialisation? A brief history of the evolution of rural industrialisation policy would be a useful way of analysing this issue. (The following account draws heavily upon Kim, (op. cit.) and Moon, (op. cit.).) Korea's efforts to engage in rural industrialisation really started on a large-scale basis with the Saemaul factory programme in 1973. The objective was two-fold. First, the goal was to shift industrial activity away from overcrowded metropolitan centres, especially the areas surrounding Seoul and Pusan. Second, the aim was to provide rural residents with non-agricultural opportunities for income and employment. A set of fiscal and financial incentives was offered to prospective firms that expanded or located in the designated areas.

The Saemaul programme was not particularly successful. Even a decade after the inception of the programme, only 50 per cent of the designated factories were in operation. Moreover, the proportion of Saemaul factories in high growth factories was lower than the national average. In addition, many of the Saemaul factories had in fact located in areas around the three major metropolitan areas (Seoul, Pusan and Taegu).

Two factors were responsible for the lack of success of the Saemaul programme. First, the factories had, given their location in small townships, difficulty in securing a steady supply of cheap labour and in finding skilled managers and technicians. Second, and most critically, the designated areas did not have the necessary infrastructure and services to attract a complementary flow of establishments and labour. An adequate rural network was missing, restricting the mobility of rural residents to travel to industries in proximate locations. The designated rural areas also had inadequate access to banking, marketing and information services.

The government, recognising these limitations of the Saemaul programme, initiated a Rural Industries Estate (RIE) programme in 1984. The RIE focused on those rural population centres which could adequately provide the necessary infrastructure and services for a conducive business environment. In addition, the package of fiscal and financial incentives was made more broad-based and generous. Local governments were also given more discretionary power and financial resources to implement these rural estates. Kim is generally positive about the RIE programme.

[T]he RIE programme has played a significant role in expanding sources of non-agricultural income and raising overall rural household income ... RIEs have made a noticeable impact on regional development through the improvement of infrastructure.

(Kim, op. cit.: 19–21)

However, he qualifies these generally positive assessments in the following manner:

It is of primary importance that only those optimal locations which can provide the necessary infrastructure and service to attract rural factories be designated as rural industrial estates. Currently, the RIE (programme) faces the potential problem of having too many designated estates whose locations are determined not by economic considerations, but rather by political ones. Thus, the current number of rural industries should be reduced such that rural growth centres are concentrated around small and medium sized cities which are more conducive to business activity than remote and small villages.

(Kim, ibid.: 21)

THE EVOLUTION OF AGRICULTURAL PROTECTION IN THE EAST ASIAN NIEs

The agricultural sector is subject to large-scale government intervention in almost all economies. A wide variety of instruments are used – the pricing of farm products and inputs in conjunction with ad valorem tariffs, non-tariff barriers and so forth. The pattern of intervention varies. In some cases, the net effect is to depress farm prices; in other cases, the net effect is to raise farm prices. Thus, nominal rates of agricultural protection can either be negative or positive. In cases where the nominal protection rate is negative, the primary objective seems to be to transfer income from rural to urban areas in order to support urban-based industrialisation. This, of course, is the standard pattern that has been observed in many developing countries intent on pursuing import substituting industrialisation (ISI). In cases where the nominal agricultural protection is positive, the primary objectives seem to be to provide food security and to maintain farm incomes broadly in line with rising non-farm incomes.

The evolution of agricultural protection in Korea and Taiwan seems to have gone through various phases. As recorded in the early 1980s, the nominal protection was rather steep and, in the case of Korea, it was one of the highest in the world. This has turned out to be a costly burden for consumers and tax payers in these countries, given that they faced food prices two to three times higher than in international markets. In light of these stylised facts, the purpose of this section is to offer a brief historical sketch of the evolution of agricultural protection in Korea and Taiwan and focus on the political economy of agricultural protection.

The substantive issues in agricultural protection in East Asia have been analysed by several authors, most notably by Anderson (1983), Chisolm and Tyers (1985), Anderson and Hayami (1986), Yoon (1989) and DeRosa (1988). A good survey can also be found in Johnson (1991). The discussion that follows draws upon these sources. One way of measuring the nominal rate of protection in the agricultural sector is to focus on the 'nominal protection coefficient' (Johnson, op. cit.: 287). In other words, the objective is to measure the ratio of domestic farm prices to adjusted border prices, where the adjustments reflect marketing and transportation costs, quality differences and distortions in the equilibrium exchange rate. If the coefficient is equal to 1, then the agricultural sector approximates the free trade regime. If the coefficient is less than 1, then there is negative protection, entailing the use of domestic prices below international prices. If the coefficient is greater than 1, then agriculture is receiving positive protection.

There are of course other ways of estimating nominal protection. DeRosa (op. cit.), for example, has focused on average *ad valorem* tariff rates, non-tariff barriers (NTBs) and their frequency ratios, i.e. the extent to which an import restriction is imposed within a given trade category. Thus the higher the average value of tariffs, the higher (*cet. par.*) is the degree of protection. Furthermore, the higher the frequency ratio of NTBs, the higher (*cet. par.*) the nominal rate of protection. It is well known, of course, that the effective rate of protection is theoretically more rigorous than the nominal protection rate, but the best research in this area seems to have focused on nominal rates, presumably because of data constraints.

Johnson (op. cit.) has drawn attention to the fact that one can depict a stylised relationship between the nominal protection coefficient and per capita income (as a crude proxy for economic development). As an economy proceeds from low- to middle-income ranges (below US$ 1,000 in 1982 prices to US$1,500–2,000), the protection coefficient shifts as well: from minus 1 to greater than 1. The evolution of agricultural protection in Korea and Taiwan broadly conforms to this stylised pattern, but if one takes a broader historical perspective then the picture is more complex. Anderson (op. cit.) has emphasised that agricultural protection in Korea and Taiwan has deeper historical roots and can be traced to Japanese colonisation.

At the turn of the century, Japan began to lose comparative advantage in rice production and became increasingly dependent on rice imports. This led to lobbying by farmers and bureaucrats to impose controls on rice imports. The government responded by declaring a policy of reducing dependence on rice imports from non-colonial sources and achieving self-sufficiency in rice production within the Japanese colony, i.e. within Japan and its two major colonies – Korea and Taiwan. Korean and Taiwanese rice farmers thus received positive protection largely as a result of this colonial policy. The broad pattern seems to corroborate this view. The apparent nominal rate of protection within the Japanese empire increased from 16 per cent in 1903–7 to 87 per cent in 1938 (Saxon and Anderson, 1982).

Table 4.4 Nominal rates of agricultural protection (%)

	1955–9	1960–4	1965–9	1970–4	1975–9	1980–2
South Korea						
Rice	−14	−9	6	55	138	154
Wheat	−22	8	18	16	47	128
Barley	−14	7	−6	35	77	107
Corn	NA	31	17	43	67	101
Soyabean	−23	5	51	63	109	226
Beef	3	5	55	88	281	326
Pork	−11	−5	82	111	113	208
Chicken	−27	7	132	103	153	140
Weighted average	−15	−5	9	55	129	166
Taiwan						
Rice	−31	−8	−13	4	58	144
Wheat	48	25	39	32	57	92
Barley	15	73	67	33	49	99
Corn	2	21	37	29	41	91
Soyabean	69	47	37	13	16	56
Beef	−4	8	20	37	162	153
Pork	15	32	40	38	13	3
Chicken	−50	−2	21	27	29	36
Weighted average	−21	2	2	17	36	55

Source: Anderson (1983: 332).
Note: Nominal protection is defined as the percentage by which the domestic price exceeds the border price.

The positive protection rates were not maintained after the two countries achieved independence from Japanese colonisation. As is well known, the two countries embarked on ISI during the 1950s, through the familiar route of using low food prices as a means of income transfers from the rural sector to finance ISI. This was reflected in significantly negative protection rates. When the economies shifted to an EOI regime in the 1960s, the degree of negative protection tended to dissipate. Thus, the weighted average protection rate fell from −15 per cent in 1955–9 to −5 per cent in 1960–4 in Korea, while in Taiwan it shifted from −21 per cent to 2 per cent and stayed at that level throughout the 1960s (Anderson, op. cit.: 332). The pattern changes radically in the 1970s. The overall nominal protection rate rose sharply, from 9 per cent in the 1965–9 period to 166 per cent by 1982, while in Taiwan the corresponding numbers are 2 per cent and 55 per cent (Anderson, ibid). If one focuses on rice only, the protection rates in the two economies, as recorded in the early 1980s, are rather similar. Full details can be found in Table 4.4.

DeRosa's (op. cit.) estimates, based on 1986 data, show evidence of more modest protection. Certainly average tariff rates for food products in Korea are lower than in most of South Asia as are the frequency ratios for NTBs. It may well be that the evidence culled by DeRosa reflects efforts at tariff reform in the agricultural sector. Li (1988: 137) has emphasised that, in Taiwan, '[t]ariffs on most agricultural products have recently been reduced to fairly low levels'. One can detect similar trends in Korea. Yet, it must be emphasised that tariff reform in particular, and agricultural protection in general, has still got some way to go in the two economies. In particular, the rice market continues to be significantly protected.

How can one explain the pattern and evolution of agricultural protection sketched above? This inevitably entails a discussion of the political economy of agricultural protection in East Asia. In light of this discussion, it will be suggested that the evidence on agricultural protection embodies uncomfortable implications for the statist interpretation of East Asian economic success.

Anderson and Hayami (op. cit.) have tried to explain the rapid increase in agricultural protection using the standard tools of neoclassical political economy. This, in turn, entails the use of a demand–supply framework. Thus, farmers are the advocates on the 'demand' side, while politicians 'supply' protection, given their motivation to maximise the probability of staying in office. The average level of protection will change as a result of shifts in demand and supply. During the process of economic development, the comparative advantage of agriculture declines or shifts in favour of industry. This increases the demand for agricultural protection. Furthermore, as the agricultural sector contracts, it increases the ease with which farmers can organise to lobby for their interests. At the same time, the decline of the importance of food in the urban household budget means that consumers are willing to tolerate a higher degree of agricultural protection. Anderson and Hayami (ibid.) test the model using an econometric framework. Their model fits the Taiwanese data very well (for the 1965–80 period), but is much less successful in the case of Korean data (also for the 1965–80 period).

The Anderson–Hayami analysis does not have the last word on the subject. Timmer (1988) has raised doubts on the empirical robustness of the results, given the discrepancy in the performance of the econometric model between Taiwan and Korea. Furthermore, Timmer (ibid.) notes that the Anderson–Hayami framework pays insufficient attention to the fact that both farmers and consumers display a strong desire for food price stability and that this preference plays an important role in the demand for agricultural protection. Admittedly, the issue of food price stability is discussed in the context of food security, but it is not integrated as a key explanatory variable in the econometric model. Johnson (op. cit.: 307) also arrives at a similar conclusion: 'none of the studies of protection ... have included food security as a persuasive argument for positive protection'.

Despite these limitations, the Anderson–Hayami framework remains so far the most comprehensive and coherent account of the political determinants of agricultural protection in East Asia. More importantly, such an analysis conveys uncomfortable implications for the statist interpretation of East Asian economic development. The strong state hypothesis enthuses over the fact that East Asian policy makers have an unusual capacity to restrain the influence of protection-seeking lobbies and pursue policies that are in the societal interest. What the hypothesis needs to explain is why this capacity is asymmetric, being so futile in the sphere of agricultural policy, but so potent in other spheres of economic policy. This lacuna in the statist literature becomes more evident when one realises that Korea and Taiwan are populated by small farmers, rather than a powerful lobby of large, oligopolistic farmers in the Batesian mould (Bates, 1981).

One could argue that East Asian policy makers have legitimate concerns about food security and that it is this motive, rather than the protection-seeking interests in the farming sector, that drives them to intervene in the agricultural sector. The point, however, is that there are less costly alternatives to protection in achieving food security (see subsequent discussion). One needs to explain why efficiency-driven bureaucrats do not pursue these options.

CONCLUDING REMARKS

This chapter has tried to convey the message that the sparkling economic success of the East Asian NIEs does not seem to extend to the agricultural sector. This conclusion is particularly valid for Korea. The much-acclaimed land reform of the 1940s and 1950s now seems to be an impediment to rural development. The achievement of rural development through rural industrialisation still has some way to go. Perhaps the most pressing contemporary issue is the relatively high levels of agricultural protection – and this applies to both Korea and Taiwan. It is an intriguing fact that East Asian policy makers, so well known for their efficient policy-making capacities, should succumb to the cause of inefficient protection.

What are the potential gains from policy reform in the agricultural sector and what types of reform need to be made? The benefits from reduced protection are well documented. For instance, Chisolm and Tyers (1985) have estimated the welfare gains of full agricultural trade liberalisation to be US$158 per capita for Korea and US$66 per capita for Taiwan. Less costly alternatives to protection for achieving the objectives of food security and rural–urban parity have been forcefully argued by Anderson (op. cit.) and Anderson and Hayami (op. cit.). In any case, it is doubtful whether food security can be achieved through agricultural protection, given that import dependence on crucial inputs to the farm sector (fertiliser, etc.) remains intact. As Anderson notes:

> Probably the most efficient means (of achieving food security) is simply to depend on import supplies and, if necessary, to borrow to finance the import bill in years when world prices are high or domestic production is low. Domestic stockpiles, futures markets, and long-term contracts with

exporting countries can be used to increase the security of depending more on food imports.

(Anderson, ibid.: 335)

On the issue of achieving rural–urban parity through protection, Anderson (ibid:335) has stressed the need to rely on adjustment assistance to farm families, through retraining and more investment in formal schooling in rural areas. It remains to be seen to what extent these policy options will be taken up in the future as viable alternatives to inefficient agricultural protection.

5

TRADE LIBERALISATION AND ECONOMIC GROWTH

There has been sustained improvement in the export performance of developing countries during 1965–80. The developing countries' share in world exports rose from 21 per cent in 1965 to nearly 29 per cent in 1980. Since then, however, it has declined and in 1989 their share in world exports stood at 21.8 per cent. It took less than a decade to lose what had been achieved in nearly two decades.

The East Asian NIEs, on the other hand, continued to increase their shares in world exports. The shares of these four economies rose from a meagre 1.6 per cent in 1965 to 7.6 per cent in 1989 (Table 5.1). This occurred despite the slow-down in the growth of world trade in general since the 1970s and increased protectionist barriers in developed countries. Thus, the East Asian NIEs have shown a remarkable ability to penetrate export markets.

The rise in the East Asian NIEs' export shares in world total matches the rise in their shares of world exports of manufactured goods from 1.6 per cent to 8.8 per cent, with manufactured exports accounting for almost 90 per cent of all East Asian NIEs' exports in 1989. This indicates that manufacturing played a major role in their export expansion. This chapter will examine various aspects of East Asian NIEs' exports of manufactured goods. An important objective will be to reflect on the debate concerning the link between trade liberalisation (or export orientation) and economic growth.

EXPORT ORIENTATION OF EAST ASIAN NIEs

A common measure of an economy's export orientation is its share of exports in gross domestic product (GDP). From Table 5.2, one can see that exports of goods and services contributed quite significantly to Hong Kong and Singapore's GDP in the 1960s. This is not surprising given their historical development as entrepôts. Re-exports are still quite substantial from Hong Kong and Singapore and this explains why exports of goods and services account for more than 100 per cent of GDP.

In the late 1980s, nearly half of Korea's output was exported while exports of goods and services accounted for less than 10 per cent in 1965. In the case of Taiwan, the share of exports in GDP rose from less than 20 per cent in 1965 to

Table 5.1 Indicators of export expansion

Economy	Share of exports in world total (%)			Share of manufactured exports					
				In world total (%)			In own total (%)		
	1965	1980	1989	1965	1980	1989	1965	1980	1989
World	100.0	100.0	100.0	100.0	100.0	100.0	59.3	61.6	76.8
Developed	78.9	71.2	78.2	92.8	85.0	82.1	69.7	73.6	80.6
Developing	21.1	28.8	21.8	7.2	15.0	17.9	20.4	32.0	63.2
East Asian NIEs	1.6	4.1	7.6	1.6	5.4	8.8	58.4	80.7	88.9
Latin American Three[a]	2.6	2.5	2.5	0.4	1.1	1.5	7.4	26.3	46.3

Source: Martin and Panoutsopoulos (1991: Table 1).
Note: a Argentina, Brazil and Mexico.

Table 5.2 Indicator of export orientation

Economy	Exports of goods and services (% GDP)			Percentage points change in the share 1965–87
	1965	1980	1987	
Hong Kong	71	88	123	52
Korea	9	34	45	36
Singapore	123	205	191	68
Taiwan	19	53	58	39
Argentina	–	7	10	3
Brazil	7 (1970)	9	9	2
Mexico	7 (1970)	11	20	13
India	4 (1970)	7	6	2
Developed market economies	11 (1960)	20	17	6
Developing market economies	16 (1960)	26	24	8

Sources: UNCTAD (various issues).

nearly 60 per cent in 1987. These figures appear quite staggering compared with developed or developing countries as a group and Latin American countries.

The policy switch from ISI to EOI in the early and mid-1960s had contributed quite significantly to the growth of exports from the East Asian NIEs. The episode has been summarised quite succinctly by Little:

> Starting in the years around 1960, these countries (i.e. Korea, Taiwan and Singapore) made policy changes that by the middle of 1960s combined selective protection for certain import competing sectors with a virtual free trade regime for exporters – by which we mean that exporters could obtain inputs ... at world market prices, while the effective exchange rate for exporters was close to that which would have ruled under free trade. Overall effective protection for industry was zero for Korea, and, of course, Hong Kong, and low for Taiwan and Singapore. The consequential growth of exports was phenomenal, far exceeding what anyone could have predicted or did predict.
>
> (Little, 1982: 141)

Table 5.3 Top exporters of manufactures among developing countries

Economy	Shares in developing countries' exports of manufactures (%)	
	1980	*1985[a]*
Taiwan	17.33	
South Korea	13.46	18.5
Hong Kong	12.59	12.2
Singapore	8.51	12.3
China	7.82	
Brazil	6.37	9.5
India	4.16	2.6
Malaysia	2.32	5.0
Kuwait	2.00	
Argentina	1.65	3.0
Mexico	1.62	7.1
Thailand	1.50	2.9
Pakistan	1.20	1.6
Philippines	1.12	1.5
Indonesia	2.60	
Chile		1.4

Sources: 1980: Linneman *et al.* (1987: Table 2.4). 1985: UNCTAD (1989: Table III.3).
Note: a Does not include Taiwan.

EXPORTS OF MANUFACTURES

Table 5.3 shows that developing countries were able to increase their share in world manufactured exports, even though they failed to maintain their gain in total world exports. However, this gain is not shared by most developing countries. The four East Asian NIEs are responsible for roughly half of manufactured exports from developing countries.

Table 5.4 shows that manufactures dominate the East Asian NIEs merchandise exports. In Korea and Taiwan, 89–90 per cent of merchandise exports in 1988 were accounted for by manufactured goods. This is phenomenal, especially when manufacturing contributed only 14 per cent to Korea's total merchandise exports in 1960. The emergence of Korea and Taiwan as major exporters of manufactures is described by James *et al.* in the following words:

These countries are now so thoroughly identified as exporters of manufactures that it is hard to remember that only a couple of decades ago they were predominantly agricultural. In 1960, primary goods, mainly agricultural, accounted for 86 per cent of Korea's exports and 73 per cent of Taiwan's. At that time, exports were less than 10 per cent of the GNP in

75

Taiwan and 5 per cent in Korea. . . . and by 1970, manufactures accounted for over 20 per cent of total exports.

(James *et al.*, 1989: 31)

The performance of Singapore is also quite remarkable. It has been able to increase the share of manufactures in merchandise exports from 26 per cent in 1965 to 65 per cent in 1988. The role of manufactures in Hong Kong's merchandise exports, however, has declined since 1960. This trend is consistent with the declining share of manufacturing in Hong Kong's GDP, which has been discussed in Chapter 1. As will be shown in the next chapter, there is a close correspondence between East Asian NIEs' performance in manufactured exports and the pattern of their industrialisation. This correspondence has often been termed 'export-led industrialisation' (E. Lee, 1981).

Although the East Asian NIEs began their export drive with labour-intensive manufactured products, over time they have been able to shift the composition of their manufactured exports towards more sophisticated products. Table 5.5 presents the changing pattern of their manufacturing exports. It shows that the shares of sophisticated products like office machines, telecommunication equipments, switchgear and transistors rose from less than 2 per cent in 1966 to more than 30 per cent in 1987 in both Singapore and Korea. For Hong Kong, the rise in export share of similar products has been roughly 13 percentage points during 1966–87. One can observe a similar trend in Taiwan. Taiwan's export shares of electrical and non-electrical machines, transport equipments and precision instruments rose from 16.4 per cent in 1970 to 28.3 per cent in 1983.

In most cases, the increase in the export shares of sophisticated products in the East Asian NIEs has exceeded the increase of such products' shares in world exports. Thus, the export structures of the East Asian NIEs reveal their comparative advantage in the production of sophisticated products. A country is said to reveal comparative advantage in the production of a good if the export share of the good in question in that country's exports exceeds the share of the product in total world exports. As can be seen from Table 5.6, the revealed comparative advantage (RCA) index for human capital-intensive products has risen in all East Asian NIEs (Taiwan excepted) during 1970–85, and Korea has attained comparative advantage in the production of such products. Even though their RCA in technology-intensive products has declined during the 1980s, they still reveal comparative advantage (RCA > 1) in the production of these products. Their RCA (Korea excepted) in physical capital-intensive products shows an increasing trend. However, the East Asian NIEs export structures continue to reveal comparative advantage in the production of unskilled labour-intensive products vis-à-vis the rest of the world. The conspicuous exception to this pattern is Singapore. Its export structure reveals comparative disadvantage in labour-intensive products and comparative advantage in technology-intensive products.

Table 5.4 Merchandise and manufactured exports (growth rates and shares)

Economy	Average annual growth rates of merchandise exports (%)					Shares of manufactures in merchandise exports (%)				Compounded growth rate of manufactured exports^{a}* (%)
	1960–70	1971–4	1975–9	1980–4	1989	1960†	1975^{a}	1982†	1988^{a}	1970–85
Hong Kong	12.7	29.0	21.3	14.1	15.8	80.0	73.7	97.0	41.5	15.0
Korea	34.7	63.0	28.2	14.4	2.7	14.0	80.2	90.0	90.3	28.2
Singapore	4.2	50.0	20.7	11.7	37.0	26.0	38.1	56.0	65.3	24.8
Taiwan	23.7	40.7	25.0	14.0	9.3	–	79.4	89.0	89.2	26.4
Developing countries										21.7
World										13.9

Sources: *James et al. (1989: Table 2.3).
†Barrett and Chin (1987: Table 5); Asian Development Bank (various issues).

Notes: a Includes basic manufactures, machines, transport and equipment and miscellaneous manufactured goods.

Table 5.5 Composition of manufactured exports (% total exports)

SITC class	Commodity	1966	1976	1987
Hong Kong				
2	Crude materials excluding fuels	3.7	2.9	2.9
5	Chemicals and related products	4.1	3.4	4.7
65	Textile yarn, fabrics, etc.	16.8	9.7	11.7
66	Non-metal mineral manufactures	4.8	3.7	4.0
69	Metal manufactures	2.6	2.3	2.0
75	Office machines, ADP equipment	0.0	1.0	3.8
76	Telecommunications and sound equipment	3.4	5.9	7.1
775	Household type equipment	0.0	1.0	2.1
776	Transistors, valves, etc.	0.0	1.9	3.1
831	Travel goods, handbags	0.8	1.7	2.0
84	Clothing and accessories	27.0	34.1	22.1
851	Footwear	2.5	0.9	1.0
885	Watches and clocks	1.1	4.5	4.8
894	Toys, sporting goods	6.2	5.9	5.8
899	Other manufactured goods	5.9	2.5	2.1
	Total	78.9	81.4	79.1
Korea				
0	Food and live animals	16.5	6.6	5.1
1	Beverages and tobacco	2.8	1.0	0.2
2	Crude materials, excluding fuels	18.6	2.5	1.1
5	Chemicals and related products	0.3	1.5	3.2
63	Wood, cork manufactures	12.2	4.7	0.2
65	Textile yarn, fabrics, etc.	13.8	12.4	10.0
67	Iron and steel	3.2	4.8	5.7
69	Metal manufactures	1.7	2.9	3.9
75	Office machines, ADP equipment	0.0	0.0	3.9
76	Telecommunications and sound equipment	1.3	2.6	12.1
775	Household equipment	0.0	0.5	2.2
776	Transistors, valves, etc.	0.0	4.1	5.8
78	Road vehicles	0.3	0.3	8.7
793	Ships and boats, etc.	0.1	3.6	2.8
84	Clothing and accessories	13.3	23.9	18.4
851	Footwear	2.2	5.2	6.7
89	Miscellaneous manufactured goods	7.6	6.3	7.6
	Total	93.8	83.0	97.8
Singapore				
0	Food and live animals	12.3	5.8	4.5
23	Crude rubber	20.6	12.3	2.6
3	Mineral fuels, etc.	15.9	29.7	16.1
5	Chemicals and related products	3.2	3.7	6.2
65	Textile yarn, fabrics, etc.	3.5	2.7	2.2
69	Metal manufactures	1.7	1.1	2.2
74	General industrial machinery	3.2	3.4	3.0

75	Office machines, ADP equipment	0.0	1.1	11.7
76	Telecommunications and sound equipment	0.3	4.0	9.9
772	Switchgear, etc.	0.4	0.6	2.3
776	Transistors, valves, etc.	0.0	7.1	8.3
778	Electrical machinery	0.8	1.3	1.1
78	Road vehicles	3.5	1.4	0.7
793	Ships and boats	0.0	3.9	1.1
84	Clothing and accessories	1.4	2.8	1.8
89	Miscellaneous manufactured goods	1.4	1.2	3.4
	Total	68.2	82.1	77.1

Taiwan		1970	1983
	Chemicals	2.3	2.5
	Resource-based manufactures	9.2	7.1
	Textiles	13.3	7.3
	Metal manufactures	1.9	4.8
	Electrical machinery	11.9	16.1
	Non-electrical machinery	3.3	6.3
	Transport equipment	0.8	3.8
	Precision instruments	0.4	2.1
	Clothing	14.3	11.9
	Furniture	0.2	2.3
	Footwear	1.9	7.2
	Miscellaneous manufactures	10.4	15.8
	Total	70.0	87.2

Sources: Hong Kong, Korea and Singapore: Industry Commission (1990: Table B3). Taiwan: James *et al.* (1989: Table 2.5).

TRADE AND ECONOMIC GROWTH: ISSUES AND DEBATES

Which trade strategies have enabled countries to attain high growth and to develop industrial potential? The answer to this question posed in the *World Development Report, 1987* (World Bank, 1987b: 78) is not straightforward. The World Bank (ibid.: 83) itself recognises that '[t]he links between trade strategy and macroeconomic performance are not entirely clear. Does outward orientation lead to better economic performance or does superior performance pave the way for outward orientation?' Thus, it raises more questions than it answers.

Empirical studies show that there is a strong positive relationship between economic growth and the rate of growth of exports (see Lal and Rajapatirana, 1987). The World Bank (ibid.) also finds that, in the spectrum of developing countries, the rate of growth of GDP declines as one moves from strongly outward-oriented to strongly inward-oriented economies.

However, correlation or association does not imply causation. By applying the Granger–Sims causality test Jung and Marshall (1985) find a very weak causality

Table 5.6 Revealed comparative advantage (RCA) indices: Asian newly industrialising economies

Factor intensity	Year	Hong Kong	Republic of Korea	Singapore	Taiwan
Unskilled labour	1970	7.10	5.43	0.94	—
	1976	6.91	6.06	0.94	—
	1980	6.48	5.63	0.93	6.14
	1985	5.74	4.18	0.72	5.58
Human capital	1970	0.45	0.20	0.39	—
	1976	0.70	0.76	0.61	—
	1980	1.23	1.19	0.51	0.81
	1985	0.87	1.84	0.43	0.78
Technology	1970	1.59	0.62	0.63	—
	1976	2.06	1.39	1.76	—
	1980	1.59	1.46	1.80	1.81
	1985	1.45	1.16	1.19	1.44
Physical capital	1970	0.13	1.16	0.26	—
	1976	0.18	0.39	0.45	—
	1980	0.23	0.74	0.56	0.43
	1985	0.44	0.53	0.59	0.48

Source: Chen (1989b: 37).
 — not available
Notes: RCA index is $(Eih/Eh)(Wi/W)$, where Eih is export of product i by country h, Wi is the world total exports of product i, and W is the world total exports.

Unskilled labour intensive: Standard International Trade Classification (SITC) 65, 664–66, 81, 82, 83, 84, 85, 89 except 896 and 897.

Human capital intensive: SITC 55, 62, 69, 775, 78, 79, 885, 896, 897.

Technology intensive: SITC 54, 56, 57, 58, 59, 88 except 885, 752, 759, 76, 77 except 775.

Physical capital intensive: SITC 68, 67, 51, 52, 72, 73, 74, 751.

running from exports to economic growth. When Jung and Marshall's F-statistics and the World Bank's sample countries are combined, one finds very little support for the export promotion hypothesis (Dodaro, 1991: 1156). Only in the case of Costa Rica, and Indonesia, exports are found to have caused economic growth in the sense that export expansion preceded economic growth. Similarly, Darrat (1986) finds no evidence of causality between economic growth and the growth of exports for Hong Kong, Korea and Singapore. On the other hand, in the case of Taiwan, he reports that economic growth 'unidirectionally causes exports'. The most intriguing finding is that of Chow (1987) who reports the existence of a 'bi-directional' causality between manufactured exports and economic growth in all four East Asian NIEs, including Japan.

Thus, there are three, not mutually exclusive, possibilities:
1 Exports cause economic growth
2 Economic growth causes exports
3 A 'third factor' affects both exports and economic growth positively.

Arthur Lewis in his Nobel lecture took the Keynesian view that exports are demand driven and cause economic growth. Thus Lewis (1980) regards exports or trade as 'an engine of growth' driven or fuelled by industrial countries' demand for developing countries exports. Lewis describes the phenomenon as:

> The growth rate of world trade in primary products over the period of 1873 to 1913 was 0.87 times the growth rate of industrial production in the developed countries, and just about the same relationship, about 0.87, also ruled in the two decades to 1973. ... We need no elaborate statistical proof that trade depends on prosperity in the industrial countries.
>
> (Lewis, ibid.: 556)

The hypothesis that trade is an engine of growth is founded on the premise that there is a stable and mechanical relationship between economic growth in developed countries and export growth in developing countries which, in turn, drives developing countries along their economic growth track.

The idea is not new. Myrdal, Nurkse and Prebisch, who laid the foundations for import substitution industrialisation (ISI), shared the same view. Since the demand for exports from developing countries is far weaker than what it was in the nineteenth century, the solution prescribed in the 1950s was to look inward. As Riedel (1984) notes, this amounted to, in effect, scrapping the trade engine altogether. The difference between Lewis and the intellectual godfathers of ISI is that Lewis retains the trade engine, but points to the drying up of fuel, i.e. the slowing down of growth in industrial countries since the early 1970s. Therefore, Lewis suggests an alternative fuel source – trade among developing countries.

However, a more rigourous study by Kravis (1970:869) shows that, contrary to the engine of growth hypothesis, 'export expansion did not serve in the nineteenth century to differentiate successful from unsuccessful countries'. For example, Australia could develop whereas Argentina did not, having similar natural resources and stimulus from the rise in foreign demands for their primary products. This led Kravis (ibid.) to conclude that external demand may be helpful but 'is neither a necessary nor sufficient condition for growth'.

Furthermore, the critics of Lewis' proposition point out that primary products no longer serve as a proxy for developing country exports, as Lewis asserted. Except for a few sub-Saharan African countries, the developing countries have in general been able to increase their share of manufactured exports in both their own and world total (Table 5.1). Their shares of manufactured exports continued to grow in the 1970s and 1980s when the growth of industrial countries slowed down considerably. Riedel observes that:

> whereas in the 1960s LDC exports of manufactures grew almost twice as

fast as DC [industrial country] real GDP . . . in the 1970s, despite a general slowdown of growth after 1973, LDC exports maintained their rapid pace, growing four times as fast as DC real GDP.

(Riedel, op. cit.: 67)

If the causal link between export demand and export expansion, and hence economic growth, is weak and unstable as Riedel and Kravis claim, then one has to explain the observed positive relationship between exports and economic growth by examining the second possibility, i.e. economic growth increasing the supply capacity of manufactured exports from developing countries. According to Riedel (op. cit.: 69), 'Supply rather than demand factors principally determined LDC export performance in manufactures'. Based on cross-country regression analysis – classified in terms of their stages of development – Dodaro (op. cit.: 1154) also expresses a similar view that 'some degree of economic development and efficiency is necessary before a country can make any significant inroads in the world market, particularly in manufactures'.

A limitation of the demand determined export-led growth hypothesis is that it assumes unlimited supply capacity of developing countries. In reality, resources are not allocated efficiently in most developing countries and this limits their ability to respond to demand. Neoclassical trade theories demonstrate that static gains from trade result from efficient allocation of resources, as shown in Figure 5.1.

Figure 5.1 represents a small economy whose terms of trade are determined exogenously by the world market. PP shows the set of efficient production possibilities. In the absence of trade, the country will produce and consume at A where the production possibility frontier is tangential to the community indifference curve, CIC_1. However, if the country trades, it will face the world price ratio (terms of trade), WW. If the world price ratio is different from the domestic price ratio – in this example, importables are cheaper in the world market than in the domestic market – the country will produce at B and consume at C which lies on a higher CIC. Essentially, the country produces what is more profitable (exportables) and imports what is cheaper. Trade thus expands the feasible set of consumption possibilities by providing 'an indirect technology for transforming domestic resources into the goods and services that yield current and future utility for consumers' (Lal and Rajapatirana, op. cit.: 189).

There are further static gains from trade liberalisation as has already been noted in Chapter 3. Trade restrictions give rise to 'rent-seeking' and 'directly unproductive activities' (see Tullock, 1967; Krueger, 1974; Bhagwati, 1980). It is argued that tariffs and import licensing and quotas are required to create a monopoly rent in order to attract investment in 'desired' industries or to protect 'infant industries'. However, the existence of such rent may generate lobbying activities to capture rent and can involve substantial resources. This, in effect, shifts the production possibility frontier inward. Furthermore, the lack of competition itself can be a source of x-inefficiency in such industries. According to

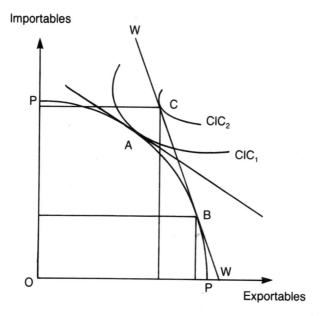

Figure 5.1 Gains from trade

Krueger (1984: 544), '[t]he welfare costs of protection would consist of the conventional production cost, plus an inefficiency cost and possibly a monopoly cost'. Thus, the welfare loss of trade protection would include:

1 dead-weight consumer/producer surplus;
2 resource cost associated with lobbying;
3 x-inefficiency of monopoly.

Bergsman (1974) estimates show that these costs for four developing countries ranged between 4 and 7 per cent of GNP in the mid-1960s:

Thus, it is argued that the removal of trade protection will generate welfare gains by:

1 preventing the emergence of welfare-reducing domestic monopolies;
2 preventing rent-seeking and directly unproductive activities;
3 inducing domestic producers to improve quality and reduce costs.

Furthermore, trade allows economies of scale to be reaped by expanding the size of the market.

While these likely gains increase the level of output, it is not clear how they induce continuous output increases or cause economic growth. In other words, for growth to occur the gains from trade liberalisation must be dynamic in nature and continuously shift a country's production possibility frontier outward. This depends on (1) the extent to which the static gains are saved and invested efficiently and (2) the introduction of new goods and, more importantly, new technology which can affect an economy's rate of technical progress. Findlay (1984) observes that 'the rate of economic growth over time ... will depend on factors such as the propensity to save and the rate of technological progress, neither of which is *directly* related to the trade regime in an obvious way'.

The World Bank (op. cit.) offers the following possible reasons why an outward trade orientation is likely to generate dynamic gains leading to a virtuous circle of growth:

1   The experience of East Asian NIEs shows that export orientation is associated with high savings rate. This may be due to the following: (a) marginal propensity to save in developing countries is found to exceed average propensity to save. Therefore, as income rises with the expansion of exports, average savings rise. (b) Marginal propensity to save out of export income is high and (c) export orientation is associated with a less distorted capital market and a positive real interest rate acts as an incentive for savings.
2   Exports generate foreign exchange and facilitate imports of raw materials and capital goods.
3   Exporting firms often benefit from foreign know-how and hence boost innovation.
4   Exporting firms must keep up with modern technology and bring managerial skills up to international standard to improve and maintain their market.

Both theoretical and empirical work on the above alleged links between export orientation (or trade liberalisation) and economic growth are ambiguous (Levine and Renelt, 1991; Tybout, 1991; Helleiner, 1990; Dornbusch, 1992; Rodrik, 1992; Kirkpatrick, 1992). Chapter 8 has an extensive discussion on the theoretical possibility of and the empirical findings on the positive relationship between real interest rate and savings. In short, the theoretical possibility depends on the relative strength of the income and substitution effects and the empirical estimates are at best weak, at worst negative or non-existent. The arguments based on 'x-efficiency' and increased managerial efforts can equally be applied to import-substituting producers. Whether managers would work harder due to incentives depends on the relative evaluation of the opportunity cost of leisure, i.e. the relative size of substitution and income effects. Similarly, the outcomes of greater markets and economies of scale due to trade liberalisation are uncertain. Extra competition from foreign producers can force producers to either expand or exit when domestic firms enjoy market power (Tybout, op. cit.). The possibility of increased innovation and acquisition of know-how due to trade liberalisation depends on two factors: the ease with which knowledge crosses international boundaries and the market size. According to Tybout (op. cit.: 7), these two can work against each other, making the net effect of trade liberalisation ambiguous.

Given the ambiguous theoretical results, it is not surprising that empirical work on trade liberalisation and productivity failed to establish any stable and predictable correlations. In a recent study, Bhagwati (1988: 38–40) concluded that there is little systematic evidence to support export promotion over import substitution on grounds of scale economies, innovation, savings or technical efficiency. According to Levine and Renelt (op. cit.: 20), the common finding that the growth of exports and GDP growth are positively correlated does not necessarily indicate that export promotion policies stimulate growth because all findings using exports can be replicated by using imports or total trade. Levine and Renelt (ibid.: 4) also question the methodological validity of the cross-country studies on the issue and note that 'almost all cross-country regression results are fragile: they are not robust to [the] slightest alternations in the list of explanatory variables'.

Despite the failure to establish the precise ways in which trade liberalisation affects economic growth, there have been ad hoc attempts to associate economic growth with export orientation. The basic premise of these studies is that if trade enhances growth through supply-side effects then one is likely to find larger contributions of total factor productivity (TFP) to growth in export-oriented countries, whatever the channels.

Table 5.7 presents estimates of the shares of TFP in output growth for selected developing countries and East Asian NIEs. Although one finds that the shares of TFP in the growth of GDP are much higher for East Asian NIEs, no easy conclusion can be drawn from it. The shares of TFP in the GDP growth are also higher in Mexico, Argentina, Chile, Peru and Turkey which are classified as inward-oriented by the World Bank (op. cit.). Moreover, the contributions of TFP in the East Asian NIEs were high before they switched to outward-oriented industrialisations in 1960. In the case of Singapore and Taiwan, the contributions of TFP declined with their increased outward orientation. Commenting on Havrylyshyn's (1990) extensive survey on trade–productivity link, Dornbusch (op. cit.: 76) concludes, 'even though the case for these productivity gains is highly plausible, it has been hard to document in a clear-cut way. The comprehensive survey by Havrylyshyn ... does identify a systematic evidence in support of the theory, but it is not overwhelming'. Even the World Bank (ibid.: 92) observes that '[t]he empirical evidence is far from conclusive'.

Thus, one finds inconclusive evidence on either demand-driven export-led growth hypothesis or the productivity enhancing role of trade liberalisation. Recent research by Rodrik (op. cit.: 103) shows that '[a] reasonable hypothesis is that trade policy plays a rather asymmetric role in economic development: an abysmal trade regime can perhaps drive a country into economic ruin; but good trade policy cannot make a poor country rich. At best, trade policy provides an enabling environment for development'. Whether entrepreneurs will take advantage of this environment to stimulate investment and growth depends on the existence of an appropriate institutional framework. In previous chapters, it has been frequently pointed out that the state can play an important role in providing an appropriate institutional environment for facilitating both economic growth

Table 5.7 Rates of growth of output and shares of TFP in selected economies

Economy	Period	Annual growth rate of output	Share of TFP in output growth
Hong Kong	1955–66	2.5	29.0
	1960–66	4.3	40.0
	1966–70	4.3	62.0
Korea	1955–60	2.0	47.4
	1960–66	4.1	59.3
	1966–70	5.1	50.1
Singapore	1955–60	3.7	69.0
	1966–70	5.1	44.0
	1972–80	8.0	−0.1
Mexico	1960–74	5.6	37.5
Argentina	1960–74	4.1	17.1
Chile	1960–74	4.4	27.3
Peru	1960–70	5.3	28.3
Turkey	1963–75	6.4	34.8

Sources: Havrylyshyn (1990: Table 2); World Bank (1987: Table 5.2).

and export expansion. Thus, the particular nature of the state in East Asia might be regarded as the missing 'third factor' in the observed positive correlation between exports and economic growth.

As has been emphasised in previous chapters, neoclassical orthodoxy maintains that a commitment to free trade is the central institutional ingredient which ensures economic success. However, a commitment to free trade is ultimately a political decision which presupposes the existence of a strong-willed government with the ability to maintain wages at competitive levels, to ensure that exchange rates do not move too far out of line from their equilibrium values and to implement stable and predictable macroeconomic policies. As the new political economy correctly asserts, governments in East Asia have in general been able to withstand the contending pressures of distributional coalitions in order to implement coherent economic policies that led to trade dependence. Once changes in domestic fortunes became closely linked to changes in world market conditions, a virtuous circle set in leading to a process of simultaneous interaction between exports and rapid economic growth.

CONCLUDING REMARKS

The East Asian NIEs have been spectacularly successful in exploiting the world market and increasing their share of manufactured exports ever since they opted for outward-oriented industrialisation. They have also been successful in moving towards more sophisticated manufactured exports. The impressive growth record and export expansion in the East Asian NIEs have rekindled the debate on whether trade has been an 'engine of growth' or a 'hand-maiden of growth'.

The empirical evidence on export-led growth or supply-led exports is inconclusive. There is little doubt that export played a very important role, but certainly the economic growth in the East Asian NIEs was not export-led in the sense that the impetus for export expansion came from abroad. The East Asian NIEs continued to grow and expand their exports even when growth in industrial countries slowed down. This shows that the resilience of the East Asian NIEs lies in their ability to exploit the world markets and their capacity to increase the supply of exports. According to Lee and Naya (1988:S149), '[w]hat has expanded the supply capacity is a question still to be answered satisfactorily and is in fact a far more interesting and challenging question than what proximate effects trade has had on economic growth'. Internal factors like the absence of strong distributional coalitions and political leadership committed to growth appear to be more important, if not crucial, in affecting a country's external trade and economic growth.

6

INDUSTRIAL POLICY AND STRUCTURAL CHANGE

The newly emerging countries of the post Second World War era, eager to shrug off the colonial past, took industrialisation as synonymous with development. From 1960, substantial industrialisation has taken place. According to the UNIDO (1985a: 5) estimates, developing countries' share in world manufacturing value added (MVA) rose from just over 8 per cent in 1963 to just under 12 per cent in 1974. However, the degree of industrialisation has not been very even among developing countries, with the growth of manufacturing output being highly concentrated in a relatively small number of countries. UNIDO (1983: 34) estimates that over 70 per cent of the increase in MVA in developing countries during 1973–80 was contributed by only ten countries and Brazil, Mexico, South Korea and India contributed over 50 per cent.

One can also observe significant differences in the rates of growth of manufacturing production in developing countries and regions. The countries of East and Southeast Asia showed the greatest dynamism after 1960 and East Asia

Table 6.1   Growth of manufacturing production

Economy	Average annual growth rates (%)		
	1960–70	*1970–80*	*1980–9*
Hong Kong	13.6	10.2	—
Korea	17.6	16.6	3.1
Singapore	13.0	9.8	5.9
Taiwan	20.1	12.8	8.1
India	4.7	4.7	7.3
Mexico	9.4	7.0	0.7
Argentina	5.7	1.3	−0.6
Brazil	9.7	8.7	2.2
Developing market economies	7.1	7.1	6.1
Developed market economies	6.3	3.7	3.4

Source: World Bank, *World Development Report* (various issues); Asian Development Bank (1991).

Table 6.2 Share of manufacturing in GDP (%)

Economy	1960	1970	1980	1989
Hong Kong	32[a]	28	22	21
Korea	12[a]	21	28	26
Singapore	9[a]	20	28	26
Taiwan	17[a]	24[a]	28[a]	27[a]
Developing countries	17[a]	18	18	—
Developed countries	41[a]	30	27	—

Sources: UNCTAD (various issues); World Bank (1991); Asian Development Bank (1991).
Notes: a At current factor cost.

became a new industrial centre in the world economy by 1980. As can be seen from Table 6.1, the growth rates of manufacturing production in the four East Asian NIEs since 1960 are much above developing and developed market economies' average. They are also substantially above the growth rates of manufacturing production in the traditional developing country industrial centres – India, Mexico, Brazil and Argentina – which together contributed 37.8 per cent of developing countries' MVA in 1980.

Due to rapid growth of manufacturing output, Hong Kong, Korea, Singapore and Taiwan have undergone significant structural changes. More than a quarter of their gross domestic product (GDP) comes from the manufacturing sector. With the rise in the importance of manufacturing, the manufacturing sector itself has experienced substantial structural changes. Their manufacturing activities are now more concentrated in the production of more sophisticated products than in the early days of industrialisation.

This chapter will examine the degree of industrialisation in the four East Asian NIEs and the changing pattern of their manufacturing activities. It will also reflect on possible causes of their achievements in industrialisation and controversies pertaining to this issue. In particular, two issues will receive prominence : (1) the extent to which the process of industrialisation follows the Chenery-Syrquin (1975) framework of 'normal' pattern; (2) the extent to which governments in East Asian NIEs have been able to pick industrial 'winners'.

INDUSTRIALISATION AND STRUCTURAL CHANGES

The most common measure of the degree of industrialisation and structural change is the share of manufacturing in GDP. As can be seen from Table 6.2, the degree of industrialisation in the East Asian NIEs is quite remarkable by the developing country standard. The shares of MVA in GDP in Korea, Singapore and Taiwan stood well above the average share of MVA in developing countries as a group in 1980. By this admittedly simple measure, the production structure

Table 6.3 Share of manufacturing in employment (%)

Economy	1971	1980	1989	1989/1971
Hong Kong	36	42	30	0.8
Korea	13	22	28	2.2
Singapore	24 (1973)	30	29	1.2
Taiwan	22	33	34	1.5

Sources: Asian Development Bank (various issues).

of these economies now looks very similar to that of developed economies. Hong Kong, however, displays a somewhat different picture. Its share of MVA in GDP declined after 1960. This is perhaps because Hong Kong was relatively industrialised in the early 1960s as is evident from its high share of industrial output in GDP in 1960. The declining trend of MVA's share in GDP in Hong Kong is not dissimilar to the pattern observed in developed countries.

A second common measure of structural change is the share of manufacturing employment. This indicator, too, shows that there had been substantial structural change in the East Asian NIEs. The share of manufacturing employment increased quite substantially in Korea and Taiwan and to some extent in Singapore (Table 6.3). Hong Kong once again shows the declining trend, the pattern detected earlier.

RESTRUCTURING OF MANUFACTURING ACTIVITIES

Along with industrialisation, there have been structural changes within the manufacturing sector itself. The manufacturing sector has moved away from simple labour-intensive activities. Table 6.4 shows that the shares of more complex activities like iron and steel products, machinery and transport equipments in MVA went up in all four East Asian NIEs. At the same time, the importance of food, beverage and tobacco declined.

UNIDO (1985b) has calculated an index of structural change. The index is derived from sixteen manufacturing branches. It is a measure of the degree of correlation between the value added shares in 1965 and 1980. A low correlation implies that the shares of individual branches have changed between the two periods and hence the index will be high. Both declining and expanding activities contribute to the index.

According to this index (Table 6.5), Singapore experienced the greatest structural change during 1965–80, followed by Korea. The degree of structural change in Singapore's manufacturing is three-and-a-half times the average for the developing country group. Hong Kong is the exception among the NIEs. (Taiwan data are not available.) Hong Kong's manufacturing sector continues to be dominated by one single activity – textiles and apparel (see Table 6.4).

90

Table 6.4 Structural change in manufacturing (shares in manufacturing value added: %)

	Hong Kong		Korea			Singapore			Taiwan[a]		
	1973–5	1983–5	1963	1973–5	1983–5	1967	1973–5	1983–5	1965	1976	1986
Food, beverage, tobacco	5.5	5.3	2.3	18.2	15.3	2.6	7.0	5.9	34.8	23.0	3.6
Textiles, appliances, leather, footwear	46.7	39.5	13.5	21.4	16.8	4.2	6.3	4.7	15.0	17.2	17.8
Wood, furniture	2.2	1.4	4.3	3.3	1.7	6.2	3.9	2.4	4.1	2.8	2.4
Paper, printing	5.2	5.9	7.9	4.2	4.7	7.3	4.6	6.3	5.1	2.5	2.8
Chemicals	1.7	1.6	7.5	9.7	9.1	2.9	4.9	7.6	8.6	10.4	17.4
Petroleum, coal, rubber, plastic	9.6	8.5	7.5	11.0	9.3	32.7	22.2	12.6		13.1	14.6
Non-metallic mineral production	0.7	1.2	8.5	5.5	4.8	4.5	3.1	3.5	6.5	3.9	2.8
Basic metals	8.6	7.5	6.1	10.1	12.1	10.1	7.0	8.2	2.2	4.7	9.2
Machinery	11.7	18.8	6.6	9.6	15.0	9.0	22.0	36.8	12.5	17.5	13.8
Transport equipment	3.3	2.3	1.3	4.3	8.4	7.4	15.5	9.3		3.5	5.2
Professional, scientific equipment	1.8	4.5	0.4	0.6	0.9	2.0	2.0	1.5		0.8	0.8
Other	2.9	3.6	4.2	2.0	2.0	1.0	1.1	1.2	1.3	2.5	3.0

Sources: UNIDO (1985a, b). Taiwan: OECD (1988: Table T1).
Notes: a Producers' value at current prices.

Table 6.5 Index of structural change and industrialisation, 1965–80

Economy	Index of structural change in manufacturing[a]	Average growth rate of MVA (%)
Hong Kong	9.87	6.05
Korea	31.37	18.99
Singapore	48.32	11.41
Taiwan	–	–
India	20.89	2.59
Yugoslavia	12.01	6.94
Malaysia	15.86	8.12
Argentina	15.90	3.12
Brazil	30.03	9.50
Developing countries	13.83	6.55

Source: UNIDO (1985b).
Note: a The index of structural change is defined as

$$0.5 \sum_{i=1}^{n} |a_{i1} - a_{i0}|$$

where a_{ij} is a 3-year average of the share of industrial branch $i = 1 \ldots n$ MVA for period 1 (1978–80) and period 0 (1965–7).

Consequently its manufacturing sector experienced the least structural change. From Table 6.5, one also observes that there is a close relationship between the average growth rate of MVA and the degree of structural change within manufacturing. (India and Argentina are exceptions.) As noted earlier, manufacturing attained importance in Hong Kong at an early stage. Similar to the trend observed in developed countries, Hong Kong registered a slow growth rate. The low structural change index is, thus, consistent with the overall findings.

Even though textiles and apparel still dominate Hong Kong's manufacturing activities, their importance has been declining, albeit at a slow rate. The OECD (1988: 48–9) notes that the electronics industry has been gaining importance. The textiles industry itself is undergoing changes. It has continued to move towards the production of high-quality, high-value and fashion items. The electronic industry is also moving up-market as is reflected in the high growth rates of electronic data processing equipment and within that area a move towards more sophisticated products. This outcome may have been influenced by the Hong Kong government's initiative to diversify the industrial structure. In 1977, the government set up an Advisory Committee on Diversification. However, Hong Kong maintained its predominantly pro-market policies, but sought to diversify the industrial structure by providing infrastructural support (Lin and Tsui, 1991).

The above-average structural change indices of Singapore and Korea are associated with their active industrial restructuring programme. The issues regarding the role of industrial policies in the industrialisation of the East Asian NIEs will be discussed later. However, at this stage it appears that their active restructuring programmes have played an important role in shifting manu-facturing towards more sophisticated activities.

In 1973, Korea launched a new phase of industrialisation which shifted the emphasis to the development of heavy and chemical industries. In the 1970s, these activities grew at an accelerated rate. At the same time, the growth of textiles and apparel slowed down substantially. The index of production of fabricated metal products, machinery and basic metal industry rose from 2.5 (1980 = 100) in 1965 to 226.5 in 1984 as opposed to a rise of textiles and wearing apparel from 4.1 to 133.1 during the same period (OECD, op. cit.). The OECD (ibid.: 34) notes that '[t]oday Korea is a very efficient producer of steel ... and a leading producer of ships.' Korea has also become a leading producer of consumer electronics and automobiles. In fact, the electronics sector has seen the fastest growing industrial activity. There has also been a substantial shift within the electronics sector itself towards more sophisticated goods, such as industrial electronic equipment. The production of electronic industrial equipment increased from 8.9 per cent of total electronics output in 1970 to 14.5 per cent in 1983.

Like Korea, Singapore initiated its industrial restructuring programme in the early 1970s. This was, however, abandoned in the aftermath of the first oil price shock and was reintroduced in 1979. The aim of this restructuring programme was to shift manufacturing activities towards certain 'priority' industries which are more skill- and technology-intensive (Chowdhury and Kirkpatrick, 1987). The machinery sector, which includes such 'priority' activities as electricals and electronics, has registered a four-fold increase in its share in MVA between 1965 and 1985. Industrial chemicals and communications equipment have also grown substantially. With the rise in importance of these activities, Singapore's manufacturing sector has become more skill- and technology-intensive and it is moving upstream into more sophisticated production (Chowdhury and Kirkpatrick, 1990).

A similar trend can also be observed in Taiwan. The OECD (op. cit.: 39–40) claims that the deliberate industrial restructuring programme has played a part in the evolution of Taiwan's manufacturing sector. The emergence of fabricated metal products, machinery and equipment as the leading industrial group by 1975 indicate that Taiwan's manufacturing sector has shifted towards more complex and sophisticated activities. At the same time more traditional industries like food, beverage and tobacco declined in importance. In line with the shift in industrial strategy in the 1980s towards high technology and skill-intensive activities (which included information, electronics, machinery and biotechnology), the electrical machinery and electrical appliances industry grew by 19.4 per cent annually between 1982 and 1984. There has also been substantial progress in the development of automation and precision machinery, especially tools and shuttle loom technology. The basic metals, chemicals and

Table 6.6   Indices of similarity of the manufacturing sector

Economy	Year of comparison	Relative to	
		Japan	USA
Hong Kong	1963	53	49
	1976	54	49
Korea	1963	66	58
	1979	68	69
Singapore	1968	65	61
	1978	64	64
Malaysia	1968	54	53
	1978	60	59
Philippines	1967	57	54
	1977	55	59
Thailand	1963	50	45
	1975	49	50
India	1963	65	49
	1978	72	49
Pakistan	1963	37	40
	1976	42	47

Source: UNIDO (1982: 25).

Notes: $I(a,b) = \{ \sum_i \text{minimum } S_i(a), S_i(b)\} \times 100$

where S_i = share of MVA in constant price of branch i; a and b are the countries compared.
If $S_i(a) = S_i(b)$ for each i, the index will be 100.
If they are totally dissimilar for each $S_i(a) > 0$, $S_i(b) = 0$ and vice versa, the index will take the value of zero.

chemical products grew at annual rates ranging from 10 to 15 per cent.

Thus, there have been significant structural changes within the manufacturing sector of the four East Asian NIEs. All of them, in particular Korea, Singapore and Taiwan, have been moving away from labour-intensive simple production activities to the more complex and skill-intensive ones. It will be interesting to see to what extent the manufacturing activities of the East Asian NIEs look similar to the ones in the 'old' industrial countries as a result of this progressive shift. Table 6.6 presents UNIDO's indices of similarities of the manufacturing sector for selected countries. It shows that during 1963–79, Korea advanced more towards the USA than towards Japan. While Singapore's manufacturing structure vis-à-vis that of Japan remained almost unchanged, it moved slightly towards the USA after 1967. Hong Kong's manufacturing structure remained unchanged vis-à-vis both Japan and the USA between 1963 and 1976.

While there is little doubt about substantial structural changes in the East Asian NIEs both in aggregate and within the manufacturing sector, the explanation of what contributed to these phenomenal changes remains controversial. At one extreme, there is a view that there is a direct link between industrialisation and the outward (export) orientation of these economies. This view attributes the transformation of these economies to the policies based on international division of labour or comparative advantage. Others highlight the role of the state and its interventionist industrial policies which 'create' competitive advantage rather than respond passively to comparative advantage determined by a country's initial set of endowments. There is also a hypothesis derived from the historical experience of the developed countries. This view does not deny the importance of exports and government policy intervention, but draws attention to the 'normal' pattern of industrialisation which follows the rise in per capita income. While these issues will not be settled here, the following section explores the main contours of this debate. It is germane to begin with a review of industrial policies in the East Asian NIEs.

INDUSTRIAL POLICIES IN EAST ASIAN NIEs

This section draws on several sources. They include Arndt (1987a), OECD (op. cit.), Deyo (1989), Haggard (1990), Lin and Ho (1984), Lin and Tsui (op. cit.), Industry Commission (1990), Islam and Kirkpatrick (1986b) and Islam (1990). Except perhaps for Hong Kong, the East Asian NIEs followed active industrial policies aimed at promoting particular types of industrial activities at different times. Being an entrepôt, Hong Kong had a substantial industrial base in the early 1960s. The labour-intensive industries in Hong Kong grew largely in response to the international division of labour as the multinational companies moved to cheaper offshore production sites.

On the other hand, industrial development in Korea has been influenced to a great extent by the guidelines of the 5-year economic plans since the early 1960s. The Korean government played a crucial role in the shift of the industrial activities from import substitution towards exportables in 1964. It was done by intervening directly in the 'choice' or 'priority' activities which were, at that time, textiles and consumer electronics. Preferential credit was the main instrument of intervention. The Korean government exercised a considerable degree of control over the financial sector. This enabled the government to channel investment funds to priority or 'strategic' industries. The Korean government removed biases against exports by reforming the exchange rate and introducing a series of incentives for the producers of exports and intermediate goods for exports.

In anticipation of shifts in international comparative advantage, the Korean government launched an industrial restructuring programme in 1973. It shifted the emphasis from labour-intensive to heavy and capital-intensive activities including the upstream end of the production chain. The priority activities included steel and non-ferrous metals, chemicals, petrochemicals, machinery, shipbuilding and electronic industrial equipment.

While the methods of direct and indirect intervention remained the same in the 1970s, the Korean government supplemented its industrial restructuring policy with active R&D and human resource development (HRD) programmes, given that without such programmes it is impossible to move up the technology ladder and upgrade industrial activities. OECD (op. cit.: 37) notes that Korea has moved very fast in increasing its R&D/GNP ratio and that it has made spectacular progress in expanding engineering education and the government 'played a very important part in augmenting R&D activity'.

Although Singapore is a very open economy in the sense that there are no or little restrictions on foreign trade and investment, the government exercises a very strong influence on the process and direction of industrialisation. The Economic Development Board (EDB) lays down its priorities for industrial activities in anticipation of changes in Singapore's comparative advantage. Accordingly, it attempts to channel both domestic and foreign investment to the 'priority' industries. More than half of the national savings are channelled into public institutions, like the Post Office Savings Bank and Central Provident Fund, and the state has made substantial investment in industrial activities such as shipbuilding and iron and steel (OECD, ibid.: 45). The EDB also administers selective grants and loan schemes for the priority industries and provides industrial infrastructure support to them.

Singapore attempted to restructure its manufacturing sector first in 1972, but this policy had to be abandoned due to problems arising from the first oil price shocks. The industrial restructuring programme was reintroduced in 1979. The main policy instrument was high wages to discourage labour-intensive activities, but there is also payroll tax and a Skill Development Fund (SDF) levy on the employers of unskilled labour. The SDF is used to upgrade the skill level of employees. These measures were intended to shift industrial activities towards more skill- and technology-intensive activities, microprocessors and other sophisticated electronic products.

The restructuring programme has suffered a setback in the mid-1980s due to both domestic and international factors. In response, the government introduced various measures which stressed cost reduction, and included additional tax incentives to attract foreign investment. There has also been a shift away from industry-specific to general investment incentives to avoid ill-conceived investment decisions by the government. It is also recognised that Singapore's ability to carry out basic research is limited due to its resource constraint. So the emphasis is on the improvement of product design, development of capability in industries that already exist and the creation of competence in new technology relevant for both established and future industries like biotechnology and electro-optics.

In line with this shift in emphasis, Singapore has stepped up its R&D and HRD programme and considerable progress has been made in this direction (Chowdhury et al., 1988). It has also improved the patent system and tightened the copyright laws in order to encourage innovation and the transfer of technology.

Government policies were instrumental in the switch of Taiwan's industrial activities towards exportables in the mid-1960s. The policies included a series of financial and fiscal measures aimed at liberalising the financial market, reforming the exchange rate system with a view to facilitating the imports of machinery and industrial raw materials by exporters and providing export financing. The government also established export processing zones to attract foreign invest-ment in the export sector – mainly textiles, agrofood and consumer electronics.

Like Korea and Singapore, the Taiwanese government promoted the develop-ment of capital and technology intensive industries in the 1970s. This had the result of broadening the country's industrial base. The shift in industrial emphasis was accompanied by a special effort to promote R&D activities by establishing publicly funded industrial parks. As a result of government emphasis on HRD, 11.3 per cent of the population 15 years old and over now has a junior or university education compared with only 4.4 per cent in the mid-1960s (OECD, op. cit.: 39).

Taiwan's industrial strategy underwent significant changes in the 1980s. One main thrust of these changes was to reduce overcapacity and make industries more flexible. The government scaled down its industrialisation plans and the authorities in shipbuilding and aluminium smelting industries revised their expansion plans downwards. The government also acted to rationalise pro-duction in state-owned enterprises and its role as an industrial entrepreneur was reduced (OECD, ibid.: 39–41).

Another aspect of the industrial strategy in the 1980s is the expansion of high technology and skill intensive activities. These 'strategic' industries included information, electronics, machinery and biotechnology.

Even in laissez-faire Hong Kong, the Advisory Committee on Diversification (ADC) realised the importance of technological upgrading as a means for industries to move up-market. It identified the lack of supporting industries and technical back-up services as the major obstacle to upgrading. On the advice of the ADC, the government set up the Industrial Development Board (IDB) in 1980. However, unlike the other three East Asian NIEs, IDB functioned pre-dominantly through the market system. Lin and Tsui (op. cit.: 4) note that this phase of industrial restructuring is still unfolding.

Thus, except for Hong Kong, East Asian NIEs have followed activist industrial policies. However, there are major differences in approaches and outcomes of their industrial policies. One notable difference is in their treatment of direct foreign investment (DFI). Both Singapore and Hong Kong are more liberal towards DFI. On the other hand Korea and Taiwan stipulate a certain level of domestic ownership. This has led to some predictable outcomes in terms of types of DFI. While joint ventures and minority ownerships are the pre-dominant form of DFI in Korea and to some extent in Taiwan, the dominant pattern of DFI in Singapore is wholly or majority foreign ownership. In the case of Hong Kong, the distribution between wholly owned and joint venture DFI is roughly equal. (See Chapter 7 for more details.)

The second difference in the industrial policies of the East Asian NIEs is government's direct participation in industrial activities. Taiwan relied more on direct government ownership of enterprises, but it is now reducing its direct ownership. In the 1950s, the state-owned enterprises accounted for over 50 per cent of total manufacturing output; it accounted for about 15 per cent in the 1980s (OECD, op. cit.: 40–1). The Taiwanese government still owns seven of Taiwan's ten largest industrial enterprises.

The Singapore government, too, made substantial industrial investment. In the early stages, it started many industries including shipbuilding, oil refineries and iron–steel which it considered 'strategic' but where private investment was limited. One estimate (Low, 1985) shows that, in 1983, the Singapore government either wholly or partially owned 450 companies involving $2.4 billion in paid-up capital and $18.2 billion in fixed assets. They employed 5 per cent of the total labour force and made up 21.4 per cent of sales in manufacturing sector. As the former Prime Minister and the architect of modern Singapore, Mr Lee Kuan Yew, recently said, '[i]n the early stages, when you try to bring up a very low level of economy to catch up with others, the government must be an activist, and catalyst to growth. But once the business got going, they would become too complex and specialised for any government to be involved. Hence private entrepreneurs and companies must be encouraged to take over' (K.Y. Lee, 1991). This aptly describes the philosophy and evolving nature of Singapore's industrial strategies.

The third difference among the East Asian NIEs, especially Taiwan and Korea, is the size of the enterprises. Taiwan gave greater importance to small and medium-sized enterprises. The credit and interest rate policies of Taiwan resulted in more small and equity-based companies. On the other hand, selective credit and low interest rate policy in Korea favoured big and debt-based enterprises (Steers *et al.*, 1989). Scitovsky observes that

> [t]he average Taiwanese firm in 1976 was only half as big as the Korean, with 34.6 employees as against 68.8 in Korea. Moreover, the very small firms, ignored by the Korean census, constituted 43 per cent of all manufacturing firms in Taiwan, bring the average size of all Taiwanese firms down to 27 employees. The disparity in firm size between the two countries seems even greater when one looks at their largest firms. In 1981, the $10 billion gross receipts of Hyundai, Korea's largest conglomerate, were three times as big as the $3.5 billion gross receipts of Taiwan's ten largest private firms combined.
>
> (Scitovsky, 1985: 224)

CAUSES OF INDUSTRIALISATION AND STRUCTURAL CHANGE: ISSUES AND DEBATES

Past studies (Chenery, 1960; Chenery and Syrquin, op. cit.; UNIDO, 1979a) of post-war industrialisation have found a systematic relationship between the level of per capita income and structural change affecting the manufacturing sector. According to these findings, the share of manufacturing in GDP rises with the rise in per capita income giving rise to an S-shaped logistic curve with an upper and lower asymptote. In summarising the studies, Nixson (1990: 318) observes that '[d]ifferences in income level alone accounted for 70 per cent of the variation in the levels of total industrial output among countries ... [T]he analysis did indicate the changes in the pattern of resource allocation that normally accompanied a rise in income'.

The spectacular transformation of Hong Kong, Korea, Singapore and Taiwan is not very different from the 'normal' pattern of industrialisation. Similar to the pattern observed elsewhere, the share of manufacturing in the East Asian NIEs rose with the rise in their per capita income. Thus, it will be interesting to examine whether the structural transformation and industrialisation of these economies can be explained by using the Chenery–Syrquin framework.

Chenery and Syrquin (op. cit.) have argued that each aspect of a country's development pattern can be described in terms of three components:

1   the normal effect of universal factors which are related to the level of income;
2   the effect of other general factors over which the government has little or no control;
3   the effects of a country's individual history, political and social objectives and particular policies that the government has pursued to achieve those objectives.

These factors can be broadly classified as exogenous and endogenous. The universal, general and country-specific sociocultural and historical factors can be regarded as exogenous in the sense that they are given and cannot be controlled or changed. The endogenous factor is the interplay of politics and policy making that define social objectives and policies to attain them within the general constraint of the exogenous factors.

The possible contributions of the country-specific, sociocultural and historical factors to the rise of the East Asian NIEs have been discussed in Chapter 2. It has been claimed that the common Confucian cultural background, the colonial past and the geopolitics of external threat and foreign aid may have played a complementary role in the structural transformation of the four East Asian economies. The most significant contribution of these exogenous factors perhaps was to provide a congenial political atmosphere for policy changes which paved the way for industrialisation and structural transformation.

Among the general factors, Chenery and Syrquin (ibid.) have identified market size and natural resource endowments as affecting a country's industrialisation process. Although Korea and Taiwan are larger economies than Hong Kong and Singapore, they are quite small compared with, say, India, Brazil and Argentina, which have larger domestic markets. By vigorously following export-oriented industrialisation policies they have successfully overcome the constraint of market size. In addition, the rise in per capita income from exports has been responsible for the increase in their savings and investment rates and the change in the demand structure, all of which have affected industrialisation favourably. It is argued that trade-dependent industrialisation is unavoidable for very small economies, as they are inevitably dependent on the rest of the world for most requirements (Little, 1979). Unlike the East Asian NIEs, many small developing countries, however, chose not to follow this path.

It is believed that there is generally an inverse relationship between a country's endowment of natural resources and industrialisation. 'The Four ... are poor in minerals. ... [They] ... have the highest population densities in relation to cultivable land of any country in the world. ... the people in such countries can become well off only through industrialization' (Little, ibid.: 449–50). Being resource poor, the East Asian NIEs never had to suffer from 'Dutch disease' problems. The Dutch disease results in a squeeze on the traded goods sector (mainly manufacturing) due to upward pressure on real wages as a result of a sudden boom in the export of primary products. In the long-run, the effect of an ample endowment of exportable natural resources is a relatively favourable balance of payments which pushes up the real exchange rate. Consequently the country's manufacturing sector suffers a loss in its international competitiveness. In other words, countries with ample exportable natural resources have comparative disadvantage in manufacturing. Further, Arndt (op. cit.: 15) argues that natural resource abundant countries may suffer the temptation of 'lotus-eating'. These countries 'do not have to work hard at doing well economically or they may think so. Countries which lack natural resources must make the most of their human resources – capacity for hard work, discipline, thrift, skills, enterprise'.

While policy makers in the East Asian NIEs could utilise the lack of natural resources to their advantage, many developing countries curse their fate for the lack of it. At the same time, many natural resource rich developing countries have made a mess of it. Thus, as discussed in Chapters 2 and 3, the politics of policy making appear to play a significant role in a country's structural transformation and industrialisation. The general association between industrial policies and industrial structure has been discussed in the previous section. The more contentious issue pertaining to a government's ability to pick a 'winning' industrial structure is assessed in the following section.

CAN A GOVERNMENT PICK A 'WINNING' INDUSTRIAL STRUCTURE?

The historical roots of this debate can be traced to the literature on the relative merits of import substituting industrialisation (ISI) and export-oriented industrialisation (EOI) of the late 1960s and early 1970s. Neoclassical orthodoxy has always maintained that the failure of ISI in a wide range of developing countries supports the contention that a government cannot create a winning industrial structure through interventionist policies. At the same time, the spectacular growth of the East Asian NIEs that closely followed the industry and trade policy reforms of the mid-1960s was approvingly and widely cited as a vindication of the neoclassical position. This conventional wisdom was reinforced by a World Bank study (Agarwala, 1983) which used a sample of thirty-one developing countries to maintain that high growth was associated with low price distortions. The natural inference is that since low price distortions measure the prevailing degree of government interventions in the industrial sector, interventionist policies have an adverse impact on economic growth. A subsequent World Bank study (World Bank, 1987b) continued to uphold the neoclassical orthodoxy, arguing that the cross-country data suggested a close association between EOI and superior economic performance in terms of a wide variety of indicators (see Chapter 5).

If the government cannot deliberately create industrial 'winners', then how do such winners emerge (in the sense of the emergence of industries with revealed comparative advantage in world markets)? The answer lies in the natural history of the development process. Balassa (1977b) maintains that the emergence of East Asian NIEs as major exporters can be explained by what he calls 'a stages approach to comparative advantage'. According to this approach a country's comparative advantage evolves in stages. Initially a typical developing country would have comparative advantage in labour-intensive activities. But as wage rates rise and living standard improves, it loses competitive advantage in such products to lower income countries. Therefore, labour-intensive activities phase out and the economic structure moves towards capital-intensive industries. A country's approaching industrial maturity can be gauged from the secular movement from capital-intensive to skill-intensive industries. The implication of this industrialisation process is that countries move through different stages of comparative advantage as the product composition of exports shifts along a spectrum of factor intensities.

An offshoot of the stages explanation has come to be known as the 'flying geese' hypothesis, a concept first developed by Akamatsu in the 1930s (cited in Kojima, 1977) to describe the rise of Japan as an industrialised nation. According to Chen (1989a), a major factor for the success of the East Asian NIEs lies in the restructuring of the Japanese economy which moved Japan towards more sophisticated activities and left markets for East Asian NIEs' labour intensive products. Japan was a large exporter of textiles in the 1950s. As real wages rose rapidly, it increasingly lost its competitive advantage in textiles and other labour-intensive products. It responded by restructuring its manufacturing sector during the 1960s and as a part of the restructuring programme relocated its labour-intensive activities to Korea and Taiwan. Arndt (op. cit.: 21) notes that '[a] considerable part of the expansion of exports of manufactures by the East Asian NICs during the 1960s and 1970s was achieved not through overall increase in demand for such products in developed countries but by their taking over markets, both in developed and in other developing countries vacated by Japan'.

Table 6.7   East Asia's share of world exports of labour-intensive manufactures, 1962–81 (%)

Economy or economic grouping	1962–8	1969–71	1972–6	1977–81
Japan	13.17	12.95	9.64	5.93
Hong Kong, Korea, Taiwan	4.23	7.20	10.26	14.11
ASEAN[a]	0.66	0.59	1.19	2.30
China	1.92	1.70	1.83	2.73

Source: Arndt (1987a: 21).

Note: a   Signapore is included in ASEAN.

This process of progressive vacation of market for more sophisticated products by Japan and taking over of these markets by the East Asian NIEs is described as 'flying geese' pattern or phenomenon, with Japan as the leader and the East Asian NIEs as followers. The East Asian NIEs themselves are being followed by ASEAN and perhaps by China. An indication of the flying geese pattern can be seen in Table 6.7.

Another variant of the neoclassical theory which is often used to explain the success of the East Asian NIEs in export expansion is known as 'product life cycle' (see Vernon, 1966; Lutz and Kihl, 1990). This theory distinguishes three phases in the life cycle of a product: introductory, growth and mature phases. New technological and sophisticated infrastructure is needed at the introductory stage of product development. Production at this stage is, therefore, skill-intensive. Since the production process is not standardised at the introductory stage, production costs are high. During the subsequent stage, production costs decline as the process becomes standardised and can be handled by relatively less skilled labour. At this phase, production may remain capital-intensive but, as it can be handled by less skilled labour, it can be transferred to developing countries to take advantage of lower wages.

If the industrial structure evolves as part of the natural history of the development process, does this mean that there is no role for activist industrial policy? Proponents of this position would maintain that the evolution of the industrial structure in line with shifting comparative advantage depends crucially on the prior existence of an appropriate policy environment. The government facilitates industrial development through the maintenance of low (ideally zero) relative price distortions. This position is often popularised by noting that the objective is to 'get prices right'. The empirical approximation of this policy prescription is, of course, the aforementioned World Bank-type studies suggesting a link between low price distortions, EOI and rapid economic growth. Furthermore, East Asian economic success is popularly seen as a glittering example of this well-known (assumed) causality.

As Chapter 3 has emphasised, this neoclassical orthodoxy has been challenged by the new political economy. This is particularly evident in the arena of industrial policy. There are several strands in the new political economy approach to East Asian industrial policy. First, it questions the empirical foundation of neoclassical orthodoxy. Second, it suggests that the nature of the debate on industrial policy has shifted from a concern with old-fashioned protection of domestic markets (inherent in ISI) to one where the policy objective is to win export markets through strategic intervention in key industries – a view that is often summarised in the phrase 'strategic trade policy'. Third, it suggests that the risk of government failure inherent in activist industrial policy can be minimised through appropriate institutional arrangements and that the East Asian experience supports such a contention.

Consider the empirical critique of neoclassical orthodoxy. It may be useful to recall at this stage that empirical approximations of the neoclassical position on the impact of industrial policy on economic development rest on systematic associations between low price distortions, EOI and a wide variety of performance indicators. Wade (1990), one of the prominent proponents of new political economy, has offered a review of the evidence and concludes that it does not stand up to critical scrutiny. In particular, the World Bank studies are afflicted by methodological problems – the classification of countries into EOI and ISI regimes are suspect, the price distortion index has limited analytic content and the conclusions on the virtues of EOI are based on an extremely limited sample. Bradford (1987a, b), has also re-examined the association between price distortion and economic growth and contrary to the World Bank's assertion finds that the 'key characteristics accounting for the above-trendline pattern of structural change in transitional economies is lower costs associated with capital formation'.

Perhaps the most popular empirical critique of the neoclassical position rests on the proposition that one cannot ignore the evidence of widespread intervention in the industrial sector in Korea, Taiwan and Singapore. It is thus tempting to infer that rapid industrial development in the NIEs is the product of such intervention – an inference that is contrary to the neoclassical position. Indeed, the conventional wisdom now seems to be that industrial policy in the East Asian NIEs differs from that in other countries not in terms of the extent of intervention, but in the quality of such intervention (Bardhan, 1990).

New political economy can seek inspiration from developments in the theory of strategic trade policy. One striking conclusion of these theories is that government assistance (subsidies, tariffs, etc.) may alter international competitiveness in favour of local export firms in oligopolistic industries. The overall outcome is that the welfare of the country in question increases (Brander and Spencer, 1985; Krugman, 1984). It must be emphasised that the theory of strategic trade policy has well known analytical limitations. As Corden notes (1991: 286): 'a fundamental problem is that (all the) models seem to be special case(s) leading to particular results, depending upon the size of the various parameters ... there has been little search for general principles'.

Other commentators have emphasised the undesirability of basing inter-ventionist policies on these theories, on the grounds that there are overwhelming political economy and information problems (Grossman, 1986; Krugman, 1987). The former pertains to the point that government assistance may trigger rent-seeking behaviour and trade retaliation across nations. The latter pertains to the information problems of engaging in optimal intervention to offset the distorting effects of oligopoly.

The adherents of new political economy could respond to this critique by suggesting that the alleged problems of rent-seeking and information problems are likely to be less severe in the case of East Asia, given the nature of the strong state and close cooperation between government and business. In other words, the risk of government failure inherent in the pursuit of strategic trade policy is less likely in the particular institutional circumstances of East Asia.

The competing propositions of the neoclassical orthodoxy and new political economy should ideally be resolved by empirical investigations. Unfortunately, this is where the available literature is most contentious – as the review of the available evidence reveals. The Korean experience has been studied most exten-sively (World Bank, 1987a; Y.C. Park, 1983a; Industry Commission, op. cit.; Islam, op. cit.; C.H. Lee, 1992; Collins and Park, 1989; Westphal, 1990; Amsden, 1989; Biggs and Levy, 1991). As documented in previous sections, the Korean government embarked on an ambitious drive to build up heavy and chemical industries (HCI) both in terms of domestic and export markets during the 1970s. The strategy was substantially toned down after 1980. To neoclassical economists, the sheer fact of policy reversal is an indication that the HCI drive was a failure. Moreover, they tend to point to evidence of declining efficiency during this period – as measured in terms of rising incremental capital/output ratio and declining TFP (World Bank, op. cit.). Furthermore, the HCI drive is also blamed for causing macroeconomic mismanagement during that period leading to acute inflationary pressures and appreciation of the real exchange rate. These developments in turn had the adverse effect of crowding out traditional export industries. The crisis point of the HCI period was a steep recession in 1980.

More positive and balanced assessments are offered by Lee (op. cit.) and Collins and Park (op. cit.). Such assessments typically emphasise that the Korean HCI drive was stalled by unfavourable and unanticipated external (the oil price shock of 1979) and internal events such as the assassination of President Park and the threat of political instability in 1979. Moreover, the picture looks much more favourable from the vantage point of the mid-1980s. Thus, while in 1982 the HCI sector as a whole did not attain international competitiveness as measured by revealed comparative advantage, by 1986 it had become the leading sector in terms of growth of value-added and exports. This has prompted Lee to ask (Lee, op. cit.: 469): 'Could Korea have successfully developed its electronics, automobile, iron and steel and petrochemical industries ... if there had been no active government for those industries?'. Biggs and Levy (op. cit.) are sympa-thetic to this question.

In the case of Taiwan, both Wade (op. cit.) and Biggs and Levy (op. cit.) document evidence of various forms of government assistance to specific industries and argue that they were made in anticipation of shifts in comparative advantage. However, none of them can satisfactorily establish the effectiveness of such policies. The Industry Commission (op. cit.: 58) maintains that the Taiwanese experience provides testimony to the failure of strategic trade policy. Thus the government's targeting of steel, shipbuilding and petrochemicals met with serious problems to the point where 'some of these ventures were closed down in the early 1980s when sector-specific interventions were wound back'. Furthermore, the Taiwanese car industry is often cited as a case of continued government assistance over two decades that failed to produce a winner in export markets (Wu, 1991). In recent years (under the 1985 car industry adjustment plan), the government has expressed the intention to promote car parts as a major export item. Informed observers have, however, expressed strong doubts about its viability in the light of global restructuring of the components industry (Wu, ibid.: 350).

In the case of Singapore, the 1979 restructuring drive saw the emergence of wages policy as a major means of phasing out labour-intensive activities and promoting more 'high-tech, high value-added' activities. It is now officially recognised that the wages policy played a role in pushing the economy into a recession in 1985 primarily through a reduction in Singapore's international competitiveness (Ministry of Trade and Industry, 1986). It must be noted, however, that external factors also contributed to the recession. As Pang notes:

> Externally, there was a world-wide excess capacity in shipbuilding and a slump in electronics – industries that account for a significant share of Singapore's manufacturing exports. The collapse in oil prices hurt regional oil-producing economies, which reduced their imports for Singapore's goods and services. It also had a serious impact on Singapore's large petroleum industry and reduced greatly the demand for oil rigs produced by Singapore's shipyards.
>
> (Pang, 1991: 226)

It thus appears that the Singapore government's attempt to create a 'winning' industrial structure was ill-timed and ill-executed, particularly in the light of recent experience. These problems were officially recognised when, after the 1985 recession, the government decided to take a more market-oriented approach to industrial policy (Ministry of Trade and Industry, op. cit.).

Finally, it is important to emphasise that critics of activist policy often approvingly cite the case of Hong Kong, as is evident in the following remarks: 'probably the most outstanding example of economy-wide success without targeting is Hong Kong. In this country rapid growth was achieved with the government restricting its activities to supporting the market' (Industry Commission, op. cit.: 59). Not all observers of the Hong Kong economy take such an optimistic view, a point well captured in the following remarks of Lin and Tsui:

> Critics have argued that the hands-off policy of the government is no longer tenable. The level of technology in Hong Kong is still quite low compared to say Taiwan or South Korea. . . . Hong Kong is extremely weak in fundamental research; it has limited capabilities in information systems, automated manufacturing, advanced materials and biotechnology, the four major fields that have experienced rapid technological advances in recent years.
>
> (Lin and Tsui, op. cit.: 74)

CONCLUDING REMARKS

Two facts stand out clearly about the phenomenal transformation of the East Asian NIEs: rapid industrialisation since 1960, and export-oriented industrialisation. Since export-oriented industrialisation depends predominantly on policies like a unified exchange rate, a liberal trading environment and a non-discriminatory tariff structure, export orientation was often identified with free market policies. This new orthodoxy argued that the successful industrialisation in the NIEs was due to 'getting their prices right'. However, there is evidence that state intervention or public policies played a substantial role in the industrialisation process of the East Asian NIEs.

But just as markets can fail, governments can fail too. The government's record in picking winners in the East Asian NIEs is mixed. This has prompted at least some observers to claim that governments in East Asia deliberately distorted prices to 'get policies right'. In other words, governments are able to 'pick winners' (Amsden, op. cit., 1991). This chapter has tried to suggest that the dichotomy between 'getting prices right' vs 'getting policies right' is a false and misleading one. The World Bank study (Agarwala, op.cit.: 46) which sparked the debate itself recognised the danger of an oversimplified dichotomy and notes, '[G]etting the prices right ... should not necessarily be interpreted as an argument for a laissez faire approach'. Similarly 'getting the policies right' should not be taken to justify wholesale government intervention. As Bradford (op. cit.: 199) puts it, '[p]art of the business of getting policies right is to provide ample scope for prices and markets to work well'.

Thus, what matters is not the 'extent' of government intervention but the 'quality' of intervention. The quality of public policies depends on flexibility, selectivity, coherence and emphasis on promotion rather than regulation (Jenkins, 1991). Obviously, as mentioned repeatedly, the nature of the state plays an important role in obtaining these criteria for 'high quality' public policies.

106

7

FOREIGN INVESTMENT AND
TECHNOLOGICAL CAPABILITIES

External resources can play a critical role in economic development. The early literature (e.g. Chenery and Bruno, 1962) on foreign capital noted the role that foreign resources may play in meeting the shortfall in domestic savings and relaxing the constraint on imports of essential raw materials and capital goods. External resource inflows can take several forms, such as aid, grants, borrowing and direct investment. Aid and grants are the main components of the official source of external finance and direct investment is the predominant form of private resource flows. While borrowing can be either from official or private sources, it is the latter that has dominated external financing in the East Asian NIEs in recent years. The important role that aid and grants have played in the early phase of industrialisation in East Asian NIEs, especially in Korea and Taiwan, has been noted in Chapter 2. The focus of this chapter is mainly the role of direct foreign investment (DFI) in the industrialisation process.

The most important contribution of foreign capital, especially DFI, is likely to come from external economies in the form of demand creation for the local suppliers and transfer of technology. Meier has succinctly summarised the role of DFI as follows:

> Direct foreign investment brings to the recipient country not only capital and foreign exchange but also managerial ability, technical personnel, technological knowledge, administrative organization, and innovations in products and production techniques.... There are also considerable scope for ... demand creation in other industries. The foreign investment in the first industry can give rise to profits in industries that supply inputs to the first industry, in industries that produce complementary products. ... A whole series of domestic investments may thus be linked to the foreign investment.
>
> (Meier, 1985: 324–5)

However, foreign resources are not costless. In the case of borrowing, it may create debt-servicing problem. The debt crisis of the 1980s is a glaring example of the danger of borrowing in the international capital market. DFI, on the other hand, may adversely affect industrial structure by raising the concentration ratio and market power. It may also 'crowd out' domestic entrepreneurial efforts by absorbing local talents. DFI may extract extra concessions from the host country as developing countries offer various special incentives to attract foreign investment. It may also adversely affect income distribution by widening the wage differentials among the blue and white collar workers and among local and foreign firms. The central problem for the recipient country, therefore, is how to devise policies that will encourage a greater flow of foreign resources and at the same time ensure that it makes the maximum contribution to the achievement of development objectives.

The East Asian NIEs are generally cited as examples of successful implementation of policies towards foreign capital inflows, in particular DFI. Both foreign borrowing and direct investment have been an integral part of industrial and trade policies in the East Asian NIEs in varying degrees. In the early phase, they were perceived to do primarily two functions: first, supplement domestic savings and relax foreign exchange constraint and thereby promote industrialisation, and second, provide markets abroad and thereby integrate the domestic economy with the world economy. With the success of East Asian NIEs in mobilising domestic savings and export expansion in the late 1960s and early 1970s, the importance of these functions of foreign capital has diminished significantly.

However, foreign capital still plays some crucial roles. The most important contribution of foreign capital, especially DFI, in the later phase of development lies in enhancing the technological capabilities of the host country. As James *et al.* (1989: 122) note, '[a]lthough the capital transfer involved is usually minimal, the technology and managerial skills transferred through DFI have often of far greater importance than the size of the capital flow'. This chapter will reflect on the costs and benefits of foreign investment in the East Asian NIEs. An issue that will receive particular attention is DFI's role as a vehicle for technology transfer to these economies. It will be useful to begin the discussion with a brief outline of key features of foreign investment in each of the East Asian NIEs.

NATURE AND TREND OF DIRECT FOREIGN INVESTMENT

The relative importance of DFI in the East Asian NIEs can be observed from the share of DFI in their GDP. In recent years (1985–8), the stock of DFI as a proportion of GDP has averaged 2 per cent in Korea, 8 per cent Taiwan, 20–26 per cent in Hong Kong and 54 per cent in Singapore (Lall, 1991: 147). The main features of external resource flow to East Asian NIEs are captured in Tables 7.1–7.4. As far as sources of foreign resource flows are concerned, Table 7.1 shows a steady decline in the flow of foreign capital from official sources and a rise in private financing. It also reveals that private flows are increasingly taking the form of direct investment. However, there are considerable variations among the four NIEs. First, external financing from official sources has become insignificant in Hong Kong and Singapore since the late 1970s, while in Korea it has constituted

Table 7.1 Total net external resource flows[a]

	1969–71	1972–6	1977–80	1981–3
Hong Kong	229.1[b]	213.2[b]	597.2[b]	1412.0[b]
Official	30.8	27.0	2.0	2.6
Private	69.2	73.0	98.0	97.4
DFI	(11.2)	(54.0)	(46.1)	(57.2)
Korea	547.2[b]	846.3[b]	1328.5[b]	1533.8[b]
Official	73.2	66.1	56.5	65.0
Private	26.8	33.9	43.5	35.0
DFI	(3.1)	(12.8)	(0.1)	(12.0)
Singapore	81.3[b]	165.5[b]	444.7[b]	1106.4[b]
Official	55.3	34.4	14.0	1.6
Private	44.7	65.6	86.0	98.4
DFI	(19.4)	(42.8)	(65.1)	(53.0)
Taiwan	186.2[b]	255.1[b]	234.9[b]	565.6[b]
Official	47.0	41.6	74.5	29.5
Private	53.0	58.4	25.5	70.5
DFI	(10.1)	(8.3)	(29.3)	(15.7)

Source: Hill and Johns (1985: Table 1).
Notes: a Net flows represent the actual international transfers of financial resources less repayments of principal in respect of earlier loans.
b The first row represents yearly averages in US$ million, percentage of total thereafter.

more than 50 per cent in the 1980s. Second, Singapore and Korea can be regarded as two polar extremes with respect to DFI (Hill and Johns, 1985: 358). DFI is the major form of net private capital inflow to Singapore and Hong Kong and constitutes a minor portion in the case of Taiwan and Korea. James *et al.* (op. cit.: 124) observe that Singapore is the only country where DFI was on average more than 10 per cent of gross capital formation during 1965–84; during the same period DFI was less than 2 per cent in Korea.

While theory provides little guidance in explaining the intercountry variations in DFI, it seems reasonable to believe that respective country policies may have played a role. Korea pursued an extremely cautious policy towards DFI until the early 1980s. Hill (1990: 25) terms Korean DFI policy as distrustful attitude and notes that there were virtually no equity inflows between 1945 and 1962. On the other hand, Singapore has been a ready recipient of foreign equity capital. In contrast to Korea, policy makers in Singapore viewed foreign investment as mutually beneficial for both Singapore and the investing countries. It provided generous incentives to foreign investors, in addition to maintaining a congenial environment for foreign investment. Hong Kong followed roughly similar open-door and non-discriminatory policies. However, it did not have special incentive

Table 7.2   Sectoral distribution of DFI (%)

Sector and year	Korea	Singapore[a]	Taiwan
Agriculture			
1967–71	1.3	0.2	0.2
1972–6	0.9	0.1	0.6
1977–82	1.0	0.5	0.2
Mining			
1967–71	0.0	0.3	0.0
1972–6	0.3	0.1	0.0
1977–82	0.2	0.5	0.0
Manufacturing			
1967–71	82.5	44.6	77.7
1972–6	75.4	52.9	82.0
1977–82	66.3	48.9	72.0
Services			
1967–71	16.2	30.2	22.1
1972–6	23.5	28.1	17.5
1977–82	32.5	32.6	27.8

Sources: Korea and Taiwan: Hill and Johns (1985: Table 5). Singapore: Lim *et al.* (1988: Table 9.5).
Note: a   For Singapore 1970, 1976 and 1981.

schemes to attract foreign investment. DFI in Taiwan is subject to a number of conditions, namely local content requirement, export performance, etc. However, policies were also designed aimed at increasing foreign investment in export processing zones. More than 80 per cent of capital in export processing zones is of the DFI type, but it forms a minor portion of total DFI (Ranis and Schive, 1985: 94–5).

Table 7.2 shows the sectoral distribution of foreign investment in the three East Asian NIEs. Given the predominance of their manufacturing sector, it is hardly surprising that foreign investment is concentrated in manufacturing. Next to manufacturing, the services sector attracts foreign investment the most and its share in DFI is increasing. The comparable data on Hong Kong are not available. Given limited investment opportunities in agriculture and mining and the dominance of manufacturing and service sectors, one can expect to find a very similar pattern in Hong Kong.

A somewhat higher share of DFI in Singapore's services sector is consistent with its status as a major financial and trading centre. On the other hand, the lower share of DFI in the services sector in both Korea and Taiwan reflects the fact that DFI in this sector has been subject to government regulations. The only areas that were allowed in the past to have DFI in Korea are hotels, merchant banks, computer and data processing companies and special-purpose storage

Table 7.3 Distribution of DFI within manufacturing (%)

Industry	Hong Kong			Korea			Singapore			Taiwan		
	1967–71	1972–6	1977–82	1967–71	1972–6	1977–82	1967–71	1972–6	1977–82	1967–71	1972–6	1977–82
Food	0.7	5.9	5.5	1.8	0.4	7.8	4.0	3.5	3.9	0.1	1.7	3.9
Textiles, clothing and footwear	21.2	8.9	10.9	6.8	13.5	1.1	14.8	5.0	1.4	6.4	7.7	3.5
Chemical	1.5	20.5	4.1	19.4	34.3	31.4	7.9	4.4	6.5	14.0	16.8	20.6
Wood, paper and products	3.0	3.3	2.2	0.0	0.1	0.2	10.7	4.5	3.6	0.4	1.3	0.3
Metal products	5.0	5.5	3.5	15.0	7.0	4.7	5.0	18.3	12.9	30.2	22.7	9.9
Non-metallic minerals	0.0	0.0	0.0	26.9	9.4	8.9	36.9	38.3	41.4	2.6	11.1	22.8
Electrical, transport equipment and machinery	37.0	34.9	45.3	26.6	32.6	40.5	16.6	19.9	27.5	45.6	38.8	39.0
Others	31.6	21.0	28.5	3.6	1.9	0.0	4.3	6.1	2.7	0.0	0.0	0.0

Source: Hill and Johns (1985: Table 6).

Table 7.4 Number of foreign companies by type of ownership

Type	Hong Kong 1984	Singapore 1981	Korea 1981
Wholly-owned	232	2,967	122
Joint-venture	214	4,098	713
Total	446	7,065	835

Sources: Hong Kong: OECD (1988: 50). Singapore: Lim *et al.* (1988: Table 9.1). Korea: Koo (1985: Table).

companies (Koo, 1985: 183). In the case of Taiwan, services like construction and banking sector were virtually no-go areas for the overseas non-Chinese DFI (Ranis and Schive, op. cit.: 103–4). The rise in DFI in the services sector in the late 1970s reflects the easing of these restrictions that followed trade and financial liberalisations.

Given the dominance of DFI in manufacturing, it is worth looking at the distribution of DFI within this sector. A few interesting phenomena can be detected from Table 7.3. First, despite the dominance of the food industry in the early years of industrialisation, DFI in this industry was very insignificant. This was perhaps due to the fact that technology in this industry is relatively simple and hence foreign firms do not possess firm-specific advantage. Second, DFI was quite significant in the textile, clothing and footwear industry until the mid-1970s. This indicates the important role that DFI played in the early phase of export-oriented labour-intensive industrialisation. Third, DFI closely followed East Asian NIEs' shifting production structure. More advanced industries such as electrical, transport and machinery and chemical attracted more DFI as the importance of textiles, clothing and footware declined. In the case of Singapore, the non-metallic minerals sector dominates the picture, because of the importance of DFI in petroleum refining.

Table 7.4 presents the type of DFI in Hong Kong, Korea and Singapore. There is a roughly equal division between wholly-owned and joint-venture DFI in Hong Kong. In the case of Singapore, the share of joint-venture is slightly higher. Korea once again displays a more nationalistic attitude towards DFI, and wholly-owned foreign companies play a very minor part. Comparable data on Taiwan are not available, but given the policy regime, one could expect to find the Taiwanese case to lie between the two polar cases.

One can note a few other interesting features of DFI in the East Asian NIEs. First, USA and Japan comprise more than 50 per cent of DFI. Second, DFI from the USA is concentrated in the financial and banking sector as opposed to Japan's concentration in the manufacturing sector, but Japan's share in finance and banking is increasing. Third, even though initial Japanese investment was in more labour-intensive activities as opposed to the US investment, the Japanese investment is moving towards skill and technology intensive industries (James *et. al.*, op. cit.). The US firms in Singapore prefer wholly-owned subsidiaries in order to maintain control over proprietary technology, especially advanced technology (Lim and Pang, 1991: 57). The European and Japanese firms also display similar preference. This feature has major implications for the transfer of the state of the art technology, an issue which will be discussed in greater detail in a subsequent section.

BENEFITS AND COSTS OF FOREIGN INVESTMENT

There is a general consensus among the observers of the East Asian NIEs that foreign investment has, by and large, benefited these economies. Some representative remarks are:

> [o]verseas investment ... brought new industries and technology.... It contributed to broadening the industrial base of Hong Kong.... They helped promote Hong Kong's exports ... they contributed to higher productivity.... The overseas firms served as a catalyst to Hong Kong's further industrialization, and this was their greatest contribution
>
> (Lin and Mok, 1985: 246, 251–2).

> [In Korea,] ... the foreign investment seems to have made a positive contribution to employment creation and the balance of payments ... foreign investors appear to have provided their domestic partners with technologies and markets ...
>
> (Koo, op. cit.: 214)

> Direct foreign investment has contributed greatly to the growth and transformation of Singapore's manufacturing sector.... Foreign firms have ... contributed greatly to the technological upgrading of Singapore's manufacturing sector.... Foreign firms ... have accounted for 80 per cent to 90 per cent of direct exports ... the balance of payments impact of direct foreign investment in Singapore is overwhelmingly positive.
>
> (Lim and Pang, op. cit.: 91–2).

> Direct foreign investment has increased the quantity and improved the quality of Singapore's entrepreneurial, managerial, marketing, technological and manpower resources. It has contributed considerably to higher rate of economic growth, full employment, healthy balance of payments, successful export oriented industrialisation and broader and more sophisticated industrial structure.
>
> (Lim *et al.*, 1988: 271)

Foreign investment has been important to Taiwan's economic success by contributing to employment, technology transfer, skill training and exports.

(Lim and Pang, op. cit.: 94).

it [DFI] undoubtedly provided important assistance to the success story ... DFI ... helped Taiwan's entry into new, more sophisticated and capital-intensive product lines and markets ...

(Ranis and Schive, op. cit.: 132–33)

While the benefits of foreign investment have been overwhelming, it is worth noting some of the reservations or costs. In the literature on foreign investment in the East Asian NIEs, one can find discussions on possible costs of DFI pertaining to: (1) factor intensity, (2) 'crowding out', (3) labour aristocracy, (4) labour subjugation/subordination and (5) linkage effects and technology transfer. Hill (op. cit.) and Lim and Pang (op. cit.) provide comprehensive surveys of the issues.

Despite DFI's favourable employment effect, most studies have found that foreign firms in the East Asian NIEs tend to be more capital-intensive. On the basis of their analysis, Lin and Mok (op. cit.) conclude that foreign firms in Hong Kong are considerably more capital-intensive than domestic firms. Chia (1985a, b) reports the same findings in the case of Singapore. However, the evidence from Korea and Taiwan is mixed. Ranis and Schive's (op. cit.) study of Taiwan and that of Korea by W.Y. Lee (1985) find support for the hypothesis of higher capital intensity in the foreign firms. On the other hand, Riedel (1975) reports opposite results for Taiwan, and Chung and Lee (1980) find no discernible difference in factor intensities among local and foreign firms in Korea. Whatever may be the differences in factor intensity among foreign and local firms, Hill (op. cit.) notes that they are minimal, especially in comparison with Latin American or other developing countries.

The domination of DFI in certain sectors (e.g. Singapore's petrochemical and Taiwan's electronic industries) in the East Asian NIEs can be a cause of concern if they 'crowd out' domestic firms. 'However, these foreign-dominated sectors have not competed with local business ...' (Chan, 1990: 56). Nonetheless, there has been concern about another kind of crowding out. In the case of Singapore, for example, it has been argued that foreign firms crowd out local entrepreneurship by monopolising local entrepreneurial talents (Lim et al., op. cit.; Lim and Pang, op. cit.). Foreign firms in Singapore and Taiwan are also found to be uniformly larger than domestic firms in the same industry (Ranis and Schive, op. cit.; Chia, 1986) and therefore can have greater market power.

The crowding out of local entrepreneurs is offset to the extent the foreign firms act as 'breeding grounds' for local entrepreneurs (Lim and Pang, op. cit.). In the case of Singapore, this does not appear to be the case. Chng et al. (1986: 24) observe that the presence of foreign firms (MNCs) did not stimulate the growth of local entrepreneurship. The class of local professional managers that have emerged are largely functionaries of foreign enterprises and, according to Chng et

114

al., they do not constitute 'Schumpeterian entrepreneurs'. On the welfare implications of increased market power, Hill (op. cit.) notes that rising concentration *per se* is not necessarily a cause of concern if the benefits of new and more efficient technologies associated with foreign firms outweigh possible welfare costs of weaker competition.

The large literature on the comparison of earnings in local and foreign firms is virtually unanimous in the findings that foreign firms are likely to pay more than the local firms (Hill, ibid.). Hong Kong appears to be the only exception to this trend. Lin and Mok (op. cit.) conclude that the earning differences between the local and foreign firms in Hong Kong are not significant. While the earning differences certainly have implications for overall income distribution and crowding out of local entrepreneurship, they can be attributed to the differences in size, skill and capital intensity. However, Hill (ibid.: 41) notes that, except for Singapore, foreign firms are not major employers in aggregate and hence the normative implications of DFI and labour markets are limited.

Political subjugation of industrial workers in the East Asian NIEs has also been a matter of concern. This phenomenon is largely seen to be a deliberate policy measure to attract foreign investment. For example, according to Lim and Pang (op. cit.: 26), '[p]olitical and labour controls were instituted to ensure that multinationals could operate in a stable and hospitable host environment'. However, as it has been pointed out in Chapter 2, labour market subordination was not a deliberate policy action designed to attract foreign capital. 'The political weakness and docility of capitalist East Asia's industrial work force can, of course, be traced to the civil wars or foreign occupation .... The perceived threat from the political Left led to a crackdown on organized labour ...' (Chan, op. cit.: 53–4). Of course, the East Asian NIEs continued to have a regimented labour market even after they achieved political stability and a disciplined work force helped attract foreign investment. (See Chapter 9 for a more detailed discussion on earning differentials and the supposed DFI-repression link.)

How much of the aggregate benefits of DFI spread throughout the economy? This depends on 'linkage' effects of DFI or local sourcing by foreign firms. Studies of the foreign firms in Singapore find a very limited local sourcing (Chia, op. cit.; Chng *et al.*, op. cit.; Lim *et al.*, op. cit.). On the other hand, Ranis and Schive (op. cit.) find a strong linkage effect in Taiwan, noting that the proportion of intermediate goods procured domestically by foreign firms rose from 41 per cent in 1972 to 50 per cent in 1978. Koo (op. cit.) reports similar findings in Korea and notes that the proportion of raw materials purchased domestically by foreign manufacturing firms increased from 32 per cent in 1974 to 47 per cent in 1978.

The linkage or spread effect has implications for technology transfer. As Enos (1989: 50) notes, 'machines, materials, persons, forms of organization – are transferred in a set of linked transactions.' According to Lim *et al.* (op. cit.: 266), the lack of linkages in Singapore is primarily due to the type of foreign investment, especially the dominance of wholly-owned foreign firms. This implies that the efficacy of foreign investment as a vehicle for technology transfer depends very much on its type rather than its size. The subsequent sections, therefore, examine this hypothesis.

FOREIGN INVESTMENT AND TECHNOLOGY TRANSFER: SOME CONCEPTUAL ISSUES

Any meaningful discussion of the issue of technology transfer must begin with defining 'technology' and what is meant by 'transfer'. Enos (op. cit.) has considered various definitions of technology and uses a wider definition to include written materials (blueprints, textbooks, technical reports, etc.), machines and human capital. A very similar definition is used by Chng *et al.* (op. cit.: 15) in their study of technology transfer to Singapore. According to Chng *et al.*, technology 'would be embodied as hardware in machines, as well as software in people who operate, maintain, and adapt/develop these machines'. This working definition will be used for the purpose of present discussion.

Among the various dimensions of transfer the one which Enos (op. cit.) calls functional definition attracts most attention. It examines the transfer of technology at different stages. In their study of Korea, Enos and Park (1987) identify seven such stages: planning, negotiations between suppliers of the technology and recipients, plant and equipment design, procurement and construction, installation and start-up, production and innovation, and subsequent innovation. An equally appealing definition of transfer takes a more economically meaningful approach and Enos (op. cit.) calls it 'project' approach. It identifies such stages as production, investment and innovation or production, investment and linkages; alternatively it includes operation, duplication, adaptation and innovation.

It is interesting to note that both functional and project approaches list innovation as the last stage of technology transfer. Innovation involves the state of the art in product and process technology. Furthermore, one can relate the stages of technology transfer to the product life cycle hypothesis (Vernon, 1966) and Porter's (1990) schema of 'national competitive development'. For example, in the 'factor-driven' stage a nation derives its competitive advantage by engaging in the production of standardised products which 'require either little product or process technology or technology that is inexpensive and widely available' (Porter, op. cit.: 547). At this phase, the standardised technology is acquired through imitation or through foreign capital and can be regarded as the 'production stage' of technology transfer. Porter's 'investment-driven' phase can be identified with the intermediate phase in product life cycle. In this phase, firms still compete in relatively standardised but capital-intensive products. 'Product designs are at least one generation behind the world's most advanced ones. Process technologies are near the state of art but do not advance it' (Porter, ibid.: 549). At this stage, technology remains readily available and can be obtained and adapted from multiple sources; it does not require highly skilled human resources. The 'innovation-driven' stage is the most dynamic phase in Porter's four distinct stages of national competitive development. Therefore, whether the state-of-the-art technology is transferred to developing countries is a crucial question.

Many observers believe that there is a close association between the vehicle of transfer and types of technology. The UN Centre for Transnational Corporations (UNCTC, 1987) provides the most comprehensive list of vehicles which fits with the broader definition of technology. The list includes DFI (wholly or majority ownership), joint ventures, licensing, franchising, management contract, marketing and technical service contracts, turnkey contracts and multinational subcontracting. These vehicles of transfer can be ranked according to the degree of control by the originator. Since the originator wants to have maximum control over the innovation with a view to earning monopoly rent, it can be argued that wholly-owned subsidiaries of the innovating firms are the only permissible vehicle for the transfer of the state of the art technology.

Furthermore, the application of the theory of transaction cost minimisation to multinational corporations (MNCs) yields an optimistic view regarding the transfer of technology by MNCs (Islam, 1990; Teece, 1986). The starting point for this optimism is that the market for technology is characterised by high transaction costs. Such transactions costs arise from the confluence of 'bounded rationality' (the notion that individual economic agents have a limited capacity to comprehend and foresee all possible contingencies and hence incorporate them into contracts), 'opportunistic behaviour' (the notion that parties to a contract are prone to seeking ways of gaining at the expense of others) and 'asset specificity' (the notion that long-term bilateral contracts entail transaction-specific investments, thereby raising the opportunity of switching to short-term, multilateral contracts). The implication is that there is unlikely to be unimpeded arm's length transactions in technology. Since MNCs are transaction cost minimisers, it is predicted that they will internalise the adoption and adaptation of technology and thus facilitate its transfer to the host country.

On the other hand, critics argue that multinational firms are motivated by their corporate goals rather than the interest of the host country and hence the technologies employed in the subsidiaries in developing countries could be either more modern or obsolete. Moreover, the product life cycle theory implies that multinational companies seek for overseas production platforms for the production of standardised products and hence they are unlikely to transfer the state-of-the-art technology. The critics also note that the transfer of technology need not be attached to ownership. They argue that, in principle, technology can be purchased and the technical knowledge can be 'unbundled' enabling the receiving country to acquire the desired technology. This view, thus, suggests regulations against DFI involving whole or majority ownership.

Which is a better vehicle for the transfer of the state of the art technology? The predominance of DFI characterised by wholly-owned foreign firms and Singapore's liberal attitudes to DFI imply that policy makers in Singapore believe that multinational corporations are better vehicles for acquiring 'high-tech' or 'core' technology. On the other hand, Korean policy makers appear to hold a different view. The relative merits of wholly owned DFI and 'purchase and unbundling', i.e. the relative efficacy of the 'Singapore' model vis-à-vis the 'Korean' model of transfer of the state-of-the-art technology, can only be settled by examining the evidence.

MNCs AND TRANSFER OF TECHNOLOGY: THE EVIDENCE

A comprehensive survey of the extent of technology transfer to Singapore by MNCs is provided by Chng et al. (op. cit.). They examine three popular channels of technology transfer: namely, training of local personnel, the use of local subcontractors and the undertaking of R&D activities in the host country and the types of technology being transferred. Their relevant survey results are summarised in Tables 7.5–7.8. The following features emerge from these tables:

1   The most important mechanism of transferring technology is foreign training of local employees.
2   There is a general reluctance to use local subcontractors.
3   R&D activities are usually located in headquarters and there is limited use of local research centres.
4   There is a reluctance to transfer the state-of-the-art 'brand new' technology.

On the training of manpower, Chng et al. (op. cit.: 70, 73) note that usually technician and supervisory personnel are sent for training in the parent companies. The in-firm training schemes for the indigenous personnel are mostly

Table 7.5   Methods of technology transfer in surveyed firms (Singapore)

Method of transfer	Wholly-local	Wholly-foreign	Joint-venture
Turnkey	0	5	1
Purchase know-how	1	3	2
Licence	1	0	2
Licence and teaching	2	8	4
Technical arrangements	0	21	4
Joint venture	2	6	7
Foreign training	2	36	9
Foreign expatriate visiting	0	26	7
Local engineers	3	17	6
Aid from suppliers	4	8	3
Customer specifications	2	7	2
Public literature	2	12	5
Management contracts	0	2	2

Source: Chng et al. (1986: Table 7.5).

Table 7.6   Local subcontracting and use of local research centres by surveyed firms
(Singapore)

Type of firm	Proportion of inputs bought locally				Use of local facilities	
	> 25%	25–49%	50–74%	+75%	Did use	Didn't use
Wholly-foreign	21	6	1	2	4	35
Joint-venture	7	1	0	1	5	7

Source: Chng *et al.* (1986: Tables 27.1, 28.1).

aimed at low level operating and problem-solving skills. The main reason for limiting training at low level manpower is the fear of disclosure of closely guarded information on product development and production techniques.

The low technological capabilities of local suppliers are cited as the major reason for low level of local subcontracting. In addition, there are reasons like high cost of monitoring and negotiating which hinder local sourcing.

A study by the Singapore Science Council (1984/85) also shows that the amount of R&D conducted in Singapore by MNCs remains small. One can

Table 7.7   Type of R&D undertaken by surveyed foreign firms (Singapore)

R&D type	Location	Wholly-foreign	Joint-venture
Basic research	Home	34	7
	Local	3	2
Product design	Home	37	7
	Local	7	4
Product development	Home	37	6
	Local	8	5
Process development	Home	31	6
	Local	13	5
Innovation technology	Home	36	7
	Local	6	2
Application technology	Home	30	5
	Local	11	6
Process adaptation	Home	22	5
	Local	7	3

Source: Chng *et al.* (1986: Table 31.1).

119

Table 7.8 Types of technology transferred by surveyed foreign firms (Singapore)

Industry/type of firm		Existing technology	Brand new
Machinery	WF	1	0
	JV	0	0
Precision equipment	WF	2	0
	JV	0	0
Electrical	WF	1	0
	JV	0	0
Electronics	WF	6	3
	JV	1	1
Total	WF	10	3
	JV	1	1

Source: Chng *et al.* (1986: Table 26.1).
Notes: WF Wholly-foreign.
 JV Joint-venture.

proffer various reasons for the absence of substantive R&D activities by foreign subsidiaries. The first is the absence of economies of scale. R&D is an indivisible, lumpy input. It may be much more economical to utilise this input jointly across a number of operating centres compared with running separate R&D centres in different locations (Chng *et al.*, ibid.: 28). Second, the receiving country may not have sufficient absorptive capacity in terms of the supply of R&D personnel and facilities (Lim *et al.*, op. cit.: 265). Third, even if the host country has absorptive capacity, the fear of intellectual theft and piracy in the absence of well-specified property rights could deter the location of MNCs R&D facilities. This may explain why only a few MNCs utilise the local R&D facilities or impart training to high level manpower. Finally, the low R&D activities can be attributed to the lack of autonomous standing of the MNC subsidiaries in Singapore (Chng *et al.*, ibid: 82). They operate as production outposts with key decisions on marketing, R&D and so forth being undertaken by the head office.

Most of the surveyed firms used the turnkey method of starting up their factories. The technology used in the turnkey projects was either obsolete or refurbished (Chng *et al.*, ibid: 69). This is consistent with the finding that MNCs mostly transferred existing technologies.

The findings of the two comprehensive surveys on the transfer of technology to Korea are summarised in Enos (op. cit.). Enos cites findings which roughly corroborate less than optimistic performance of MNCs as noticed in Singapore.

DFI transfers production capability (capability to operate and maintain a production system) but hardly investment capability (capability to set up or expand new production systems) or innovation capability (capability to innovate new products and processes).

(Kim, 1988; quoted in Enos op. cit.: 18)

Hong highlights the problem associated with the transfer of 'core' technology in the following words:

The continuous increase in exports of Korean electronic products [attracted] ... the attention and reservations of overseas manufacturers. Those who used to be cooperative for TCs [technical collaborations] became reluctant to disclose technologies for custom-designed key components .... On the other hand, as the life cycle of most ... electronic products became shorter and new functions kept being added to new models, the needs for technological improvements radically increased .... Under these circumstances, the Korean electronics industry came to recognize the crucial importance of self-reliance in developing its own technologies.

(Hong, 1991: 250)

Similar incidences involving MNCs and the transfer of advanced technology to developing countries are reported in Enos (op. cit.: 24). It seems, therefore, that there is a discrepancy between the available evidence and the optimistic predictions about MNCs' transfer of technology. This in effect casts doubts on the efficacy of the 'Singapore model' for the transfer of the state-of-the-art technology which is essential for launching 'innovation-driven' development.

INDIGENOUS TECHNOLOGICAL CAPABILITIES AND PUBLIC POLICY

If MNCs cannot be relied upon for the transfer of technology at the 'innovation stage', then, as the above quote from Hong indicates, the only option left is the development of indigenous technological competence. The Korean experience also shows that local effort has been the most significant factor in the successful acquisition of technology. The importance of indigenous technical competence is summarised by Enos as follows:

[T]he Koreans' technical sophistication and commitment to industrial development allowed them to extract other conditions, ensuring a swifter and more effective transfer of technology .... Better conditions related chiefly to large-scale training programs, ... in Korea ... and to the systematic replacement of all expatriates, both technical and managerial, by adequately prepared Korean citizens.

(Enos, op. cit.: 19)

The above observation clearly indicates the need for public policy to enhance domestic technological capabilities. Enos (op. cit.: 5) identifies Korea as 'the first developing country to systematically address the matter and to formulate and enforce public policy' starting in 1966. With a view to strengthening the supply of technological capability, the Korean government established the Korea Institute of Science and Technology in 1966 as an integrated technical training centre to meet industry's technical needs. It is a multidisciplinary research institute and covered a broad spectrum of activities in applied research, such as project feasibility studies, technical services for small and medium industries and engineering studies on a pilot plant scale. With the subsequent advancement and sophistication of the Korean economy, a number of specialised research institutes, e.g. shipbuilding, marine resources, electronics, telecommunications, energy, machinery and chemicals were set up to develop in-depth capabilities.

In order to streamline the administrative apparatus, the Korean government established the Ministry of Science and Technology in 1967 at the cabinet level to formulate basic science and technology (S&T) policies. It is responsible for basic policies of R&D, human resource development (HRD), international technical collaborations, the development of research institutions and creation of a favourable social climate for the promotion of S&T. Following the establishment of the Ministry of Science and Technology, several laws were enacted to provide incentives to local firms for promoting development and upgrading of technology.

The R&D expenditure has grown faster than GNP in Korea, and in 1989 it stood at 2.12 per cent of GNP, which is the highest R&D/GNP ratio among the East Asian NIEs. The private sector responded to government initiatives positively. The share of private sector in total R&D expenditure increased from about 10 per cent in 1966 to 80 per cent in 1986 (Hong, op. cit.: 252). Consequently, the ratio between private and government R&D expenditure rose from 0.47 in 1971 to 4.00 in 1986 (Table 7.9). The number of private R&D

Table 7.9   R&D indicators of Korea, Taiwan and Singapore

Indicator	Korea		Taiwan		Singapore	
	1983	1989	1983	1989	1978	1984
R&D/GDP (%)	1.8	2.12	0.91	1.38	0.2	0.6
Private/government expenditure (ratio)	0.47[a]	4.00[b]	0.65[c]	1.09	–	–
Private R&D institutes (No.)	1[a]	290[b]	–	–	–	–

Sources: Hong (1991: Table 2); Taiwan Statistical Data Book, 1991 (Tables 6.1, 6.8); Ministry of Trade and Industry (1986: Chart 16-1).
Notes: a   1971.
      b   1986.
      c   1980.

Table 7.10 Foreign technology transferred through technical collaboration in Korea
(No.)

Industry	Up to 1966	1967–76	1977–86	Total
Chemical	7	169	597	773
Metal	1	73	217	291
Electronic	8	172	727	907
Machinery	6	185	1,088	1,279
Others	11	120	674	805
Total	33	719	3,303	4,055

Source: Hong (1991: Table 1).

institutes also rose from 1 to 290 during the same period.

The Korean government's policies to enhance technological capabilities seem to have yielded dividends. As Table 7.10 shows there has been a clear jump in the number of foreign technologies being transferred to Korea since 1966 through technical collaborations. This is a clear indication that technical competence of local firms has been the most important factor in acquiring technology. This also explains, to some extent, the variation in the vehicles for technology transfer in the case of Singapore and Korea and lends support to the hypothesis that the proportion of vehicles which are subsidiaries of MNCs falls with the increase in the degree of technical competence of the host country.

Korea's enhanced technological capabilities is also reflected in a recent survey of 1,110 professors, researchers and business experts by the Korea Advanced Institute of Science and Technology. The questionnaire survey on the perception of the community regarding Korean technological capabilities reveals that the average time lag in the development of technologies between Korea and Japan is 4 years. It also shows that Korea is 5 years behind the world leaders in futuristic technology (Table 7.11). This is quite a quantum jump if compared with average time lag of 10–15 years fifteen years ago.

The contrasting position of the Singapore government on technological development can be gleaned from the following statement of the Senior Minister of State for National Development:

[p]ure or basic research to enlarge the frontiers of knowledge ... has led to very practical applications affecting our daily life, but ... Singapore has neither the financial resources nor human resources to indulge in it. Our efforts have to be primarily in that area of research more properly termed development, which works on bringing out new or modified products and processes based on established findings, and technology.

(Quoted in Chng *et al.*, op. cit.: 26)

Table 7.11 Time of development of future technology

Field	Average year of development		
	Korea	Japan	World
Electronics	1998.3	1993.6	1992.9
Materials	1999.9	1993.5	1994.4
Energy	2001.3	1998.1	1995.0
Resource	2002.6	1997.6	1996.1
Production	1999.9	1994.4	1993.7
Transport	2001.8	2002.4	1995.2
Bio-Tech	2003.0	1998.3	1998.4
Medical	2002.0	2001.1	1998.2
Environment	1999.7	1996.6	1994.2
Total	2001.0	1997.1	1995.7

Source: Hong (1991: Table 9).
Notes: Obtained by surveying the perception of 1,110 professors, researchers and business experts
as to the timing of the emergence of specific future technologies in Korea, Japan and the
world's first.

The above quote epitomises the Singapore government's stand on S&T policy until, at least, the late 1970s. The Economic Committee, set up in 1986 to identify Singapore's problems and to chart new directions, does not propose a radically different approach (Ministry of Trade and Industry, 1986). While it recognises the need for upgrading technological capabilities, it regards basic research as unfeasible and recommends increased efforts to improve product design and development capability in industries already established.

Chng *et al.* (op. cit.: 23) note that as a consequence of such a policy stance, tertiary institutions in Singapore have traditionally been teaching- rather than research-oriented. Thus it is no wonder that Singapore is still behind Korea and Taiwan in terms of the ratio of R&D expenditure to GNP (Table 7.9). Singapore also has fewer research scientists and engineers as a proportion of the labour force (OECD, 1988: 46).

Chng *et al.* (op. cit.: 23) further observe that this is perhaps consistent with the dominant nature of production in Singapore which remains dependent on cheap labour and locational advantages rather than skills or brain-power. However, they ask, 'how does such a strategy stand today?'

CONCLUDING REMARKS

Foreign resource flows have played an important role in the development of East Asian NIEs. However, there are some significant variations in their forms and sources. Over the years, the external resources from official sources have declined and the importance of private sources has increased. With respect to forms, wholly-owned DFI is the most dominant form in Singapore, but it is a very small proportion in Korea. Although respective country policies towards DFI may have influenced the form, in Hong Kong, which follows roughly similar policies to Singapore's, there is almost equal division between wholly-owned and joint venture DFI.

There is a broad consensus among the observers of East Asian NIEs that benefits of foreign investment have outweighed the costs. DFI in the form of wholly-owned MNCs have been particularly useful at the early stage of industrialisation ('factor-' and 'investment-driven' phases) in transferring technology. However, MNCs are found to be reluctant to transfer the state-of-the-art technology needed for 'innovation-driven' and self-reinforcing development. This indicates the need for public policy to enhance indigenous technological capabilities, including R&D and human resource development.

8

FINANCIAL DEVELOPMENT AND ECONOMIC PERFORMANCE

The early development economists, e.g. Lange, Lewis and Nurkse, regarded the lack of capital as the fundamental problem of development. Thus, accumulation of capital occupies a central position in the process of economic growth. The process of capital accumulation entails three steps. First, the volume of real savings must increase. According to Arthur Lewis, the crux of the development problem was to raise the proportion of national income saved from 4–5 per cent to 12–15 per cent, so that additional resources became available for investment. Therefore, the second step was to channel savings to investors and the final stage in the process of capital accumulation was the act of productive investment.

The most common factors that are cited as reasons for the failure to raise the saving rate, channel investable funds properly and invest them efficiently are financial repression and the absence of a developed financial sector. Financial repression means that the financial sector is not allowed to function according to the interplay of market forces. In the past, it was commonly believed that high real interest rates (due to scarcity of capital) would discourage investment and hence hamper growth. Therefore, most developing countries followed a policy of interest rates ceiling which was much below the market equilibrium. The low nominal interest rates together with high inflation produces very low (often negative) real interest rates, which are believed to generate the several adverse effects.

First, it encourages people to hold their savings in real assets such as land, gold, real estates, etc., whose prices normally rise at a faster rate than general price level and hence offer a better hedge against inflation. Savings is an act of deferred consumption. By not consuming now, people save resources to be used for investment which raises future consumption. But savers (households) are not the same people as investors (producers). Furthermore, commodities not being consumed may not be directly suitable for investment. This is a problem of the lack of double coincidences. Therefore, in a monetary economy financial institutions (banks and securities market) perform the job of (1) intermediating between savers and investors and (2) converting real savings into financial savings. Savings in real assets thus reduce the amount of financial savings available for transferring to investors and impede the development of the financial sector. The absence of a developed financial sector itself has adverse affects. A

126

'shallow' financial sector means that there is a lack of alternative financial assets in which people can save and this in turn can adversely affect the saving rate.

Second, a below-equilibrium interest rate ceiling implies an excess demand for investible funds. As a result, funds must be allocated by credit rationing. This raises the question of what criteria to use in allocating investible funds. Normally, the funds are allocated to the 'priority' industries. It has been argued earlier that the government may not always be able to pick 'winners' and hence the allocation of funds may be inefficient. Furthermore, regulations governing credit rationing may induce rent-seeking activities resulting in economic waste.

Third, the negative real interest rate encourages the potential investors to be indulgent. The result is not only an inefficient investment profile but also a capital-intensive industrial structure which is out of line with the country's factor endowments.

Therefore, a developed and efficient financial sector should play an important role in economic growth. The *World Development Report, 1989* highlights the importance of financial systems in economic development. It summarises the importance of the financial sector in the following words:

> A financial system provides services that are essential in a modern economy. The use of a stable, widely accepted medium of exchange reduces the costs of transactions. It facilitates trade and, therefore, specialization in production. Financial assets with attractive yield, liquidity, and risk characteristics encourages saving in financial form. By evaluating alternative investments and monitoring the activities of borrowers, financial intermediaries increase the efficiency of resource use. Access to a variety of financial instruments enables economic agents to pool, price and exchange risk. Trade, the efficient use of resources, saving, and risk taking are the cornerstones of a growing economy.
>
> (World Bank, 1989: 1)

Thus, financial development and liberalisation are seen to be crucial elements in promoting economic growth. A developed financial sector performs two growth-promoting functions: (1) it facilitates trade and specialisation, (2) it facilitates capital accumulation.

The spectacular financial development and growth performance of the East Asian NIEs are regarded as vindicating this hypothesis. This chapter examines the second aspect of the role of financial systems, i.e. the link between the financial sector and capital accumulation in light of the experience of East Asian NIEs. In particular, the chapter will analyse the evidence on the impact of financial development on the three aspects of capital accumulation; i.e.:

1   the relationship between real deposit interest rate and saving rate (or the volume effect of real deposit interest rate);
2   the relationship between real deposit interest rate and financial savings (or the composition/efficiency effect of real deposit interest rate);

3 the relationship between positive real interest rate and efficiency of investment.

Finally, the chapter will reflect on the issues surrounding the 'new' view of the role of finance in economic development.

DETERMINANTS OF DOMESTIC SAVINGS: THE ROLE OF FINANCIAL REFORMS

The East Asian NIEs have performed spectacularly in mobilising domestic savings, especially since 1970 (Table 8.1). The saving rates of Hong Kong and Taiwan exceeded 20 per cent of GDP in the mid-1960s, a remarkable achievement, given the fact that Hong Kong, Korea and Singapore had the lowest saving rates in Asia in 1960. In Korea and Singapore, the saving rate rose nearly eight-fold in only 5 years (1960–5), while it was nearly five-fold for Hong Kong.

What are the factors that contributed to this phenomenal success? During the 1960s, Korea and Taiwan carried out reforms which created a more liberalised financial market and allowed deposit interest rates to be market determined. As a result, real deposit interest rates became positive since the mid-1960s. Since the rise in saving rates followed financial reforms, it is quite common to attribute the phenomenon to positive and higher real deposit interest rates and the rapid development of the financial sector, usually referred to as financial deepening.

As mentioned earlier, most savings in developing countries find their way to investment in land, real estates, or precious metals. There are a number of reasons for such a behaviour. First, there are not many alternative financial assets available to the people. Even the access to financial institutions, e.g. banks, is limited. More importantly, when the deposit interest rate cannot respond to

Table 8.1   Gross domestic savings in selected Asian countries (% GDP)

Economy	Saving rate					Real deposit rate*
	1960	1965	1970	1971–80	1981–90	1961–81
Hong Kong	6	29	25	27.5	30.5	1.8
Korea	1	8	15	22.3	31.8	1.0
Singapore	−3	10	21	30.0	42.3	2.8
Taiwan	13	22	26	32.2	32.9	4.1
Burma	11	13	9	12.3	12.4	1.0
India	14	16	18	20.5	20.3	−1.1
Indonesia	8	8	11	22.6	31.8	−35.4
Malaysia	27	24	22	30.4	33.2	3.0
Thailand	14	19	22	21.5	24.5	2.6

Sources: Asian Development Bank (various issues); *James et al. (1989: Table 3.3).

market condition due to a government controlled 'ceiling', the real deposit interest rate becomes negative in an environment of high inflation. On the other hand, such real assets as land and jewellery offer an excellent hedge against inflation. They not only protect the real value of savings, but also offer the possibility of capital gains as in most cases their prices rise at a faster rate than the rate of inflation. Therefore, financial reforms that produce positive returns on deposits and increase the accessibility to financial institutions and availability of financial assets are likely to promote savings. Financial institutions can attract savings by offering assets that are safe, convenient and generate attractive returns.

However, the evidence on the supposed link between financial developments and the savings performance is not overwhelming. For example, as can be seen from Table 8.1, there are other countries, e.g. Indonesia and India, with similar saving rates as those of the East Asian NIEs, but with apparently more repressed financial sectors; this is especially true of Indonesia. At the same time, Singapore did not abolish controls over interest rates until 1975, yet its saving rate rose from −3 to 21 per cent of GDP in 10 years (1960–70). Despite consistently negative real deposit rates throughout the 1970s in Hong Kong and since 1973 in Korea (see Table 8.3), both have performed impressively in raising their saving rates.

Even the World Bank which advocates financial liberalisation recognises the uncertainty in the relationship between real deposit rates and savings. According to the World Bank (op. cit.: 27), '[w]hether financial variables affect the saving rate is still an open question. ... Empirical estimates range from a large positive effect to no effect at all'. Another leading advocate of financial liberalisation, Fry (1984), has examined the determinants of national savings in fourteen Asian countries which include the four NIEs. Among other variables, he used two financial variables – the real return on financial assets and the rural population per branch of depository institutions (banks) – as proxies for financial liberalisation/repression and financial deepening, respectively. Although the increased rural bank branches (a proxy for financial deepening) were found to be responsible for raising the national saving rates over the period 1961–81 by 1.7 percentage points in Taiwan and by 4.1 percentage points in Korea, the magnitude of real deposit interest rate effect was not found to be sufficiently large to be of substantial policy significance (Fry, ibid.: 86). In a different study, Fry (1985: 293) notes, 'the real deposit rate coefficient is not significantly different from zero in the saving rate functions for the gang of four by itself'. Individual country studies also fail to provide conclusive results. Wong's (1986: 66) econometric study of Singapore data (1960–83) reveals that interest rate has the expected positive coefficient, but is statistically insignificant.

Giovannini (1985) claims that the apparent high interest elasticity of savings found in the East Asian NIEs is due to outliers in the Korean data for periods immediately following the 1965 financial reforms. When the Korean 1967 and 1968 data are omitted from the pooled time series (1962–79 for Korea, 1964–79 for Singapore and 1962–79 for Taiwan) and cross-section regression, the coefficient of real interest rate becomes negative and insignificant. By analysing the flow-of-funds data, Giovannini (ibid.) finds that the increase in private savings after the increase in interest rate was only temporary and concludes that the largest proportion of the increase in aggregate savings can be accounted for by the improvement in government budget.

The ambiguity in the relationship between real interest rate and savings can be analysed by decomposing the interest rate effect into income and substitution effects. While an increase in real interest rate encourages savings through the substitution effect (i.e. savers substitute present consumption with future consumption), it discourages savings through the income effect (i.e. as savers become better off with the rise in their interest income, they tend to spend more). Thus, substitution and income effects work in opposite directions and savings rate responds positively to a rise in real interest rates, only if the former outweighs the latter.

Given the uncertainty in the relationship between financial development (in particular, interest rate reforms) and savings, one has to turn to other determinants of domestic, especially household, savings. In the literature, a large number of factors are identified as possible determinants of household savings. In short, they are factors that influence the sources of uncertainty facing decision makers and their opportunities for responding to such uncertainty. In developing countries, various socioeconomic factors such as economic growth, general macroeconomic environment, family structure, social security system, retirement practices, self-financing nature of investment and borrowing constraints, population growth and dependency ratio, attitude towards education, income distribution, etc., can be identified as having an influence on household savings behaviour. For example, Scitovsky (1985) cites the low population growth rate, the inadequacy of social security benefits, the limited availability of consumer credit and mortgage loans, the high proportion of individual proprietorship, the existence of a bonus component in the wages system, public expenditure on education as among some of the possible reasons for high household savings rates in the East Asian NIEs. In particular, the differences in these factors may have contributed to the variations in savings rates in Korea and Taiwan.

Fry's (1984) work on fourteen Asian countries shows that a 1 percentage point increase in the growth rate increases the savings rate by, on average, just over 1 percentage point. However, the rate-of-growth effect on national savings is found to be affected by population dependency ratio. He notes, 'on average, a reduction in the population growth rate by 1 percentage point and its concomitant reduction in the dependency ratio ... raises the national saving rate directly in the sample countries by 7 to 9.5 percentage points' (Fry, ibid.: 85). The East Asian NIEs not only experienced rapid economic growth since the mid-1960s, their rates of population growth and dependency ratios too fell significantly. The annual average population growth dropped from roughly 2.5 per cent in the 1960s to less than 2 per cent in the 1970s and it now stands in the neighbourhood of 1 per cent. The dependency ratio fell with the decline in population growth from roughly 50 per cent in the 1960s to about 40 per cent in the 1970s. Therefore, in terms of Fry's empirical estimates, these factors may have contributed significantly to the rise in the East Asian NIEs' national saving rates since the mid-1960s.

Ever since the East Asian NIEs switched to export-oriented industrialisation, they have experienced improvements in their terms of trade except during the two oil price shocks. Empirical analyses show that improved terms of trade exert a positive influence on national savings. Fry (ibid.) notes that a 10 per cent improvement in the terms of trade raises the saving rate by 0.3 of 1 percentage point.

In addition to the terms of trade effect, export-oriented industrialisation augments the saving rate by raising the rate of economic growth. Studies have found that the growth of export income has been an important factor in the rapid rise in national savings in the East Asian NIEs, particularly in Korea and Taiwan (Lin, 1973; Yusuf and Peters, 1984; Mikesell and Zinser, 1973). Among the possible reasons for favourable growth effects of exports are higher propensity to save and invest out of export income and the rise in total factor productivity due to scale economies and improved efficiency. Furthermore, higher rates of export growth means less foreign exchange constraints on investment. Esfahani's (1991: 113) work on semi-industrial countries shows that 'the major contribution of exports to GDP growth rate is to relieve the import shortage'. As the foreign exchange constraint becomes less binding, the demand for investible funds increases which, in turn, encourages savings and can be regarded as a demand-leading phenomenon.

Foreign aid and/or foreign capital inflow should have the same effect as exports on domestic savings. It, too, relaxes the foreign exchange constraint and hence can promote growth and domestic savings. As is well known, the East Asian NIEs, especially Korea and Taiwan, received massive amounts of US aid in the 1950s and early 1960s. Between 1953 and 1962, aid financed about 70 per cent of total imports and 85 per cent of current account deficit in Korea (Haggard and Cheng, 1987b; Jacoby, 1966). In the case of Taiwan, aid financed up to 40 per cent of imports of goods and services in the early 1950s (Scott, 1979). Hong Kong and Singapore received massive amounts of foreign capital. In 1983, foreign direct investment constituted about 93 per cent of gross external liabilities of Singapore (OECD, 1988). The large inflow of foreign capital/aid is believed to have contributed significantly to NIEs economic growth and in the case of Taiwan to price stability, thus creating a favourable environment for savings (Chen, 1979).

Macroeconomic policies also have played an important role in raising domestic savings in the East Asian NIEs. For example, the government current budget has mostly been in surplus since the 1970s and this contributed directly to domestic savings. An estimate shows that 64 per cent of gross national savings in Singapore came from the surpluses of the statutory boards and the government budget surplus (Lim et al., 1988: 217).

More importantly, government's fiscal position affects domestic savings via its impact on inflation and hence on private savings. Fry (1991) has found a clear negative relationship between the size of deficits and inflation. This is consistent with Harberger's (1981) finding that government deficits are typically the underlying cause of acute and chronic inflation in developing countries. A rise in fiscal deficit may induce the private sector to anticipate a higher inflation rate and/or an increased level of current account deficit in the future. The private sector may then adjust its savings behaviour as if it faced the problems of rising inflation and growing external debt. This leads to capital flights and the build up of stocks of goods, precious metals and assets denominated in foreign currency (Corden, 1987; Fry, op. cit.).

The ability of the governments of East Asian NIEs to pursue prudent fiscal–monetary–wages and exchange rate policies provided a stable macroeconomic environment with low inflation rates. A few episodes of higher inflation due largely to external shocks were not allowed to persist for long. With the exception of Korea, the inflation rate in the East Asian NIEs remained fairly low after 1960. Korea's higher inflation rate, though much lower than in Latin America, might explain its relatively poor savings performance.

Finally, one should note the importance of compulsory savings in the case of Singapore. In 1955, the government of Singapore established the Central Provident Fund in order to provide social security benefits for employees upon retirement. The scheme is fully funded by compulsory contributions from both employees and employers. In 1984, the combined rate of contribution peaked at 50 per cent and 30 per cent of gross national savings came from the Central Provident Fund. In the same year, public sector savings contributed 64 per cent to gross national savings. Therefore, only 6 per cent of gross national savings in 1984 came from voluntary private savings (Lim *et al.*, op. cit.: 217). The case of Singapore is a classic example of interactions between private and public sector savings and also between compulsory and voluntary savings.

FINANCIAL DEEPENING AND THE ROLE OF REAL INTEREST RATES

Financial deepening involves the monetisation of an economy, and the rise of financial institutions. With financial deepening savings are increasingly held in financial assets rather than in non-financial assets. This is likely to improve the efficiency of intermediation between savers and investors.

The extent of financial deepening in an economy can be judged by tracing the evolution over time of such key financial variables as currency, M_1 or M_2 ratios to GDP, the best measure being the ratio between total financial assets to total real assets. In the absence of comparable data on total financial and real assets, most researchers rely on the M_2 to GDP or GNP ratio. Table 8.2 presents the M_2/GDP ratios for selected Asian countries since 1960.

As can be seen from the table, the M_2/GDP ratio in the East Asian NIEs grew

Table 8.2 Financial deepening: M_2/GDP (%)

Economy	1961–70	1971–80	1981–90
Hong Kong	89.3[a]	85.7	155.0
Korea	19.0	33.7	36.8
Singapore	59.8[b]	61.7	78.8
Taiwan	34.1	58.1	110.2
India	24.0	31.2	44.7
Indonesia	7.5[c]	16.1	24.3
Malaysia	29.4	44.2	88.2
Thailand	26.0	35.8	57.6

Source: Asian Development Bank (various issues).
Notes: a 1965–70.
  b 1963–70.
  c 1966–70.

quite rapidly. Korea is conspicuous in having a 'shallow' financial system relative to the other NIEs, a finding that is consistent with other studies such as that of Kohsaka (1987). Hong Kong has the 'deepest' financial system, a point emphasised by Arndt (1983) in his study of financial deepening in Asia during 1955–80. Nonetheless, as Cole (1988: 28) points out, one should interpret Hong Kong's figure with caution. While the ratio of more than 100 shows Hong Kong's importance as an offshore financial centre, the exceptionally high M_2/GDP ratio may well be due to the fact that Hong Kong does not make any distinction between local residents' and non-residents' bank deposits. On the other hand, Singapore does not include offshore deposits in M_2 and hence its lower ratio should not be interpreted as an indication of a less 'deep' financial system. The M_2/GDP ratio in Taiwan has exceeded 100 since 1985. Emery (1987, as cited in Cole, op. cit.: 36) suggests that the rapid growth of M_2 reflects some loss of monetary control due to the build-up of foreign exchange reserves.

A high M_2/GDP ratio and its rapid growth indicate that a large amount of loanable funds flows through the organised financial sector in Hong Kong, Singapore and Taiwan. On the other hand, slower financial deepening in Korea implies that the growth of financial assets lagged behind the growth of non-financial assets. As a result, savings are held either in non-financial or in informal (curb/black) markets rather than in financial assets and there has been less reliance on financial institutions for intermediations between savers and investors. For example, after the government decree in 1972 requiring all informal loans to enterprises to be registered, it was found that informal-sector lending amounted to one-half of commercial bank lending (Cole and Patrick, 1986: 59). As fewer real loanable funds were directed through the organised financial sector, Korea had to make up for the shortage of domestic loanable funds by borrowing heavily abroad (McKinnon, 1984: 5).

There can be no doubt about the spectacular financial deepening in the East

Table 8.3 Real deposit interest rates, 1966–83

	Hong Kong	Korea	Singapore	Taiwan
1966	5.4	6.4	3.5	7.4
1967	2.9	7.0	4.1	5.4
1968	2.1	8.5	4.9	3.1
1969	2.2	8.5	3.9	3.5
1970	−2.4	6.3	4.0	6.3
1971	−3.9	5.9	2.3	6.0
1972	−2.9	0.2	0.3	2.9
1973	−4.3	−1.9	−3.8	−5.0
1974	−3.2	−2.5	−5.2	−14.5
1975	0.3	−4.0	0.1	9.3
1976	−0.6	−4.1	3.8	5.8
1977	−1.3	−3.6	4.4	3.5
1978	−0.5	−3.7	4.2	4.5
1979	−1.2	−0.8	4.1	−0.3
1980	−2.0	2.1	4.0	−3.1
1981	2.8	−0.4	5.3	1.4
1982	3.5	−5.4	6.7	6.9
1983	1.8	−5.3	2.3	5.6

Source: Fry (1985: Table 11.2).
Notes: Deposit interest rate: simple nominal rate of interest on 12-month deposits.
Real rate: nominal rate minus expected inflation.
Expected inflation: estimated as a polynomial distributed lag of current and past changes in the rate of inflation.

Asian NIEs, especially in Hong Kong, Singapore and Taiwan. This section will examine the possible causes of financial deepening in East Asian NIEs. As mentioned earlier, the East Asian NIEs, especially Taiwan and Korea, undertook financial reforms in the 1960s and adopted a policy of maintaining positive real deposit rates. This was done by raising the nominal deposit interest rate and controlling inflation, particularly in Taiwan. As mentioned earlier, it is argued that when the nominal interest rate is below the inflation rate, the resulting negative real interest rate restricts the demand for financial assets, since savers are encouraged to invest in real rather than in financial assets. With the fall in financial savings, the supply of loanable funds declines and the financial sector becomes shallow. Therefore, policies that produce positive real interest rates are believed to accelerate financial development.

However, as can be seen from Table 8.3, the relationship between real deposit interest rates and growth in financial assets is not unambiguous and casts doubt on the possibility of a positive relationship between real deposit interest rates and financial deepening. For example, Hong Kong's M_2/GDP ratio during the 1970s was much higher than that of Singapore, despite the fact that Singapore had positive real deposit interest rates throughout the sample period (except in 1973 and 1974), as opposed to Hong Kong's persistently negative real deposit interest rates. While to some extent this anomaly may be due to their differences in the treatment of non-resident deposits, it remains puzzling in view of the fact that Singapore shares many of Hong Kong's characteristics. Both are international financial centres and Singapore's currency is widely used as both a medium of exchange and store of value in neighbouring countries.

Due to the ambiguity in the relationship between real deposit interest rate and financial deepening in the East Asian NIEs, one has to turn to other factors to explain their financial development. In general, the growth in financial development went hand in hand with economic growth in East Asia. This raises the possibility of a causal link between economic and financial growth. Even though financial deepening and savings are found to be generally correlated, the nature of the causal relationship is not very clear. According to Patrick (1966), there are two possible patterns in the causal relationship between financial development and economic growth. First, economic growth induces an expansion of the financial system as the demand for financial services increases with the expansion of economic activities and is termed 'demand-following'. Second, the expansion of financial system precedes the demand for its services and by facilitating inter-mediations between savers and investors promotes growth. This pattern is regarded as 'supply-leading'.

Jung (1986), by examining time series data for each of fifty-six developed and developing countries which include Korea and Taiwan, has found only moderate support for supply-leading relationships. According to him, in the early stage of development, the financial sector is more important in facilitating transactions (demand-following) than intermediations (supply-leading) and financial development consists more of substitution from currency to non-currency financial assets than of substitution from real to financial assets as implied by the McKinnon hypothesis (McKinnon, 1973). Jung has also found some support for the hypothesis of changing causality with economic development. In other words, the direction of causality changes from supply-leading to demand-following as the economy develops. However, his findings are very much sensitive to the proxies used to measure financial developments.

The preceding discussion shows that empirical findings are inconclusive as regards the relationships between (1) real deposit interest rate and the rate of saving and (2) real deposit rate and financial deepening. This poses a serious research problem: how to explain the positive association between economic and financial growth. Attempts have been made to explain this by invoking the impact of interest rate policy on the efficiency of capital.

Real interest rate

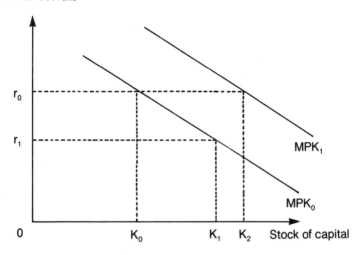

Figure 8.1 Marginal efficiency of investment

EFFICIENCY OF INVESTMENT AND THE ROLE OF REAL INTEREST RATES

It is argued that when real interest rates are negative, there is very little incentive to use capital more efficiently since excess capacity is costless. Fry observes:

> Overtime, shift work and other measures that increase the effective utilization of plant and machinery are not worthwhile when keeping the capital stock idle is costless. Under such circumstances, the measured capital stock exceeds the effective capital stock.
>
> (Fry, 1991: 30)

In his study of ten Asian countries which include Korea and Taiwan, Fry (ibid.) has found that the effective capital stock rises when the real deposit interest rate is raised to its market equilibrium level. He also has observed a positive and significant relationship between the growth contributions of total factor productivity and the real deposit interest rates. In the case of Korea and Taiwan, the incremental capital/output ratios have been found to be the lowest among the sample countries. In other words, marginal product of capital/returns to capital in both Korea and Taiwan are higher than in the other eight countries included in Fry's sample.

The above contention of Fry can be illustrated by using a simple diagram (Figure 8.1). Suppose MPK_0 measures the returns to capital before the interest rate reforms. Let r_0 be the equilibrium real interest rate which is higher than the ceiling real interest rate, r_1. The corresponding equilibrium (effective) capital stock is K_0 and the measured capital stock is K_1. When real interest rate moves towards the equilibrium rate, the measured capital stock approaches the effective stock (K_0) along MPK_0 as a result of profit-maximising producers' attempt to equate marginal product of capital with the real interest rate (efficiency effect). The positive association between real interest rate and total factor productivity implies that the interest rate reforms also induces technological progress. This shifts the marginal product curve to MPK_1. The corresponding effective capital stock (K_2) on MPK_1 is higher than the effective stock prior to the interest rate reforms (productivity effect).

Thus, one can conclude that the sources of East Asian NIE's high growth are (1) growth in effective capital stock and (2) changes in total factor productivity. Both these factors are, in turn, affected by real interest rates.

This has also been suggested by the aforementioned World Bank study. According to the World Bank (op. cit.), less than half the growth in output in the fastest-growing countries is attributable to increases in labour and capital. The rest is due to higher productivity. It finds that investment productivity is significantly higher in the fastest-growing countries and argues that this is suggestive of a link between financial development and growth. The World Bank (ibid.) suggests two channels through which this link may be established. First, through the favourable effect of real interest rate on financial savings and second, through improvement in the productivity of investment. But it emphasises the improvement in productivity and states that 'positive real interest rates helped growth mainly by improving the quality of investment and not just by increasing the quantity of investment' (World Bank, ibid.: 32).

However, neither Fry nor the World Bank showed how real interest rate affects total factor productivity (TFP) or technological progress and one cannot conclude causality from an observed correlation between real interest rate and the growth contributions of TFP. Moreover, the observed correlation could be coincidental if neutral technological progress was occurring due to some other reasons (e.g. government's efforts to increase R&D and the skill of labour force) during the period when the interest rate reforms were carried out.

There are also question marks about the World Bank study. It has already been noted that the relationship between the real interest rate and both real and financial savings is ambiguous. On the basis of a similar study, which uses the International Monetary Fund (IMF) classification of countries according to real interest rates, McKinnon (1986: 323) comments that any positive link between real interest rates and personal saving is much less apparent. On the other hand, by using the data generated by the International Price Comparison Project, Bradford (1987a, b) has found that the high capital formation in high growth countries is associated with lower cost of capital.

Moreover, from Figure 8.2 (reproduced from the World Bank, op. cit.), one can see that the relationship between the efficiency of investment and real interest rates is very loose. The straight line through the origin measures the average

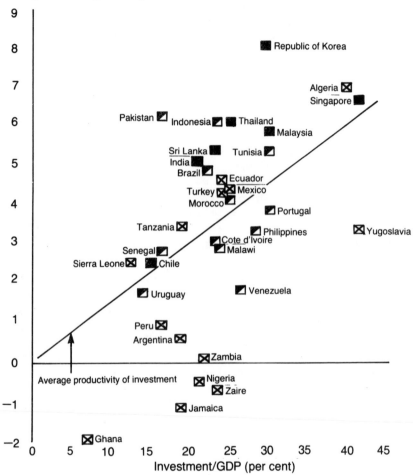

Figure 8.2 Real interest rates, investment, productivity and growth

Source: World Bank (1989: 33)

productivity of investment in the sample countries. Any deviation from it is due to differences in the productivity of investment among individual countries. Thus, countries above the average line have higher productivity and those below the average line have lower productivity of investment. As can be seen from Figure 8.2, there are countries which have been classified as having either strongly or moderately negative real interest rates that have above average productivity of investment. More interestingly, the magnitude of deviations from the average productivity indicates that investment in Algeria, Ecuador, Mexico and Turkey which have been classified as having strongly negative real interest rates, is more productive than Singapore or Chile which have strongly positive real interest rates. In fact, such cross-country studies are hazardous because they are very sensitive to 'outliers'. As Dornbusch notes:

> Most of the evidence about the harmful consequences of misdirected capital market policy come from the outliers – countries that have vastly negative asset returns. Once these outliers are isolated, the evidence no longer supports the claim that positive real interest rates help growth.
>
> (Dornbusch, 1991: 37)

The classification of countries can itself be questioned. Typically the World Bank and the IMF studies use real deposit interest rates to classify the countries. Fry (op. cit.) has also used deposit interest rates. But the relevant interest rate for the investors is the lending rate and hence one should use real lending rates and not the deposit rates. The use of the deposit rate can be justified provided the lending rate is above the deposit rate as one may expect in a liberalised financial market. However, the existence of widespread credit rationings in Korea and Taiwan imply that, despite positive real deposit rates, the real lending rates are below the equilibrium rate. According to Cole and Park (1983: 190) and the World Bank (1987a: 83), export and investment finance in Korea were made available at rates that were lower than market rates by between 5 and 24 percentage points in the 1960s and 1970s. This phenomenon, coupled with relatively high inflation rates throughout the 1960s and 1970s, certainly implies that real lending rates were negative. Therefore, if real lending rates are used, one may find that countries like Korea will end up as having either moderately or strongly negative real lending rates.

Even the existence of a positive association between real deposit interest rates and economic growth in the case of East Asian NIEs is doubtful. As can be seen from Table 8.3, between 1966 and 1983 the real deposit interest rates were negative for 10 years in both Hong Kong and Korea. Yet they registered a very high GDP growth. To be more specific, the real deposit interest rates were negative throughout the 1970s (except in 1975) in Hong Kong, but the average annual growth of real GDP was 9.5 per cent during the 1970s. In the case of Korea, the real deposit interest rates were positive only in 1971 and 1972 while the average annual growth rate of GDP during the 1970s was 8.7 per cent.

The preceding discussion is not meant to discredit any claim about the possibility of positive relationships between real deposit rates and growth in both real GDP and financial assets. However, it does caution one against facile generalisations. As the study by Levine (1992: 37) shows, 'it is the provision of specific financial services that will be related to long-run growth, not necessarily the size of the financial system or of any particular financial institution'.

THE STRUCTURALIST CRITIQUE AND THE 'NEW' VIEW OF THE ROLE OF FINANCE IN ECONOMIC DEVELOPMENT

It would be fair to maintain that the the the literature on financial development has, since the mid-1970s, been dominated by the hypothesis of financial liberalisation (see Fry, 1988, 1989; McKinnon, 1988, 1989; Park, 1990; Patrick, 1990). It is argued that, by providing payment services, mobilising savings, allocating credit and allowing to pool, trade and price risks, the financial system improves the flow of information, the allocation of resources and the management of firms that promote economic growth. The position adopted in this chapter is that the empirical foundation of the financial liberalisation hypothesis is not robust. This lack of robustness has been compounded by burgeoning arguments that directly challenge the doctrine of financial liberalisation. One variant of the critique, known as 'new structuralist', takes much comfort in Wijnbergen's (1982, 1985) findings that the major effect of financial reforms in Korea was a huge portfolio shift from the unregulated (informal) to the regulated (formal) market without any concomitant increase in the volume of savings. Given Wijnbergen's empirical results, the arguments for financial reforms, therefore, depend on the relative efficiency of the formal financial sector in allocating investible funds. Choo (1990) and Fischer (1989) claim that informal credit market is less efficient because it has a narrow information base and a limited capacity for risk pooling. On the other hand, the informal credit market can economise on overhead costs which may outweigh its limitations pertaining to risk pooling. The implication is that one cannot make an a priori statement about the efficacy of the formal vis-à-vis informal credit market.

As part of the new structuralist critique of the financial liberalisation hypothesis, one should also mention the 'Cavallo effect' (Cavallo, 1977). The essence of the argument is that in developing countries firms depend on borrowing for their working capital. According to new structuralists, the diversion of funds from the informal market as a result of financial liberalisation will reduce the supply of loanable funds as bank deposits require reserves. As a result, there will be a credit squeeze and a rise in working capital cost with a predictable outcome of stagflation (Bruno, 1979; Taylor, 1979, 1983). The validity of this argument hinges on the substitutability between time deposits and informal market loans. That is, there will be a large portfolio shift (as observed in Korea) from the informal to formal market following the rise in real deposit rates if time deposits and informal loans are close substitutes.

A stronger critique of the financial liberalisation hypothesis maintains that a repressed financial system facilitates rapid economic growth (Amsden, 1989, 1991; C.H. Lee, 1992; Wade, 1988). For ease of reference, this critique can be characterised as the 'new' view of the role of finance. In developing this argument, it would be useful to start with the distinction that Zysman (1983) makes between a capital market-based and credit-based financial system. In a capital market-based financial system, securities (stocks and bonds) are the main sources of long-term business finance. Borrowers can choose from a broad spectrum of capital and money market instruments offered competitively through a large number of specialised financial institutions.

In a credit-based system, the capital market is weak and firms rely heavily on credit to finance investment. This makes them heavily dependent on banks – to the extent that banks are the main suppliers of credit. However, if banks are themselves dependent on the government, then firms become heavily dependent on the government. One thus has a case of a state-controlled, credit-based financial system. In such an institutional environment, financial repression (in the form of control of credit allocation by the government) becomes the norm, and firms exhibit high debt/equity ratios.

Wade (op. cit.: 133) maintains that Korea and Taiwan can be characterised as exhibiting the classic features of government-dominated credit-based systems. During the 1970s, debt/equity ratios were 300–400 per cent in Korea and 100–200 per cent in Taiwan. The corresponding figure in Latin American countries such as Brazil and Mexico was 100–120 per cent. In the industrialised countries, the figures were below 100 per cent. Furthermore, in Taiwan, virtually the entire banking system has, until very recently, been government-owned. In Korea the same was true until 1980–3 and even after the financial deregulation of the mid-1980s the government exercises de facto control of the banking system through personnel policies, appointment of senior managers, range of services and the like.

There are, according to the new view of the role of finance in development, distinct advantages that flow from the operation of a state-dominated, credit-based system. Wade (op. cit.: 134), for example, identifies the following alleged advantages. First, 'a credit-based system permits faster investment in developing country conditions than would be possible if investment depended on the growth of firms' own profits or on the inevitably slow development of securities market'. More importantly, productive investment is less affected by speculative stock-market booms and busts.

Second, a credit-based system tends to avoid the bias towards short-term profitability that often appears to be associated with a stockmarket system. This stems from the argument that lenders of long-term finance are interested in the ability of borrowers to repay the loans over the long term. Hence, long-term performance becomes the dominant consideration entailing a focus on such issues as the ability of organisations to develop new products, cost competitiveness and so on. These therefore become the criteria that managers are concerned with rather than short-run performance in the stockmarket.

Finally, a state-dominated financial system provides the government with the necessary political clout to implement its industrial strategy. As Wade (ibid.: 134) puts it: 'firms are dissuaded from opposing the government by knowledge that opponents may find credit difficult to obtain'.

The notion that a credit-based financial system can be seen as a political device to assist governments in the implementation of industrial strategy is the crux of Amsden's (op. cit.) argument that financial repression is an essential feature of 'late industrialisation' (of which Korea and Taiwan are classic examples). In her model of late industrialisation, governments deliberately use selective credit allocation in order to speed up the process of industrialisation. However, industrialising nations run the risk that costs of financial repression can outweigh its alleged benefits in the sense that it can provoke a subsidy mentality and induce wasteful rent-seeking behaviour. Yet, governments in late industrialisation can circumvent this difficulty by ensuring that abuse of preferential credit allocation is minimised through the imposition of strict performance standards. If such standards are based on good approximations of ex-ante social rates of return, then politically determined credit allocation will lead to socially profitable investments in 'desirable' industries and sectors. Hence, financial repression will lead to rapid growth.

A more sophisticated argument in favour of financial repression stems from transaction cost economics. This view is closely associated with the work of Lee (op. cit.) and can be characterised as the 'internal capital market hypothesis'. This hypothesis was discussed in some detail in Chapter 2 in the broader context of the role of the state in economic development, but the issues encapsulated by this hypothesis are also highly germane to this chapter.

It can be shown that when transaction costs and corresponding information asymmetries between borrowers and lenders are high and pervasive, lenders cannot efficiently monitor the activities of borrowers (Stiglitz, 1989). A predictable outcome is credit rationing (Stiglitz and Weiss, 1981). This implies that, in a freely functioning capital market, firms relying on external finance may find that investment projects entailing high ex-ante social rates of return are crowded out. Under such circumstances, reliance on the 'internal capital market' (reliance on finance generated through retained earnings or out of depreciation charges) can minimise transaction costs.

Lee (op. cit.) has tried to adapt this argument to the East Asian case by suggesting that a state-dominated credit-based system operates as a de facto internal capital market. The state cultivates a long-term and close relationship with borrowing firms. The atmosphere of trust and cooperation created as a result of this close relationship allows 'lender monitoring' to be carried out effectively and efficiently. The outcome is that transaction costs are minimised. Hence, what is apparently considered a phenomenon of financial repression is in effect a de facto internal capital market that is more efficient than private capital markets.

While the above arguments are suggestive and interesting, one can construct cogent counterarguments. First, one should be careful not to confuse a credit-based system with a state-controlled credit-based system. Financial repression is a necessary feature of the latter, not the former. More importantly, the major advantages of a credit-based system as identified by Wade do not require the existence of state control (and hence financial repression). The only way in which financial repression can contribute to economic growth in this framework is to presuppose that a strong-willed government has the capacity to overcome the inadequacies of private capital markets without the corresponding risk of government failure.

The inadequacies of the internal capital market hypothesis have been noted in considerable detail in Chapter 2. It is sufficient to emphasise that the notion of transaction cost minimisation is not unique to a state-controlled financial system. It is also worth noting that the efficacy of the internal capital market has been exhaustively studied in the case of Japan, but in the Japanese internal capital market the state does not play a major role (Frankel, 1991).

The hypothesis of the superiority of 'lender monitoring' in a state-controlled financial system is also questionable when one takes account of the interactions between formal and informal credit markets. This point can be developed using an argument expounded by Cole and Patrick (op. cit.). When formal financial institutions are regulated, informal credit markets expand. Such markets provide funds to those who cannot obtain credit from formal sources. In addition, privileged borrowers in regulated markets have an incentive to re-lend to users in unregulated markets (and hence profit from arbitrage). The net outcome is that informal credit markets act as a channel for diverting official (regulated) credit to more profitable investment opportunities, thus invalidating the notion that the state can effectively monitor the behaviour of borrowers. Some evidence can be offered to substantiate these arguments by focusing on the Korean experience. Thus, in 1972, approximately 50 per cent of commercial firms in Korea financed their investment needs through the informal credit market. In addition, credit diversion was quite extensive (Cole and Patrick, op. cit.).

One can produce additional evidence which casts further doubt on the efficacy of a state-controlled financial system. In the case of Korea, the early 1980s was characterised by frequent financial bail-outs of large financial corporations (Kwack, 1990; Haggard and Moon, 1990). As Kwack (op. cit.: 236) emphasises: '[f]requent bailouts have not only created moral hazard problems but given firms a strong incentive to maximise borrowing'.

A final point – the 'new' view can be seen as a reaction to the popular perception that financial liberalisation is synonymous with a laissez-faire approach. Current developments in the literature as well as the experience of a wide range of countries with financial reforms have brought to the fore the issue of prudential regulation of the financial system (Long and Vittas, 1991; Park, 1991b). This point can be best illustrated by recent financial scandals in Taiwan, graphically described by Lau as follows:

Early in 1986 Taiwan was rocked by a series of banking scandals that jeopardised public confidence [and] posed a serious economic threat to the nation. ... The executives of several large credit cooperatives and trust companies ... had violated banking laws and regulations through illegal borrowing and lending [and] forgeries.

(Lau, 1990a: 207)

Fry (1990), a protagonist of financial liberalisation, too, reports that the newly liberalised financial systems of Korea, Taiwan, Indonesia and Thailand have been subject to financial crises and panics.

In order to avoid the recurrence of such financial scandals, prudential regulations which entail, inter alia, enforceable legislations on audits and disclosures are necessary. Thus, the choice is not between a laissez-faire approach vs dirigiste system, but a competitive financial sector within the institutional context of prudential regulation.

CONCLUDING REMARKS

The notion that financial development is a key element in economic development is the crux of the financial liberalisation hypothesis. The empirical analogue of this analytical proposition is that movements in the real interest rate enhance the aggregate savings rate, induce financial deepening and improve investment efficiency. These salutary effects in turn contribute to rapid economic growth. While there is no doubt that East Asian economic development has been characterised by remarkable increases in the aggregate savings rate, progressive financial deepening and improvements in capital productivity, it cannot be concluded that interest rate policy played a central role in such developments. Admittedly, the interest rate reform of the mid-1960s was an important policy and political development in Korea and Taiwan, but the point is that these reforms were counteracted by protracted periods of financial repression. Even in Hong Kong, usually an acknowledged international financial centre, one can find periods when the real interest rate was negative. Moreover, a detailed scrutiny of cross-country studies (which typically includes some or all of the East Asian NIEs) tends to provide inconclusive evidence in favour of the financial liberalisation hypothesis.

This does not necessarily discredit the importance of financial development in economic development. Nor does it imply that one has to accept the 'new' view which maintains that financial repression leads to rapid growth. Although the new view is characterised by some interesting and novel arguments, it is also vulnerable to important analytical limitations and does not seem to be supported by the available evidence.

In sum, the chapter adopts an eclectic position on the role of finance in economic development. This entails taking account of a complex set of variables (demographic factors, the government's fiscal stance, technical change, etc.) that affect the process of savings and investment in an economy. It also implies that the relationship between financial and economic development is characterised by simultaneous interactions – and it is this simultaneity that is not easy to disentangle in empirical studies. Finally, the eclectic position emphasises the need for prudential regulations as a central element in the efficient management of the financial sector.

9

THE LABOUR MARKET, HUMAN RESOURCE DEVELOPMENT AND THE POLITICS OF LABOUR SUBORDINATION

The labour market has played a central, but contentious, role in East Asian economic development. There are those who maintain that the state in East Asian NIEs has systematically controlled the labour movement in order to maintain the competitive edge of the NIEs in labour-intensive manufactures. This was primarily done by ensuring a steady supply of low-cost, docile and disciplined workers. Such a view also typically draws attention to pervasive labour market discrimination of female workers in East Asia. The hypothesis of 'labour subordination' (Frobel *et al.*, 1980; Deyo, 1987b, 1989) has, however, been challenged by those who maintain that there is no correlation between weak labour movements and export-manufacturing success. Furthermore, given that tight labour market conditions are the norm rather than the exception in the NIEs, deliberate attempts to repress wages or ensure labour peace are prone to failure (Lim, 1989). Those sympathetic to such a view would also maintain that labour markets in East Asia are generally competitive and that this feature, combined with outward-oriented industry and trade policies, have yielded substantial benefits to the working population (Addison and Demery, 1987; Fields, 1985). In addition, it is often claimed that the key reason behind East Asian success is the presence of flexible, hard-working, educated and well-trained workers (Oshima, 1988).

It is thus clear that the role of the labour market in the development of East Asian NIEs is the subject of some debate. The purpose of this chapter is to review the nature of this debate. It aims to assess the impact of labour market performance on East Asian economic development. This entails the coverage of a number of key issues in labour market performance in East Asia: the implications of growth accounting estimates, the impact of human resource planning (or education and training policies), the extent to which labour markets are indeed competitive in East Asia and, finally, the political economy of labour subordination.

The chapter makes the basic point that the issue of labour market performance can be judged from two distinct, but interrelated, perspectives: efficiency and equity. Thus, one would be interested in establishing the extent to which labour market outcomes are efficient and the extent to which they are equitable. Efficiency aspects form the subject of this chapter; issues in equity form the subject of Chapter 12.

LABOUR MARKET PERFORMANCE: CONCEPT AND MEASUREMENT

Given that the thrust of this chapter is efficiency, it follows that the measurement of labour market performance should start with some notion of labour market efficiency. In an economy characterised by perfect competition in both product and factor markets, the notion of labour market efficiency is unambiguous: it pertains to a situation where full employment prevails (all those willing and able to work at the prevailing wage can do so) and where workers are paid what they are worth (as reflected in their marginal productivities). A related implication is that wage differentials reflect productivity differentials. Hence workers of homogeneous quality receive the same wage.

The competitive model sketched above points to two basic performance indicators – wages and employment – as capturing the entire array of information on a given labour market. These indicators would be sufficient in a static context. In a more dynamic context, the issue of 'human capital formation' (the process via which future and current members of the labour force acquire skills) assumes considerable importance. Hence, it is necessary to focus on performance indicators that impinge on the process of human capital formation and provide some information on the 'quality' of the workforce. Furthermore, the labour market is not simply an abstract entity; it is also a social and political institution entailing the interaction of two social groups: labour and management. Thus, it would be useful to focus on performance indicators which have some bearing on the dynamics of labour–management relations in the workplace.

It is thus clear that one would need a wide array of performance indicators in assessing labour market efficiency – whether at the aggregate or sectoral level – in any given economy. Putting these performance indicators into practice entails the clarification of a number of methodological points and the recognition of data constraints. Consider first the case of employment. Here, one requires not only the overall volume of employment in terms of numbers employed but also its intensity in terms of work-hours. In examining the behaviour of wages, one should distinguish between measures focusing on the living standards of workers and measures that deal with labour costs as borne by employers. The former is critical when measuring labour market equity; the latter is far more relevant when dealing with labour market efficiency. It should be emphasised that it is not the absolute level of labour costs, but labour costs in relation to productivity (commonly referred to as unit labour costs), that is the appropriate concept.

Consider now the relevant performance indicators to assess the 'quality' of the workforce. One obvious way of capturing this aspect of the labour market would be to focus on education and training levels of different members of the workforce. Beyond these obvious indicators are such data as absenteeism, turnover, the flexibility of workers in terms of accepting retraining and new technology, and the relevance of training to industry needs. All of them convey useful information concerning the 'quality' of workers. Thus, a high degree of absenteeism and high turnover may well be reflected in poor-quality products. Furthermore, high turnover reduces the opportunity for individual workers to acquire on-the-job training. If workers are flexible enough to undergo retraining and to accept new technology, it enhances the capacity of firms to upgrade production methods and product quality. Finally, the more closely geared the training of workers to industry needs, the greater the opportunity of appropriate utilisation of skills.

The interaction between labour and management in the workplace can be examined in a number of ways. A common indicator is the degree of industrial unrest as measured by the number of industrial disputes, the duration of such disputes and working days lost.

In summary, one can suggest a wide array of performance indicators that would shed some light on the nature of labour market efficiency. For ease of reference, one may compile (based on the above discussion) the following list of performance indicators:

1   employment and employment intensity (as measured by work-hours);
2   unit labour costs (as measured by total labour costs in relation to productivity);
3   educational and training attainments of the workforce;
4   other indicators of 'quality' of the workforce in terms of absenteeism, turnover, flexibility of workers, relevance of training to industry needs;
5   labour–management interactions as reflected in the degree of industrial unrest.

In compiling such indicators, it is important to give due recognition to data constraints. Employment and wage data, at least at the aggregate level, are relatively easy to obtain, as are data on educational attainments. It is much more difficult to obtain information on the array of indicators encapsulated in (4). Fortunately, a recent survey by a particular organisation has allowed access to these rarely available indicators, although the information is not available on a consistent time-series basis.

LABOUR MARKET PERFORMANCE IN EAST ASIAN NIEs: AN OVERVIEW

The previous discussion has indicated a broad set of indicators which can be used to depict the East Asian experience. Table 9.1 shows a common measure of labour utilisation: the open unemployment rate for selected years covering the period 1960–89. It confirms the familiar perception of low unemployment rates in East Asia suggesting relatively high labour utilisation rates. Within this broad

Table 9.1   Open unemployment rates (%) for selected years

Economy	1960	1965	1970	1975	1980	1985	1989
Korea	—	—	4.5	4.1	5.2	4.0	2.6
Taiwan	2.5	1.9	1.0	2.5	1.3	2.9	1.6
Hong Kong	1.8	—	4.8	9.1	3.2	3.1	1.1
Singapore	—	8.6	6.0	4.5	3.5	4.2	2.1

Sources: Asian Development Bank (1990) for 1970–89 period for South Korea, Singapore, Hong Kong, Taiwan *except*: Taiwan, 1960, 1970, (Li, 1988: 165); Hong Kong, 1961 (Lin and Ho, 1984: 11); Singapore, 1965 (Chew, 1986: 136).

pattern there are important variations both over time and across time. First, the period of the mid-1960s was a period of conspicuously high unemployment rate for Singapore. Year-to-year variations show an unemployment rate that ranged between 8.1 and 8.6 per cent (Chew, 1986: 136). Second, the distinction between the pre-oil shock and post-oil shock period seems to be particularly important for Hong Kong, when the unemployment rate reached a high of 9.1 per cent in 1975 and subsequently tapered off to less than 5 per cent. Third, Taiwan seems to have the lowest unemployment rate for this group of exceptionally successful economies (with the exception of 1989 when Hong Kong had the lowest unemployment rate). Indeed, if the data are projected back to 1952, there is not a single recorded case when the unemployment rate reaches above 3.0 per cent (Li, 1988: 165). It is impossible to establish the extent to which this reflects the manner in which labour market data are collected in Taiwan vis-à-vis the other economies. To the extent that one is willing to accept the superficial evidence, the data suggest a rather flexible labour market (at least in terms of one measure). Moreover, given evidence of very low unemployment rates even in the 1950s, one is inclined to suggest that the popular perception that export-oriented industrialisation had a dramatic impact on labour market performance in Taiwan is only partially true.

One must also draw attention to the fact that there have been transitional increases in unemployment in all these economies primarily in response to slow growth and recessions. This is evident in the case of Korea (1980), Taiwan (1975, 1985), Hong Kong (1975, 1985) and Singapore (1975, 1985). Finally, recorded unemployment rates of less than 3 per cent since the mid-1980s in all these economies only confirms the perception of tight labour markets and suggestive evidence of, at best, frictional unemployment.

So far, the interpretation of open unemployment rates has entailed the implicit assumption of a homogeneous workforce all of whom face the same unemployment experience. Table 9.2 attempts to rectify this inadequacy by providing some information on youth unemployment (which is typically higher than more experienced workers), on the prospects facing the long-term unemployed and

148

Table 9.2 Youth unemployment, long-term unemployment and employment prospects in the 1990s

Economy	Youth unemployment Youth unemployment as proportion of total unemployment, 1981 (%)	Long-term unemployment Those unemployed over 1 year expected to increase/decrease between 1989 and 1991 0 = increase 100 = decrease	Job prospects Reduction/creation of new jobs 0 = severe reduction 100 = many new jobs	
			In 1989	Beyond 1989
Korea	38.5	50.6	58.0	72.3
Taiwan	34.4	60.0	58.8	60.8
Hong Kong	46.9	72.9	78.2	61.7
Singapore	37.2	80.0	67.7	64.7

Source: World Competitiveness Report (1989: 115).

overall job prospects in 1989 and beyond as perceived by the private sector. Thus the information provided in this table is more forward-looking and disaggregated than in the previous table. As can be seen, youth unemployment accounts for more than 30 per cent of total unemployment in all the economies (as recorded in 1987). The pattern seems to be conspicuous in the case of Hong Kong where 47 per cent of the total unemployment is due to youth unemployment. The data are consistent with the view that a significant proportion of unemployment in these economies can be accounted for by first-time job-seekers attempting to find a sustainable niche in the labour market. The table also shows that the prospects facing the long-term unemployed is least promising in Singapore and Hong Kong and most promising in Korea. The private sector in all these economies expect good job prospects beyond 1989, with this perception being particularly notice-able in Korea. Hence, the data confirm the pattern of a continuing tight labour market in East Asia.

Table 9.3 provides information on working hours in East Asia. This appar-ently innocuous statistic is subject to diverse interpretations. Radical scholars would seize upon them to point to the presence of labour subordination in the sense that long working hours represent appropriation of labour's earning power by industrial capitalists or the state acting on its behalf (Frobel et al., op. cit.; Deyo, 1989). Others would regard the same statistic as symptomatic of the Confucian work ethic entailing diligence and hard work (Hofheinz and Calder, 1982). Economists steeped in the neoclassical tradition would regard working hours as the outcome of a utility maximising decision by the worker between work and leisure. These diverse interpretations should be borne in mind when one examines the data in Table 9.3.

The feature that is most prominent in the table is the rather long working

149

Table 9.3 Employment intensity as measured by hours of work per week in
manufacturing, 1980 and 1987

Economy	Hours worked per week (manufacturing)	
	1980	1987
Korea	53.1	54.0
Taiwan	44.0	41.0
Hong Kong	49.1	44.5
Singapore	48.0	49.2

Sources: Korea, Hong Kong, Singapore: ILO *Yearbook of Labour Statistics* (various issues). Taiwan: *Taiwan Statistical Data Book, 1990.*

hours (per week) that characterises East Asia. In recent years (1987) they have ranged from 54 hours per week (Korea) to 45 hours per week (Hong Kong). Furthermore, working hours have increased slightly in Korea and Singapore, although they have fallen to some extent in Taiwan and Hong Kong – most noticeably in the latter. As noted earlier, the normative interpretation of the extent of working hours is difficult to resolve. They could reflect some degree of labour subordination; they could be the consequence of a Confucian work ethic; equally, the rational choice of the individual worker may well be at work. What the data in the table show is a certain anomaly in East Asian development. Usually, rising affluence is accompanied by a steady decline in working hours as the demand for leisure increases and as unions are able to successfully negotiate with employers and the state to reflect the increased preference for leisure in a shorter working week. This relationship between affluence and working hours is clearly absent in East Asia. Whether this should be condemned or condoned is by no means clear, but it is likely to emerge as a socially and politically sensitive labour market issue in the future.

Any review of labour market performance must include indicators which shed some light on the degree of national competitiveness – the latter being broadly defined to mean the ability of a country's labour and management to design, produce and market goods and services that are better and/or cheaper than other international competitors. The notion of quality is rather difficult to capture in empirical terms, but the notion of cost competitiveness has often been measured by the real exchange rate or some variant of it – such as unit labour costs (ULC). The latter is defined as total labour costs as a proportion of average labour productivity. It is thus rooted in the labour market and can be justified by appealing to the profit-maximising behaviour of employers. Thus, a rise in ULC entails a decline in cost competitiveness and a decline in profitability. The ULC measure that is recorded in Table 9.4 has been compiled in US$ and in relative terms (that is, relative to major competitors). It covers the 1970–91 period.

A number of patterns can be discerned in Table 9.4. First, the ULC seems to

Table 9.4 Unit labour cost (ULC, in US$) relative to major competitors, 1970–91

| Period | ULC (1987 = 100) | | | |
	Korea	Taiwan	Hong Kong	Singapore
1970–9	107	70	137	97
1980–4	108	92	133	124
1985–8	106	100	113	117
1989	150	130	109	114
1990[a]	145	132	107	132
1991[a]	143	131	106	142

Source: Industry Commission (1990: Table 1, Appendix F, Tables F4–F6).
Notes: a Indicated forecasts.

have remained fairly stable between 1970 and 1988 in Korea, but there has been a sharp increase since that time. In Taiwan, the ULC shows a steady upward trend between 1970 and 1984, a period of stability between 1984 and 1988, and a noticeable increase after that. In Hong Kong, the ULC has consistently fallen between 1970 and 1991, and there is no evidence of a sharp worsening of the status quo. In Singapore, a period of a rise in the ULC (1980–4) has been juxtaposed with a fall (1985–8), but, in common with Korea and Taiwan, there is clear evidence of a rise in ULC after 1989. Thus, what the data show is a case of worsening cost competitiveness in recent years in East Asia – with the possible exception of Hong Kong. This raises an important policy issue. A rising ULC can only be offset on a sustainable basis if there are sustained productivity improvements. This, in turn, suggests the need to maintain and enhance, inter alia, labour market efficiency.

A constant refrain in East Asian economic development is that one reason behind their success has to do with the fact that the economies are endowed with a highly literate and well-trained workforce (e.g. Oshima, op. cit.; Garnaut, 1989). Tables 9.5–9.8 provide some relevant data on this dimension of the labour market in the NIEs. The data can be classified into two groups: those

Table 9.5 Primary school enrolment ratios (%), 1960–85

Economy	1960	1970	1980	1985
Korea	94	102	101	96
Taiwan	96	98	100	101
Hong Kong	87	117	109	105
Singapore	111	105	108	114

Sources: 1960: James *et al.* (1989: 193). 1970–85: Asian Development Bank (1990).

Table 9.6   Adult literacy rates (%), 1960–85

Economy	1960	1970	1980	1985
Korea	71	88	92	–
Taiwan	54	85	90	92
Hong Kong	71	77	90	88
Singapore	50	72	84	86

Sources: 1960: James *et al.* (1989: 195). 1970–85: Asian Development Bank (1990).

which focus on inputs (as reflected in enrolment ratios) and those which focus on outputs (as reflected in educational attainments).

Table 9.5 provides information on primary school enrolment ratios covering the 1960–85 period. Many observers regard this as a very important indicator of the development potential of a society. This point is emphatically made by Bowman (1980: 37–8): 'unless the primary school enrolment ratio is over 80 per cent, the performance of the socio-economic system seems fundamentally constrained in the long run ...' Easterlin (1984) makes essentially the same point when he maintains that the establishment of an effective primary school system is the single most important factor in explaining the diffusion of economic growth. Taking these considerations into account entails the clear implication that the East Asian NIEs did possess the requisite condition for growth even in 1960. As Table 8.5 shows, even in 1960 the East Asian NIEs could boast enrolment ratios that ranged from 87 per cent (Hong Kong) to 111 per cent (Singapore) – significantly above the 80 per cent mark suggested by Bowman (op. cit.). In recent years (1985). Enrolment ratios have ranged from 96 per cent (Korea) to 114 per cent (Singapore).

Table 9.6 looks at actual educational achievements as reflected in a rather basic indicator – adult literacy rates. As can be seen, all the NIEs have made

Table 9.7 Secondary and tertiary education enrolment ratios, 1960–85

Economy	Secondary school enrolment ratio as % of relevant age group		Higher education enrolment ratio as % of relevant age group	
	1960	1985	1960	1985
Korea	27	94	5	32
Taiwan	30	76	3	22
Hong Kong	20	69	4	13
Singapore	32	71	6	12

Sources: 1960: James *et al.* (1989: 194). 1985: World Competitiveness Report (1989: 120).

Table 9.8 Distribution of the labour force by educational attainment (%), 1980

Economy	Primary	Secondary/ post-secondary	Tertiary
Korea	56.7	33.7	9.6
Taiwan	52.4	37.4	10.2
Singapore	58.5	38.3	3.2

Source: Lim *et al.* (1988: 170).

substantial progress in terms of this measure: from 71 per cent to 92 per cent in Korea (1960–80); from 54 per cent to 92 per cent in Taiwan (1960–85); from 71 per cent to 88 per cent in Hong Kong (1960–85); and, finally from 50 per cent to 86 per cent in Singapore (1960–85). The table also reveals that underachievement in adult literacy was a problem in Taiwan and Singapore in the 1960s; Korea and Hong Kong were well-endowed in this respect.

Table 9.7 shifts attention to achievements in secondary and tertiary education. Enrolment ratios are given for the 1960–85 period. The improvements in this area have been rather substantial, with Korea registering the most progress. Thus, secondary enrolment ratios have risen from 27 per cent in 1960 to 94 per cent in 1985. In all the other NIEs, the relevant statistic is below 80 per cent as measured in 1985, having risen from enrolment ratios that ranged from 20 per cent (Hong Kong) to 32 per cent (Singapore) in 1960.

When one considers enrollment ratios in higher education (Table 9.7), the Korean performance once again stands out among the NIEs. Thus, enrolment ratios have increased from 5 per cent in 1960 to 32 per cent in 1985. In the other NIEs, the relevant numbers are: 3 per cent to 22 per cent (Taiwan), 4 per cent to 13 per cent (Hong Kong), 6 per cent to 12 per cent (Singapore). Thus, there is a clear difference in achievements in enrolment ratios in higher education between the two city states and the larger NIEs.

Tables 9.5–9.7 have primarily concentrated on inputs to the education and training system without the outputs from such a system and the manner in which they are reflected in the labour market. One way of measuring this phenomenon is to consider the highest educational qualifications attained by the members of the workforce. Comparable data for the NIEs in this respect are unfortunately not easy to find. Given such a constraint, Table 9.8 provides information on the distribution of the labour force by educational attainments in 1980 for the NIEs except Hong Kong. Taiwan seems to have the best-endowed workforce, with 10 per cent possessing tertiary qualifications compared with 9.6 per cent in Korea and only 3.2 per cent in Singapore. Despite higher enrolment ratios at the tertiary level (6 per cent in 1980 compared with 3 per cent in Taiwan for the same year), Singapore appears not to have been able to achieve the performance levels of Taiwan or Korea. This could well reflect higher wastage rates in Singapore at

Table 9.9 Various indicators of labour market efficiency

Variable	Korea	Taiwan	Hong Kong	Singapore
	Score (0 = minimum, 100 = maximum), with higher values indicating higher performance			
Absenteeism[a]	42	49	74	74
Worker motivation[b]	58	57	68	70
Worker flexibility[c]	50	58	71	61
Worker turnover[d]	41	48	33	53
Acceptance of labour-saving technology[e]	50	71	82	84
Relevance of vocational training to industry needs[f]	47	51	50	68
Employment and labour cost flexibility[g]	39	64	85	77

Source: World Competitiveness Report (1990) as cited in Industry Commission (1990: 42).
Notes: All data based on 1990, except absenteeism which is a 1986–8 average.
  a Extent to which workers' absenteeism adversely affects enterprises.
  b Willingness to identify with corporate objectives and priorities.
  c Willingness of workers to relocate, retrain and/or assume new work functions.
  d Extent to which high worker turnover adversely affects enterprise level performance.
  e Willingness of workers to accept labour-saving technology.
  f Extent to which vocational training meets the requirements of a competitive economy.
  g Extent to which enterprises can adjust employment and compensation levels to cope with changing economic circumstances.

that point in time, in which case this raises issues pertaining to the efficiency of the education and training system in that country.

A somewhat novel approach to the measurement of labour market performance is presented in Table 9.9. The data in that table present a broad range of indicators as revealed by questionnaire surveys of the community's perceptions (business, media, labour representatives) of labour market efficiency in the East Asian NIEs. The survey is based on 1990 data and forms part of the World Competitiveness Survey conducted by IMD in Switzerland. It considers such issues as absenteeism, worker turnover, and the extent to which they affect the efficiency of enterprises. It also deals with such issues as workers' 'willingness to identify with corporate objectives and priorities, the willingness of workers to accept labour saving technology, the relevance of vocational training to industry needs, and the extent to which enterprises can adjust employment and compensation levels to cope with changing economic circumstances'. The results reveal some interesting patterns. First, on most indicators, the two city states seem to have a significantly better performance than the two larger NIEs of Korea and Taiwan (measured on a scale of 0, which is the minimum, to 100, which is the maximum). Moreover, Singapore has the best performance in terms of all indicators. Worker turnover is a problem but less than in the other NIEs. In the case of Hong Kong, worker turnover is the most serious problem (receiving a score of only 33 compared with numbers that range from 41 to 53), followed by the relevance of training to industry needs. They are compensated by low absentee-ism, high worker motivation, high worker flexibility and so forth. In Taiwan, worker turnover, absenteeism and relevance of industry training to industry needs seem to be relatively significant problems. Korea seems to be the worst performer in terms of all indicators, largely reflecting the fact that, since the democratisation initiatives of 1987, Korea has been beset with a turbulent industrial relations climate. This is also to some extent true in the case of Taiwan after the lifting of martial law in 1987. These observations provide a convenient juncture to introduce the issue of industrial conflict as an important dimension of labour market performance in the NIEs.

Table 9.10 provides two broad indicators of industrial conflict in East Asia: work stoppages and working days lost (in thousands). Korea again seems to stand out with a surge of industrial unrest in 1987. Thus, for example, the number of work stoppages increased from 265 in 1985 to 3,617 in 1987. The degree of industrial unrest has eased to some extent, but the turbulent industrial relations climate continues to be of central concern to policy makers (Bai, 1989, 1990). Taiwan has ceased reporting data on working days lost since 1975, but on the basis of number of work stoppages, the degree of industrial conflict seems to have worsened in the 1980s. Data from Hong Kong suggest that the problem of industrial unrest is moderate, while in Singapore there have been no recorded work stoppages since the mid-1970s.

In sum, this broad-ranging review of labour market performance of the East Asian NIEs has revealed a number of interesting issues. It has confirmed the familiar point of a tight labour market. Despite such a labour market condition, ULC have been generally contained. Forecasts, however, reveal that ULC may increase significantly in the 1990s, implying the need to sustain productivity improvements. The review has also identified that Korea has experienced a rather sharp decline in labour market performance in the late 1980s against a back-ground of a turbulent industrial relations climate. In the city states of Hong Kong and Singapore, industrial conflict is not really significant. Some observers claim that industrial unrest has become an issue in Taiwan, although relevant statistics are difficult to find. In all the NIEs, worker turnover is a significant problem and is particularly acute in Hong Kong. This has important implications for edu-cation and training policies – a point that will be discussed subsequently.

LABOUR MARKET PERFORMANCE AND ECONOMIC DEVELOPMENT: A GROWTH ACCOUNTING APPROACH

It has been shown in the preceding discussion that the labour market in the East Asian NIEs has performed relatively efficiently during most of the past decades. The question is how to assess the impact of such performance on economic development. Analysing and measuring the impact of labour market performance on economic development is a challenging task.

Table 9.10 Industrial conflict in East Asia, 1960–87

Period	Korea		Taiwan		Hong Kong		Singapore	
	Work stoppages	Working days lost (thousands)	Work stoppages	Working days lost (thousands)	Work stoppages	Working days lost (thousands)	Work stoppages	Working days lost (thousands)
1960	12	–	52	3	12	30[a]	45	304
1965	13	19	15	11	13	67[b]	30	46
1970	47	9	92	24	47	47	5	3
1975	17	14	458	–	17	18	7	
1980	206	613	628	–	37	8.9	0	0
1985	265	64.3	1,443	–	3	21.1	0[c]	0
1987	3,617	6,946.9	1,609	–	14	2.8	0	0

Sources: 1980–7: ILO, Yearbook of Labour Statistics (various issues). 1960–75: Deyo (1989: 56–64). Singapore: Deyo (op. cit.), Taiwan: Gee (1992).

Notes: a 1959–60.
        b 1965–6.
        c There was one work stoppage in 1986.

Table 9.11　Contribution of factor inputs and TFP to economic growth

| Country | Period | Contribution to economic growth | | |
		Rate of growth of capital stock (%)	Rate of growth of labour force (%)	TFP (%)
Korea	1961–7	0.6	1.6	4.5
	1968–74	4.1	1.8	3.4
	1975–81	4.6	1.8	0.4
	1982–8	3.6	1.2	5.3
Taiwan	1961–7	1.6	2.2	5.3
	1968–74	4.4	2.1	2.9
	1975–81	4.2	1.8	2.6
	1982–8	2.2	1.0	5.0
Hong Kong	1955–70	3.5	1.9	4.3
Singapore	1966–72	5.4	2.7	4.4
	1972–80	5.9	2.1	0.0

Sources:　Korea and Taiwan: Fry (1991: 19). Hong Kong: Chen (1979, as quoted in Industry Commission, 1990: 65). Singapore: Yuan (1986: 27).
Notes:　Economic growth = rate of growth of capital stock + rate of growth of labour force + rate of growth of TFP.

One way of assessing the impact of labour market performance on economic growth is to adopt a growth accounting approach. In this framework, economic growth (defined as a sustained increase in per capita income) can be seen as the product of increases in the volume of factor inputs (labour and capital) as well as the efficiency with which such factor inputs are used. The last would be typically reflected in changes in total factor productivity (TFP).

A well-functioning labour market should not only be reflected in growth in labour inputs as a significant source of growth, but more importantly in terms of growth of TFP. An attempt is made to substantiate these points empirically in Table 9.11. Consider first the case of Korea. In the 1961–7 period, the dominant sources of growth were growth of labour inputs and TFP. Since, 1968 growth of capital inputs has been a major source of growth along with TFP. The one exception is provided by the 1975–81 period when TFP fell to a negligible 0.4 per cent from 3.4 per cent in 1968–74. Since 1982, TFP has emerged as a dominant source of growth. What inference can one draw between this pattern of TFP growth and the role of labour market performance in Korean economic development? Some observers of the Korean economy (Park, 1983a; World Bank, 1987a) maintain that the sharp decline in TFP was primarily due to capital market distortions rather than labour market distortions. At the same time, the strong resurgence of growth in TFP has coincided with a marked deterioration in industrial relations in the late 1980s. Thus, there does not seem to be a simple relationship between labour market performance and the pattern of TFP in the Korean case. Of course, one must note that the turbulent industrial relations climate is of very recent origin in Korea and its ramifications will probably be reflected in growth accounting data in the 1990s.

For Taiwan, the pattern is identical to the Korean case for the 1961–7 period, with the growth of labour inputs and TFP being the dominant sources of growth. Since 1968, growth of capital inputs and growth of TFP have been the dominant sources of growth. As in the case of Korea, there have been periods when the growth of TFP has shown a decline, particularly in 1975–81. Once again, the inefficient use of the capital stock, rather than labour market distortions, is the major factor behind the results (Little, 1979). Over this period, the Taiwanese government embarked on a series of ill-planned and inefficient investments in infrastructure and heavy industries. The resurgence in the growth in TFP is evident in the 1980s. One cannot unambiguously attribute this to an improvement in labour market performance, although one can make the general point that the trends in TFP could have been, and probably have been, affected by the cumulative effects of human capital formation.

In the case of Hong Kong, the available data only cover the 1955–70 period. In common with the other NIEs, growth of capital inputs and TFP are the dominant sources of growth. In Singapore, growth accounting data extend over two subperiods: 1966–72 and 1972–80. The conspicuous feature about Singapore is the rather sharp deceleration of the growth of TFP, from 4.4 per cent in 1966–72 to virtually zero in 1972–80. Despite this, aggregate growth was very rapid because of very rapid growth of factor inputs. At least one analyst (Yuan, 1986: 30) has maintained that 'the manpower policies of the government during the 1970s may have held down the rate of TFP increase'. The government's manpower policies are the subject of detailed discussion at a later stage. It is sufficient to note here that in the wake of the first oil price increase the government attempted to restrain the growth of nominal and real wages through a combination of centralised wage policy and the recruitment of foreign labour, particularly in low-skilled activities. The net effect is that 'this may have been a deterrent towards greater efforts at increasing the efficiency of labour and TFP' (Yuan, op. cit.: 30).

In sum, the growth accounting exercises for the NIEs show that the growth of TFP has been the dominant source of economic growth, but that there have been episodes of a significant deceleration of the rate of TFP increase. This pattern is particularly acute in the case of Singapore. The discussion also suggests that the inefficient use of capital is the main reason for adverse developments in TFP in the case of Korea and Taiwan, but labour market distortions in Singapore seem to be an important factor behind its zero growth of TFP in the 1970s.

The results reported here carry several implications. First, the importance of maintaining and enhancing the growth of TFP in the NIEs has to be seen in the context of long-term trends in labour supply. As Manning and Pang (1990: 61) have emphasised: 'By the early 1980s ... labour force growth rates had begun to decline in all the NIEs'. This was primarily the reflection of rapid fertility decline. Admittedly, substantial increases in female labour force participation – and, in the case of Singapore, the additional impetus of labour immigration – managed to sustain labour force growth, but the irreversible decline in long-term growth of labour supply has to be recognised. To appreciate the importance of this decline, one may note the following statistics. In the 1965–73 period, labour force growth rates were: 2.9 per cent in Korea; 4.2 per cent in Taiwan; 3.5 per cent in Hong Kong; 3.4 per cent in Singapore (James et al., 1989: 181). Over the 1980–2000 period, they are projected to decline to: 1.9 per cent (Korea); 2.3 per cent (Taiwan); 1.1 per cent (Hong Kong and Singapore) (James et al., op. cit.). Clearly, the NIEs have become labour-constrained economies, a phenomenon confirmed by the previous discussion on the behaviour of employment. Against such a context, the momentum of growth can only be maintained through policies directed towards maintaining the efficiency of both labour and capital markets.

Second, the key policy issue of factor market efficiency and TFP are intimately linked, given that the former is the foundation of the latter. The previous discussion has already highlighted how distortions in both labour and capital markets have led to episodic declines in the growth of TFP in the NIEs. Moreover, one has to emphasise that changes in TFP represent the cumulative effects of education and training. This suggests the need to ensure that education and training policies continue to respond flexibly to changing economic circumstances. In sum, the growth accounting exercises suggest that the role of the labour market in East Asian economic development embraces the wider issue of factor market efficiency in both a static and a dynamic sense.

HUMAN RESOURCE PLANNING AND LABOUR MARKET PERFORMANCE

The previous section has confirmed that TFP is the dominant source of growth in East Asia – although there are conspicuous episodic exceptions. Both theory and evidence also confirm that TFP is influenced by human capital formation. The latter in turn is influenced by prevailing education and training policies – or what is sometimes referred to as the framework of human resource planning (Amjad, 1987). What is the optimal human resource planning framework and how does the practice of human resource planning in East Asia measure up to this optimal standard? These are the issues that occupy this section. The debate on education and training policies can, for expositional purposes, be classified into two generic types: the 'interventionist approach' (IA) and the 'market-oriented approach' (MA). The essential propositions of IA can be summarised in the following way:

159

1 Industrialisation entails an increase in the demand for specific skills, particularly when the economic structure moves towards 'high-tech' activities.
2 Policy makers should forecast the demand for such skills and aim to produce them through the publicly funded education and training system. In addition, private firms should be forced to produce a certain level of on-the-job training in accordance with official guidelines. Without such intervention, a shortage of critical skills can serve as a major bottleneck and abort efficient industrial development.
3 The private sector cannot be expected to solve the problem of critical skill shortages for several reasons. First, institutional rigidities in the labour market and insufficient information available to prospective trainees mean that private economic agents are unable to anticipate and respond to shifts in labour demand patterns. Second, firms will underinvest in on-the-job training because of externalities attached to such training.

The MA takes a position markedly different from IA. It suggests:

1 There is no simple, predictable relationship between the changes in industrial structure and demand for specific skills. Hence, manpower forecasting is certain to fail.
2 The appropriate way of guiding resources into different areas of training is to adopt a cost–benefit approach. Thus, if the social rate of return to particular levels of education is high, then it provides evidence that human capital formation is socially efficient. Manpower forecasts can play a role, but only when used in an indicative fashion and in conjunction with cost–benefit analysis. Furthermore, attempts should be made to reduce institutional rigidities in the labour market and enhance information flows to prospective trainees.
3 On-the-job training is best left to the private sector. The problem of externalities (the notion that firms will not provide an optimal amount of training because trained workers may leave for better opportunities elsewhere) is exaggerated and is primarily limited to small firms where labour turnover is high. The publicly funded education and training system can complement on-the-job training by providing prospective workers with broad-based, flexible skills.

What has been the experience of the NIEs in terms of the aforementioned debate? It seems that elements of IA are clearly present in Singapore and Korea, but are less evident in Taiwan and Hong Kong. Both Singapore and Korea have produced manpower forecasts to guide enrollments in the education and training system, but the forecasts have invariably produced large prediction errors (Islam, 1990, 1987). This pattern is consistent with what has been observed across a large set of countries (Debeauvais and Psacharopoulos, 1985). Both these economies have also used training levies on an ambitious scale in order to induce firms to enhance the amount of on-the-job training undertaken by the private

160

sector. While Singapore's experience has been successful in aggregate, smaller firms have benefited less from the operation of the training levy, known as the Skill Development Fund (Salome and Charmes, 1988: 89; Islam, 1990: 52). In the case of Korea, the training levy appears to have proven ineffective in inducing firms to undertake a greater amount of in-service training. In 1988, for example, 87 per cent of firms preferred to pay the training levy rather than carry out the required training (Bai, 1990: 23). These results, it seems, are not atypical when seen in a cross-country context (Bas, 1988).

In Taiwan, an attempt was made to introduce a training levy in 1972. It was, however, withdrawn in 1974 in the wake of the first oil crisis. The idea was re-introduced in 1982, but its actual promulgation remains in doubt (Salome and Charmes, op. cit.). Hong Kong does not seem to operate a training levy as part of compulsory in-service legislation. It is useful to reflect on the fact that both Taiwan and Hong Kong represent a contrast to Singapore and Korea. Yet, the lack of an interventionist approach to in-service training in the two economies does not seem to have hampered their growth potential. Furthermore, the data in Table 8.9 showed that Korea, despite its highly interventionist approach towards in-service training, had the worst perceived record among the NIEs in terms of the relevance of such training to meeting the needs of industry.

Finally, as a means of summing up the efficiency of the human resource planning framework in the NIEs, it would be useful to offer some observations on the private and social rate of return to education. The social rate of return seems to be the same for secondary and higher education in Hong Kong, lowest for higher education in Singapore and Taiwan and highest for higher education in Korea. It also seems to be the case that the private rate of return seems to exceed the social rate of return largely because students do not pay the full cost of their schooling (Gannicott, 1990). While policy inferences should not really be drawn from ex-post-historical data, this admittedly sketchy empirical analysis suggests that policy makers should pay greater attention to lower levels of education even in the NIEs, given that the social payoffs seem to be higher. Furthermore, one way of harmonising private and social rates of return to education is to ensure that students bear a greater proportion of the social costs of running the education and training system.

LEWISIAN, COMPETITIVE OR SEGMENTED? IN SEARCH OF AN APPROPRIATE LABOUR MARKET PARADIGM FOR EAST ASIAN NIEs

A deeper understanding of the role of the labour market in East Asian economic development entails a closer scrutiny of the way in which labour markets function in the NIEs. One can, in fact, identify three labour market paradigms: Lewisian, competitive and segmented. The general perception seems to be that East Asian labour markets are competitive (Fields, 1984, 1985; Kuznets, 1988). Yet, those who subscribe to the competitive paradigm also note concurrently that:

1   East Asian labour markets operated in a Lewisian fashion (Lewis, 1954) in their early stage of industrialisation. This is often summarised as the 'turning point' hypothesis (Bai, 1982; Fei *et al.*, 1979; Lindauer, 1984).
2   Singapore represents a conspicuous case where the government implemented a highly centralised wage or incomes policy, thus entailing a departure from competitive and efficient outcomes (Fields, op. cit.). This phenomenon is noticeably absent in Taiwan and Hong Kong, but some attempt at incomes policy is evident in Korea after 1977 (Nam, 1991; Collins and Park, 1989).

Consider first proposition (1). The notion that the East Asian labour markets operated in a Lewisian fashion in their early stages of development can be summarised as follows. Underdevelopment is characterised by labour surplus conditions in the rural-based agricultural sector. Economic development entails the progressive reallocation of such workers from the agricultural sector to urban-based manufacturing sector. Given labour surplus conditions, the urban-based manufacturing sector faces a very flat – virtually horizontal – labour supply curve with respect to the prevailing real wage rate. As rapid capital accumulation increases labour demand, the growth of real wages still remains sluggish or remains constant as long as labour surplus conditions are not fully eliminated. Once surplus labour is fully exhausted, the labour supply curve turns upward – signalling the onset of a sustained general rise in real wages. The economy thus reaches Lewis' 'turning point'. From that point onwards, labour markets behave in a competitive fashion.

This framework has been used by some authors (cited above) to interpret the behaviour of real wages – particularly in Korea and Taiwan. Manning and Pang

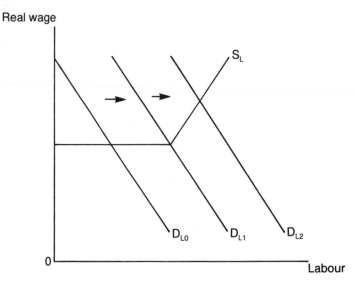

Figure 9.1 Lewisian labour market

162

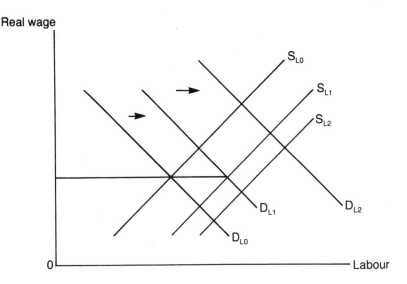

Figure 9.2 Neoclassical labour market

(op. cit.: 65) summarise the work of such authors in the following way: 'A number of studies have concluded that the Lewis' turning point ... occurred in Korea and Taiwan in the early to mid-1970s'. Park (1988: 109) has cautioned that 'there are still some differences of opinion on exactly when the Korean economy passed the Lewis-type "turning point" '. Nevertheless, the early to mid-1970s appear to be the most commonly cited range. Similar interpretations, using similar time-ranges, have been offered for Hong Kong (Pang and Ong, 1988), but it is more problematic for Singapore. As Manning and Pang (op. cit.: 65) note: 'In Singapore, a sharp spurt in real wage growth in the early 1970s was followed by moderate real wage increases in the late 1970s. It was only in the 1980s that real wages ... jumped quickly'. As will be seen subsequently, such a behaviour of real wages is more consistent with the impact of government intervention than with a Lewis-type interpretation.

It is thus clear that those who subscribe to the notion of a competitive labour market paradigm in East Asia also concurrently subscribe to the notion of a Lewisian framework – with the possible exception of Singapore. They are used jointly to describe the history of labour market behaviour during the course of economic development. Yet, despite the enduring popularity of such interpretations, one could easily argue that a Lewisian framework is not really necessary to explain the behaviour of real wages. In order to establish this point, consider Figures 9.1 and 9.2. The former shows a Lewisian labour market and the latter a textbook-style, competitive labour market. In Figure 9.1, real wages remain constant over the horizontal range of the labour supply curve and rise in the upward-sloping segment. In Figure 9.2, exactly the same outcome is replicated without assuming any horizontal labour supply curve. All that has happened is that the (upward) sloping labour supply curve has shifted to the right by exactly the same amount as the right ward shifts of the labour demand over the initial phase of the development process – thus causing real wages to remain constant. Eventually, the shifts in the labour demand curves outstrip the shift in the labour supply curve. The nature of these intertemporal shifts can be justified by suggesting that, during the early stage of development, rapid labour force growth (fuelled by rapid population growth) keeps pace with growth of labour demand (fuelled by capital accumulation and technical progress). Subsequently, as the rate of labour force growth decelerates (in response to a secular decline in fertility), and capital accumulation and technical progress maintain their momentum, the shifts in labour demand outstrip the shifts in labour supply.

Consider now proposition (2). The purpose is to illustrate how state intervention in a particular NIE affects the validity of the competitive labour market model. Economic management in Singapore in the post-oil shock period of 1973 has been dominated by the National Wages Council (NWC). Set up in 1972, the NWC soon became a prominent body which issued annual wage guidelines. During the 1973–9 period, an official wage restraint policy was followed on the grounds that, as a result of the oil shock, domestic inflation had to be restrained through attempts to control labour costs. Although the NWC maintained that wage guidelines were voluntary, there was 100 per cent compliance in the public sector, while statistical analysis suggests a significant correlation between actual wage increases and the official guidelines in the private sector (Islam and Kirkpatrick, 1986b). The wage restraint policy was abandoned in the post-1979 period in favour of a 3-year 'wage correction' policy, the argument being that wages need to be raised to their equilibrium levels in order to compensate for the prior period of wage restraint. Accordingly, wages were to be increased by 20 per cent across the board.

The post-1979 wage policy experiment is acknowledged by the government to be a failure and is seen as a contributory factor in the 1985 recession (Ministry of Trade and Industry, 1986) and the NWC now no longer operates with its pre-1985 mandate. What is germane to the discussion in this chapter is that evidence of intervention through a centralised wage policy in Singapore is not fully compatible with a competitive labour market paradigm. It is consistent with the popular perception that the empirical behaviour of real wages followed a pattern – sluggish growth in the 1970s, a sudden spurt in the 1980s – that is distinct from the pattern observed in the other NIEs.

It is important to note that, in questioning the relevance of the competitive labour market paradigm, one should not overstate the impact of the NWC. The Singapore government employed an array of labour market policies, rather than merely relying on centralised wage policy. Attempts to recruit foreign workers and to encourage female labour force participation which went on during the period under review may also be seen as equally important ways to restrain wage growth – a point that is emphasised by Lim et al., (1988). Furthermore, the spurt of growth in ULC that one observes in the early 1980s was also due to the growth of non-wage costs – rather than merely to NWC-inspired wage guidelines. The behaviour of overall labour costs has been significantly influenced by the Central Provident Fund (CPF), an all-pervasive scheme whereby employers (and employees) make compulsory contributions. These contributions were repeatedly raised up until the mid-1980s. As an illustration of the impact of the CPF scheme, one may note that it accounted for 17.5 per cent of average hourly earnings in 1975 and rose to approximately 29 per cent of average hourly earnings by 1984 (Islam, op. cit.: 45). Other components of labour remuneration show no such massive increase.

The degree of state intervention in the labour market is by no means as pervasive – or as effective – in the other NIEs. A centralised wage policy has not been pursued on any significant scale in Taiwan and Hong Kong. The role of wage policy in Korea is summarised by Nam in the following manner:

> wage guidelines in Korea have a rather short history. They first appeared in ... 1977. Since the fall of 1981, government announcements of planned pay increases for public servants have served as informal wage guidelines for the private sector ... the government also tried to keep wage increases low by having banks restrict credit to firms that increased wages beyond government guidelines ... however ... government efforts to stabilise wages have been ineffective.
>
> (Nam, op. cit.: 231–2)

Collins and Park (op. cit.: 281) take a more circumspect view, noting that 'government attention to incomes policies clearly increased. This concern, together with the increased leverage of the banking system over private firms, expands the scope for intervention'.

In sum, the evidence for a competitive model of wage determination varies among the NIEs. It is much less clear for Singapore in the 1973–85 period. Opinion is divided on the extent to which state intervention in the Korean labour market in the form of wage policy was effective, particularly after 1977. No analyst has as yet suggested that wage policy was attempted on any significant scale in Taiwan and Hong Kong.

Critics of the competitive model of wage determination in the NIEs go beyond merely pointing out that wage policy was pursued in some of these economies. They point out that the labour market in the East Asian NIEs is segmented in many fundamental respects and that this segmentation is often the result of government policy (Islam and Kirkpatrick, 1986a). The labour market segmentation hypothesis (LMSH) will be expounded at two levels. First, a general conceptual framework will be developed which will allow one to isolate the impact of segmentation on the labour market. Second, particular aspects of segmentation will be noted and their relevance to East Asia will be highlighted. Throughout the discussion the terms labour market segmentation will be treated as synonymous with labour market discrimination.

165

LMSH has its origins in the early 1970s (Norris,1989) and the way it is discussed here draws on the exposition by Gannicott (1986). The latter, in turn, has depended on the seminal contributions of Oxaca (1973) and Malkiel and Malkiel (1973). The starting point of this framework is that the observed wage gap between two groups of workers has both a 'productivity' component and a 'discrimination' component. The former measures the observed wage gap as a function of observed differences in human capital endowments between the relevant groups of workers. Typically, these include such basic variables as education and experience – the latter being a proxy for the impact of skills acquired on the job. The 'discrimination' component is, in effect, a residual – that part of the gross differences in earnings which cannot be explained by varying human capital endowments. Although this framework was originally developed to measure sex discrimination in the labour market, it is clear that it can be interpreted in a general way. Thus, if the competitive labour market paradigm is valid, one would expect the 'productivity' component to be significant and the 'discrimination' component to be insignificant. Conversely, if LMSH is valid, one would expect the 'discrimination' component to be significant.

Many variants of LMSH have been developed in the development literature. Perhaps the most popular is the Harris–Todaro model (Todaro, 1969; Harris and Todaro, 1970), where the urban labour market is split into an informal sector and a formal sector. Wages in the formal sector are kept above market-clearing levels by institutional factors (minimum wage legislation, stiff hiring and firing rules, influence of labour unions, etc.). As a result, a wage gap exists between the formal and informal sector, even if workers in the latter have the same productivity characteristics as the former. Thus, in terms of the general framework discussed above, the 'discrimination' component is highly significant. The Harris–Todaro view of the urban labour market in developing economies is seen as a part of a broader model of rural–urban migration, where risk-neutral migrants flock to the urban areas in search of formal sector jobs, but a significant proportion end up in the informal sector. Such a model – discussed in greater detail in Chapter 12 – conveys the stark prediction of rising urban unemployment and poverty.

The Harris–Todaro model does not really apply to the East Asian NIEs. First, as Chapter 12 will show, the prediction of rising urban poverty cannot be supported by the evidence in the case of East Asia. Second, although, the so-called informal sector is of some significance in East Asia as a source of employment (Salome and Charmes, op. cit.: 29), the notion of a wage gap in favour of the formal sector that is above the market-clearing level is difficult to sustain, given evidence of rather low unemployment rates.

This does not mean that the notion of segmentation is unimportant or irrelevant in the case of the East Asian NIEs. LMSH applies – or is alleged to apply – in specific ways, these being:

1   segmentation in terms of export and non-export sectors;

2   segmentation in terms of competitive and non-competitive industries (applies primarily to Korea);

3   segmentation in terms of foreign and domestic workers (applies to Singapore);

4   segmentation in terms of male and female workers.

Before delving into details, it would be useful to note that LMSH, as expressed in (1) to (4), is often associated with the hypothesis of 'labour subordination'. This entails deeper political ramifications and it seems best to discuss the political economy of labour subordination in a separate section. The discussion at this juncture will abstract from the political dimensions of labour market policy.

Consider now proposition (1). The notion is that policy makers in the East Asian NIEs have tried to distinguish between export-oriented industries and the non-traded or non-export industries in terms of applying their labour market policies. Accordingly, through a combination of coercion and legislation, wages and working conditions have been kept artificially different from the rest of the economy: below-average wages, long working hours, substantial dependence on low-skilled, female workers. This type of segmentation is best epitomised by wages and working condition in export processing zones (EPZs). The standard rationale is that policy makers intervened in export-oriented industries in order to maintain their comparative advantage in labour-intensive industries.

The evidence is the subject of some debate. Collins and Park (op. cit.: 312) focus on Korean data to claim that 'wages are kept artificially low in (export-oriented) industries compared with elsewhere in the economy'. On the other hand, Addison and Demery (op. cit.: 20), on the basis of comparative data on all the NIEs, claim that there is no evidence that 'wages are deliberately kept low in these sectors'. E. Lee(1984: 18) summarises the evidence on South East Asia (which includes Singapore) in the following way: 'wages in export processing zones are not significantly lower than wages in urban zones outside the zones'.

A major weakness of the empirical analysis as it pertains to proposition (1) is that it fails to distinguish between the 'productivity' component and the 'discrimination' component in the observed wage gap between the export and non-export sectors. In other words, it is not enough to show that export sector wages are below the rest of the economy; one needs to establish that this is due largely to factors unrelated to differences in human capital endowments. At a conceptual level, this is difficult to establish. One could argue that as long as workers are mobile between industries, then below-average wages in export-oriented industries would simply induce a high labour turnover. Indeed, those who support the notion of segmentation in export-oriented industries typically refer to the high labour turnover that is alleged to prevail in such industries (Lee, op. cit.).

The notion of segmentation in terms of competitive and non-competitive industries (proposition (2)) has been applied mainly in the case of Korea. The point is that oligopolistic industries pay their 'core' workers above their perceived productivity as a 'rent-sharing' mechanism. In other words, oligopolies earn excess profits or 'rent' as a result of their market power and share part of this rent with their 'core' workers through payments in excess of productivity. This could be due to a number of reasons, such as the need to avoid a bad image in order to avoid a strict enforcement of antimonopoly legislation (Park, 1986: 30) and the need to reduce labour turnover which can be costly in the long run. These considerations apply to Korea mainly because the incidence of oligopolistic industries – as measured by the degree of industrial concentration – in that economy is one of the highest in the world (Amsden,1989). Park (ibid.: 41), based on econometric investigation, has concluded that 'substantial wage premiums due to the degree of industrial concentration in an industry exist in Korea, even after adjusting for the quality of labour and/or compensating factors'. However, the magnitude of the wage premium is small, being only 4 per cent when the measured degree of industrial concentration rises by 50 per cent (Park, op. cit.: 37).

Consider proposition (3) which is specific to the case of Singapore. As has been noted at several stages in the discussion, the Singapore government has, particularly in the mid-1970s and early 1980s, relied heavily on foreign workers. Although, the recruitment of foreign workers covers two groups – low-skilled manual workers and skilled professionals – comparatively greater restrictions are placed on the former. The use of work permits that are tied to specific jobs in specific industries means that mobility of workers can be regulated allowing wages and working conditions in foreign labour-intensive industries to diverge persistently from the rest of the economy. As a crude illustration of the importance of this type of segmentation, it may be noted that between 1970 and 1980 the share of foreign workers in total employment increased from 2 to 11 per cent. More importantly, foreign labour during that period was concentrated in manufacturing and construction which accounted for 46 per cent and 28 per cent respectively of total non-permanent residents (Islam and Kirkpatrick, op. cit.). It should be noted that the Singapore government is committed to the scaling down of low-skilled foreign workers (Ministry of Trade and Industry, op. cit.). Thus, this form of segmentation is likely to reduce in the future.

Proposition (4) is perhaps the one that has become a major current policy issue. Even those who subscribe to the notion of a competitive labour market paradigm in East Asia concede that sex discrimination in the labour market is the least desirable feature in the NIEs (Lindauer, op. cit.; Kuznets, op. cit.). Gannicott (op. cit.) tried to estimate the 'productivity' and 'discrimination' components in the male–female wage gap in Taiwan using the 1982 Labour Force Survey. His empirical results suggest that the 'discrimination' component is as high as 60 per cent, leading him to conclude: 'wage discrimination in the labour market is a strong feature of the Taiwanese labour market' (Gannicott, op. cit.: 725).

A Gannicott-type analysis has not been applied to the other NIEs. A crude indication of the male–female wage gap can be found in Table 9.12. As can be seen, female wages were only 48 per cent of male wages in Korea in 1985,

Table 9.12   Male–female wage differentials in non-agricultural activities, 1980–90

Economy	Female wage/earning as proportion of male wages (%)		
	1980	*1985*	*1990*
Korea	44.4	47.8	–
Hong Kong	75.9	76.8	80.2
Singapore	–	59.4[a]	–

Sources: ILO *Yearbook of Labour Statistics*, (various issues).
Notes: a   1986.

although this is a slight improvement over 1980 when female wages were only 44 per cent of male wages. In Singapore, the picture is somewhat better, with female wages being 59 per cent of male wages in 1985. Hong Kong represents the most promising case among the East Asian NIEs, with female wages being 76 per cent of male wages and rising to 80 per cent by 1990. Thus, the pattern seems to be that Korea has the worst case of male–female wage disparity. It is doubtful whether one can justify such acute disparity on the basis of observed disparities in human capital endowment between the two groups. Thus, for example, in 1985, the average years of educational attainment for females in Korea was 7.6 years compared with 9.7 years for males. The stark implication of these findings is aptly summarised by Manning and Pang (op. cit.: 72): 'the persistence of gender discrimination may slow economic growth in the future because it discourages human capital accumulation among females'.

THE POLITICAL ECONOMY OF LABOUR SUBORDINATION: SOME CONCLUDING REMARKS

One of the conventional wisdoms surrounding East Asian economic development is that their governments deliberately manipulated the industrial relations system in order to produce and maintain a steady supply of docile and low-cost labour. East Asian governments adopted a combination of coercion (e.g. anti-union legislation, strikes, etc.) and cooption (e.g. making the labour leaders part of the political leadership). These measures were seen as necessary for the maintenance of free labour markets with its predictable outcome of competitive wage levels. It is in such an institutional environment that the East Asian economies have maintained their competitive edge in the export of labour-intensive manufactures.

Radical scholars have often seized upon these popularly perceived features of East Asian economic development to express concern about 'labour subordination' beneath the 'economic miracle'. Others have taken a more sanguine view, emphasising that labour subordination at least delivered desirable outcomes. As Bhagwati notes:

169

[t]hese countries appear to have used authoritarian methods to keep trade-union wage demands under control and to build on this basis a successful macro policy of low inflation ... without which one would likely lapse into repeated overvaluations, occasional exchange controls, and the attendent inefficiencies of implied import substitution.

(Bhagwati, 1987: 100)

Such remarks convey the implication that labour subordination is a necessary condition for export-oriented industrialisation. This chapter takes a rather more circumspect view of the hypothesis of labour subordination in the East Asian NIEs and suggests that the conventional wisdom is in many respects factually and analytically inadequate.

There are a number of points that need to be highlighted. To start with, the conventional wisdom implies that coercive controls on the labour movement were consciously implemented as part of the initiation of the EOI regime during the mid-1960s. Yet, the historical evidence on labour legislation does not support such a simplistic interpretation. As Deyo (1989: 143), a prominent proponent of the labour subordination hypothesis, concludes, 'East Asia does not support a supposed link between EOI and state repression of labour'. Haggard (1990), well known for his concern about 'development without democracy' in East Asian NIEs, takes a very similar position.

A review of the historical evidence suggests that, in most cases, control of the labour movement started as a response to political circumstances and was un-related to conscious considerations about EOI. Thus, in the case of Singapore, coercive labour legislation can be traced to 'the fierce political contest between leftists and moderates as each sought to consolidate power in newly independent Singapore' (Deyo, op. cit.: 65). In Taiwan, strict political and labour controls were systematised in the late 1940s (J.S. Lee, 1989) – at least a decade before the onset of the EOI strategy. Moreover, attempts to coopt the trade-union movement and bring it under the control of the ruling party (the Kuomintang) in the 1950s was largely motivated by the need to mobilise 'workers for defense purposes in the case of a Communist Chinese attack' (Lee, ibid.: 17). In Korea, strict labour legislation (e.g. ban on strikes), assault on leftist labour unions and firm control over union activities and finances are the product of the 1940s and 1950s rather than the invention of the EOI regime of the 1960s (Park, 1987). Finally, in Hong Kong, the authorities have always maintained a permissive attitude towards unions and workers' rights in terms of full freedom to strike and picket peacefully, in terms of prescription of criminal sanctions against employers' refusal to pay back-wages and in allowing employees to seek redress in cases of violation of existing protective labour laws. These provisions have been maintained in spite of restrictive controls over labour legislation (Turner, 1981).

A variation on the argument that East Asian governments deliberately imposed strict controls on the labour movement as an instrument of economic

170

policy is offered by Froebel *et al.* (op. cit.). They point out that an industrial relations environment characterised by compliant, low-cost labour is necessary for the attraction of DFI which in turn fuels the momentum of EOI. Deyo has responded to this view by emphasising that the evidence does not support this contention:

> With the exception of the 1970 legislation protecting foreign investors from labour militancy, Korea's most repressive years ... are most easily linked to political crises than to the imperatives of foreign investment. Moreover, in the cases of Singapore, Hong Kong, and Taiwan, foreign investors receive no greater protection from labour than do domestic employers, thus casting further doubt on the DFI–repression link.
>
> (Deyo, op. cit., 144)

It must also be emphasised that the notion that coercive labour legislation has been implemented in order to attract foreign capital presupposes that multi-national companies are sensitive to such factors. In fact, survey data reveal that the dominant factor influencing the perception of foreign investors is the predict-ability of the overall economic environment (Chng *et al.*, 1986).

The view that labour subordination is an instrument of economic policy in East Asia typically abstracts from the industrial structure that the economies in this region operate. A good illustration of this point can be provided by the case of Hong Kong. Despite permissive labour legislation, the degree of industrial strife is low as are unionisation rates, particularly in export-oriented manufactur-ing. This is because of an industrial structure dominated by small and medium-sized firms and of a labour market characterised by a high degree of labour mobility. In such an environment, entrenched unions are difficult to develop and labour militancy finds it difficult to strike root. Such an argument has also been forcefully applied for Taiwan. Thus, Lee and Park paraphrasing Gee (1992), note that:

> Taiwan's private sector is dominated by either small or medium-sized enterprises ... since there is only a small number of workers in an establish-ment, effective and direct communication between the workers and the owners of the enterprise is easy. Thus, incipient labour disputes have tended to be settled informally and open confrontation has been avoided. Also, because of a large number of establishments in a given industry, the cost of organising an industry-wide union is very high in Taiwan ... the rate of labour turnover in Taiwan is very high. [This] indicates that workers in general do not expect to stay very long in a given establishment and this translates into relatively less interest in organising an establishment-based union.
>
> (C.H. Lee and Park, 1992: 12–13)

The thrust of the discussion so far is that the EOI–labour subordination link represents a gross oversimplification, at least when seen in terms of the historical evolution of industrial relations in the East Asian NIEs and variations in industrial relations practices within the NIEs. There are good reasons to believe that labour subordination is not a unique feature of the EOI regime. One could still argue that while coercive labour legislation and cooption of the labour movement developed in response to particular political circumstances and pre-dates the onset of EOI, policy makers eventually converted the process into an explicit policy instrument as an aid to the maintenance of international competitiveness. If this was indeed the motivation behind labour subordination, then this was misdirected. As argued above, even in the absence of stringent labour legislation, the prevailing industrial structure in combination with labour mobility can act as 'natural' constraints on union militancy. One is thus tempted to suggest that the process of labour subordination – to the extent that it was effective – led to avoidable political and social costs.

It is appropriate to wrap up the discussion by focusing on the future evolution of industrial relations in the East Asian NIEs. As Table 9.10 has indicated, labour unrest is increasingly becoming a problem in Korea and Taiwan against an evolving environment of democratisation. The former has been particularly badly hit with over 3,000 strikes in 1987. Although the incidence of strikes has tapered off quite significantly since then, close observers are worried that if the country fails to find a solution to the problem of labour disputes there may be chronic instability and perhaps long-run stagnation (F.K. Park, 1992). In Taiwan, industrial unrest appears to be on the increase, particularly after the 1984 promulgation of the Labour Standards Law. Industrial unrest in Taiwan has been exacerbated by the opposition of public sector unions to the government's privatisation of banks, steel mills, passenger transportation companies, shipbuilding yards, and construction companies. Given these developments, some observers expect a period of turbulent industrial relations in the future (Gee, op. cit.).

Current developments in industrial relations in the East Asian NIEs have their origins in the way industrial relations have been managed in the past. Studies have documented that, in Korea and Taiwan, lack of trust between labour and management, inexperienced union leadership and inadequate knowledge of laws and regulations have led to the use of strikes when mediation or arbitration may have worked (Lee and Park, op. cit.). These problems are really the product of a 'top-down' approach to industrial relations which has characterised the East Asian NIEs. One hopes that in the wake of the recent surge of labour disputes, policy makers will realise that the practice of labour subordination led to avoidable infringements on workers rights. As these economies approach maturity, and as they seek to achieve comparative advantage in knowledge-based, innovation-driven activities, policy makers will need to move away from a 'top-down' approach to industrial relations to a more consultative framework.

10

MACROECONOMIC MANAGEMENT

The East Asian NIEs, except Hong Kong which has no central bank and does not possibly engage in active macroeconomic management, are often cited as examples of how consistent application of sensible macroeconomic policies can counterbalance adverse internal and external developments. The setting of a *right* macroeconomic environment is believed to be an important factor for the success of these economies. Singapore and Taiwan, despite their highly interventionist attitudes, have been very prudent in using traditional fiscal and monetary policies. In contrast to most developing countries and many industrial economies, the public sector in both Singapore and Taiwan has been persistently in surplus since the late 1960s. As a result, there has been no pressure for monetary expansion for deficit financing and beyond the needs of a growing economy. Even in Korea, which had overall budget deficits for most of the time, '[g]overnment policies have sustained relative financial stability by never allowing massive money financed deficits' (Dornbusch and Park, 1987: 401).

Another feature is that fiscal and monetary policies in the East Asian NIEs have been designed as supply-side tools rather than as predominantly demand management instruments. The supply-oriented macroeconomic policies are perfectly sensible for economies whose output is export demand determined. In the 1960s, they did not have to worry about the lack of effective demand. The problem was to unlock supply rigidities and to make supply responsive to export demand. Therefore, the *immediate* aims of the macroeconomic policies were predominantly to ensure a realistic exchange rate, labour market flexibility and relatively stable price level.

The issue of *fine-tuning* the economy by using the traditional macroeconomic tools was seriously confronted for the first time only in the 1970s in the aftermath of oil price shocks and the consequent world recession. There is evidence that governments in all four East Asian NIEs have used public investment programmes in varying degrees to stabilise their economies and to minimise the effect of declines in export demand. In addition, incomes policy and statutory charges and tariffs have been used to offset the supply-shock impact on inflation. The exchange rate, too, has been used to insulate the domestic economy from foreign inflation.

While details of adjustment to external shocks (adverse movements in the current account) are discussed in Chapter 11, the main focus here is the short-term stabilisation aspects of macroeconomic policies. In particular, this chapter will seek to explore macroeconomic trade-offs faced by these growing economies and their experience with policy instruments. However, one must bear in mind that in small open economies such as East Asian NIEs, the internal balance (growth/unemployment and inflation) and external balance (current account) are intimately related. Therefore, it will be useful to begin with an overview of their macroeconomic performance – both internal and external.

MACROECONOMIC PERFORMANCE OF THE EAST ASIAN NIEs: AN OVERVIEW

Conventional measures of macroeconomic performance are growth and un-employment rates, price stability and external balance. According to these aggregate indicators, the four East Asian NIEs look very impressive. As can be seen from Table 10.1, GDP grew between 7 and 10 per cent on average during the past three decades. They maintained their growth momentum, however, with slightly higher inflation rates even during the 1970s when most other countries were struggling with stagflation. Singapore outperformed the other three NIEs with respect to price stability while Korea was more prone to inflation until the mid-1980s. Their unemployment record is equally impressive. For most of the time, these economies operated at or near full employment. Their unemployment rates were generally below 4 per cent during the 1980s.

Table 10.2 shows the external balance of the four East Asian NIEs. They have been able to turn current account deficits into surpluses by the mid-1980s. Taiwan's international reserves stood at 19 months' imports in 1989. The comparable figures for Singapore and Korea have been 5.3 and 3.2 months, respectively. Taiwan became a net exporter of capital in the 1970s. The resource balance (exports minus imports of goods and services) for Hong Kong and Singapore, too, has been positive since the mid-1980s, implying that they have also become net exporters of capital.

The impressive macroeconomic performance was, however, disrupted period-ically by both internal and external factors. The common external factor that affected them all was two oil price shocks in the 1970s and the consequent world recessions. However, there were also episodes of downturn in individual econ-omies. Thus, Singapore experienced a recession in 1985 when GDP fell by 1.6 per cent and unemployment rose to 6.5 per cent, the highest rate since 1970. In the case of Hong Kong and Korea, the recessions were rather steep. The annual GDP growth rate fell to −5.1 per cent for both Hong Kong (in 1985) and Korea (in 1980) (Industry Commission, 1990). Only Taiwan did not have a recession in the technical sense of negative growth rate, although its growth rate decelerated in 1974.

Besides such external factors as drops in exports to ASEAN partners and

Table 10.1 Macroeconomic performance: internal balance (selected years)

Economy	Growth rate of real GDP (%)			Inflation rate (CPI) (%)			Unemployment rate (%)		
	1960–70	1970–80	1980–90	1960–70	1970–80	1980–90	1960–70	1970–80	1980–9
Hong Kong	10.1	9.5	6.8	2.4	8.5	6.7	4.7	4.2	2.9
Korea	9.5	8.7	8.9	17.4	16.4	5.0	5.4	9.5	3.6
Singapore	9.2	9.0	7.0	1.1	6.7	1.2	0.6	5.4	3.6
Taiwan	9.6	9.7	8.0	4.1	11.1	3.2	7.7	6.5	2.2

Sources: Asian Development Bank (various issues).
Notes: CPI: Consumer Price Index.

Table 10.2 Macroeconomic performance: external balance (selected years)

Economy	Current account balance (% GNP)						Resource balance (% GDP)			
	1970–5	1976–8	1979–82	1985	1988	1990	1970–80	1981	1985	1989
Hong Kong	—	—	—	6.2	5.7	5.0	1.0	−5.6	5.6	6.4
Korea	−7.4	−1.2	−6.4	−1.0	8.3	1.3	−6.6	−5.6	1.4	−0.1
Singapore	−18.0	−6.6	−9.9	0.0	7.0	4.5	−11.1	−4.6	−1.9	3.3
Taiwan	−0.7	4.3	1.2	14.8	8.3	7.6	1.6	0.7	13.8	7.8

Sources: As for Table 10.1.

sluggish export demand from OECD countries, the 1985 Singapore recession was also the result of policy failure. In 1979, the Singapore government initiated an ambitious industrial restructuring programme. With a view to discouraging the use of unskilled labour, the National Wages Council adopted a high wages policy which involved large increases in wages and employer contributions to the Central Provident Fund (CPF). In addition, employers were required to contribute to a newly created Skill Development Fund (SDF). These measures contributed to the rise in total labour costs by 13.4 per cent per annum in nominal terms (and 10.1 per cent in real terms) during 1979–84. The rise in labour costs meant a fall in the rate of profit and as a result investment in the manufacturing sector stagnated during this period. The decline in the marginal return to capital relative to the world profit rate was perhaps also responsible for the decline in foreign investment during 1979–84 (Kirkpatrick, 1988; Lim et al., 1988).

The rise in labour costs had further implications for a small open economy such as Singapore. It seriously affected Singapore's international competitiveness. The high dollar policy did not help the situation. The Singapore dollar, as measured by the export weighted effective exchange rate index, appreciated by 27.9 per cent between 1980 and 1985, which significantly contributed to the erosion of Singapore's international competitiveness.

The strong tendency to generate surpluses by the public sector and the statutory boards also contributed to the downturn of the economy. For example, between 1984 and 1985 the combined surplus of the general government, public sector and statutory boards was S$12,394 million, in line with the government's high savings policy. The high savings policy at the time of falling investment, therefore, produced a 'textbook' result of the 'paradox of thrift'.

In addition, public policy created distortions in the allocation of resources. For example, the government used infrastructure development as a means of keeping up economic activity in the face of the oil price shocks for too long. The government also encouraged investment in housing as part of its pump-priming and home-ownership policy. This resulted in lopsided investment in the non-traded construction sector.

Korea, too, experienced self-inflicted wounds due to the industrial restructuring programme. The programme of investment in heavy and chemical industries was launched in 1973 and coincided with the first oil price shock. Due to the ambitious investment programme, the ratio of fixed investment to GNP rose to 33 per cent in 1979 from its historical value of 25 per cent. Since the domestic savings ratio remained at its historical level, the shortfall was financed by foreign borrowing. Consequently, the external balance and debt situation worsened. The debt/GNP ratio jumped from a low of 28.5 per cent in 1978 to 53.5 per cent in 1982 (Collins and Park, 1989: Table 3.3).

The bulk of this increased investment took place during 1977–9 in the midst of high inflation. Inflation caused real appreciation but failed to generate sufficient expenditure switching to tradables and resource switching to non-tradable sectors due to the government's policy of channelling investment to chemical and heavy industries. The result was an excess demand in the non-tradable sector, with inflationary consequences (Corden, 1991). On the other hand, there was also excess demand for such tradables as food and other consumer goods, while the chemical and heavy industries had excess capacity. This disequilibrium in demand and supply widened the trade gap and the current account deficit rose to 7.2 per cent of GNP in 1979 from a small surplus in 1977 (Park, 1986).

The restructuring programme also caused cost-push inflation. The massive investment took place when a significant number of skilled workers were migrating to booming Middle East countries. The skill shortage pushed wages up and the ULC (unit labour cost) index more than doubled between 1975 and 1979 (Park, ibid.).

The downturn in the Korean economy during 1970–2 can also be attributed to some extent to policy mismanagement. The financial reform of 1965 and the liberal attitude towards foreign borrowing saw a massive inflow of foreign capital in the late 1960s. The government, worried about the expansionary monetary consequence of the rapid build up of reserves, raised the reserve requirement for commercial banks in order to limit credit expansion. This policy was contradictory as the monetary reform was designed to enhance the supply of credit. The domestic credit squeeze forced the firms to borrow from the curb market and from overseas. The latter exacerbated the pressure on domestic money supply.

The devaluation of the won in 1971 caused a serious financial problem for those firms that had borrowed abroad as the won cost of foreign debt-servicing rose. The government eventually had to bail these firms out and accepted the monetary and inflationary consequences (Park, ibid.).

After a period a sustained growth in the 1960s, Taiwan experienced cyclical fluctuations in 1973–5. The sharp rise in growth (13.0 per cent) in 1973 was followed by a fall in growth rate (1.1 per cent) in 1974 when the industrial production declined. While the cause of this deceleration of growth was predominantly external, internal factors were also responsible. An accommodative monetary policy validated a large wage claim during 1973–5 and money wages rose by nearly 30 per cent, while the growth of labour productivity during this period was only 6.0 per cent. This saw a rise in real ULC by 23.5 per cent as opposed to a fall by 1.2 per cent between 1961 and 1973 (Lundberg, 1979: 297). In addition, Taiwan let its real exchange rate appreciate by 23 per cent in 1974 compared with its '1972' level (Balassa, 1980). The rise in the ULC and the real appreciation of currency obviously affected Taiwan's international competitiveness at a time when the world economy was hit by the first oil price shock. Despite the accommodative nature of nominal money supply, the real money supply declined by 24 per cent in 1974 and aggravated the contractionary impact of declining export shares.

While the East Asian NIEs are generally hailed for prudent macroeconomic management, the above discussion shows that there were periodic episodes of policy misjudgements. However, unlike many other countries, the NIEs were quick to recognise the problem and take corrective measures. '[They] never allowed these problems to get far out of hand for long. Adjustment invariably came rapidly, before economic agents became accustomed to and adjusted to instability and inflation' (Dornbusch and Park, op. cit.: 395). One can cite the example of Singapore where the recovery package included a host of measures designed to cut labour costs in terms of reductions in the employer contributions to the CPF from 25 per cent to 10 per cent and reductions in the SDF levy and payroll tax. These measures achieved a significant reduction in total labour cost. As a result, it did not take long for the economy to recover in 1986.

The Korean government also initiated a rescue effort in 1972 with the intention of stimulating economic activity and alleviating the interest burden. This was achieved by bailing out the firms having difficulties with servicing foreign debt and by abrogating the existing informal loan contracts. Even though this action had adverse inflationary consequences, it helped restore confidence among foreign lenders. The measures were able to turn the economy around and GDP grew at 15.3 per cent in 1973. The government was also quick in responding to the crisis in the late 1970s with a comprehensive programme which consisted of tight fiscal and monetary policies, readjustment of investment in heavy and chemical industries and clamping down on the real estate speculation. Largely due to these drastic measures, Korea brought down its annual inflation rate to less than 5 per cent by the mid-1980s.

Taiwan's recovery plan involved a rise in real interest rate to 19 per cent in 1975. This measure reduced inflation rates to the 7–9 per cent range and at the same time enhanced the supply of investible funds. While the supply of loanable funds was growing, increased investment incentives were provided through amendments to the Statute for Encouragement of Investment. The share of gross domestic investment in aggregate expenditure rose from 28 per cent in 1971–3 to 33 per cent in 1974–6. Finally, Taiwan's real exchange rate depreciated and towards the end of 1975 reached its '1972' average (Balassa, op. cit.). The rise in investment and improvements in its competitive position contributed to the recovery of the economy in 1976 when GDP grew at 13.6 per cent.

An admittedly crude measure of the success in stabilising the economy may be based on two criteria. The first is the magnitude of deviations from the trend growth path, known as the amplitude of business cycles and the second is the duration of cycles (recessions and booms). As can be seen from Table 10.3, the average amplitude of business cycles during both booms and recessions in the period 1960–88 is the greatest in Singapore, followed by Taiwan. The average duration of cycles is also longer in Singapore and Taiwan. Thus, there appears to be a trade-off between the nature of expansions and contractions. The severe downturn in Singapore and Taiwan is matched by stronger and longer periods of expansions (Koh, 1990).

The above survey shows that, despite similar aggregate growth performance, the East Asian NIEs differ in stabilising their growth path. Singapore and Taiwan's growth has not been particularly smooth, but Singapore was more

Table 10.3 Amplitude and duration of business cycles, 1960–88

Economy	Amplitude (%)		Duration (years)	
	Expansions	Contractions	Expansions	Contractions
Hong Kong	6.5	7.5	2.2	1.5
Korea	5.5	5.9	2.0	1.8
Singapore	10.4	14.4	4.0	4.3
Taiwan	7.7	9.9	3.5	3.7

Source: Koh (1990: Table 6.5).

successful in stabilising the price level. While Taiwan and Hong Kong were relatively less successful in controlling inflation, Korea had the worst record among the four, although it was able to bring down inflation successfully in the late 1980s. There are also differences in their performance with respect to external balance. Taiwan's resource balance has been positive since the early 1970s. Hong Kong and Singapore have become net exporters of capital only in the mid-1980s. Korea's positive current account balance appears to be short-lived, which may be due to such internal factors as political unrest (Park, 1991b).

MACROECONOMIC GOALS AND TRADE-OFFS

Treadgold (1990) provides a comprehensive survey of macroeconomic goals and trade-offs in the the East Asian NIEs. This and the following section draw heavily on Treadgold (op. cit.). The other sources include Garnaut (1991), Park (1983b, 1986), Peebles (1988), Scitovsky (1985), Dornbusch and Park (op. cit.) and Pangestu (1991).

Policies cannot be analysed without considering the official declarations of policy goals. However, it is often very difficult to distinguish between aims and means of economic policy from the official statements. In most situations, macroeconomic objectives are specified in terms of magnitudes that should perhaps be more accurately regarded as *intermediate* variables, not pursued in their own right and better regarded as providing links between policy actions or instruments and ultimate goals. The problem is classically illustrated in the following quote in the context of Taiwan.

> One of the government aims in the 1950s was to bring down or eliminate the large budget deficits. ... The derived policy intention implied the aim of cutting down the rate of monetary creation and ultimately dampening the rate of inflation. The necessary rise of tax rates or limitation of government expenditures would also result in more resources for investment and export and thereby would have positive effects on economic growth.
>
> (Lundberg, op. cit.: 269)

Table 10.4a Macroeconomic developments, 1972–5

Economy	GDP growth rate (%)				Inflation rate (%)			
	1972	1973	1974	1975	1972	1973	1974	1975
Hong Kong	9.7	16.4	1.8	2.2	6.1	18.2	7.0	0.5
Korea	6.1	15.3	8.3	8.1	11.9	3.1	23.8	26.3
Singapore	13.4	11.5	6.3	4.1	2.1	19.5	22.4	2.6
Taiwan	13.2	12.9	1.1	4.8	3.0	8.3	47.4	5.3

Sources: As for Table 10.1.

Fast economic growth based on exports has been and is a high priority macroeconomic goal in all four East Asian NIEs. However, fast economic growth may overheat the economy, and generate inflationary pressure and cause external imbalance. Among the East Asian NIEs, Korea has been willing to sacrifice some degree of price stability and external balance to maintain the growth momentum. As Park (1983b: 323) puts it, '[a]ll groups including business in Korea ... have seldom been willing to put up with the possible setbacks to growth that price stability may require. ' On the other hand, Taiwan always had a firm anti-inflationary attitude and has shown the willingness to slow down economic activities if there has been any sign of overheating. As one commentator (Wu, 1985: 7) observes, 'that [in Taiwan] unrestrained economic growth has never been pursued single-mindedly, at all costs, as it was for a time in the 1970s ... in South Korea and in some Latin American countries, seems quite indisputable'. According to Lundberg (op. cit.: 268), the apparently genuine anti-inflationary attitude in Taiwan is rooted in its historical experience. The Taiwanese policy makers were influenced by a belief that the downfall of the nationalist regime on the mainland was related to hyperinflation and this attitude 'was probably strengthened by Taiwan's own inflationary experience during the years 1946–60'. Singapore appears to lie between Taiwan and Korea in terms of adherence to the macroeconomic goals of growth rate and price stabilisation. The government of Hong Kong believes in the efficacy of the self-equilibrating mechanisms inherent in the free-market city economy and its macroadjustment policies are dictated by the balance of payments situation. Its primary objective is to keep Hong Kong competitive in the international market by controlling inflation.

As mentioned earlier, the East Asian NIEs confronted the question of macroeconomic management only in the early 1970s. Therefore, their stance on stabilisation can be gleaned from the macroeconomic developments and responses of this period. From Table 10.4a one can find that the decline in the growth rates in Hong Kong and Taiwan due to the first oil-price shock were dramatic in comparison with Korea and Singapore. Hong Kong's GDP growth rate fell, respectively from 16.4 per cent in 1973 to 1.8 per cent in 1974 and that of Taiwan

Table 10.4b Responses to macroeconomic developments, 1972–5

Economy	Money supply growth (%)				Money supply/GDP (%)				Total government expenditure/GDP (%)				Capital expenditure/total expenditure (%)			
	1972	1973	1974	1975	1972	1973	1974	1975	1972	1973	1974	1975	1972	1973	1974	1975
Hong Kong	45.3	−6.0	2.5	22.9	37.3	26.8	23.9	28.1	11.5	12.9	13.9	16.3	37.1	61.3	51.5	42.3
Korea	45.1	40.6	29.5	25.0	12.8	13.8	12.8	11.9	20.3	15.7	18.0	19.9	14.7	14.6	13.0	14.3
Singapore	35.5	10.4	8.6	21.4	29.2	25.8	22.8	26.0	18.6	18.0	18.9	19.7	28.9	31.6	40.3	34.3
Taiwan	37.8	49.4	7.0	26.9	17.5	20.2	16.2	19.1	12.4	11.6	9.4	12.0	21.0	25.6	21.0	25.4

Sources: As for Table 10.1.

Table 10.5a Macroeconomic developments, 1978–81

Economy	GDP growth rate (%)				Inflation rate (%)			
	1978	1979	1980	1981	1978	1979	1980	1981
Hong Kong	9.5	11.7	10.9	9.4	5.8	11.6	15.6	14.0
Korea	9.7	7.6	−2.2	6.7	14.2	18.2	28.5	21.3
Singapore	8.6	9.3	9.7	9.6	4.8	3.9	8.5	8.3
Taiwan	13.6	8.2	7.3	6.2	5.8	9.8	19.0	16.2

Sources: As for Table 10.1.

dropped from 12.9 per cent to 1.1 per cent. In contrast, Korea and Singapore's GDP growth rates fell from 15.3 per cent and 11.5 per cent in 1973, to 8.3 per cent and 6.3 per cent in 1974. The sharp drop in growth rates in Hong Kong and Taiwan is, among other things, an indication of their willingness to accept the trade-off in terms of lower inflation. The sharp fall in inflation in Taiwan was achieved by reducing the growth rate of money supply (Table 10.4b). The reduction in money supply growth resulted in the decline of money supply/GDP ratio from 20.2 per cent in 1973 to 16.2 per cent in 1974, with a contractionary effect on economic activities. The same result was realised in Hong Kong by drastic public capital expenditure cuts which reduced domestic economic activities. Since money supply was endogenous and linked to domestic activities during this period, the money supply/GDP ratio fell accordingly. This pro-cyclical money supply response accentuated the economic slowdown and the rate of inflation in Hong Kong dropped sharply, from 18.2 per cent in 1973 to 0.5 per cent in 1975.

On the other hand, Korea's inflation rate remained above 20 per cent and it maintained its growth rate at about 8 per cent, showing that Korea was more interested in growth than price stability. The minor downward adjustment of money supply growth did not have much effect on its money supply/GDP ratio or on economic activities. There was no adjustment in government expenditure either.

Singapore's belated acceptance of the growth–inflation trade-off is also clear from Tables 10.4a and 10.4b. The rate of inflation remained around 20 per cent in 1973 and 1974 when the GDP growth was maintained at a reasonably high rate. The rate of inflation was brought down in 1975 to 2.6 per cent at the cost of reducing the GDP growth rate to 4.1 per cent. This was achieved by reducing money supply growth to the extent that the money supply/GDP ratio declined considerably. The slashing of public capital expenditure from 40.3 per cent of total government expenditure in 1974 to 34.3 per cent in 1975 boosted the anti-inflationary programme. The continued decline in the rate of inflation paved the way for slow recovery of the economy in 1976.

Table 10.5b Responses to macroeconomic developments, 1978–81

Economy	Money supply growth (%)				Money supply/GDP (%)				Total government expenditure/ GDP (%)				Capital expenditure/ total expenditure (%)			
	1978	1979	1980	1981	1978	1979	1980	1981	1978	1979	1980	1981	1978	1979	1980	1981
Hong Kong	11.2	3.7	15.7	4.1	28.9	24.2	22.7	15.3	14.4	14.2	15.4	16.8	30.7	32.9	37.5	41.3
Korea	24.9	20.7	16.3	4.6	11.8	11.0	10.6	8.7	16.4	18.2	20.2	17.7	16.1	17.2	24.4	13.8
Singapore	11.6	15.8	7.5	18.0	27.9	29.0	27.3	25.7	21.7	21.2	21.7	34.4	32.6	33.8	34.6	53.6
Taiwan	34.1	7.0	19.8	13.8	24.5	21.9	21.0	25.6	12.8	12.5	8.8	15.0	30.0	31.6	33.2	42.6

Sources : As for Table 10.1.

From the macroeconomic developments and responses during 1978–81 (Tables 10.5a and 10.5b), it appears that the emphasis of macroeconomic goals and policy objectives in all four East Asian NIEs have changed since the late 1970s. Hong Kong, Singapore and Taiwan have shown greater tolerance to inflation in the aftermath of the second oil price shock. On the other hand, Korea seems to have shown more concern for inflation since 1979 (Mitchell, 1981). Cole and Park (1983: 214) observe: '[r]ecently ... inflation has become the most important issue in Korea, and there is some indication that both the government and the general public would be willing to trade 1 or 2 per cent growth for greater stability of prices'. Thus Korea responded with much more restrictive monetary and fiscal policies. The drop in money supply growth was sufficient to reduce money supply/GDP ratio from 11.8 per cent in 1978 to 8.7 per cent in 1981. The contractionary effect was enhanced by a deep cut in the government capital expenditure programme which saw its share in total expenditure dropping from 24.4 per cent in 1980 to 13.8 per cent in 1981. Korea's growth rate became negative in 1980 with inflation rising by only 10 percentage points in 1980 and declining to 21.3 per cent in 1981. This contrasts sharply with a more than 20 percentage points rise in inflation rate following the first oil price shock.

With inflation seemingly under control and economies growing at reasonable rates, external balance has been attracting more attention in recent years. Taiwan's current account surplus has been steadily increasing since 1981. Korea, which had accumulated substantial external debt during a decade of chronic current account deficit, has also been turning out significant current account surpluses since 1986; its current account surplus in 1988 was 8.3 per cent of GDP. Both Hong Kong and Singapore have been running a current account surplus since the mid-1980s. In 1989, the current account surplus stood at 5.6 and 8.3 per cent of GDP in Hong Kong and Singapore, respectively.

The strategy of labour-intensive industrialisation has been a tremendous success in increasing employment. However, stabilisation of employment in the face of exogenous shocks may still require some attention. A relatively un-regulated labour market appears to have enabled Hong Kong and Taiwan to avoid or overcome shortfalls of employment opportunities and served to down-grade interest in employment as an objective of macroeconomic policy (Treadgold, op. cit.). In Korea, 'unemployment, or under-employment, which used to be one of the most pressing problems, by 1978 no longer appeared to be a pressing issue' (Cole and Park, op. cit.: 238). Singapore is the only East Asian NIE where interest in employment as a macroeconomic goal has increased noticeably in recent years. This is mainly due to the sharp deterioration in labour market performance during the recession in 1985 when unemployment rose from 2.7 per cent to 6.5 per cent, its highest level since the 1960s. Without the buffer of foreign 'guest' workers, the situation would have been even worse.

INSTRUMENTS OF MACROMANAGEMENT

Following the well-known Tinbergen rule, there must be as many *effective* policy instruments as there are objectives. To be effective, the instruments must be *controllable* and *reliable*. Controllability refers to the extent to which the policy makers can control such policy variables as aggregate money supply or fiscal deficits. Reliability, on the other hand, refers to the extent to which the policy variables are reliably linked to the ultimate target variables of macroeconomic policy.

Of the two conventional macroeconomic instruments, monetary and fiscal policies, the former seems to be least controllable in small open economies such as those of the East Asian NIEs. This is because of the link between money supply and the balance of payments outcome, particularly when there is an attempt to target exchange rates. In the case of Singapore, most observers appear to agree with the view that:

> [A] domestic monetary target that differs significantly from that arising as a by-product of foreign exchange policy is most difficult to achieve. Since the domestic money stock is largely endogenous, there is limited scope for independent monetary policy in Singapore.
>
> (Lim *et al.*, op. cit.: 323)

This seems to be the official line, too. To quote Dr Goh, the former First Deputy Prime Minister and the Chairman of the Monetary Authority of Singapore (MAS):

> [M]onetary policy – that is, control of money supply – has no place in Singapore. ... Nobody in the Monetary Authority of Singapore (MAS) bothers if M_1, M_2 or M_3 is going up or down.
>
> (Goh, 1982)

Of course, this does not imply that the MAS has no control over money supply at all. The authority in Singapore has both external and internal means for varying the size and rate of change of money supply. It has accumulated large foreign assets, which can be liquidated and the proceeds remitted to Singapore to enhance the volume of local currency in circulation. It can also use its control over the banking sector to put pressure on the commercial banks to repatriate their foreign assets. (The largest commercial bank, Development Bank of Singapore, is government owned.) In addition, the government can sterilise a portion of the net inflow of private funds by requiring that it be deposited by the banks at the MAS as it did in 1972–3 to counteract an anticipated inflationary net inflow of short-term capital (Geiger and Geiger, 1973: 189). In addition to using traditional internal means of monetary control, such as cash-reserve requirement and open market operations, the Singapore government can shift its deposits from commercial banks to MAS and vice versa and thereby affect money supply.

The Singapore government also has the will to use its control as it deems fit. This is evident from the following comments of Dr Goh:

> When public sector accounts are in surplus, there is a draining of money from commercial banks to government accounts. ... From time to time the MAS has got to make good the liquidity shortage. It does so by selling the Singapore dollar against the US dollar. This is the way our assets have been growing over the years.
>
> (Goh, op. cit.).

The cases of Taiwan and Korea are not much different. Through their control over the banking sector and capital flows, both Taiwan and Korea have been able to control money supply even when they have targeted exchange rates. However, it is possible that such control may have become weaker with the passage of time. Park cites both external and domestic reasons for the weakening of monetary control in the following words:

> [W]ith the growth of the external sector, both in size and importance, the increased foreign capital transactions have weakened the effectiveness of monetary policy. Despite supposedly strict government control of capital movements, business has somehow managed to borrow from abroad when domestic financial markets have become tight. ... The bulk of subsidies to preferred industries and fiscal deficits have been financed by borrowings from the central bank ... those types of central bank credit that could not be controlled through the manipulation of traditional policy instruments accounted for anywhere from 30 per cent to 45 per cent of the reserve base in the 1970s.
>
> (Park, 1983b: 322–5)

Fry (1985: 310) observes a similar trend in Taiwan. He cites the example of loss of periodic monetary control in 1971–3 and 1977–80 due to rapid increases in net foreign assets. According to Emery (1987), the rapid growth of broad money since 1985 indicates some loss of monetary control in Taiwan.

The trust in the efficacy of the market mechanism is perhaps the reason why the Hong Kong government has hitherto refused to equip itself with traditional instruments of monetary control. It does not have any central bank, no mandatory cash-reserve requirement, no discount facility (variations in central bank credit to commercial banks) and the government does not engage in open market operations. Until 1972 Hong Kong operated a fixed exchange rate currency board system under which two private banks were entitled to issue bank notes subject to the matching purchase (using foreign exchange) of Exchange Fund certificate of indebtedness; and correspondingly they were required to withdraw notes from circulation, equivalent to the amount of certificates of indebtedness they surrendered to the Fund. Money supply adjusted automatically to maintain equilibrium in the balance of payments under this system.

However, the link of money supply with balance of payments was severed during its 9-year (1974–83) experiment with floating exchange rates. During this period Hong Kong probably provided the purest example of an *endogenous* money supply, linked to domestic economic activities (Treadgold, op. cit.: 23). In 1972, the two note-issuing banks were permitted to acquire certificates of indebtedness by simply crediting the account of Exchange Fund held at these banks with Hong Kong dollars instead of foreign exchange. This broke the link between net foreign exchange receipts and new issues of notes. Moreover, 'the fact that the currency issue could be increased on demand by the note-issuing banks ... meant that the monetary base was not subject to any direct policy influence' (Treadgold, op. cit.: 24).

Besides the supposed link between money supply and balance of payments, the controllability issue also concerns the nature and efficacy of the specific instruments of monetary control. The principal instruments are rediscounting, open market operations, variable reserve requirements, moral suasion and quantitative credit and interest rate controls.

In the case of Korea, Fry (op. cit.) has found that the use of rediscounting has ironically jeopardised control over the monetary base. Even though the open market operations are believed to be the most flexible monetary policy instrument, the absence of, or lack of depth in, secondary financial markets in Korea, Singapore and Taiwan render it largely inappropriate. (Hong Kong does not have a central bank to conduct open market operations.) It is commonly held that reserve requirements have limited effectiveness in Singapore and Taiwan. With more than 100 commercial banks and a highly competitive banking sector, moral suasion is unlikely to have much effect in Hong Kong. In the case of Singapore, moral suasion is judged to be effective only as a selective credit policy rather than as an aggregative monetary policy (see Hewson, 1981; Sung, 1985; Lundberg, op. cit.).

The reliability aspect of the effectiveness of monetary policy entails two issues. The first is the existence of a stable relationship between demand for money and interest rate and the second is the sensitivity of economic activities (in particular investment) to changes in interest rate. The limited attempts to test these relationships in four East Asian NIEs have produced mixed results. Most observers (e.g. Lim *et al.*, op. cit.; Greenwood, 1979) doubt the existence of any reliable link between monetary aggregates and economic activities in Singapore and Hong Kong. However, Wijnbergen (1982, 1985) has found some evidence of a positive relationship between credit expansion and economic growth and a negative relationship between real interest rates and economic acitivities.

Thus, the monetary policy is found to be generally less effective in the East Asian NIEs, in terms of both its controllability and reliability. In addition, the nature of monetary policy is found to be by and large accommodating in the sense that money supply responds *endogenously* to domestic economic activities. This is particularly true for Hong Kong, Korea and Singapore. However, the degree of accommodation varies among them. In Hong Kong, for example, the response to domestic demand for credit has been almost automatic, especially between 1972 and 1983. Only once (in 1979) did the government intervene by imposing direct controls on the expansion of domestic credit and pressure on the interest rate fixing bank cartel to raise interest rates. This was done, however, to stabilise the dollar rather than price level.

On the other hand, Singapore's monetary policy has been more active and there has been little reliance on automatic adjustment. Singapore appears to have followed a more pragmatic approach. As mentioned earlier, it imposed temporary credit ceilings on bank lending in response to inflationary pressures in 1973. It has also used moral suasion to control bank lendings and money market operations. Compared with Singapore and Taiwan, Korea showed very little discipline in monetary management. Money supply has accommodated fiscal deficits – the net claim of the government on domestic credit was positive until mid-1980s. This phenomenon explains, in large part, why Korea had the highest rate of inflation among the East Asian NIEs until very recently. However, the monetary management in Korea is far better than that of Latin American countries. This was, in a way, due to a repressed financial sector which offered very little or no substitutes for domestic money such as dollar deposits or foreign assets. Moreover, Korea never liberalised the financial sector to an extent which would have reduced bank deposits and hence reserves. As a result, the velocity did not rise and, according to Dornbusch and Park (op. cit.: 415), these factors helped finance budget deficits in a less inflationary way.

Only Taiwan seems to have pursued an 'active monetary policy both to steril-ise the effects of the large overall balance of payments surpluses on the supply of money and to counteract monetary disruptions generated domestically' (Fry, op. cit.: 310), although as mentioned earlier it periodically lost control over monetary aggregates due to rapid build up of foreign reserves. In order to cope with the situation, Taiwan revalued its exchange rates and raised reserve require-ments in 1971. The reserve requirement system was modified in 1975 to make it more effective.

The effectiveness of fiscal policy is concerned mainly with both real and finan-cial crowding-out and the net effect on the economy. That is, the government's claims on real and financial resources are likely to disadvantage the private sector and thereby reduce the size of the multiplier. In open economies such as the East Asian NIEs, the multiplier effect is likely to be further reduced through import leakages and exchange rate appreciation. Exchange rate appreciation not only discourages exports, but also boosts import leakages.

On average, budgetary changes have been found to have a net positive impact on GDP in the East Asian NIEs. Yu and Chen (1982) have estimated that, between 1952 and 1979, budgetary changes in Taiwan contributed a net 3.8 percentage points to the annual rate of growth of GDP. According to S. Lee (1978), the net effect of the budget on GDP has also been consistently expansion-ary in the case of Singapore. Given the overall credit ceiling and government's control over credit, the crowding-out of private investment is likely to be large in Korea. Hence, it is argued that the net effect of budgetary changes in Korea is small. However, two studies (Sundararajan and Thakur, 1980; Wijnbergen, 1982) on the issue produced conflicting results – the former cited the evidence of large crowding-out and the latter found large and positive effects of public investment on private investment.

With regard to its controllability, the discretionary component of fiscal policy has been widely held to be a cumbersome and inflexible arm of macromanagement due to institutional rigidities, administrative bottlenecks and political pressures, known collectively as 'inside lag'.

However, there is agreement among the observers of the East Asian NIEs that the governments of these nations have much greater control over the fiscal tool. This control stems from the nature of the state. In East Asian NIEs, the 'activities of autonomously organized social and political groups are limited and . . . these groups lack effective access to centres of decision-making power within the state structure' (Haggard and Cheng, 1987b: 101). This makes the state relatively insulated from the pressure of interest groups than in, say, Latin American countries. This view is also reflected in the following quote from Dr Goh:

> Democratically elected governments tend to overspend because politicians make election promises of all kinds. [So] expenditure exceeds revenue. That's the source, the root of all the troubles. . . . In Singapore, our position is reverse . . . a state of chronic surplus.
>
> (Goh, op. cit.)

The relative weakness of pressure groups makes the 'inside lag' of fiscal measures very low in the NIEs. The governments of East Asian NIEs have been very quick in adjusting their revenue and expenditure structures and there is ample evidence of the use of the public investment programme to stabilise the economy, especially during recession. As mentioned in the previous section (Tables 10.4b and 10.5b), public investment programmes have also been used to combat inflation.

However, the possibility of crowding-out weakens the effectiveness of fiscal policy. The use of monetary policy remains a difficult option due to the lack of controllability of monetary aggregates. Therefore, it is often suggested that small open economies such as that of Singapore should use the exchange rate and incomes (wages) policies for short-term macroeconomic management. The former should be used to insulate the domestic economy from foreign inflation, while the money wage should be set in the light of exchange rate/price level policy to yield a real wage conducive to the achievement of the employment (and output) target (Corden, 1984; Lim et al., op. cit.). This seems to be the official line of thinking, too, as indicated in the annual report of the MAS:

> Underlying this shift in emphasis away from targets for interest rates and money supply growth in the conduct of monetary policy is the view that the exchange rate is a relatively more important anti-inflation instrument.
>
> (Monetary Authority of Singapore, 1982: 4)

The existence of the bonus system and various statutory levies, such as employers' contribution to the CPF, payroll tax and SDF, makes it easier for the government to achieve a desirable real wage outcome. It may be recalled that wages policy was used quite successfully to combat recession in 1985, when employers' contribution to the CPF was cut by 15 percentage points. This, together with cuts in payroll tax and SDF levy, achieved a significant one-shot reduction in total labour cost. The buffer of foreign workers provides the government with one more instrument to manipulate the labour market. According to Y. Lee (1987: 165): '[t]he existence of the a pool of foreign workers can act as a buffer so that the adjustment of real wages which is required need not be severe.'

Although assigning the exchange rate for inflation and wages for employment (and output) targets has been recommended for Singapore, it is equally applicable in other East Asian NIEs (Garnaut, op. cit.). However, the Hong Kong government adopted a fixed exchange rate system in October 1983 and pegged the Hong Kong dollar to the US dollar, making Hong Kong more vulnerable to macroeconomic instability. For example, the Hong Kong dollar appreciated in 1985 with the record appreciation of the US dollar and this contributed to the steep recession as exports declined by 6 per cent. The depreciation of the US dollar in the following year improved Hong Kong's competitiveness and GDP grew at 8.7 per cent in 1986. Such fluctuations, however, can be mitigated by pegging the Hong Kong dollar to a basket of currencies, as in Singapore, rather than maintaining a rigid link with the US dollar, so as to maintain the nominal effective exchange rate constant (Balassa and Williamson, 1987: 33).

Korea, too, used exchange rate and incomes policies for stabilisation purposes. It devalued the exchange rate by 20 per cent against the US dollar and switched to a floating exchange rate system in the early 1980s. To offset the inflationary effect of devaluation, Korea adjusted a wide range of interest rates upward. Exchange rate management was kept somewhat rigid during 1981–2 to minimise inflationary pressure of rising import costs. However, since 1983, exchange rate management has been free of any price stabilisation bias and tilted toward stimulating exports and growth. Stabilisation efforts have relied substantially on incomes policy since 1981, including the imposition of informal wage guidelines to moderate wage increases, control of interest rates and dividends and sharp adjustments to the government's purchase price for rice. According to Nam (1988: 86–7), this wage moderation resulted in real wage increases below the labour productivity gains during 1981–4, although he is generally suspicious about the impact of incomes policy (Nam, 1991). The Korean experience with macroeconomic management has been succinctly summarised by Dornbusch and Park in the following way:

> Except in 1979–81, government policy has avoided an overvaluation of exchange rate. By standing in the way of strong union movement, the government sanctioned the market pressure on wages generated by rural–urban migration. Wages thus rose slowly despite strong productivity

growth in manufacturing. Growth in employment and continuing profitability of the export sector rather than much faster growth in manufacturing real wages were the result.

(Dornbusch and Park, op. cit., 403)

Taiwan's strong anti-inflationary attitude is responsible for more active
exchange rate policy. It did not hesitate to revalue its currency when it was
considered necessary. Thus, it was revalued in 1972 and 1978 to sterilise the
monetary consequences of large overall balance of payments surpluses and to
offset imported inflation. As the balance of payments surplus is growing steadily,
Taiwan continued to revalue its dollar in the 1980s. A relatively flexible labour
market always produced the desirable outcome – the average annual unemployment has been at an enviable rate of 1.8 per cent during the period 1971–89 and
ULC increased by only 10 per cent during 1980–84. This was predominantly due
to an elastic labour supply and the absence of active labour unions. As observed
by Lundberg:

> [T]here existed no, or very little, active wage push or wage policy as an
> independent factor in the inflation process. Without active trade unions
> and with a relatively elastic supply of labour, at least up to the 1970s, the
> price of labour can be regarded as a passive factor, adjusting to market
> conditions, including change in prices and productivity.

(Lundberg, op. cit., 295)

THE POLITICAL ECONOMY OF MACROMANAGEMENT: SOME CONCLUDING REMARKS

Export-led growth appears to be still a dominant macroeconomic objective of the
East Asian NIEs. Price stability attracted attention to the extent that it affected
international competitiveness. These economies adopted an outward-oriented
policy at a time when world output and trade were expanding rapidly. In such a
situation, there was very little need for traditional stabilisation programmes.
Therefore, the conventional fiscal and monetary policies were mainly used to
mobilise domestic resources and channel investment to the 'desired' sector to
complement the overall development programme.

The need for stabilisation arose only in the 1970s and despite periodic cyclical
downturns and inflationary episodes, the East Asian NIEs were in general
successful in smoothing out their difficulties. Hong Kong, being very close to a
free market economy with flexible factor and commodity markets, relied mostly
on the automatic adjustment mechanism for overcoming the periodic difficulties
(Peebles, op. cit.).

In general, the key to successful macroeconomic management in the East
Asian NIEs lies in the flexibility of the labour market and the short inside lag of
fiscal measures. The political structure of the East Asian NIEs is such that
governments, including that of Hong Kong, are able to quickly respond with

adjustments in public expenditure (investment) to fine-tune the economy. In addition, the repressed financial market, especially in Korea and to some extent in Taiwan, helped finance government expenditure in a less inflationary way by keeping money substitutes out of reach. The rural–urban migration in Korea, migration from mainland China to Hong Kong and Taiwan and the existence of buffer foreign labour provided the necessary flexibility in the labour market in these economies. In addition, a weak labour movement means that the wages can be effectively manipulated to achieve desirable macroeconomic outcomes. One must, however, emphasise political developments since 1987 in Korea and Taiwan (as was noted in Chapter 9), which cast doubt on the extent to which macroeconomic management can continue to rely on labour market flexibility.

There is a general agreement that in small economies, dependent on foreign trade, there is a little scope for monetary policy even when there are controls on the financial sector. In such a situation, the exchange rate is a better instrument in so far as stability is concerned. The absence of substitutes for domestic currency, especially in the form of dollar deposits or external asset holdings in Korea and Taiwan, prevented wild fluctuations of their currencies by discouraging speculative attacks. Singapore achieved the same result by pegging its currency to a basket of undisclosed currencies. The pegging of their currencies (except for the Hong Kong dollar) to a basket of currencies rather than one single currency, helped them maintain their effective real exchange rate at a competitive level even when there were variations in the bilateral rates.

11

MANAGING EXTERNAL SHOCKS

The slowing down of world trade in the 1970s meant a substantial shock for the highly trade-dependent East Asian NIEs. Furthermore, world recessions added to protectionist pressures in industrial countries. As trade restrictions on labour-intensive products proliferated, there were secondary reductions in the export volumes of the East Asian NIEs. In addition to the decline in export volume, the events of the 1970s had other adverse effects on these nations. Being net importers of oil, Hong Kong, Korea, Singapore and Taiwan faced much larger import bills as a result of two sharp rises in oil price. The decline in export volume and high import bills meant a substantial loss of resources for the trade-dependent East Asian NIEs. Estimates by Balassa (1980) and Naya and James (1986) show that the impacts of external shocks – measured by 'additional' current account deficit as a percentage GNP – were larger in the more open smaller economies of Hong Kong and Singapore (Table 11.1). Their estimates also show that Singapore and Korea were more vulnerable to terms of trade shocks, particularly oil price increases. As can be seen from Table 11.2, the terms of trade effects accounted for almost all of Singapore's external shocks during 1974–82. Taiwan was affected roughly equally by both oil price increases and declines in export demand. Hong Kong displayed more vulnerability to changes in export volume.

This chapter examines the nature of East Asian NIEs' adjustment to external imbalances in the aftermath of the two oil price shocks in the 1970s. It draws primarily on Chowdhury (1992) and such works as Jaspersen (1981), Corden (1979), Aghevli and Marquez-Ruarte (1985), Park (1983b, 1986), Collins and Park (1989), Nam (1988), Naya and James (op. cit.) and Balassa (op. cit.).

STRUCTURAL ADJUSTMENT IN THE EAST ASIAN NIEs: AN OVERVIEW

An adverse external shock means that a country has command over fewer real resources. Adjustment to the decline in the availability of real resources can occur in at least three ways. First, the adjustment could be autonomous or self-correcting. The decline in terms of trade, for example, reduces income and hence expenditure.

193

Table 11.1 The size of external shocks (% GNP)

Economy	External shocks/GNP (%)	
	1974–8	*1974–82*
Hong Kong	—	−26.7
Korea	−6.9	−13.3
Singapore	−23.3	−46.3
Taiwan	−6.5	−12.7

Sources: 1974–8: Balassa (1980).
1974–82: Naya and James (1986: Table 14.6).
Note: External shock = additional current account deficits due to the rise in import bills and decline in exports.

The reduced expenditure cuts imports and releases goods and services for exports, which, in turn, closes the resource gap. There are also indirect monetary effects. The increased deficit in the current account means a loss of foreign reserves. If the country is not following a fully flexible exchange rate system, this will reduce the monetary base and hence the money supply. The reduction in money supply raises interest rates and reinforces the contractionary impact of the terms of trade effect on income and expenditure.

The second way to adjust is to replace the lost real resources by foreign savings (external borrowing). Adjustments through external borrowing can be very short-lived unless it is used for investment to enhance a country's productive capacity – either for exports or import substitutes – to eventually pay off the loans.

The sustained improvement in the resource balance ultimately depends on the third means of adjustment. This involves restructuring the economy towards the tradable sector, especially in accordance with the changing pattern of comparative advantage.

Table 11.2 Terms of trade and export volume effects of external shocks

Economy	Terms of trade effect		Export volume effect	
	1974–8	*1974–82*	*1974–8*	*1972–82*
Hong Kong	—	35.6	—	64.4
Korea	74.5	83.2	25.5	16.8
Singapore	71.8	98.1	28.2	1.9
Taiwan	41.0	43.8	59.0	56.2

Sources: As for Table 11.1.

The second and third means of adjustment are policy-induced and distinguish *positive* adjustment from *negative* adjustment. Positive adjustment enhances development by increasing the growth potential and restructuring the economy while the negative adjustment places the entire burden on internal demand. The existing consumption level perhaps can be maintained through external borrowing for a short period of time, but absorption must be reduced to service and ultimately to pay off loans.

However, the autonomous or self-correcting reduction in absorption may be costly as it may affect various sections or sectors of the economy unevenly. Furthermore, while the cut in absorption improves the external balance, it produces internal imbalance. As the output of non-traded sector is domestic-demand determined, the drop in domestic absorption results in increased un-employment in the non-traded sector. This will not happen if prices and wages in the non-traded sector are flexible downward. The fall in prices of non-tradables will increase the relative price of tradables and, as a result, resources will move to the traded sector. In the absence of such flexibility, the absorption reduction must be supplemented by a switching policy to shift resources away from the non-traded to the traded sector. A common switching policy is exchange rate devaluation; it makes the domestic price of tradables rise relative to non-tradables. This induces movements of resources to the traded sector and the supply of tradables rises. The rise in relative price of tradables in domestic currency also encourages a shift in expenditure away from tradables to non-tradables. The combined effect of resource and expenditure switching maintains the internal balance while the external balance is restored (Corden, op. cit.).

The East Asian NIEs' adjustments to external shocks were mainly positive. They were characterised by policy-induced reduction in absorption, particularly current government expenditure, and the growth of the traded sector. These were also supplemented by switching policies. The devaluation of their currencies was the main switching device (Garnaut, 1991: 9–10). As mentioned in the previous chapter, the flexibility of labour markets in the East Asian NIEs aided their macromanagement and, in this particular case, it meant that the extent of required devaluation was much less than what is often suggested for countries characterised by labour militancy.

Table 11.3 presents the percentage contributions of absorption reductions, switching and growth of traded sector to the cumulative changes in resource balances of the East Asian NIEs in the 1970s and the 1980s. The contributions of absorption reduction is further decomposed into policy-induced reduction and autonomous (self-correcting) components. As explained earlier, the self-correcting reduction in absorption works via reduction in income due to terms of trade loss and the decline in economic activities. Likewise, the switching effect is decomposed into expenditure and resource switching components. As can be seen from the table, while the East Asian NIEs were generally successful in restoring positive resource balance, with the exception of Korea, they were less successful in increasing the share of the traded sector. This indicates that despite

Table 11.3 Sources of adjustment in resource balance

Percentage attributable to	Hong Kong[a]		Korea		Singapore		Taiwan	
	1974–8	1980–6	1974–8	1980–8	1974–8	1980–8	1974–8	1980–8
Absorption reduction	−146.99	−150.26	−399.0	−177.39	−20.93	−111.18	−216.82	−134.15
Autonomous	−301.85	−275.23	−157.3	−259.67	–	–	−230.20	−72.33
Policy-induced	154.86	124.97	131.3	82.28	–	–	13.38	−61.83
Switching	−104.96	85.29	−25.1	51.36	68.68	80.89	49.94	18.71
Expenditure	−298.70	122.88	−39.1	49.09	72.87	85.85	51.65	30.27
Output	193.74	−37.58	14.0	2.27	−4.19	−4.96	−1.71	−11.56
Growth of traded sector	151.94	164.97	324.1	226.03	52.26	130.28	266.88	215.43
Total	−100.00	100.00	−100.00	100.00	100.00	100.00	100.00	100.00

Sources: Asian Development Bank (various issues); World Bank, World Tables, 1987.
Note: a Hong Kong exports and imports of goods and services.

the growth of their traded sector – which was the main contributing factor to the improvement of resource balances – it lagged behind the non-traded sector. The general perception is that, given the flexibility of relative prices in the East Asian NIEs, there is considerable scope for switching production from the non-tradable to the tradable sector (Garnaut, op. cit.: 9–10). Thus, the decomposition exercise reveals contrary results. The autonomous decline in absorption did not occur in any of these countries. The decline in terms of trade was perhaps perceived to be temporary by economic agents and the optimism was supported by continued growth of the economy (though at a subdued rate). The restrictive macro-economic policies were successful in reducing domestic absorption, but they were not enough to offset the negative impact of autonomous growth of demand. The positive impact of expenditure switching was more than enough to offset the negative effect of the failure to shift resources away from the non-traded sector.

ADJUSTMENT EXPERIENCE OF HONG KONG

Among the East Asian NIEs, only Hong Kong relies mostly on the automatic adjustment mechanism of the market. From the evidence, though, it seems that the self-equilibrating mechanism did not work in Hong Kong. Unemployment rose from 4.4 per cent in 1971 to 9.0 per cent in 1975 and the inflation rate dropped from 14.2 per cent in 1973 to 4.0 per cent in 1975. Table 11.3 shows that the autonomous adjustment did not occur in response to either the first or the second external shock. On both occasions, reductions in domestic absorption were achieved by policy actions.

Due to the policy-induced reduction in domestic demand, capital expenditure as a percentage of total government expenditure fell from 61.3 per cent in 1973 to 42.5 per cent in 1975. There were also de facto policy-induced effects. It was noted in the previous chapter on macromanagement that the money supply mechanism in Hong Kong was changed in 1972 and it was made dependent on domestic activities. As domestic activities fell due to the first oil price shock, the real money supply fell by 6.7 per cent. This had a contractionary effect on domestic demand.

Apparently the self-correcting adjustment mechanism also failed to achieve the required amount of switching, especially in response to the first external shock of the early 1970s (see Table 11.4 for year-to-year adjustments). The pattern of domestic expenditure favoured tradable goods and offset the positive contribution of output switching. The shift of the production structure towards tradables and the growth in the traded sector were not enough to prevent the deterioration of the real resource balance in the 1970s.

Hong Kong's real resource balance did improve in the 1980s. Similar to the 1970s, the policy-induced reduction in domestic absorption and growth of the traded goods sector contributed positively. However, this time, switching had an overall positive impact. The large positive expenditure switching was probably due to the depreciation of Hong Kong dollar that followed the depreciation of

Table 11.4 Hong Kong: adjustment decomposition (in constant 1980 prices) (% distribution)

	Absorption effect				Switching effect				Total change in resources balance
	Total	Terms of trade effects[a] on income and expenditure	Output effect of income and expenditure	Policy-induced effect	Total	Expenditure switching	Output switching	Growth of traded goods effect	
1972	−24.7	−101.6	−36.0	112.8	86.3	75.1	11.2	38.4	100.00
1973	−188.6	−679.5	−190.0	680.9	14.4	−148.9	163.2	274.2	100.00
1974	1.4	−130.7	−8.1	140.3	87.1	96.2	−9.1	11.5	−100.00
1975	−7.9	−60.2	−0.4	52.9	−93.2	−142.8	49.5	−1.1	−100.00
1976	−34.2	−74.2	43.1	83.1	74.0	−218.6	292.6	60.2	100.00
1977	−106.6	−115.2	−81.7	90.3	−107.5	−87.4	−20.1	−114.1	−100.00
1978	−56.9	−2.9	−34.6	−19.5	−84.2	−80.8	−3.3	41.1	−100.00
1979	−1,632.0	−344.9	−1,632.6	345.5	1.9	−214.3	216.2	1,530.1	−100.00
1980	−103.9	0.0	−79.8	−24.1	−71.0	−42.2	−28.8	74.9	100.00
1981	−856.7	942.0	−923.9	1,009.2	185.3	403.7	−218.4	771.4	100.00
1982	−236.6	−658.7	−272.6	694.6	104.4	918.8	−814.3	232.2	100.00
1983	−35.5	1.9	−60.6	23.3	83.8	14.4	69.5	51.7	100.00
1984	−22.8	2.2	−45.9	21.0	78.7	57.2	21.5	44.1	100.00
1985	−17.5	−69.6	2.6	49.6	−79.5	160.3	−239.8	−3.1	−100.00
1986	90.2	−86.0	−106.1	101.9	68.8	41.8	27.0	121.5	100.00

Sources: As for Table 11.3.
Notes: a Terms of trade adjustment: changes in terms of trade from base year × exports of goods and services (in constant prices).

the US dollar after September 1985. To the extent it failed to shift resources towards the tradables sector, the long-run sustainability of this improvement remains in doubt.

The main source of adjustment, like other NIEs, was the growth of the traded sector during the 1970s and 1980s, even though it lagged behind the non-traded sector in the 1980s. Table 11.5 shows that the growth of exports contributed the most. More than 100 per cent of GDP growth was due to the growth of exports, except for 3 years when export demand fell either due to external shocks and recession in the industrial economies or to the loss of competitiveness through real appreciation. There was unprecedented appreciation of the US dollar in early 1985. Since the Hong Kong dollar was linked to the US dollar, it meant a serious loss of international competitiveness and exports registered a decline. The growth of import substitutes was primarily negative. This finding is consistent with previous studies (Naya et al., op. cit.). Given the small domestic market, there is a very little scope for import substitution.

ADJUSTMENT EXPERIENCE OF KOREA

Korea is unique in its adjustment to external shocks. It is characterised by a positive output shift towards traded sector. (See Table 11.6 for the contributions of various factors to the year-to-year changes in real resource balance.) Despite substantial losses in real resources, Korea did not experience any slowdown in the pace of development. It replaced the lost resources with foreign savings (borrowing). Rather than using foreign loans for maintaining the consumption level, it initiated an ambitious plan to restructure the economy towards heavy and chemical industries (see Chapter 6). According to Balassa (op. cit.: 24–5), these measures contributed to the rise in the share of investment in the GNE from 23 per cent in 1971–3 to 30 per cent in 1977–9.

Korea also took positive steps to encourage exports and switching by devaluing the won by 20 per cent towards the end of 1974 (Nam, op. cit.: 75). Devaluation contributed to positive output switching in the absence of real wage resistance. The growth of real wages in manufacturing fell from 14.1 per cent in 1973 to 2.8 per cent in 1975 while labour productivity grew from 8.3 per cent to 11 per cent during the same period (Park, 1983b: Table 5). However, output switching became negative since 1976 when the growth of real wages exceeded the growth of labour productivity. The switching policy was also supplemented by steps to enhance the supply elasticity of exports: it ensured that the expansion of exportables was not hindered due to the lack of needed imported raw materials and equipments. Bank credit was expanded by almost 50 per cent to help finance the needed imports (Park, ibid.: 303). The favoured status of the export sector for bank credit was extended to cover industries producing for the export sector.

Since the high rate of imports was maintained with the help of foreign borrowing during the 1970s, the cumulative real resource balance did not

Table 11.5 Hong Kong: sources of GDP growth (%)

	Real GDP growth	Total	Non-traded output	Exports	Import substitutes	Non-exported exportables
1972	11.00	100.00	84.2361	67.7287	48.5694	−100.5346
1973	12.70	100.00	79.9574	70.1669	14.1295	−64.2538
1974	2.20	100.00	97.2711	−154.6392	349.8025	−192.4344
1975	0.20	100.00	−481.0458	180.3922	−1,256.204	1,656.858
1976	17.10	100.00	16.1892	126.9846	−30.1332	−13.0406
1977	12.50	100.00	79.8434	25.8254	30.2427	−35.9115
1978	9.49	100.00	77.9919	105.8744	−90.1170	6.2508
1979	12.57	100.00	72.8265	123.8600	−43.4653	−53.2212
1980	10.87	100.00	85.1328	114.8523	−60.6175	−39.3676
1981	9,41	100.00	83.3333	129.1570	−33.7085	−78.7818
1982	3.02	100.00	156.8619	−46.1437	151.2465	−161.9648
1983	6.50	100.00	52.2714	185.9434	−55.6376	−82.5772
1984	9.48	100.00	67.2287	194.3394	−50.0686	−111.4994
1985	−0.11	100.00	−1,714.778	−4,952.217	5,798.142	968.8527
1986	11.89	100.00	74.4160	133.5685	−11.1574	−96.8271

Sources: As for Table 11.3.

Table 11.6   Korea: adjustment decomposition (in constant 1985 prices) (%)

	Absorption effect					Switching effect			
	Total	Terms of trade effects on income and expenditure	Output effect of income and expenditure	Policy-induced effect	Total	Expenditure switching	Output switching	Growth of traded goods effect	Total change in resources balance
1971	−241.5	−61.8	−211.2	31.6	−23.4	−6.5	−16.9	164.9	−100.00
1972	−4.5	42.3	−70.6	108.4	50.8	46.8	3.9	53.8	100.00
1973	1,683.9	−621.0	−1,901.0	838.0	182.8	86.2	96.6	1,601.1	100.00
1974	118.0	−19.9	−69.0	−29.1	−41.8	−60.8	19.0	59.8	−100.00
1975	−54.2	–	−126.7	72.5	53.8	42.6	11.3	100.3	100.00
1976	−306.2	−118.3	−393.7	205.7	68.9	7.2	61.8	337.4	100.00
1977	−841.8	−533.7	831.2	523.1	−8.4	84.0	−92.4	750.2	−100.00
1978	−154.1	−71.1	−104.6	21.6	−40.1	−28.4	−11.6	94.1	−100.00
1980	74.0	22.8	26.2	25.0	47.2	103.1	−55.9	−21.2	100.00
1981	−72.4	48.2	−125.6	4.9	63.1	−7.4	70.5	109.4	100.00
1982	−782.9	127.0	−857.3	−52.6	87.7	182.5	−94.8	795.2	100.00
1983	−209.9	26.8	−262.4	25.7	63.5	48.8	14.7	246.4	100.00
1984	−2,554.1	0.0	−2,615.7	61.5	77.2	−279.2	356.4	2,576.9	100.00
1985	−127.2	0.0	−172.78	45.5	56.2	78.2	−22.0	171.0	100.00
1986	−130.1	−54.2	−171.3	95.5	53.7	29.5	24.3	176.4	100.00
1987	−277.8	−144.8	−307.9	174.9	40.7	54.3	−13.7	337.1	100.00
1988	−936.2	−575.4	−930.1	569.4	−8.5	−51.2	42.8	1,044.6	100.00

Sources: As for Table 11.3.

improve. Korea's external debt more than doubled to $8.5 billion during 1974–5. The situation would have been worse had there been no policy-induced reduction in absorption. The dampening of the growth of consumption raised the savings ratio from 19 per cent of GDP in 1971–3 to 26 per cent in 1974–6. The major source of this saving came from the reduction in government budget deficit. With the exception of 1975, the current account of the government budget produced surpluses since 1973.

Korea's adjustment to the second oil price shock was distinctly different from the first. The growth-first strategy during the first oil crisis resulted in substantial price instability. The rate of inflation (in terms of GDP deflator) was more than 20 per cent during the period 1974–8. This prompted more attention being paid to inflation in the latter half of the 1970s. The change in policy response was also necessitated by persistent high interest rates and the diminished availability of external finance (Scitivosky, 1985; Park, 1983b, 1986). Therefore, the Korean government responded to the second oil price shock with much more restrictive policies. These included tight fiscal and monetary policies and readjustment of the investment programme in heavy and chemical industries. As part of tighter fiscal measures 15,000 public sector jobs were slashed between 1981 and 1984 and the rate of growth of government expenditure fell from 22 per cent in 1981 to zero in 1984 (Haggard and Moon, 1990: 221). The monetary policy was tightened by an upward adjustment of bank deposit and lending rates by 5–6 percentage points. To discourage the use of oil, it increased energy prices for end-users by 60 per cent. In order to discourage imports and encourage exports, the won was devalued by 20 per cent in January 1980 (Park, 1983b, 1986). The switching effect of devaluation was enhanced by a moderation of wages growth and by clamping down on real estate speculation. The growth of real wages in manufacturing declined from 18 per cent in 1978 to −1.6 per cent in 1981. During the same period, labour productivity grew between 12 and 15 per cent per annum (Park, 1983b: Table 5). The subsequent drop in real estate price encouraged resources to move away from the non-traded construction sector while expenditure on housing increased.

The policy package largely succeeded in achieving its objectives. The cumulative change in the real resource balance became positive. This improvement was brought about by positive contributions from policy-induced reduction in absorption, expenditure switching towards non-tradables, and output switching towards tradables and the growth in tradable goods. In fact, Korea appears to be the most successful of all. To the extent it succeeded in restructuring its economy in accordance with emerging comparative advantage, its long-term growth prospects have been enhanced.

The rise in investment in aggregate expenditure contributed to the acceleration of economic growth. As can be seen from Table 11.7, growth in both the traded and non-traded sectors contributed positively to the growth of real GDP during the 1970s as well as in the 1980s. However, as the economy was restructured, the share of exportables increased more than proportionately by the

Table 11.7 Korea: sources of GDP growth (%)

	Real GDP growth	Total	Non-traded output	Exports	Import substitutes	Non-exported exportables
1974	8.8	100.00	32	−8	29	47
1975	8.8	100.00	39	51	36	−26
1976	15.0	100.00	35	86	−38	17
1977	17.4	100.00	63	54	−9	−8
1978	11.3	100.00	55	61	−72	56
1980	−2.16	100.00	−63.7888	−118.9438	−54.0799	336.8125
1981	6.72	100.00	30.3916	72.0353	4.9282	−7.3551
1982	7.30	100.00	61.1983	21.1602	22.3401	−4.6986
1983	11.78	100.00	53.6950	54.8901	−0.7159	−7.8693
1984	9.41	100.00	49.9462	30.2536	7.9688	11.8313
1985	6.93	100.00	61.2288	22.7628	39.0932	−23.0848
1986	12.40	100.00	49.8054	72.8670	−14.5533	−8.1191
1987	12.04	100.00	57.0227	69.5867	−21.3991	−5.2102
1988	11.48	100.00	53.5763	45.8590	−4.3897	4.9544

Source: As for Table 11.3.

end of 1980s. Import substitutions also played a role, but to a lesser extent. In some years, there were, in fact, negative import substitutions. This was largely a result of continued appreciation of the real exchange rate due to high inflation.

ADJUSTMENT EXPERIENCE OF SINGAPORE

The decomposition of the absorption effect into autonomous and policy-induced components is not possible due to data limitations. However, Balassa (op. cit.: 28) noted that in 1974 and 1975, domestic policies added slightly to the adverse effects of external shocks in Singapore. The nature of adjustment to both external shocks in the early and late 1970s was primarily the same. Overall, the growth in domestic absorption added to the cumulative loss of real balances. The positive improvement came from the switching of expenditure toward the non-traded sector and the growth of the traded sector.

Singapore responded to the first oil price shock with depreciation of its dollar. The real exchange rate fell by 20 per cent between 1972 and 1974 (Balassa, ibid.: 28). Despite depreciation of the dollar, resources moved away from the traded sector and there were large negative contributions to changes in real balances in 1974 and 1975 (Table 11.8). This was predominantly a result of the government's policy of using infrastructure development in order to prevent unemployment from rising due to the external shock. That is, the government's expansionary policy negated the switching effect of devaluation. In addition to dampening the inflationary pressure, the government put a halt to its economic restructuring programme – initiated in 1972 and based on a high wages policy. The moderation of wages growth that followed enhanced the positive resource switching effect of devaluation. Thus, between 1976 and 1979 output switching contributed positively to the improvement in the real resource balance. However, it was not enough to offset the large negative impact of 1974 and 1975, and the cumulative contribution of output switching remained negative during 1974–8.

The concern for price stability led the government eventually to adopt tighter macroeconomic policies. After rising from 31.6 per cent in 1973, the share of capital expenditure in total government expenditure fell from 40.3 per cent in 1974 to 34.3 per cent in 1975. In line with contractionary government expenditure policy, the annual growth rate of the money supply fell from 21.4 per cent in 1975 to 10.3 per cent in 1977.

In 1979, the Government of Singapore resurrected its restructuring programme to accelerate the shifting of resources away from the non-tradable sector and, particularly, from the production of low-skill, labour-intensive products in which it was apparently losing its comparative advantage. Partly due to this, there was a large positive contribution of output switching to the improvement of real resource balance in 1979.

However, the instrument of high wage policy to achieve the restructuring of the economy seems to have back-fired. It increased Singapore's unit labour costs. In addition, Singapore let its dollar appreciate after 1980. These two events

204

Table 11.8 Singapore: adjustment decomposition (in constant 1985 prices) (% distribution)

	Absorption effect	Switching effect			Growth of trade goods effect	Total change in resources balance
		Total	Expenditure switching	Output switching		
1972	-163.5	137.1	135.6	11.5	126.4	100.00
1973	-0.2	70.1	63.3	6.8	30.1	100.00
1974	63.8	51.5	74.9	-23.3	-15.4	100.00
1975	7.1	68.9	102.0	-33.1	24.0	100.00
1976	-114.3	94.5	20.9	73.6	119.8	100.00
1977	-20.4	74.2	68.0	6.2	46.2	100.00
1978	-159.9	-60.3	-87.0	26.6	120.24	-100.00
1979	-401.1	-32.1	-174.4	142.2	333.3	-100.00
1980	-528.6	-18.0	15.1	-2.9	446.6	-100.00
1981	-199.4	89.0	101.4	-12.3	210.4	100.00
1982	-107.8	-61.8	41.4	-103.2	69.6	-100.00
1983	-203.2	98.5	229.6	-131.0	204.6	100.00
1984	-346.7	111.2	151.7	-40.5	335.5	100.00
1985	67.2	67.8	170.7	-122.9	-35.0	100.00
1986	11.8	74.6	32.4	42.2	13.6	100.00
1987	-95.2	71.5	-19.1	90.8	123.7	100.00
1988	-28.4	70.2	38.5	31.7	58.2	100.00

adversely affected Singapore's international competitiveness. Resources moved away from the traded sector. This movement was accelerated by the government's policy of encouraging the housing sector as part of its home-ownership programme. Between 1981 and 1984 investment in residential construction grew at an average annual rate of 47 per cent. In 1984, 63 per cent of total capital formation (29 per cent of GDP) was in construction, particularly in residential buildings (Ministry of Trade and Industry, 1986: 29–30). Thus, the overall macroeconomic policy setting was not in congruence with the restructuring programme. The impact of this incompatibility is reflected in the negative contributions of output switching to the changes in real resource balance during 1980–5.

The Government of Singapore was reasonably swift in recognising the problem and responded with substantial cuts in labour costs and depreciation of the dollar in 1986. It also adjusted the construction programmes of the Housing Development Board and Housing and Urban Development Corporation.

The improvement in Singapore's real resource balance came mainly from the growth of the traded sector, despite the apparent failure to increase its share in GDP. Being politically stable, Singapore remains attractive to foreign investment. The foreign direct investment was further motivated by various tax exemption schemes. Direct foreign investment constituted 17.3 per cent of total investment during 1977–85. Foreign investment remained concentrated in the traded sector, especially in exportables. The share of foreign-invested firms' exports from Singapore was estimated to be 92.9 per cent in 1980 (Haggard and Cheng, 1987b).

Due to data limitations it is not possible to identify the contributions of exportables and import substitutes to the growth of the traded sector. However, given the small domestic market, it is likely that import substitution did not take place. Other studies (e.g. Naya and James) show that it was the case. According to Balassa (op. it.: 29): '[i]mprovements in Singapore's competitive position were translated into rising export shares while negative import substitution continued.'

ADJUSTMENT EXPERIENCE OF TAIWAN

Taiwan's responses to the two oil price shocks were markedly different (Table 11.9). In the case of the first oil price shock, it took much more restrictive policies. Taiwan had expansionary monetary and fiscal policies in place in 1973 prior to the first oil price shock. However, the money supply growth rate fell from 49.4 per cent in 1973 to 7.0 per cent in 1974 and the share of capital expenditure in total government expenditure dropped back to the 1972 level (see Table 10.4b). It also raised discount rates from 8.5 per cent to 12 per cent during 1973–4 and restricted credit (Nam, op. cit.: 75; Scitovsky, op. cit.: 255). As a result, the policy-induced reduction in absorption contributed positively to improvements in real resource after 1975.

The contractionary monetary policy, however, did not deter investment in the

Table 11.9 Taiwan: adjustment decomposition (in constant 1986 prices) (% distribution)

	Absorption effect				Switching effect				
	Total	Terms of trade effects on income and expenditure	Output effect on income and expenditure	Policy-induced effect	Total	Expenditure switching	Output switching	Growth of traded goods effect	Total change in revenue balance
1972	-120.2	-106.3	-164.7	150.8	54.2	40.2	14.0	116.0	100.00
1973	-1,006.1	-599.3	-1,012.8	605.8	8.7	-13.9	22.6	1,097.4	100.00
1974	-50.4	-7.9	-6.3	-36.1	-56.5	-35.9	-20.6	6.9	-100.00
1975	-21.2	-11.0	-70.3	60.1	56.7	86.9	-30.2	64.5	100.00
1976	-132.2	5.8	-177.0	39.0	57.7	11.2	46.5	174.5	100.00
1977	-97.5	25.4	-137.5	14.5	52.2	52.5	-0.4	145.4	100.00
1978	100.0	36.1	-134.6	-1.5	48.2	33.8	14.3	151.7	100.00
1979	-122.7	40.2	-75.7	-87.2	-69.2	-53.9	-15.3	91.9	-100.00
1980	-292.6	361.3	-322.9	-331.0	40.9	5.1	35.8	351.7	100.00
1981	-34.4	105.3	-73.6	-66.1	53.0	47.1	5.9	81.4	100.00
1982	-30.7	148.9	-66.4	-113.1	51.6	78.2	-26.5	79.0	100.00
1983	-51.4	67.5	-82.4	-36.4	48.2	39.2	9.0	103.1	100.00
1984	-75.4	64.9	-100.0	-40.4	40.6	19.0	21.6	134.9	100.00
1985	-27.3	54.1	-55.5	-25.9	47.9	72.2	-24.2	79.3	100.00
1986	-29.1	0.0	-53.7	24.6	46.4	32.8	13.6	82.7	100.00
1987	-1,391.4	-321.2	-1,142.0	71.8	-521.4	-408.6	-112.8	2,012.8	100.00
1988	-86.8	-7.8	-43.7	-35.3	-85.2	-44.7	-40.5	72.0	-100.00

traded sector perhaps because of the introduction of enhanced investment incentives through amendments to the Statute for Encouragement of Investment. More importantly, interest rate and selective credit policies meant that investment did not suffer despite contractionary monetary policy. By raising the deposit rate, Taiwan managed to increase the supply of credit to some extent and greater control over the financial sector allowed credit to be allocated selectively to the traded sector. Balassa (op. cit.: 27) notes: '[t]he increased investment and improvements in its competitive position, in turn, contributed to increases in export shares and import substitution in Taiwan'.

As mentioned in the previous chapter, unlike Korea, Taiwan has always put price stability first. Thus, in order to curb inflation, which rose to more than 40 per cent in 1974, Taiwan let real exchange rate appreciate by nearly 23 per cent (Balassa, op. cit.). While this was successful in reducing inflation rate to less than 5 per cent in 1975, there were large negative output and expenditure switchings in 1974–5. The negative output switching was perhaps compounded as the growth of real wages exceeded productivity growth by about 4 percentage points during 1974–5 (Nam, op. cit.: Table 5). The positive output switching in the later years after the the new Taiwan dollar was allowed to depreciate was not enough to fully offset negative effects in the first 2 years of adjustment.

Unlike the deflationary response to the first oil price shock, the overall macroeconomic policy setting in the aftermath of the second oil price shock was expansionary. The growth rate of money supply grew from 7.0 per cent in 1979 to 19.8 per cent in 1980 and the ratio of money supply to GDP rose from 21.9 per cent in 1978 to 25.6 in 1981. At the same time 'Taiwan kept total investment up through an accelerated program[me] of infrastructure investment' (Scitovsky, op. cit.: 255). The share of capital expenditure in total government expenditure increased from 30.0 per cent in 1978 to 42.6 per cent in 1981. The expansionary macroeconomic policies were responsible for the policy-induced negative impact on the cumulative change in real resource balance in the 1980s.

Despite the failure to increase the share of the traded sector, like other East Asian NIEs, the improvement in real resource balance came primarily from the growth in tradable goods supply. The growth of exports, in particular, contributed positively to economic growth since 1975 even though it was slightly less than that of the non-traded sector (Table 11.10). The contribution of import substitution to economic growth varied from negative to positive. Positive import substitution took place in the early 1980s. As expected, import liberalisation in the latter half of the 1980s led to negative import substitutions.

THE POLITICAL ECONOMY OF ADJUSTMENT: SOME CONCLUDING REMARKS

There is no denying that the East Asian NIEs fared much better than most developing countries. They have shown remarkable resilience in the face of rising import costs and falling export demand. The success is clearly vindicated by the

Table 11.10   Taiwan: sources of GDP growth (%)

	Real GDP growth	Total	Non-traded output	Exports	Import substitutes	Non-exported exportables
1972	13.32	100.00	50.9091	75.4545	−17.7944	−8.5692
1973	12.82	100.00	53.3333	65.8333	−29.1880	10.0214
1974	1.4	100.00	191.6667	−258.3333	−372.5379	539.2024
1975	4.78	100.00	76.4706	11.7647	96.8440	−85.0783
1976	13.67	100.00	45.0980	88.8889	−24.4848	−5.5021
1977	10.22	100.00	55.3846	51.5385	18.2245	−25.1476
1978	13.55	100.00	51.0526	67.8947	−1.1172	−17.8302
1979	8.17	100.00	62.3077	33.8461	−45.6397	49.4859
1980	7.32	100.00	40.7936	50.7936	2.7874	−4.3748
1981	6.17	100.00	51.7544	65.7895	30.1663	−47.7102
1982	3.57	100.00	70.0000	27.1429	68.9399	−66.0827
1983	8.42	100.00	51.4620	90.0585	−10.2187	−31.3018
1984	10.62	100.00	47.8632	81.1966	−10.5051	−18.5547
1985	4.92	100.00	68.3333	25.8333	70.0335	−64.2002
1986	11.65	100.00	47.6510	120.4698	−31.0272	−37.0936
1987	12.33	100.00	56.8182	89.2045	−48.6134	2.5903
1988	7.36	100.00	80.0848	47.4576	−66.9387	39.3963

fact that their current accounts have been in surplus since the mid-1980s. However, there seems to be a resurgence of balance of payments deficits in Korea since 1990 which Park (1991c) attributes to political unrest.

The policy responses and the adjustment pattern of the East Asian NIEs were very similar. They all responded to external shocks with absorption reducing and switching (expenditure and resource) policies with varying degrees. The absorption reduction was achieved mainly through public sector savings and the East Asian NIEs were able to cut public expenditure reasonably quickly due to the relative weakness of organised interest groups. The selective credit policy and the control over the financial sector ensured that the absorption reduction did not reduce investment and hence retard growth. The main switching device, devaluation, was not met by significant real wage resistance due to the weakness of the labour movement. Thus, devaluation enhanced export expansions and import substitutions, which ultimately produced current account surpluses in the East Asian NIEs.

Having succeeded in overcoming adverse external shocks, soon they may have to think of how to adjust to success. The current account surplus in the East Asian NIEs (Korea excepted) may become chronic. The policy response to current account surplus should be the reverse – increase absorption and appreciate the exchange rate (Balassa and Williamson, 1987; Corden, op. cit.). In the wake of the current democratisation movement, it will be interesting to see whether there emerge strong distributional coalitions seeking to influence the allocation of higher level of government expenditure envisaged in increased absorption. More importantly, one must consider how the export sector is going to respond to the appreciation. Appreciation of the exchange rate will lower real profits in the tradable sector, and eventually in the economy as a whole (Corden, ibid.: 30). Having become accustomed to higher real profits, exporters might resist any significant real appreciation. On the other hand, the real wage will increase as a result of appreciation. The tax cuts and/or increased government expenditure on social infrastructure will mean even higher real wages (in terms of a higher 'social' wage). Therefore, the final outcome will depend on the relative strength of wage earners vis-à-vis profit earners. Thus, while the relative weakness of the labour movement aided the East Asian NIEs to cope with adverse external shocks, they may need an organised labour movement in adjusting to success and the current democratisation movement should not be seen with apprehension.

However, the potential distributional consequences of appreciation can be avoided in an 'innovation-driven' society where rapid technological progress continuously shifts the wage–profit frontier outward, thus enabling both labour and capital to enjoy more real wages and profits. Whether the East Asian NIEs can graduate to an innovation-driven stage of development depends on their commitment to in-house R&D – a theme expounded in Chapter 7 – and their progress in democratisation as democratic institutions offer a wider gate through which innovations have to pass – a point elaborated in Chapter 13.

APPENDIX: THE METHODOLOGY OF DECOMPOSING THE SOURCES OF ADJUSTMENT TO CHANGES IN RESOURCE BALANCE

The methodology of decomposition was developed by Jaspersen (1981) from the theoretical framework of Corden (1979) and Salter (1959).

The real domestic demand or absorption is defined as:

$$DD = C + I = GDP - XGS + MGS \qquad (1)$$

where: DD = domestic demand
C = consumption
I = investment
GDP = gross domestic product
XGS = exports of goods and services
MGS = imports of goods and services

It is assumed that GDP is divided into (tradables (GDT) and non-tradables (GDN). For this exercise tradables are defined to include agricultural, mining and manufacturing output, while non-traded goods consist of GDP less tradables.

For any two consecutive years, say $t-1$ and t, the real resource balance (RB) is:

$$RB_{t-1} = XGS_{t-1} - MGS_{t-1}$$
$$RB_t = XGS_t - MGS_t$$

Therefore, the change in RB in year t is:

$$\Delta RB_t = RB_t - RB_{t-1} \qquad . \qquad (2)$$

where a positive difference indicates an improvement in real resource balance and a negative difference shows a deterioration.

The contributions of absorption reduction and switching to the changes in resource balance are derived as described below.

Absorption effect

To begin with, it is assumed that output of tradables is held constant, so that exports are residual after domestic absorption of exportables and import substitutes. It is further assumed that output of non-tradables is domestic demand determined.

If $h = DD_t/DD_{t-1}$

then $DD_t = hDD_{t-1}$
$$= h(GDT_{t-1} + GDN_{t-1} - XGS_{t-1} + MGS_{t-1})$$
$$= hGDN_{t-1} + hMGS_{t-1} + h(GDT_{t-1} - XGS_{t-1}) \qquad (3)$$

where $(GDT_{t-1} - XGS_{t-1})$ is the previous year's domestic consumption of

211

traded goods. In the current year, if $h(GDT_{t-1} - XGS_{t-1})$ is consumed domestically, then the surplus of tradables available for current exports (XGS^*) is:

$$XGS^* = GDT_t - h(GDT_{t-1} - XGS_{t-1}) \tag{4}$$

By assumption, $GDT_t = GDT_{t-1}$. Therefore,

$$XGS^* = GDT_{t-1} - h(GDT_{t-1} - XGS_{t-1})$$

or, $h(GDT_{t-1} - XGS_{t-1}) = GDT_{t-1} - XGS_t^* \tag{5}$

Substituting (5) in (3), we obtain:

$$hDD_{t-1} = hGDN_{t-1} + GDT_{t-1} - XGS_t^* + hMGS_{t-1} \tag{6}$$

The resource balance in current year is:

$$RB_t = XGS_t - MGS_t$$

But in the current year only XGS_t^* is available for exports. Also, equation (3) implies that

$$MGS_t = hMGS_{t-1}$$

Therefore, $RB_t = XGS_t^* - hMGS_{t-1}$

The change in resource balance due to absorption effect is, then

$$\Delta RB_1 = RB_t - RB_{t-1}$$
$$= (h-1)(XGS_{t-1} - MGS_{t-1} - GDT_{t-1}) \tag{7}$$

When an economy suffers an external shock, say, due to the decline of terms of trade, there will be a self-correcting reduction in absorption as income is reduced. If the growth is affected, it will also have an effect on resource balance through changes in import demand. Therefore, the absorption effect is further decomposed into terms of trade and output effect as follows:

Let $\quad a = (GDP_t - GDP_{t-1})/GDP_{t-1} = k - 1$

where $\quad k = GDP_t/GDP_{t-1} \tag{8}$

Also let $\ b = TOTA_t/GDP_{t-1}$

and $\quad d = (TOTA_t + GDP_{t-1})/GDP_{t-1} = b + 1$

where $TOTA_t =$ terms of trade adjustment in year t, defined as
$TOTA_t = GDP_t^* - GDP_{t-1}$, where GDP_t^* is GDP_{t-1} adjusted for changes in terms of trade.
Therefore,

$$GDP_t^* = GDP_{t-1} + \Delta TOT(XGS_t)$$

Thus, $d = (GDP_{t-1} + \Delta TOT(XGS_t)/GDP_{t-1}$

Finally, we let $c = h - 1$

The changes in domestic demand as a result of changes in output and terms of trade adjustment under the general assumption of absorption effect are, respectively:

$$kDD_{t-1} = kGDN_{t-1} + GDT_{t-1} - XGS'_t + kMGS_{t-1} \tag{9}$$

and

$$dDD_{t-1} = dGDN_{t-1} + GDT_{t-1} - XGS'_t + dMGS_{t-1} \tag{10}$$

where XGS'_t and XGS'_t are the levels of exports (residuals) after domestic absorption of exportables. Equations (9) and (10) are obtained by the same procedure as equation (6).

The changes in resource balance due to output and terms of trade effects, respectively, are:

$$\Delta RB_{11} = a(XGS_{t-1} - MGS_{t-1} - GDT_{t-1}) \tag{11}$$

$$\Delta RB_{12} = b(XGS_{t-1} - MGS_{t-1} - GDT_{t-1}) \tag{12}$$

also by the same procedure used to obtain equation (7).

By implication, the residual absorption effect is policy induced. Therefore, the policy induced effect is:

$$\Delta RB_{13} = (c - a - b)(XGS_{t-1} - MGS_{t-1} - GDT_{t-1}) \tag{13}$$

Switching

The switching effect is decomposed into expenditure and output effect. The expenditure switching to non-tradables is estimated as:

$$\Delta RB_{21} = GDN_t - hGDN_{t-1} \tag{14}$$

By assumption, output in the non-traded sector is demand-determined. Therefore, any change in total demand will be reflected in the output of the non-traded sector. In equation (14), $hGDN_{t-1}$ is the expected expenditure on non-traded goods and GDN_t is the actual expenditure. Therefore, the difference is due to expenditure switching.

Output switching occurs when the composition of GDP shifts from non-traded to traded sector and is estimated as:

$$\Delta RB_{22}' = GDT_t - kGDT_{t-1} \tag{15}$$

where $kGDT_{t-1}$ is the expected tradable output, if the traded sector grew at the national average rate and GDT_t is the actual tradables output. Therefore, the difference measures the extent of output shift towards traded sector.

Growth of traded goods

Finally, allow for the growth of the economy. From the point of view of external balance what matters is the growth of traded sector. This is estimated as:

$$\Delta RB_3 = \Delta GDT_t$$
$$= GDT_t - GDT_{t-1}$$
$$= kGDT_{t-1} - GDT_{t-1} = (k-1)GDT_{t-1} \tag{16}$$

12

POVERTY, INEQUALITY AND
ECONOMIC DEVELOPMENT

Three critical dimensions of economic development are evident in Meier's (1985: 6) popular definition of development: it is 'a process whereby the per capita real income of a country increases over a long period of time – subject to the stipulation that the number below "an absolute poverty line" does not increase, and that the distribution of income does not become unequal'. Despite its popularity, this definition fails to offer a clear guideline in cases where growth in per capita income (or economic growth) is accompanied by a reduction in poverty but a simultaneous increase in inequality. Does such a case constitute development? In the light of this anomaly, the chapter adopts an 'absolute poverty approach', where the emphasis is on a sustained improvement in the living standards of the poor within the context of per capita income growth. This approach, unlike the one espoused by Meier, does not allow regressive movements in income inequality to dominate the poverty criterion. Applying this approach to the East Asian NIEs reveals the familiar story that these economies have truly experienced development in the sense that they have shown a sustained – and rapid – decrease in poverty within the context of rapid growth. Their record on income inequality is more mixed. Some of the countries have experienced episodic increases in inequality – as will be documented in greater detail at subsequent stages – although they still remain among the most egalitarian countries in the developing world.

Issues in poverty and inequality during the process of development form the substance of this chapter. It briefly examines conceptual issues and evidence from the East Asian NIEs. This sets the background for considering the various determinants of poverty and inequality during development. The analytical discussions are then used to find clues in understanding changes in income distribution in East Asia.

INEQUALITY AND POVERTY DURING THE PROCESS
OF DEVELOPMENT: SOME CONCEPTUAL ISSUES
AND EVIDENCE

Any measure of income inequality is a scalar representation of the differences of income across n units in a given population. For convenience, it is assumed that the n units – persons, families, households or other suitable criteria – are comparable in all respects and that the information on incomes is a good proxy of the well-being of each unit. All known measures of inequality have in common a notional state of complete equality – everybody has the same income – and a correspondingly notional state of complete inequality – one person/income unit has all the income. Within these bounds, what constitutes an 'appropriate' depiction of the level of inequality depends upon the extent to which the measures used satisfy a set of axioms (Sen, 1973; Cowell, 1977).

The empirical analysis in this chapter utilises two inequality measures – the Gini ratio and the L-index – that satisfy the acceptable criteria that any measure should have. The L-index is unbounded above and takes the minimum value of zero. It has the useful property of being additively decomposable.

Consider now the issue of poverty measurement. The first step in the analysis of poverty is to compute a poverty line based on some notion of 'minimum need' which truncates the overall distribution such that anyone whose income is below the poverty line is counted as poor. Once having decided on a poverty line, the next task is to provide a single-valued statistic (or statistics) that would adequately reflect the following dimensions of poverty:

1   the absolute number (or size) of the poor;
2   the overall extent of the poverty gap (i.e. the extent to which the average income of the poor falls below the poverty line);
3   interpersonal differences in the poverty gap or inequality among the poor.

One of the most widely used measures – known as the head count ratio – examines the cumulative proportion of households or individuals lying below the poverty line. A more composite measure that takes account of absolute number (size) of the poor, the overall poverty gap and inequality among the poor – such as the Sen Index (Sen, 1976) – is much more robust. The empirical analysis unfortunately relies exclusively on the head count ratio. Data constraints precluded the use of such composite measures as the Sen Index. In particular, reliable estimates of Sen-type indices require detailed information on the lower tail of the income distribution. Islam (1983) has shown that when income distribution data are not sufficiently disaggregated, the head count ratio and the Sen Index have a near-perfect correlation. These arguments can be used to justify the extensive reliance on the head count ratio, despite its theoretical inadequacy.

Assuming that one has overcome the task of measuring inequality and poverty in a reasonably reliable manner, one has to face the equally formidable task of making normative judgements on changes in income distribution during development. One way to proceed is to adopt an explicit social welfare function where poverty, inequality and average income are arguments in the function such that welfare declines with a rise in poverty and inequality and increases with income.

Within this approach, one could take the extreme egalitarian view that social welfare can only be regarded as enhanced if the increase in per capita GDP and poverty reduction is accompanied by a reduction in inequality. The chapter,

Table 12.1   Gini coefficients for household income distribution, 1961–85

Year	Korea	Taiwan	Singapore	Hong Kong
1961		0.440		
1963				0.462
1964		0.360		
1965	0.344			
1966		0.358	0.498	0.467
1968		0.362		
1970	0.332	0.321		
1971				0.409
1972		0.318		
1974		0.319		0.398
1975			0.448	
1976	0.391	0.307		0.409
1977				
1978		0.306		
1979			0.424	0.373
1980		0.303		
1981			0.443	0.453
1982	0.357	0.308	0.465	
1983				
1984		0.312	0.474	
1985		0.317		

Source: Rao (1988: 28).

however, takes a more eclectic view. The 'first-best' position is one where all the arguments in the social welfare function move in the desired direction. In cases where the movements in poverty and inequality are in conflict (poverty falls, inequality rises), these are still regarded as welfare-improving and it is the 'absolute poverty' approach which is adopted in this chapter.

Two patterns seem to stand out from the data provided in Table 12.1. First, inequality – measured by the Gini ratio – is noticeably higher in the city states of Hong Kong and Singapore (0.48 in recent years) compared with South Korea and Taiwan (0.32–0.36 in recent years). Second, inequality seems to have fallen in all the economies during their phases of rapid growth. More recent trends seem to represent a mixed picture. Inequality seems to have increased between 1970 and 1980 in Korea, with a hint of a decline between 1980 and 1982. In Taiwan, inequality seems to have remained roughly constant, after registering a perceptible fall between 1964 and 1970. In Singapore, inequality seems to have risen sharply between 1979 and 1984, while a similar trend is observed in Hong Kong between 1976 and 1981.

Table 12.2 Trends in poverty incidence (% of households in poverty)

Country	Year	Poverty incidence total (%)	Remarks on poverty line
Hong Kong	1963–4	35.6	Poverty lines vary according to household size. For a four member household the
	1973–4	3.5	poverty line was HK$580 per month in January 1974
Korea	1965	40.9	Absolute poverty line was 121.000 won per month in 1981 prices
	1976	14.8	
	1982	7.7	
Singapore	1953–4	19.2	Poverty line in 1982–3 was S$60 per person per month
	1972–3	7.0	
	1977–8	1.5	
	1982–3	0.3	
Taiwan	1975	5.0	Estimates from World Bank (1979)

Source: Rao (1988: 38).

One can now turn to the evidence on poverty and inequality in the economies under review. Table 12.2 presents the trends in poverty in the East Asian NIEs. It reveals that there has been a large fall in aggregate poverty in these countries under review. Thus, in Korea, the proportion in poverty fell from 40.9 per cent in 1965 to 7.7 per cent in 1982. The corresponding figures in Singapore are: 19 per cent in 1953–4 to a negligible 0.3 per cent in 1982–3; in Hong Kong, 35.6 per cent in 1963–4 to 3.5 per cent in 1973–4; and in Taiwan, the head count ratio was a modest 5.0 per cent in 1975.

The task now is to explain the above trends in poverty and inequality in the East Asian NIEs. The following section attempts to do so in terms of a series of hypotheses.

STRUCTURAL DETERMINANTS OF INEQUALITY AND POVERTY DURING DEVELOPMENT

It would be useful to commence the discussion in this section by making a distinction between the structural determinants of poverty and inequality and policy-induced effects on these variables. The distinction is, of course, artificial, given that structure and policy interact concurrently and continuously. Neverthe-less, the development literature typically takes as its point of reference the hypothesis, first developed by Kuznets (1955), that there are inevitable trends in income distribution during the course of development which occur independently of policy interventions. At the same time, the development literature in the 1970s was replete with attempts to identify appropriate policy measures to reduce poverty and to bring about a more equal distribution of income (Ahluwalia et al., 1974; Streeten et al., 1981). In the 1980s, this preoccupation has changed in form but not in substance. The current concern – which received insufficient attention in the 1970s – is with the impact of macroeconomic stabilisation measures and World Bank/IMF-led structural adjustment programmes on the poor (World Bank, 1990; Heller, 1988; Demery and Addison, 1987). Thus, the distinc-tion between structure and policy, which will be consistently maintained in this chapter, is meant to capture cross-currents in the development literature.

Kuznets' U-shaped hypothesis

As noted earlier, in a classic paper, Kuznets (op. cit.) noted a systematic link between inequality and development. He hypothesised a secular trend in inequality for nations undergoing development – with an increase in inequality in the early stages followed by a decrease in the later stages. Although Kuznets adopted a time-series perspective, the revival of interest in the U-shaped hypothesis in the development literature in the 1970s has been dominated by a cross-section view and analysis. Practitioners working with cross-country data have generally tended to support the U-shaped hypothesis (Adelman and Morris, 1973; Paukert, 1973; Ahluwalia, 1976; Lydall, 1977; Cromwell, 1977; Ahluwalia et al., 1979). This has prompted at least one practitioner to note that the U-shaped hypothesis has 'acquired the force of economic law' (Robinson, 1976).

The U-shaped hypothesis, however, has its critics (Beckerman, 1977; E. Lee, 1977; Anand and Kanbur, 1981). The critique highlights a number of points: the hypothesis, as resurrected in the development literature, is based on cross-country data which are not comparable; the database encompasses countries with different policy and political environments, and hence is not relevant to an examination of a hypothesis pertaining to the 'natural' history of the develop-ment/growth process; cross-section data cannot be used to make time-series inferences; and finally, the hypothesis is highly sensitive to the data set and the functional form used (Anand and Kanbur, op. cit.).

The evidence on the U-shaped hypothesis is thus surrounded by controversy. One way of coping with the controversy is to consider the theoretical foun-dations of the U-shaped hypothesis and identify reasons for believing that the development process is characterised by inexorable forces generating short-run increases in inequality. Kuznets tried to explain the inequality–development relationship in terms of what Anand and Kanbur (op. cit.) have called the 'inter-

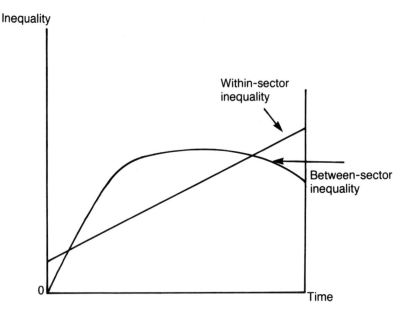

Figure 12.1 Trends in inequality

sectoral shifts theory' (ISST) which focuses on a progressive shift of the population from rural-based agricultural activities to urban-based industrial activities.

A formalisation of the Kuznets model can be offered in an intuitively
appealing way by making use of decomposable inequality indices. In the case of
indices such as the L-index, overall inequality can be written as the weighted sum
of the inequality values of the subgroups of the population plus a component
arising from differences arising from subgroup mean incomes.

Following Anand and Kanbur (op. cit.: 19–22), the predictions on inequality
can be derived in the following way. First, the within-group component of
inequality (Iw) increases monotonically as the weight of the more unequal sector
(Iu) increases through a progressive population shift. Second, the behaviour of
the between-group component (Ib) is non-monotonic, rising at first and
decreasing subsequently. This is because at the start of the development process
there is no between-group inequality given that everybody is in the low-income
rural sector. Similarly, at the end of the development process, there is no
between-group inequality, given that everybody is in the high-income urban
sector. From this the inference can be made that there must be a turning point in
between sector inequality as the intersectoral population transfer takes place.

The intertemporal behaviour of both the between-sector and within-sector
inequality components of inequality are summarised in Figure 12.1. As is obvious
from this diagram, the effect on aggregate inequality of these changes is ambiguous. If the fall in between-sector inequality dominates the monotonic rise in
intrasector inequality, the aggregate inequality will eventually fall – as predicted

by Kuznets; otherwise it may not. The upshot of this detailed analysis is that, even in the case of an extremely primitive version of ISST (typified by the artificial assumption of constancy in sectoral income distribution), the U-shaped behaviour of inequality during development is a probable outcome, but not the only possible outcome.

Poverty under the Kuznets process: the impact of labour market segmentation

The U-shaped hypothesis focuses exclusively on inequality. This is an unfortunate omission, given that poverty is the fundamental aspect of development. However, one can easily draw inference on poverty from the simple version of ISST. It may be recalled that the ISST contains an extremely simple view of the intersectoral migration process: the typical migrant in the low-income rural sector transfers to a typical high-income (at least higher than the average rural income) urban occupation. On the plausible assumption that the prevailing poverty line lies below the average urban income level, the clear inference is that intersectoral migration worsens inequality but monotonically decreases poverty. The normative implications of the U-shaped hypothesis are thus rather favourable: the benefits of development will 'trickle down' to the poor without the need for active policy intervention.

Those who maintain that there is evidence of both worsening poverty and inequality in the developing world argue, however, that the 'ugly facts' do not fit the predictions of 'fancy models' (Griffin and Khan, 1978; Griffin and Ghose, 1979). Anand and Kanbur (1984) have tried to amend the U-shaped hypothesis in order to cope with the alleged ugly fact of growing poverty during the course of development. They want to explore whether absolute poverty exhibits a U-shaped time-path under the Kuznets process. Their amendment entails a depiction of a Todaro-type migration process (Todaro, 1969; Harris and Todaro, 1970) where the urban labour market is split into a low-income informal sector and a high-income formal sector. In fact, the strong assumption is made that the average income in the informal sector is lower than the average income in the rural sector.

The significance of the Anand–Kanbur contribution lies in making explicit the implications of the migration process for a general class of poverty indices. Following Fields (1979), they consider two types of sectoral changes: a 'modern sector enlargement effect' (entailing a progressive increase in the size of the formal sector), and a 'modern sector enrichment effect' (entailing a rise in the formal sector wage, but where the size of the formal sector remains constant). They show that in the case of 'modern sector enlargement', the head count ratio monotonically declines or improves, depending upon the configuration of relevant parameters (the probability of formal sector employment, the sectoral poverty indices). The Sen Index, however, at first rises and then falls – thus depicting a U-shaped time-path. In the case of 'modern sector enrichment', both the head count ratio and the Sen Index monotonically worsen. This is because the 'modern sector enrichment' by definition increases the average income in the formal sector without a corresponding increase in formal sector employment opportunities. Thus the urban rich (located in the formal sector) get richer while the urban poor (located in the informal sector) get poorer. In other words, there is a corresponding increase in both urban inequality and urban poverty.

The amendment made to the Kuznets model by Anand and Kanbur thus provides ample ammunition to those who maintain that the development process is characteristically immiserising – in both an absolute and a relative sense. Thus, it necessitates active government intervention to deal with the paradoxes of development. Despite its greater realism compared with first-generation Kuznets-type models, the Anand–Kanbur proposition is sensitive to an unproven assumption – imperfections in the urban labour market. It is this assumption – common to all Todaro-type migration models – which generates the notion of a formal sector/informal sector dichotomy or a segmented labour market. What needs to be established is the extent to which segmented urban labour markets are endemic structural features of developing economies and the extent to which they are the product of past and continuous policy interventions with respect to product and factor markets. If it is primarily the latter, then a change in the overall policy environment will eliminate or reduce the segmentation in the urban labour market and thus neutralise the stark implications of the Anand–Kanbur model. The subsequent analysis of the income distribution experiences of East Asia seems to substantiate the above observations.

THE U-SHAPED HYPOTHESIS, LABOUR MARKET SEGMENTATION AND INCOME DISTRIBUTION IN EAST ASIAN NIEs

Consider first the naive version of the Kuznets model which predicts a U-shaped trend in income distribution. Although the trends in poverty (Table 12.2) are compatible with the U-shaped hypothesis, it is quite obvious that the income inequality trends in East Asia, depicted in Table 12.1, do not follow a phase of growing inequality followed by a phase of declining inequality. Contrary to the prediction of the U-shaped hypothesis, the observed pattern of income inequality in these countries, in fact, seems to be the reverse – a phase of falling inequality juxtaposed with a phase of growing inequality, with the possible exception of Taiwan.

Another way of examining the validity of the U-shaped hypothesis is to consider sectoral income distributions, in terms of both intersectoral inequality and intrasectoral inequality. The sectoral analysis is usually couched in terms of the rural–urban divide, so that it is not readily applicable to the city states of Hong Kong and Singapore. The sectoral analysis can be amended for these particular cases by taking into account the pattern of income distribution within and between the manufacturing and service sectors. This reflects the view that

Table 12.3 Trends in rural–urban household income differentials and intrasectoral Gini coefficients (Korea, 1965–83)

Year	Rural–urban income disparity ratio (1975 = 100)	Gini ratio	
		Urban	Rural
1965	108.5	0.416	0.344
1966	87.7		
1967	66.9		
1968	69.4		
1969	71.1		
1970	74.7	0.346	0.332
1971	88.2		
1972	91.6		
1973	91.4		
1974	103.1		
1975	100.0		
1976	92.7	0.412	0.391
1977	88.6		
1978	75.1		
1979	67.3		
1980	69.0	0.405	0.389
1981	73.8		
1982	76.2	0.371	0.357
1983	72.6		

Source: Kim (1986: 75).

economic development in the two city states has entailed a reallocation of labour from the low-productivity service sector to both high-productivity service and manufacturing sectors.

Consider first the case of Korea. Relevant information is provided in Table 12.3. Recall that in the original version of the U-shaped hypothesis as propounded by Kuznets, the intersectoral inequality component first rises and then falls during the course of development. As can be seen, no such trend is evident. Intersectoral inequality, as measured by the rural–urban differential, falls between 1965 and 1968, rises between 1969 to 1973, falls yet again from 1975 to 1979 and fluctuates thereafter. In other words, the short-run movements are too erratic to be consistent with the simple version of the U-shaped hypothesis.

The Kuznets model also suggested that urban inequality would be greater than rural inequality and that intrasectoral inequality would remain constant. However, overall inequality would still increase because of the progressively larger weight of the unequal urban sector in the overall economy. As can be seen from Table 12.3, urban inequality in South Korea is indeed greater than rural

Table 12.4 Trends in intrasectoral Gini coefficients (Taiwan, 1964–72)

Year	Gini ratio	
	Rural	Urban
1964	0.34	—
1966	0.36	0.36
1968	0.32	0.37
1970	0.32	0.31
1972	0.32	0.30

Source: Kuo (1975: 94–6) as reported in Rao (1988: 32).
Notes: Rural = farm households.
　　　　Urban = non-farm households.

inequality (the urban sector Gini ratio in 1965, for example, was 0.42 compared with 0.28 in the rural sector). However, the crucial assumption of constant intra-sectoral inequality is not valid. Both urban and rural inequality fell between 1965 and 1970; they rose equally significantly between 1970 and 1976. The trend between 1976 and 1982 is more mixed. Urban inequality fell consistently over that period, while rural inequality continued to rise significantly up to 1980 before registering a decline.

The Taiwanese experience is depicted in Table 12.4. The striking feature is the insignificant difference between rural and urban inequality (proxied by income distribution of farm and non-farm households). There is 1 year (1968) in which urban inequality is perceptibly higher than rural inequality. On the other hand, after registering a decline between 1964 and 1968, sectoral income distributions have been more stable compared with Korea.

The Hong Kong case is shown in Table 12.5 for only one year. While time-trends clearly cannot be inferred from the table, a Kuznets-type sectoral analysis is also difficult to apply. It was noted that a modified sectoral approach to the

Table 12.5 Mean income and Gini coefficient by sector (Hong Kong)

Sector	Mean income ($)	Gini ratio
Manufacturing	875	0.36
Utilities	1381	0.53
Construction	899	0.39
Trade	1236	0.46
Transport	1068	0.41
Finance	2435	0.57
Community, social and personal services	1482	0.50

Source: Chia (1975: 607–15) as reported in Rao (1988: 29).

Table 12.6   Trends in intrasectoral Gini coefficients (Singapore, 1966–75)

Sector	Gini ratio		Mean real income rank[a] (1976)
	1966	*1975*	
Manufacturing	0.48	0.45	4
Commerce	0.50	0.46	3
Transport	0.40	0.34	2
Personal and professional services	0.52	0.47	1

Source: Rao and Ramakrishnan (1980: 45–59).
Note: a   1 = highest, 4 = lowest.

East Asian city states could be applied in terms of a manufacturing service sector distinction. It was implied that manufacturing inequality would be higher. The data suggest the reverse. The manufacturing Gini of 0.36 is noticeably lower than the diverse service sector, where the Gini ratio varies from 0.39 (construction) to 0.57 (finance and insurance). More importantly, manufacturing is the lowest-income sector in the economy. This suggests that it would be incorrect to characterise economic development in Hong Kong as a process of labour reallocation from the low-productivity service sector to the high-productivity manufacturing sector. It would be more appropriate to depict the Hong Kong case as one of unemployed members of the workforce moving into manufacturing employment. Despite its low-income status, manufacturing employment was still able to provide an adequate income to alleviate poverty.

The Singapore experience is depicted in Tables 12.6–12.8. Once again, manufacturing is not the most unequal sector. There are several service-oriented industries (transport and communication) in which the Gini ratio is conspicuously higher. Sectoral income distributions have not remained constant – they have fallen across all sectors between 1966 and 1975. As shown in Table 12.6 manufacturing was in fact among the lowest paid sectors as recorded in 1976. Thus, as with Hong Kong, the manufacturing sector made a dent on poverty and inequality by providing jobs to previously unemployed people at a tolerable wage

Table 12.7   Earnings disparity ratios for selected industries (Singapore, 1973–84)

Sector	*1973*	*1976*	*1979*	*1982*	*1984*
Utilities/manufacturing	1.6	2.1	2.3	2.9	2.5
Transport/manufacturing	1.7	1.8	2.0	2.4	2.6
Finance/manufacturing	2.2	2.0	2.1	1.8	1.9

Source: Islam and Kirkpatrick (1986b: 97).

225

Table 12.8 Inequality by sector: decomposition estimates (Singapore)

| Year | Intersectoral inequality | | Intrasectoral inequality | |
	L-index	Contributon to aggregate inequality (%)	L-index	Contributon to aggregate inequality (%)
1973	0.02	4.9	0.39	95.1
1976	0.01	2.9	0.33	97.1
1979	0.02	6.3	0.30	93.7
1980	0.01	3.2	0.30	96.8
1981	0.01	3.2	0.30	96.8
1982	0.01	2.7	0.37	97.3
1983	0.01	2.4	0.42	97.6

Source: Islam and Kirkpatrick (1986b: 95).

which was nevertheless well below the ones prevailing in other sectors of the economy. Table 12.7 shows some trends in intersectoral inequality by showing some sectoral earnings disparity ratios for selected industries using the manufacturing sector as a base. There is no clear trend. Some indicators show an increase, others show a decline.

A more direct evaluation of the Kuznets model can be shown by sectoral decomposition analysis, using a decomposable index (the L-index). Some illustrative examples are provided for Singapore in Table 12.8. As can be seen for the period 1973–83, intersectoral inequality contributed to only between 4.9 per cent and 2.4 per cent of inequality. The bulk of the contribution to total inequality was thus provided by intrasectoral inequality. These estimates have implications for the validity of the Kuznets model. Recall that the Kuznets model, when couched in terms of a decomposition framework, suggests that the fall in intersectoral inequality will have to be greater than the rise in intrasectoral inequality to generate a fall in overall inequality in the later stages of development. This central assumption cannot be supported by the decomposition estimates provided here.

The previous discussion has shown that if the original Kuznets model is adapted by incorporating the assumption of a segmented urban labour market, then it can generate the stark prediction of a monotonic increase in urban inequality and urban poverty as a sustained population transfer takes place between urban and rural areas. This central prediction is clearly not applicable to the East Asian economies. As the sectoral trends in poverty shown in Table 12.9 confirm, there has been a sustained fall in both rural and urban poverty. Urban inequality has increased in some cases, but these are of an episodic rather than a sustained nature. Does it mean that the segmented labour market model is not applicable to East Asia? The structure of the labour market is the subject of Chapter 9, but it is sufficient to note here that a particular form of segmentation

Table 12.9 Trends in intrasectoral (rural and urban) poverty (Korea, 1965–82)

Year	Rural poverty (%)	Urban poverty (%)
1965	35.8	54.9
1976	11.7	18.1
1982	8.2	7.0

Source: Rao (1988: 38).

does prevail in some East Asian economies. However, the nature of the segmentation is that it does not conform to the stark scenarios of the modified Kuznets model.

The labour markets of the city states of East Asia have been affected by the influx of migrants and government-controlled inflow of foreign workers. The case of refugees is relevant to Hong Kong, that of controlled short-term immigration to Singapore. The nature of labour market segmentation reflects these features. To appreciate this point, consider the case of refugees. Lin (1985) has noted that in Hong Kong the deterioration of overall inequality – but not poverty – during 1976–81 coincided with a sudden influx of over 300,000 refugees. Given their uncertain residential status and lack of familiarity and experience in the Hong Kong labour market, one would expect the majority of such refugees to seek and find employment in the low-income segment of the labour market. This would stretch the lower tail of the income distribution and contribute to worsening inequality. Yet, the available data do not show any intensification of poverty. A plausible reason could be that the wages earned by recently arrived migrants are still above their pre-migration income levels. This is contrary to the segmented labour market model of Anand and Kanbur (op. cit.) where the equilibrium earnings of migrants in the low-income segment of the urban labour market are lower than their pre-migration earnings.

Consider now the case of Singapore. As discussed in a previous chapter, the Singapore government – in the late 1970s and 1980s – inducted foreign workers into selected industries and occupations to meet a domestic labour shortage. This, as Kapur (1983) has noted, has the effect of effectively segmenting the labour market: foreign workers, given their particular status, cannot move freely between sectors and occupations in response to ex-ante wage differentials. Islam and Kirkpatrick (1986a, b) have argued that such a form of segmentation has contributed to worsening inequality between 1979 and 1983. The broad mechanism generating such an outcome may be depicted as follows. According to Singaporean policy makers, the labour market was characterised by excess demand in certain low-skilled occupations (e.g. construction) as well as excess demand for skilled professionals. One would expect that the supply price of foreign workers moving into low-skilled occupations would be lower than the comparable supply price of Singaporean workers, given the evidence that foreign

227

workers were largely recruited from poorer Asian economies. On the other hand, the attempt to recruit skilled professionals from abroad would have entailed setting wages in line with, if not in excess of, those prevailing in comparable occupations in the industrialised countries. These developments led to a predictable 'stretching' of the wage structure at both the upper and lower end of the occupational scale.

As Islam and Kirkpatrick (op. cit.) are careful to emphasise, and as shown in this chapter, this particular form of segmentation has not entailed an intensification of poverty as envisaged by Anand and Kanbur (op. cit.). Once again, the reason lies in the fact that foreign workers in the low-income segment of the Singaporean labour market still earned in excess of their pre-migration income levels. More importantly, such migrants were carefully selected to move into pre-arranged employment. This is unlike a Todaro-type world where risk-neutral migrants flock to the cities in search of uncertain jobs.

Apart from the segmentation of the labour market caused by the immigration of workers from foreign countries, are there any other forms of segmentation in East Asia which have distributional implications? A useful way of examining this issue is to look at the large firm/small firm dichotomy. Wages and working conditions may be different between the two sectors due to factors that lie beyond differences in worker characteristics. In other words, the higher wages of workers in large firms may not just be due to the higher human capital endowments of such workers. Deyo (1989) has assembled evidence which shows that the average firm size is higher in South Korea and Singapore, and significantly lower in Hong Kong and Taiwan. Comparable data on trends in wage differentials by firm size are not available. Some information exists in the case of South Korea, but the evidence is debatable. Amsden (1989) claims that segmentation by firm size is significant and seems to be increasing. Park (1987) claims that substantial wage premiums due to the degree of concentration in an industry exist in Korea even after adjusting for the quality of labour and/or compensating factors. On the other hand, Lansbury and Zappala (1990) have assembled evidence which shows that wage increases actually fall as firm size increases.

In summing up the issue of segmentation in East Asia, two points may be worth emphasising. First, in at least two of the East Asian NIEs, Taiwan and Hong Kong, segmentation may be less important because of the dominance of small firms. Moreover, in Taiwan, there has been a process of decentralised industrialisation, with a significant number – as high as 55 per cent – of manufacturing establishments locating in rural areas (Amsden, 1979; Ho, 1979; Gallin and Gallin, 1982). This acted as a brake on excessive rural–urban migration and restrained the expansion of an impoverished urban informal sector. Finally, in all the East Asian economies, the onset of full employment in the late 1960s is perhaps the most important evidence against the significance and persistence of labour segmentation. If the latter did exist on a significant scale, this should have been reflected in considerable urban unemployment and underemployment. The macroevidence indicates otherwise.

228

INEQUALITY, POVERTY AND ECONOMIC DEVELOPMENT: SEN'S ENTITLEMENTS APPROACH

So far the discussion on the structural determinants of inequality and poverty during development has focused on one primary variable, namely the intersectoral migration process and the way it affects poverty and inequality. This inevitably abstracts from the complex array of other structural factors which influence movements in inequality and poverty. This has led some practitioners, such as Bigsten (1989) and Sundrum (1990), to provide a checklist of structural factors (e.g. intersectoral labour allocation, population pressure, asset distribution, technology, factor market performance) which affect income distribution. However, as Lal (1976) has warned, it is not enough to have a checklist. It is necessary to show how the various structural factors interact. It would be fair to maintain that a robust and general model of income distribution is yet to be constructed. Sen (1981a, b), however, has made an ambitious attempt in this direction in his 'entitlements approach'. This section is devoted to a brief discussion of this approach. As will be argued in greater detail at a later stage, the advantage of the Sen's work lies in the fact that it allows the prevailing policy environment to be easily incorporated as a major influence on income distribution.

As Sen puts it:

> Each economic and political system produces a set of entitlement relations governing who can have what in that system. For a market economy, the determining variables of entitlements can be broadly split into:
> (i) ownership vector
> (ii) exchange entitlement mapping
>
> (Sen, 1981a: 308)

The former pertains to the portfolio of physical and human capital assets which a person owns. The latter pertains to the ability of an individual to acquire, given his or her ownership bundle, the alternative bundles of commodities through production or trade.

Sen maintains that:

> Poverty removal ... is ultimately dependent on a wide distribution of effective entitlements, and this – for any given level of per capita income – would tend to be reflected in the low level of inequality in the distribution of income.
>
> (Sen, ibid.: 311)

What causes a 'wide distribution of effective entitlements'? There are two generic forces corresponding to the distinction that Sen makes between ownership vector and exchange entitlement mapping. Thus, any factor or set of factors which affect the ownership vector would directly influence both poverty and inequality. Common examples include a sustained increase in the overall volume

229

of assets and asset redistribution, such as land reform. Similarly, any factor or set of factors which influence the exchange entitlement mapping will in turn affect poverty and inequality. Examples include the shifts in terms of trade faced by poor peasants, the availability of employment opportunities for semi-skilled and unskilled workers and the direct provision of 'basic needs' (primary education, basic health care services, low-cost housing, etc.) by the state.

As should be obvious, the 'entitlement approach' does not make neat predictions concerning the time-path of inequality and poverty during the course of economic development as do models that belong to the Kuznets genre. All that it suggests is that the key structural determinant of inequality in a market economy is the set of entitlement relations. Any market economy at any stage of development will experience either a decline or rise in poverty and inequality depending upon the nature of changes in its set of entitlement relations.

Critics of the 'entitlement approach' may seize upon its lack of predictive capacity as a weakness. One could also argue that the distinction between ownership vector and exchange entitlement mapping is rather stylised and is not always helpful. Thus, to take one example, rapid expansion of primary education affects both the exchange entitlement mapping as well as the ownership vector. The position maintained by this paper is that, despite these alleged limitations, the 'entitlement approach' represents a marked improvement on Kuznets-type views on inequality and poverty in developing economies. The predictive capacity of the Kuznets model is gained at the expense of analytical content. Refinements to the first-generation Kuznets model inevitably entail a focus on the intersectoral migration process to the exclusion of all other factors germane to the understanding of poverty and inequality. More importantly, the prevailing policy environment does not seem to play any explicit and important role in the determination of income distribution. The advantage of the 'entitlement approach' is that it assigns an explicit and significant role to public policy in terms of its impact on poverty and inequality. Public policy thus becomes the subject of discussion in the next section.

THE POLICY ENVIRONMENT AND ITS IMPACT ON POVERTY AND INEQUALITY

Policy measures which influence both the ownership vector and the exchange entitlement mapping will in turn influence outcomes on poverty and inequality. This seems to be the key message of the 'entitlement approach'. One obvious example of a policy measure which directly affects the ownership vector in a developing economy is asset redistribution through land reform. Since land is a key asset in many, if not most developing countries, land reform has understandably been the subject of much discussion in the development literature. Indeed, as the subsequent discussion of the experience of the NIEs will show, land reform is central to an understanding of the historical circumstances which underpin the relatively low inequality of the NIEs vis-à-vis other developing countries.

However, as is well known, land reform is a politically costly exercise and is thus not a readily usable policy option in most cases. This suggests the need to consider more feasible policy alternatives which have poverty alleviating potential.

Employment creation and basic needs

There are two broad policy measures which have considerable relevance in influencing the set of entitlement relations in a market economy: employment creation and direct provision of basic needs by the state. Consider first the case of employment creation. One could argue that it affects both the ownership vector and exchange entitlement mapping. Thus, the principal asset of the poor is their labour services. Employment creation, by enhancing the value of this asset, would influence the prevailing ownership vector. At the same time, the enhanced purchasing power of the poor generated by employment creation allows them to acquire the preferred bundle of alternative commodities – thus affecting the exchange entitlement mapping. Given that employment creation works through both channels, it is a powerful redistributive tool.

What is the most effective way to create employment of the labour services of the poor on a sustainable basis? It is at this juncture that the notion of export-oriented industrialisation becomes highly relevant to the discussion. As is well known, and as has been emphasised at various stages in this book, export-oriented industrialisation provides the opportunity for developing economies to intensively utilise a key resource which is in plentiful supply: semi-skilled and unskilled workers. Given that such workers are typically represented in poverty groups, the enhanced purchasing power of such groups reduces poverty. At the same time, this strategy has an equalising influence on income distribution by increasing the income share of poorer groups in society.

It is worth pointing out that, according to Sen, the key issue is labour-intensive industrialisation rather than export-oriented industrialisation. Employment creation is a means of entitlement raising and whether this is generated via the domestic market or the export market is a secondary issue (see Sen, 1981a: 299). This point has some appeal but it should be treated with caution. While large economies may rely on domestic markets to foster labour-intensive industrialisation, this is unlikely to be a feasible option for economies with a limited domestic market size. Furthermore, monopoly imperfections which inhibit the growth of labour demand are more likely to crop up in narrow domestic markets than in the global terrain of export markets.

Employment creation may be seen as an indirect means of entitlement raising. It operates through the labour market to enhance the purchasing power of the poor who then acquire their preferred bundle of commodities. A more direct method of entitlement raising is the selective provision of 'basic needs' to the poor by the state (Streeten et al., op. cit.). Thus, public investments in primary education, basic health delivery systems, low-cost housing, sanitation facilities may all be seen as basic needs which enhance the endowments of the poor as well as their exchange entitlement mapping. Advocates of basic needs would emphasise that as a strategy it is consumption-oriented in appearance but productivity-enhancing in substance. In other words, there are large human capital components in the various basic needs items. The productivity-enhancing effect of education is, of course, well known but it has also been argued that improved nutritional standards and better health facilities raise the productive potential of an individual, have beneficial effects in reducing fertility and generally enhance a person's adaptability and capacity to change. Thus, the basic needs strategy alleviates poverty both by boosting the current consumption bundle of the poor and by raising their productivity.

Which strategy – employment creation or basic needs provisions – is more effective in alleviating poverty and generating a more equal distribution of income? It is best to regard the two as complementary rather than competing strategies. As the World Bank puts it:

> Both elements are essential. The first provides the poor with opportunities to use their most abundant asset – labour. The second improves their immediate well-being and increases their capacity to take advantage of the newly created possibilities. Together, they can improve the lives of ... the poor.
>
> (World Bank, op. cit.: 51)

For ease of reference, the above issues are summarised in Figure 12.2 (adapted from Sen, 1981a). As can be seen, the provision of basic needs works primarily through the path designated by 'c'. The employment strategy works through two paths – 'a' and 'b'. The former increases the demand for semi-skilled and unskilled workers through export-oriented industrialisation, while the latter achieves the same outcome through inward-oriented industrialisation. The principal way in which 'c' differs from 'a' or 'b' is that the 'c' enhances the non-income advantages of the poor (better health standards, higher longevity, higher literacy, etc.) while 'a' or 'b' enhances the purchasing power of the poor. All have the common effect of reduced poverty and a more equal distribution of income through widespread diffusion of entitlements.

As a means of rounding up the discussion on these policy issues, it would be useful to note that, even with the successful implementation of labour-intensive industrialisation and basic needs provisions, some subgroups in poverty – such as the infirm, the aged, and those in resource-poor areas – may still need specific assistance in the form of carefully designed transfers and safety nets (e.g. public employment schemes, subsidies and other social security provisions). A comprehensive policy of poverty alleviation cannot ignore these considerations.

Macroeconomic policy, structural adjustment and poverty

While employment creation and basic needs provisions were core policy issues in

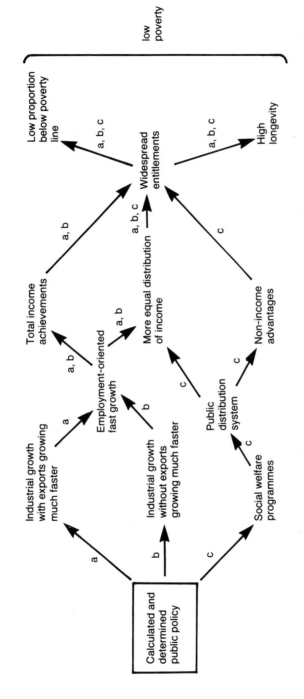

Figure 12.2 Consequential links and levels of explanation (a, b = employment strategy; c = basic needs)

the 1970s and they continue to be so today, the 1980s have added a new dimension to the debate on the impact of the policy environment on poverty and income distribution. This stems from the fact that a number of developing economies have experienced serious macroeconomic imbalances manifested in unsustainable fiscal deficits, rising external indebtedness, balance-of-payments problems and rampant inflation. This has prompted the governments of these countries to implement orthodox stabilisation measures – fiscal restraints, tight credit controls, etc. – in order to restore macroeconomic equilibrium. In addition, many developing economies have followed structural adjustment policies recommended by the international economic agencies – the World Bank and the International Monetary Fund – as the condition for loans to deal with their macroeconomic disequilibrium. These structural adjustment policies usually entail efforts to implement policy reform as a means of boosting aggregate supply. The intention is not only to offset the aggregate demand reduction caused by orthodox stabilisation measures but to provide the basis for future growth. The typical elements in structural adjustment measures entail minimising distortions in the relative price structure through trade liberalisation, deregulation of product and factor markets as well as privatisation. The primary objective is to achieve a more internationalised, private sector-driven economy. While sound in principle, the practice of macroeconomic stabilisation-cum-structural adjustment led, in many cases, to unanticipated adverse consequences on poverty and income distribution. This has prompted many development observers to seek macroeconomic adjustment with a 'human face' (Cornia *et al.*, 1988).

Why have these stabilisation-cum-adjustment measures led to adverse income distribution consequences? The reduction in aggregate demand engenders a rise in unemployment and this, in turn, directly affects the living standards of the poor. More ominously, faced with the exigencies of restoring macroeconomic equilibrium, many developing countries cut back public expenditure on essential social services, many of which are critical in maintaining the well-being of the poor. The long-term implications are adverse, as these developments can be seen as de facto divestment of human capital.

It is important, in making an assessment of the link between adjustment measures and poverty, that a number of factors need to be taken into account. First, the adverse impact of adjustment measures on poverty is essentially of a short-run nature. In principle, adjustment measures should boost output growth in the medium to long run and thus create sustainable employment opportunities for the poor. Second, there are important components of adjustment measures, such as exchange rate depreciation, which have distributional consequences. Exchange rate depreciation typically boosts demand for labour-intensive exports in the manufacturing sector and also assists small farmers who produce exportables. Third, the income distribution consequences are in many cases quite complex, creating a diverse range of gainers and losers so that the net effect is not always clear. Thus, for example, deregulating controls on food prices – a favourite item in the adjustment agenda – will boost living standards of small farmers who are net producers of food, but hurt landless rural workers and the urban poor.

Despite the above qualifications, the fact remains that adjustment measures can cause at least a transitional increase in poverty. Thus the current policy challenge is to find means of cushioning these unfavourable effects of adjustment. The World Bank (op. cit.: Chapter 7) has called for attempts to protect public expenditure on basic needs-type services through a temporary pause in investment and, more importantly, through a restructuring of the government's fiscal position. This would entail, as Sundrum (op. cit.: 282) puts it, 'increasing public revenue mainly by taxes falling on the upper-income groups, and by reducing public expenditure on services whose benefits accrue mainly to these groups'. Several studies of country-specific experiences have in fact shown that countries which have been able to adopt measures similar to the ones mentioned were successful in offsetting the adverse effects of stabilisation-cum-adjustment policies on the poor.

There is a more fundamental lesson which one learns from the discussion so far. Efficient macroeconomic management and correspondingly efficient micro-economic policies may not always be seen as poverty alleviating and redistributive strategies in the same spirit that such measures as, say, land reform are. However, macro-cum-micro policies, taken in their entirety, are critical in creating an environment in which equitable growth can take place.

THE ENTITLEMENTS APPROACH, POLICY INFLUENCES AND INCOME DISTRIBUTION IN THE EAST ASIAN NIEs

At this juncture an attempt will be made to provide an interpretation of the evidence in the light of the analytical propositions reviewed in the previous two sections. The entitlements approach considers distributional changes as the product of changes in the ownership vector and changes in exchange entitlement mapping. Changes in a key ownership vector – land ownership in the rural areas of Taiwan and South Korea – have been influenced by historical circumstances (see Chapter 4). In both these countries, land reform programmes were implemented at the end of the 1940s – often under foreign (American) supervision. In the case of South Korea, land reforms were instituted between 1947 and 1949, with the net outcome being a redistribution of land owned by big farmers and absentee landlords. The effect on the size of distribution of land ownership can be gleaned from the following statistics. In the late 1930s, 3 per cent of all farm households had owned over 66 per cent of all land, whereas by the end of the 1940s, less than 7 per cent of all households were landless (Amsden, 1989: 38). In addition, it must be noted that the destruction caused by the Korean war had a levelling effect on asset distribution (Choo, 1975).

In the case of Taiwan, land reform entailed the following elements: rent reduction, sale of public land and the 'land to the tillers programme'. The net effect was that between 1949 and 1957, owner farmers as a proportion of all farmers

Table 12.10   Growth of real wages in manufacturing (1970 = 100)

Year	Korea	Taiwan	Singapore	Hong Kong
1948				59.9
1954		56.0		
1960		55.7	90.0	62.9
1962	59.6			
1965	55.7	72.9		94.0
1968				
1970	100.0	100.0	100.0	100.0
1975	130.3	124.2	100.0	116.2
1980	192.7	192.1	120.0	151.5
1985	251.2	252.8		

Source: Haggard (1990: 230).
Note: 1970 = 100.

increased from 36 to 60 per cent (Kuo, 1975). Thus, in the case of both Taiwan and South Korea, early land reforms played an important role in generating a relatively equitable distribution of income in the initial stages of their rapid economic growth.

While asset redistribution in South Korea and Taiwan explains the trend towards lower equality in the early stages of their rapid economic growth, the same analysis cannot be applied to the cases of Singapore and Hong Kong. Moreover, even in the cases of South Korea and Taiwan, one has to consider durable factors – rather than one-shot asset redistribution – in explaining long-term trends in inequality and poverty. As the entitlement approach emphasises, in a developing labour-surplus economy, the utilisation and returns to labour services represent the major mechanisms for reducing poverty and generating more equitable growth. Seen from this perspective, labour-intensive industrialis-ation – entailing the utilisation of semi-skilled and unskilled workers – represents the key route to lower poverty. All the four NIEs are, of course, characterised by labour-intensive industrialisation fostered by an export-oriented regime. This produced full employment and rapid growth of real wages within the span of a decade.

Table 12.10 shows trends in real wage growth covering the 1940s to the mid-1980s. While the fall in aggregate poverty has occurred against a background of rapid real wage growth in South Korea, Taiwan and Hong Kong during the period when labour-intensive industrialisation consolidated itself, the conspicu-ous exception is Singapore. As can be seen, there was virtual stagnation of real wage growth between 1970 and 1975. Thus, at least in the case of Singapore, real wage growth cannot be regarded as the central mechanism which led to the rise in the living standards of the poor. This suggests that poverty alleviation occurred primarily through the provision of employment at constant real wages.

While labour-intensive industrialisation undoubtedly led to an alleviation in poverty in East Asia – as predicted by the entitlement approach – a balanced assessment has to take account of a number of complicating factors. First, some radical scholars take a slightly jaundiced view of improvements in labour welfare in the NIEs by emphasising that improvements in the living standards of the poor occur primarily through long working hours and income supplementation by secondary household earners. Deyo provides a clear expression of this view:

> [the] positive appraisal of East Asian equality must be tempered by other sharing in the fruits of growth as, rather very high levels of labour extraction among low income earners and families. In the early 1980s, South Korean manufacturing workers averaged fifty-four hours per week on the job, one of the highest levels in the world. ... In Hong Kong, male factory workers put in the longest average work week in Southeast Asia. ... In all four Asian cases, a large proportion of employment expansion in export industries involves a rapid entry of secondary household earners, especially young women from low-income families into low wage jobs. Thus, Asian household income equality partially reflects only intensified outlays among poor families.
>
> (Deyo, op. cit.: 98)

Second, labour-intensive industrialisation loses some of its explanatory significance in the light of episodic increases in inequality in East Asia. As can be seen from Table 12.10 – and as elaborated in previous sections – clear phases of rising income inequality can be seen in the case of Hong Kong (1976–81), South Korea (1970–80) and Singapore (1979–84). The only exception seems to be Taiwan where relative inequality appears to have remained roughly constant. It is important to emphasise that these phases of rising inequality seem to have co-incided with a change in the policy environment in East Asia – from labour-intensive industrialisation to a more interventionist phase of industrial restructuring entailing emphasis on shifting resources towards more skill-intensive and capital-intensive activities. While a detailed analysis of the process of industrial restructuring is the subject of another chapter, the distributional implications that follow from such a shift in the policy environment is germane to the subject of this chapter.

The very success of export-oriented industrialisation in eliminating labour surplus conditions in East Asia provided the momentum for a policy shift emphasising industrial restructuring. A growing phase of labour scarcity entailed an inevitable upward pressure on labour costs which, without a compensating increase in productivity, posed an inevitable threat to sustained competitive advantage in labour-intensive products. This was the common driving force towards the adoption of restructuring policies in East Asia during the 1970s. The precise timing, scale and intensity of these policies varied across the countries. In Singapore, the restructuring policies were pursued vigorously between 1979 and 1984; in Korea, these policies were particularly evident between 1973 and 1979. Restructuring efforts in Taiwan and Hong Kong have been less intensive and

Table 12.11 Average income growth rates by educational group (Singapore 1973–83)

	Income rank[a] (1976)	Average change (%) 1973–79	Income rank[a] (1983)	Average change (%)	
				1979–83	1973–83
No education	(5)	9.8	(7)	12.1	10.7
Below PSLE[b]	(4)	10.1	(4)	12.1	8.6
PSLE[b]	(6)	10.5	(5)	12.9	11.5
Post-primary	(7)	0.4	(6)	18.6	11.5
Secondary	(3)	7.7	(3)	18.1	7.0
Post-secondary	(2)	5.5	(2)	21.5	12.4
Tertiary	(1)	2.3	(1)	14.7	7.6
Total		8.7		18.3	12.8

Source: Islam and Kirkpatrick (1986b: Table 19).

Notes: The growth rates are in nominal terms. The lack of group-specific price deflators precludes the possibility of providing real income estimates. Figures in parentheses show income ranks in 1976 and 1983. The 1976 rather than the 1973 level was used since observations on all categories were not available in 1973.

  a 1 = highest paid, 7 = lowest paid.

  b Primary School Leaving Examinations.

vigorous, with such policies being primarily effective in the financial sector in Hong Kong.

The impact of restructuring on income distribution works primarily via income adjustments in the labour market. Incentives to guide resources in capital and skill-intensive sectors tend to increase the demand for skilled and professional workers at the expense of semi-skilled and unskilled workers. At the same time, efforts to increase the supply of skills through the education and training system takes time to catch up with the changes in labour demand patterns. Thus, one probable outcome is that income distribution turns unfavourably against workers with lower human capital endowments. Suggestive evidence can be found in Tables 12.11 and 12.12 for Singapore. As can be seen, income growth rates for workers with lower educational attainments grew well below the national average for the same time period. Decomposition analysis substantiates this finding, with intergroup inequality for workers with different educational levels rising from 25.0 per cent of aggregate inequality in 1979 to 30.0 per cent of aggregate inequality by 1983.

Table 12.13 depicts the South Korean experience in terms of wage behaviour for workers with different educational endowments between 1971 and 1978 – the period most pertinent to the government's efforts towards restructuring. As can be seen, wage differentials have shifted sharply in favour of workers with higher educational attainments.

Specific policies associated with the restructuring process probably contributed to the worsening inequality in South Korea and Singapore. In the former,

Table 12.12   Educational inequality: decomposition estimates (Singapore, 1973–83)

Year	Intersectoral inequality		Intrasectoral inequality	
	L-index	Contribution to aggregate inequality (%)	L-index	Contribution to aggregate inequality (%)
1973	0.11	26.8	0.30	73.2
1976	0.08	23.5	0.26	76.5
1979	0.08	25.0	0.24	75.0
1980	0.08	25.8	0.23	74.2
1981	0.09	29.0	0.22	71.0
1982	0.11	28.9	0.27	71.0
1983	0.13	30.2	0.30	69.8

Source: Islam and Kirkpatrick (1986b: 100).

the government explicitly tried to favour large firms – and in particular the chaebols (large diversified business groups) – by offering them preferential credit so that they could play a leading role in moving the economy towards heavy, capital-intensive industries. This led to a sharp increase in industrial concentration and offset the relatively equitable asset distribution which Korea had in the 1950s (Amsden, 1989; Kim, 1986). In the case of Singapore, it was noted that selective immigration policy caused labour market segmentation and contributed to rising inequality. It is necessary to add to this observation that the selective immigration policy was pursued as an adjunct to the process of industrial restructuring.

Table 12.13   Trends in wage differentials by education (Korea 1971–8)

	1971 (%)	1975 (%)	1978 (%)
High School (12 years of education)	100.0	100.0	100.0
Middle School (9 years of education)	67.3	61.9	65.6
Junior School (14 years of education)	–	136.2	149.2
College and University (16 years of education and more)	175.2	214.4	230.9

Source: Kim (1986: 73).

Comparable information on the impact of industrial restructuring on income distribution in Hong Kong and Taiwan is unfortunately not available. However, Lin (op. cit.) has noted that the worsening income distribution in Hong Kong between 1976 and 1981 coincided with an increase in the size of the service sector, particularly financial services. It is significant that the latter has played a leading role in the restructuring process. In the case of Taiwan it appears that industrial restructuring has not worsened income distribution.

The entitlement approach also emphasises that the direct provision of basic needs by the state is an effective mechanism for reducing poverty and inequality. The common perception, strongly endorsed by Sen (1981a), is that this mechanism was less important in East Asia. The process of acquiring basic needs by the poor occurred through the market rather than through deliberate public action. In other words, the higher income generated through labour-intensive industrialisation to large segments of the population provided them with the necessary purchasing power to acquire basic needs. This view is only partially correct. Admittedly, social welfare expenditure by the government is relatively less in East Asia compared with other economies at a similar stage of development. Surprisingly, however, this conclusion is less valid in the case of Hong Kong – apparently the epitome of laissez-faire policies. As Lin and Ho note:

[t]he government spends something approaching one-fourth of the national income providing various sorts of physical infrastructure ... compulsory primary education, extensive medical and health services, subventions for numerous social welfare agencies, and public low-cost housing for well over 40 per cent of the population.

(Lin and Ho, 1984: 50)

An ambitious low-cost public housing programme is also a key feature of Singapore (Lim et al., 1988). In addition, it is well known that, in all the NIEs,

Table 12.14 Physical Quality of Life Index (selected years)

Year	Korea	Taiwan	Singapore	Hong Kong
1950		63		
1951				
1957	58			
1959				
1960		77		76
1968	76			
1970		87	83	
1971				86
1980	85	88	86	92
1985	88	94	91	95

Source: Haggard (1990: 231).

240

Table 12.15 Recession and recovery in the East Asian NIEs (per capita GNP growth, %)

Year	Korea	Taiwan	Hong Kong	Singapore
1973	12.0	11.0	11.1	7.0
1974	6.6	−0.4	0.9	4.3
1975	4.8	1.9	−2.5	6.4
1976	11.9	11.4	14.9	4.2
1979	5.4	6.4	3.7	7.7
1980	−6.1	5.3	9.7	4.8
1981	4.4	3.8	6.9	7.9
1982	5.6	1.2	2.5	6.8
1983	11.2	6.4	4.3	9.5
1984			7.6	9.8
1985			−6.5	−1.0
1986			10.3	0.8
1987			12.3	7.9

Source: Industry Commission (1990: Statistical Appendix).

large-scale public investment in education and training ranging from basic levels to tertiary levels was made. Thus, in many respects, the NIEs followed a 'basic needs' strategy that not only improved social well-being but was also investment-oriented in the sense of augmenting the productivity of human resources.

The combination of selective basic needs provision by the state and enhanced purchasing power of the population caused by labour-intensive industrialisation led to marked improvements in key 'quality of life indices'. Table 12.14 substantiates this point by showing changes in a broad-based index (Physical Quality of Life Index: PQLI) covering the 1950s to the 1980s. The improvements are steady and significant, with Taiwan and Hong Kong showing near-perfect scores in terms of PQLI. Moreover, cross-country analysis shows that these two countries in particular, and the NIEs in general, have among the best records in terms of achieving adult literacy and higher life expectancy (Sen, op. cit.).

A previous section has indicated how attempts at macroeconomic stabilisation combined with structural adjustment measures in order to cope with external shocks has had the unintended consequence of worsening poverty and inequality in many developing countries. How empirically significant is this issue for the East Asian NIEs?

To start with, the discussion of the impact of macroeconomic policies on income distribution can be seen as an attempt to distinguish short-run, cyclical factors from more long-term structural factors that influence income distribution. All the NIEs have had phases of slow growth and recession in the 1970s and 1980s. The relevant details are shown in Table 12.15. As can be seen, during the 1973 oil shock, Hong Kong was the most severely affected with a decline in per capita GDP growth of −2.5 per cent. Taiwan also had a recession, with growth slowing down to −0.4 per cent (on a per capita GDP basis) in 1974. In Korea and Singapore, there was a relatively sharp deceleration of growth (per capita GDP growth was nearly halved between 1973–4 and 1975) but not an actual recession. The recession after the 1979 oil shock was particularly severe in Korea (−6.6 per cent per capita GDP growth in 1980) but the other economies fared considerably better; 1985, however, was a year of sharp recession for the two city states – with per capita GDP growth falling to −6.5 per cent in Hong Kong and −1.0 per cent in Singapore.

Annual data on poverty and basic needs indicators are unfortunately not available to gauge the extent to which the aforementioned phases of slow growth and recession affected income distribution. There is broad evidence to indicate that real wages either fell or grew very slowly over those phases. Under such circumstances it is reasonable to surmise that average living standards of the poor would have been adversely affected. One must, however, emphasise that, compared with international standards, the NIEs have been remarkably successful in resuming rapid growth after every recessionary phase – as the relevant details in Table 10.15 show. This has primarily occurred because of the fact that policy makers took quick and decisive action in terms of pushing through macroeconomic stabilisation measures, in ensuring that expenditure on social services was protected during the recessionary phase and in being able to maintain the momentum of export-oriented policies (e.g. through exchange rate devaluations). Such favourable policy developments ensured that the adverse impact of cyclical factors on poverty was quickly reversed.

THE POLITICAL ECONOMY OF POVERTY ALLEVIATION AND INCOME REDISTRIBUTION

One theme of this book is the need to understand the political process that underpins any effective development strategy. This theme has considerable relevance in the context of the current discussion. How serious are the political obstacles to poverty alleviation and income redistribution? Are the political constraints facing antipoverty and egalitarian policies different from the ones facing growth-promoting policies? These are the issues which form the substance of this section.

Political constraints on poverty reduction and political constraints on improving economic growth often have common origins. This is where neoclassical political economy – extensively reviewed in Chapter 3 – is of considerable relevance. Recall that a central proposition of neoclassical political economy is that an economy characterised by widespread state intervention in specific sectors and industries – as is evident under import substituting industrialisation – would engender endemic rent-seeking behaviour. Powerful rent-seeking groups will not only impede growth but also impede progress in poverty alleviation. Given that such groups are likely to perpetuate distortions in product and factor markets, labour-intensive industrialisation is unlikely to develop. A previous section has argued that labour-intensive industrialisation is a central mechanism for equitable growth.

In an economic regime characterised by widespread rent-seeking behaviour, public investment in basic needs may not be effective. This is because poor growth in such a regime reduces the tax base and constrains the capacity of the government to finance basic services. Such regimes are also likely to lack the political resolve to maintain macroeconomic equilibrium. A previous section has argued how efficient macroeconomic management can be an important component in poverty alleviation.

In sum, in an economy exposed to the ravages of rent-seeking behaviour, the prospects for both rapid growth and poverty alleviations are unfavourable. This is a stark example of 'government failure' in economic development.

One can construct arguments to counter the pessimism of neoclassical political economy. It is easy to overlook the fact that the self-interest of the ruling elite and the non-poor can actually act as a powerful force supporting income transfers to the poor. One can construct a variety of examples and circumstances to support this contention. Thus it is plausible to suggest that the externalities inherent in general improvements in educational and health standards of the poor may provide sufficient incentives for rich industrialists to support a strategy of state-sponsored basic needs provision. Furthermore, when there is an improvement in both the quantity and quality of basic education and health care, the providers of services – middle-class doctors and teachers – also gain directly through better earnings and working facilities. They can thus become important constituents supporting public investment in basic needs. These examples suggest that self-interest of the ruling elite and the non-poor can create implicit political coalitions that cut across the poor/nonpoor divide. These examples also suggest that a basic needs provision as a strategy of poverty alleviation is likely to be much more feasible than one which entails reshuffling the existing stock of community assets and income.

Finally, advocates of neoclassical political economy would readily concede that rent-seeking behaviour can be restrained through a variety of institutional arrangements, as has been extensively discussed in Chapter 3. Such restraints would thus create the necessary environment for equitable growth.

THE POLITICS OF EQUITY AND THE EAST ASIAN NIEs: SOME CONCLUDING REMARKS

East Asian experience suggests that early and decisive land reform, labour-intensive industrialisation, and selective provision of basic needs (particularly of education) go a long way towards explaining sustained reductions in poverty and a relatively equal distribution of income. What are the political circumstances that permit these forces to achieve their full potential? The analytical discussion suggests that institutional arrangements that restrain rent-seeking behaviour and the self-interest of the ruling elite are two important factors. Both these conditions were fulfilled in the case of the East Asian NIEs. Policy makers in these economies developed authoritarian institutional arrangements that endowed them with relative autonomy to implement labour-intensive industrialisation. This in turn led to predictable effects on poverty and income distribution. The emphasis on public investment in education can be linked to the self-interest of the ruling elite. The NIEs (Korea and Taiwan) were also fortunate in implementing land reform at a stage when trenchant political opposition from rural interests could not develop.

The above discussion raises the contentious issue of the relationship between authoritarian political structures and equity. Certainly, East Asian-style authoritarianism managed to protect policy makers from the regressive influence of collective action, but (as noted in Chapter 3) this is only one possible way of dealing with the problem of collective action. Alternatives include democratic corporatism (Haggard, 1990: 267) and the standard neoclassical solution of restricting state action to specified areas. Furthermore, one could even argue that East Asian policy makers are reacting to the limits of authoritarianism. Thus, one could suggest that the uncertain outcomes of the industrial restructuring experiments of the 1970s (with their potential regressive influence on income distribution) created the momentum for maintaining 'good' policies that combine growth with equity. The democratisation decree of 1987 in South Korea and the lifting of martial law for the first time in Taiwan (also in 1987) may also be seen as partial responses to the political aspirations of an increasingly equity-conscious society.

There are also other cogent reasons why the link between authoritarianism and income distribution should be severed. If one accepts that the self-interest of the ruling elite and the non-poor is a progressive force leading to public action on basic needs provision, then one also has to accept that such a factor is, in principle, neutral with respect to the political system. Furthermore, cross-section evidence shows that '[civil and political] liberties appear to be strongly and positively associated with measures of welfare improvement such as women's education, overall education, and infant mortality declines' (World Bank, 1991: 50). Kohli (1986: 161) has assembled evidence to conclude that 'authoritarian–exclusionary regimes tend to worsen income inequalities, while democratic regimes stabilise them'. Such considerations inspire one to suggest that the political dimension of poverty alleviation and income redistribution need not degenerate to the cruel paradox of 'equity without democracy'.

APPENDIX: L-INDEX

The L-index may be defined as follows:

$$I_L = \frac{1}{n} \sum_{i=1}^{n} \ln(\bar{Y}/Y_i) \tag{1}$$

where: n = population size
$\bar{Y}$ = average income
Y_i = income of the ith group in n
$\ln$ = natural log operator

It takes a minimum value of zero and is unbounded above. It correlates rather well with the Gini ratio.

The decomposition of the L-index may be expressed as follows:

$$I_L = \sum_{j=1}^{m} \lambda_j I_{Lj} + \sum_{j=1}^{m} \lambda_j \ln(\lambda_j/s_j) \tag{2}$$

where: I_{Lj} = L-index for jth group ($j = 1 \ldots m$)
λ_j = population share of jth group
s_j = income share of the jth group

The first term in equation (2) represents 'within-group' inequality, the second term 'between-group' inequality.

13

THE CHALLENGES OF THE 1990s

This survey of the rise of the East Asian NIEs has entailed a long journey through a vast and diverse terrain of issues and debates. The literature seems to be caught in the cross-currents of two competing paradigms. On the one hand, one has to contend with the neoclassical view that East Asian success is largely the outcome of 'getting prices right'. In particular, this view traces the ascendancy of the NIEs to the policy reforms of the early 1960s, entailing a combination of trade and financial liberalisation. These reforms were in turn buttressed by a well-functioning labour market and prudent macroeconomic management. This neoclassical resurgence has been challenged by the statist 'counterrevolution'. In terms of this view, one can only understand the policy-making process in conjunction with the underlying political process. The East Asian NIEs have the common institutional feature of a 'strong, developmental state'. Such a state is insulated from the contending pressures of distributional coalitions which enables policy makers to engage in sector-specific interventions to overcome market failure without the corresponding burden of government failure. The interplay of policies and politics has to be set within the broader sociocultural, historical and strategic context within which the East Asian NIEs have evolved.

The enduring lesson to be learned from this survey is that neither the extreme neoclassical position nor the strong statist view is validated by the available evidence. East Asian policy makers were not immune to policy mistakes but what sets them apart from other less successful economies is their consistent capacity to contain these mistakes from becoming protracted. What remains to be seen is the extent to which this enviable track record can be maintained in the future. This concluding chapter will reflect on the key issues that are germane to this question.

THE EAST ASIAN NIEs IN THE YEAR 2000

The NIEs of East Asia are now poised to move into the select club of the developed economies in the 1990s. Indeed, two of the city states are already classified by the World Bank as 'high-income' economies. In terms of the targets and objectives set by the policy makers in these economies, the NIEs have still some way to go.

In the case of Singapore, the government has often expressed the view that its citizens should aspire to reach the prevailing Swiss living standards by the year 2000 (Lim *et al.*, 1988; Ministry of Trade and Industry, 1986). In the case of Korea, the government-sponsored think-tank – the Korea Development Institute – has offered projections and analyses of the economy's prospects of achieving advanced country status by the year 2000. The consensus seems to be that, if Korea can maintain a per capita growth rate of 6 per cent a year, then it will reach advanced country status by the target year (Song, 1990). Some international experts have suggested that, by the target year, Korea's per capita income will become aprroximately US$5,900 (in 1981 dollars) (Song, ibid.). In the case of Taiwan, the Economist Intelligence Unit (1991: 11) has noted that '[t]he government's economic think-tank, the Council for Economic Planning and Development, in 1987 set out the broad parameters of government policy up to 2000'. Only in the case of Hong Kong does one observe a noticeable lack of a declared vision of where the economy should be heading in the current decade – a feature that seems to be compatible with the city state's 'laissez-faire' spirit. In sum, with the predictable exception of Hong Kong, all the NIEs of East Asia seem to embody the message of achievement of advanced country status by the year 2000.

THE FUTURE OF THE EAST ASIAN NIEs: TWO VIEWS

How feasible is the target set by the policy makers of the East Asian NIEs? There is no simple answer. A lot depends on one's assessment of the constraints and challenges facing the NIEs in the 1990s. Garnaut sums up the nature of these constraints and challenges in the following manner:

> Serious questions have arisen through 1989 about the sustainability of rapid growth in each of the [East] Asian economies ... [D]omestic political tensions ... have challenged social cohesion around the growth objective. ... The international situation, too, has seemed less than ideal for the continuation of rapid internationally-oriented growth.
>
> (Garnaut, 1989: 106)

Thus, the feasibility of the East Asian NIEs achieving advanced country status by the end of the century depends very much upon the extent to which the domestic and international conditions that are necessary for rapid growth are likely to continue. Close observers of the East Asian scene have offered quite different assessments of such prospects. The most pessimistic scenario is painted by Bello and Rosenfeld (1992). They depict a case of 'dragons in distress', arguing that Korea, Taiwan, Singapore and Hong Kong are headed for crisis. The contention seems to be that the stresses and strains created by the rapid growth of the past decades are unlikely to be contained any further under the prevailing social and political system. A more 'mainstream' interpretation is that, provided the world economy is not afflicted by a new tide of protectionism and fractious trading blocs, one can remain optimistic about the future of the East Asian NIEs. The following is a representative sample of this mainstream genre.

> While the economy of Taiwan faces major challenges, there are reasons to be cautiously optimistic about the future. First, Taiwan has an extremely good track record in responding to adversities and crises. ... Second, there is now an enlightened and far-sighted leadership, a high-caliber government bureaucracy, and a well-educated electorate. Third, while labor strife and special interest group militancy have become almost constant fixtures in the economy, there is no need for despair ... the labor strife in Taiwan, serious as it may appear, will pass as management and labor discover new modes of operation and cooperation.
>
> (Lau, 1990a: 214–15)

> Democratisation in ... Korea since 1987 has been accompanied by high levels of industrial tension and disputation... There may be one or two years of ... modest growth during which ... Korea absorbs the far-reaching political changes. The economy's powerful growth momentum, and the commitment of the Korean elite to reaching the economic and political standards of advanced industrial countries, will then take over.
>
> (Garnaut, op. cit.: 117)

> Singapore enters the 1990s with considerable assets: a well-run economy, industrial harmony, excellent relations with its leading trading partners, an increasingly better educated and trained population, and political and social stability. ... The emerging issues that will confront Singapore in the 1990s relate to the management of economic success and transformation, not the containment of industrial and political conflicts.
>
> (Pang, 1992: 89)

A SPECIAL CASE: POST-1997 HONG KONG AND THE 'CHINA FACTOR'

It must be emphasised that, even within this mainstream genre, observers have expressed considerable uncertainty about growth prospects in Hong Kong, largely because of the worrying presence of the 'China factor'. As is well known, the signing of the Sino-British agreement in 1984 has provided for the transfer of sovereignty to China in 1997. This has prompted debates about the likely reactions of the managerial and professional classes in Hong Kong to 'life' under Chinese sovereignty. One possibility is that the threat of a curtailment of individual and political liberties in the post-1997 constitutional arrangements will be taken so seriously that it could precipitate large-scale emigration of skilled personnel, together with capital flight. This would understandably seriously diminish Hong Kong's continued economic expansion. Recent events suggest

248

that such a scenario is not unduly pessimistic. The rate of emigration increased dramatically – amounting to approximately 1,200 per week – after internal political turmoil in China in mid-1989 (declaration of martial law on 29 May, 4 June massacres) brought disillusionment with Hong Kong's prospects under Chinese sovereignty (Sunday Mail, 13 October 1991).

Even if China did not deal with Hong Kong in a heavy-handed way, and allowed the current economic and political system to remain largely intact, internal political instability in China is likely to remain a significant threat. This is because of the way the Hong Kong economy has become increasingly integrated with parts of mainland China (Southern China) through trade and investment links. Lin and Tsui (1991: 43)) note that, in 1988, 91 per cent of direct investment in Guangdong province in China came from Hong Kong. There are also extensive subcontracting arrangements with Chinese firms. These links will be threatened with the onset of any sustained political instability in China.

One could of course argue that the scenario painted above is unduly pessimistic. China is treading cautiously, but persistently towards market- and internationally oriented policy reforms. The events of 1989 are unlikely to permanently stall this steady pace of reform. Experience with the 'special economic zones' (SEZs) in Southern China have shown that the Chinese government can maintain a pragmatic policy of non-interference based on the proverbial argument that one should not kill the 'goose that lays golden eggs'. It is possible that Hong Kong will be regarded as one such 'goose' by the Chinese government and that it will operate as yet another SEZ. Only time will tell whether this positive interpretation of post-1997 Hong Kong will turn out to be a reasonably accurate forecast.

THE CHALLENGES FACING THE EAST ASIAN NIEs: INTERNAL VS EXTERNAL FACTORS

It would be appropriate at this juncture to move away from the specific and special circumstances of Hong Kong and revert to the general discourse on the future of the rest of the NIEs in East Asia as they make their self-proclaimed journey to advanced country status by the end of this century. How should one choose between the apocalyptic scenario of 'dragons in distress' and the unmitigated optimism of the mainstream tradition? A lot depends upon the extent to which one considers 'internal factors' as more important than 'external factors' in influencing the future growth path of the NIEs. Internal factors pertain to the political and social institutions within which future policy options will have to be decided. External factors pertain to the global economic and political environment facing the NIEs.

Some commentators, most notably Ariff (1991) and Park (1991c), have expressed concern that the way the USA manages the domestic economy will have important repercussions for the rest of the world, and particularly for the East Asian NIEs for whom the USA represents the key export market. The essence of the argument is that the USA will have to engage in a sustained fiscal correction through cutting its budget deficit as a means of rectifying its persistent trade imbalances with the rest of the world, and in particular East Asia. The problem is that if the USA brings about such corrections too rapidly, then it will lead to a 'reduction in world demand, adversely affecting many export-oriented economies' (Ariff, op. cit.: 3). Park (op. cit.: 116) is more emphatic: 'Any unilateral budget cut in the United States will unleash serious deflationary effects, triggering a recession in the East Asian NIEs ...' Takenaka (1991: 65) has supported these scenarios by demonstrating that a 2 per cent decline in American GNP will lead to a 4.6 per cent decline in Korean GNP and 3.4 per cent decline in Singapore's GNP. These estimates take account of the trilateral trade relationship among the USA, Japan and the NIEs.

Garnaut (1991) has offered a rebuttal of these pessimistic scenarios by suggesting that a fiscal correction does not inevitably mean lower US output. As he puts it:

Analytically, if policies to reduce demand were combined efficiently with policies to switch production towards, and demand away from, tradables goods and services, there is no reason why a reduction in the budget deficit should be associated with a decline in total United States production.

(Garnaut, 1991: 19)

There is the more general point that a focus on the repercussions of US domestic economic management abstracts from the way the trading partners of the USA will respond. Changes in the global environment arising from such a factor will, by its very nature, affect *all* regional economies. Of course, the extent of this impact will vary – in the same manner that the external shocks of the 1970s affected the East Asian NIEs to a greater extent than some other regional economies. Yet, the NIEs adjusted to the external shocks in a much more effective way than others, largely because of favourable internal policy and political environment. It is this very logic that leads one to suggest why internal factors are more likely to play a decisive role in shaping the future growth path of the East Asian NIEs.

One could argue that the very success of the NIEs has bred bilateral trade frictions. Major trading partners, such as the USA, reeling from the politically sensitive issue of persistent bilateral trade deficits, are consistently urging the NIEs to provide greater 'market access' and are also retaliating through a battery of non-tariff barriers. Thus, changes in the global environment facing the NIEs are more likely to occur in the form of bilateral trade frictions – and by their very nature such frictions will be NIE-specific rather than being a uniform phenomenon affecting all regional economies.

One could respond to the above position in the following manner. First, there is no obvious reason to suppose that bilateral trade conflicts will inhibit the future growth prospects of the NIEs. Indeed, there are good reasons to suppose that such trade frictions will prove to be a boon rather than a bane for the economic high-fliers of East Asia. If, as a result of pressures from their major trading partners, the NIEs rationalise agricultural protection, induce greater competition in domestic product markets (through import-liberalisation programmes), generate greater competition in the financial sector (through easier entry of foreign banks and general relaxation of capital controls), then these should be deemed to be desirable developments. Second, how efficiently bilateral trade conflicts are handled will depend on internal political circumstances.

In sum, there are good grounds for arguing that one should focus on internal political and social institutions in appreciating the future growth prospects of the NIEs. Yet, 'internal political and social institutions' represent a rather generic – and distressingly vague – category. It is necessary to provide a sharper focus to this issue.

THE KEY CHALLENGE: HOW TO ACHIEVE INNOVATION-DRIVEN DEVELOPMENT

One could make a start by developing an analytical framework by drawing upon several independent, but complementary, contributions: Porter's (1990) work on the competitive advantage of nations, Sah's (1991) analysis of the advantages of centralisation and decentralisation, and Friedman's (1988) explanation of Japanese industrial success as a result of the greater diffusion of flexible manu-facturing strategies compared with other nations. Hidden in Porter's massive treatise on how nations develop – and lose – competitive advantage in inter-national markets is the interesting idea that the trajectory of an economy may be conceptualised as proceeding along a continuum that may be summarised as factor-driven, investment-driven, and innovation-driven phases of development. These analytical categories have already been discussed in a previous chapter (in the context of foreign investment). What is germane to the guts of the analysis is that the central challenge facing the NIEs is the transition to innovation-driven development. This is a particular translation of the idea that the NIEs are poised to join the ranks of the developed countries by the end of this century.

The East Asian NIEs have been remarkably successful in achieving factor-driven development – i.e. in deriving national competitive advantages from basic factors of production (disciplined, hard-working, educated workforce, rapid capital accumulation), diligently applying them to foreign-designed products, and competing effectively in international markets largely through sourcing arrangements with Japanese and Western firms. Korea, according to Porter, has also fully achieved investment-driven development, but now faces inevitable constraints because this phase of development is only possible in a 'certain class of industries: those with significant scale economies and capital requirements, standardised products, low service content, technology that is readily transfer-able' (Porter, op. cit.: 551). Innovation-driven development, however, requires in-house technological capability, so that firms can not only appropriate and improve technology and products from other countries but create them. More importantly, they require the greater diffusion of flexible manufacturing strategies (Friedman, op. cit.). What is crucial to the thrust of this discussion is that the internal institutional framework has to adapt to facilitate the development sequencing from the factor-driven to the innovation-driven phase.

Much has been made of the virtues of the 'strong state' in East Asia. Indeed, an important theme of this book is that the state in East Asia has been able to insulate itself from the disruptive influence of distributional coalitions. This has provided policy makers with the capacity to pursue coherent economic policies. Critics of this view have however been quick to point to the social costs imposed by the machinery of the strong state. While these social costs have been masked in the past as a result of rapid growth and a hierarchical political system, they have emerged on a significant scale in the more open, democratised environment of the 1990s. Sen (1991) has raised similar concerns in the broader context of economic development. As he notes: 'the view ... that the "harder" the state the more effective it must be, [is] dead wrong' (Sen, ibid.: 425). One can add the following important point to this popular critique of East Asian economic development: the strong state certainly facilitated factor-driven and investment-driven development, but this framework is inappropriate in achieving innovation-driven development.

In order to develop such a view, one has to make a distinction between 'macropolitics' and 'micropolitics'. The former focuses on the way the state develops and implements rules for resource allocation through a process of interaction with various societal groups. In fact, this is the typical domain of the statist literature on East Asia. The latter focuses on the rules of the game as they are developed and implemented at the level of the firm – between workers and managers within the same firm/organisation, and between different firms. This novel interpretation of politics was first noted by Piore and Sabel (1984) and developed in some detail by Friedman (op. cit.) in the context of Japan. Micropolitics would entail such debates as the nature of production technology to be used, the degree of worker control and supervision, the extent to which workers should have the right to broad training, the autonomy of small-firm suppliers and so on. An economic order thus evolves as a result of countless political choices that are more or less consciously made at the level of the organisation. As will be shown subsequently, the analytical device of micropolitics is particularly useful in gaining some insight into the process of innovation-oriented development.

The next building block in the argument is the distinction that one needs to make between 'mass production' and 'flexible production' (Friedman, op. cit., drawing upon the work of Piore and Sabel, op. cit.). Mass production entails the adoption of standardised technology to produce standardised products. Its driving force is the achievement of economies of scale, and as a strategy it works best in price-sensitive mass markets. Flexible production, on the other hand, 'is the effort to make an ever-changing range of goods to appeal to specialised needs and tastes with tailored designs' (Friedman, op. cit.: 15). Its driving force is the achievement of economies of scope and product differentiation. Mass production is the distinguishing feature of factor-driven and investment-driven development; flexible production is the distinguishing feature of innovation-driven development. As Porter (op. cit.: 554) puts it: '[f]irms in an innovation-driven economy compete internationally in more differentiated industry segments. ... Price-sensitive, less sophisticated segments are ceded to firms from other nations'.

Mass production and flexible production entail different approaches to the political economy of industrial relations. The imperatives of mass production drives management 'to control closely the autonomy of ... workers, (and the reduction) of costs through discipline and supervision' (Friedman, op. cit.: 15). A flexible producer, on the other hand:

> requires a high level of skill in the workforce, to facilitate rapid changes in manufacturing processes and to reduce oversight costs; workers need to be able to make changes on their own, lest the burden on top management inhibit the firm's ability to meet or create new demand. Hence worker supervision is much less extensive than under mass production.
>
> (Friedman, op. cit.: 16)

It thus seems that mass production is compatible with a hierarchical organisational mode, where firms are endowed with a 'top-down', relatively unified governance structure, while flexible production is compatible with a more decentralised governance structure. Sah's (op. cit.) work on the relative merits of hierarchies nicely complements the implications of the above arguments. Using a stylised analytical framework, he shows that hierarchically organised firms usually do not perform well in choosing innovation-oriented projects. As he concludes:

> If the decision making process is highly hierarchical ... then the gates that an innovation has to pass through may be undesirably narrow ... it may in the longer run also affect the distribution of project types that is generated within an economy. If unfamiliar innovation-oriented projects are almost surely rejected in an economy, then inventors and research scientists are unlikely to come up with many such projects.
>
> (Sah, op. cit.: 81)

It is important to emphasise that the 'culture' of hierarchy is independent of firm size. In Sah's analytical framework, hierarchical and decentralised decision-making systems are compared for organisations of the same size. The point is that small and medium-sized firms can be just as hierarchical as large, bureaucratised corporations if both of them have the same top-down, centralised governance structure. It is in this important sense that Korea, with its large-firm dominant economy, has a similar organisational mode to Taiwan with its small-firm dominant economy (Whitley, 1990).

The central premise of the above arguments – that innovation-oriented development entails a greater diffusion of flexible production supported by decentralised organisational modes – is broadly consistent with the available evidence. In the USA the share of significant industrial innovations has apparently been produced by relatively decentralised firms (Sah, op. cit.; Oster, 1990). Friedman (op. cit.) argues that his thesis is consistent with the Japanese experience, particularly in the machine tools industry. Friedman's work is nicely complemented by Aoki's (1990) analysis of the nature of the Japanese firm. In fact, he has gone so far as to suggest that industrial organisations can be classified into two generic organisational modes, the 'H-mode' (hierarchical mode) and the 'J-mode' (Japan mode), the latter, of course conforming to the ideal-type, decentralised governance structure. Koike (1988) has also argued that the push towards flexible manufacturing strategies in Japan has been accompanied by employer-led restructuring of workplace organisation, with its central focus on human development at the firm level.

The final building block in the discussion on the appropriate institutional framework for facilitating innovation-driven development is to draw the links between the macropolitics of the state and the micropolitics of industrial organisation. As has been noted earlier, factor-driven and investment-driven development can be achieved within the framework of the strong state. The hallmark of these phases of development is the application of mass production. The basic ingredients of this production paradigm – hard-working, disciplined, relatively skilled workers and easily available standardised technology – can be adequately provided by the strong state and effectively applied by hierarchically organised firms. This nexus between macropolitics and micropolitics – which can prove so effective during factor-driven and investment-driven development – can turn out to be increasingly inadequate in the context of innovation-driven development. Emphasis has to shift from mass production to flexible production, from hierarchical control to decentralised governance, both at the level of the state and at the level of the firm.

Decentralised governance at the level of the state needs to be carefully delineated. It means more than a mere emulation of liberal democratic institutions. Indeed, mere emulation of this type can be counterproductive. It is likely to impair the proven capacity of the East Asian state to implement coherent economic policies by containing the contending pressures of special interests. The objective of decentralised governance at the level of the state, therefore, is to ensure that this proven capacity of coherent policy making is maintained and enhanced. This in turn entails an appreciation of the point that:

> Government's essential task at the innovation-driven stage is to create an environment in which firms are and continue to be innovative and dynamic. Its role must shift from actor and decision maker to facilitator, signaller, and prodder. Intervention must decrease substantially. ... Unless national policy toward industry shifts as a nation moves to the threshold of a more advanced stage, the upgrading of industry will be retarded or blocked.
>
> (Porter, op. cit.: 673).

The state cannot create decentralised management at the level of the firm, but through deconcentrating economic power and ensuring industry competition it can at least provide an environment where firms themselves recognise the benefits of flexible production and the consequent restructuring of workplace organisation.

In sum, the transition to innovation-driven economic progress entails a virtual reconstruction of the ideology of development. In carrying out such a reconstruction, the policy makers in East Asia face twin pressures from the democratic reform movement and conservative hardliners. While the democratic reform movement has become particularly popular and intense in Taiwan and Korea (Far Eastern Economic Review, 1990), its limitation is the lack of a coherent national agenda for achieving innovation-driven development. The risk is that the government may react to the populist elements in the movement by a mere emulation of liberal democratic institutions with its predictable outcomes. Conservative hardliners also pose a danger in the sense that they may yearn for old policies and political philosophies based on the argument that it is best to stick to a proven formula of success. It remains to be seen how the much-acclaimed East Asian policy makers will juggle with these twin pressures in their bid to achieve advanced country status by the year 2000.

BIBLIOGRAPHY

Addison, T. and Demery, L. (eds) (1987) *Wages and Labour Conditions in the Newly Industrialising Countries of Asia*, London: Overseas Development Institute

Adelman, I and Morris, C.T. (1973) *Economic Growth and Social Equity in Developing Countries*, Stanford: Stanford University Press

Agarwala, R. (1983) 'Price Distortions and Growth in Developing Countries', *World Bank Staff Working Papers*, No. 575

Aghevli, B. and Marquez-Ruarte, J. (1985) *A Case of Successful Adjustment: Korea's Experience During 1980–84*, Washington, DC: International Monetary Fund

Ahluwalia, M. (1976) 'Inequality, Poverty and Development', *Journal of Development Economics*, 3(4): 307–42

Ahluwlaia, M., Chenery, H., Bell, C., Duloy, J. and Jolly, R. (1974) *Redistribution with Growth*, New York: Oxford University Press

Ahluwalia, M., Carter, N.G. and Chenery, H.B. (1979) 'Growth and Poverty in Developing Countries, *Journal of Developing Economies*, 6(3): 299–34

Ahmed, Z. (1975) *Land Reforms in South-East Asia*, New Delhi: Orient Longman

Allen, G.C. (1980) *Japan's Economic Policy*, London: Macmillan

Amjad, R. (ed.) (1987) *Human Resource Development: The Asian Experience*, New Delhi: ILO–ARTEP

Amsden, A. (1979) 'Taiwan's Economic History: A Case of Etatisme and a Challenge to Dependency Theory', *Modern China*, 5(3): 341–80

Amsden, A. (1989) *Asia's Next Giant: South Korea and Late Industrialization*, New York: Oxford University Press

Amsden, A. (1991) 'Diffusion of Development: The Late Industrializing Model and Greater Asia', *American Economic Review*, Papers and Proceedings, 81(2): 282–6

Anand, S. and Kanbur, S.M. (1981) 'Inequality and Development: Critique', *Mimeo*, London: SSRC Development Economics Study Group

Anand, S. and Kanbur, S.M. (1984) 'Poverty Under the Kuznets Process', *Economic Journal*, (Supplement), 95: 42–9

Anderson, K. (1983) 'Growth of Agriculture Protection in East Asia', *Food Policy*, 4(8): 330–36

Anderson, K. and Hayami, Y. (1986) *The Political Economy of Agricultural Protection: East Asia in International Perspective*, Sydney: Allen & Unwin

Aoki, M. (1990) 'Toward an Economic Model of the Japanese Firm', *Journal of Economic Literature*, 28(1): 1–28

Ariff, M. (ed.) (1991) *The Pacific Economy: Growth and External Stability*, Sydney: Allen & Unwin

Arndt, H. (1983) 'Financial Development in Asia', *Asian Development Review*, 1(1): 86–100

Arndt, H. (1987a) 'Industrial Policy in East Asia', *Industry and Development*, 22: 1–66

Arndt, H. (1987b) *Economic Development: The History of An Idea*, Chicago, London: University of Chicago Press

Asian Development Bank (1991) *Asian Development Outlook,1991*, Manila: Asian Development Bank

Asian Development Bank (various issues) *Key Indicators of Developing Asian and Pacific Countries*, Manila: Asian Development Bank

Atkinson, A.B. (1987) 'On the Measurement of Poverty', *Econometrica*, 55: 749–64

Axelrod, R. (1984) *The Evolution of Cooperation*, New York: Basic Books

Bai, M.K. (1982) 'The Turning Point in the Korean Economy', *The Developing Economies*, 20(2): 117–39

Bai, M.K. (1989) 'Korean Industrial Relations in Transition', *Mimeo*, Seoul: Korea Labour Institute

Bai, M.K. (1990) 'Education and Training in Korea', *Mimeo*, Seoul: Korea Labour Institute

Balassa, B. (1968) *Economic Growth, Trade and the Balance of Payments in Developing Countries, 1960–65*, Washington, DC: IBRD

Balassa, B. (1977a) *Policy Reforms in Developing Countries*, Oxford: Pergamon

Balassa, B. (1977b) 'A Stages Approach to Comparative Advantage', *World Bank Staff Working Papers*, No. 256

Balassa, B. (1980) 'The Newly Industrializing Countries After the Oil Crisis', *World Bank Staff Working Papers*, No. 437

Balassa, B. (1981) *The Newly Industrializing Countries in the World Economy*, New York: Pergamon

Balassa, B. (1983) 'Outward Versus Inward Orientation Once Again', *The World Economy*, 6(2): 215–18

Balassa, B. and Williamson, J. (1987) *Adjusting to Success: Balance of Payments Policy in the East Asian NICs*, Washington, DC: Institute of International Economics

Ballance, R. and Sinclair, S. (1983) *Collapse and Survival: Industry Strategies in a Changing World*, London: George Allen & Unwin

Barclay, G. (1954) *Colonial Development and Population in Taiwan*, Princeton: Princeton University Press

Bardhan, P. (1990) 'Symposium on the State and Economic Development', *Journal of Economic Perspectives*, 4(3): 3–8

Barrett, R. and Chin, S. (1987) 'Export-oriented Industrializing States in the Capitalist World system: Similarities and Differences', in Deyo, F. (ed.), *The Political Economy of the New Asian Industrialism*, Ithaca and London: Cornell University Press

Bas, D. (1988) 'Cost effectiveness of Training in Developing Countries', *International Labour Review*, 127(3): 355–69

Bates, R.H. (1981) *Markets and States in Tropical Africa: The Political Basis of Agricultural Policies*, Berkeley: University of California Press

Bauer, P.T. (1972) *Dissent on Development*, London: Weidenfield & Nicholson

Bauer, P.T. (1984) *Reality and Rhetoric: Studies in the Economics of Development*, London: Weidenfield & Nicholson

Beckerman, W. (1977) 'Some Reflections on Redistribution with Growth', *World Development*, 5(8): 665–76

Bello, W. and Rosenfeld, S. (1992) *Dragon's in Distress: Asia's Miracle Economies in Crisis*, London: Penguin

Berger, P.L. (1988) 'An East Asian Model' in Berger, P.L. and Hsio, M. (eds), *In Search of an East Asian Development Model*, New Brunswick: Transaction Books

Berger, P.L. and Hsiao, H.M. (eds) (1988) *In Search of an East Asian Development Model*, New Brunswick: Transaction Books

Bergsman, J. (1974) 'Commercial Policy Allocative and X-Efficiency', *Quarterly Journal of Economics*, 58 (August): 309–33

Bhagwati, J. (1978) *Foreign Trade Regimes and Economic Development: Anatomy and Consequences of Exchange Control Regimes*, Cambridge: Ballinger

Bhagwati, J. (1980) 'Lobbying and Welfare', *Journal of Public Economics*, 14(3): 355–64

Bhagwati, J. (1984) 'Development Economics: What Have We Learned?', *Asian Development Review*, 2(1): 23–38

Bhagwati, J. (1986) 'Rethinking Trade Strategy' in Lewis, J.P. and Kallab, V. (eds), *Development Strategies Reconsidered*, New York and Oxford: Transaction Books

Bhagwati, J. (1987) 'Protectionism: Old Wine in New Bottles', in Salvatore, D. (ed.) *The New Protectionist Threat to World Welfare*, New York: North-Holland

Bhagwati, J. (1988) 'Export-promoting Trade Strategy: Issues and Evidence', *World Bank Research Observer*, 3(1): 27–37

Bhagwati, J. and Srinivasan, T. (1975) *Foreign Trade Regimes and Economic Development: India*, New York: NBER

Biggs, T. and Levy, B.D. (1991) 'Strategic Interventions and the Political Economy of Industrial policy in Developing Countries', in Perkins, D.H. and Roemer, M. (eds), *Reforming Economic Systems in Developing Countries*, Harvard: Harvard University Press

Bigsten, A. (1989) 'Poverty, Inequality and Development', in Gemmel, N. (ed.), *Surveys in Development Economics*, Oxford: Basil Blackwell

Bowman, M.J. (1980) 'Education and Economic Growth: An Overview', in King, T. (ed.), *Education and Income, World Bank Staff Working Papers*, No. 402, Washington, DC: World Bank

Bradford, Jr, C.I. (1982) 'The Rise of the NICs as Exporters on a Global Scale', in Turner, L. and McMullen, N. (eds), *The Newly Industrializing Countries: Trade and Adjustment*, London: George Allen & Unwin

Bradford, Jr, C. (1987a) 'NICs and the Next-tier NICs As Transitional Economies', in Bradford, C. and Branson, W. (eds), *Trade and Structural Change in Pacific Area*, Chicago: Chicago University Press

Bradford, Jr, C.I. (1987b) 'Trade and Structural Change: NICs and Next Tier NICs as Transitional Economies', *World Development*, 15(3): 299–315

Bradford, Jr, C. and Branson, W. (eds) (1987) *Trade and Structural Change in Pacific Area*, Chicago: Chicago University Press

Brander, J. and Spencer, B. (1985) 'Export Subsidies and International Market Rivalry', *Journal of International Economics*, 18: 83–100

Bruno, M. (1979) 'Stabilization and Stagflation in a Semi-Industrialized Economy', in Dornbusch, R. and Frenkel, J. (eds), *International Economic Policy, Theory and Evidence*, Baltimore: Johns Hopkins University Press

Cardoso, F. and Faletto, E. (1979) *Dependency and Development in Latin America*, Berkeley: University of California Press

Cavallo, D. (1977) 'Stagflationary Effects of Monetarist Stabilization Policies', unpublished Ph.D. Thesis, Harvard University

Chan, S. (1990) *East Asian Dynamism*, San Francisco: Westview Press

Chee, C.H. (1971) *Singapore: The Politics of Survival, 1965–1967*, London: G. Bell & Sons

Chen, E. (1979) *Hyper-Growth in Asian Economies*, London: Macmillan

Chen, E. (1989a) 'Trade Policy in Asia', in Naya, S., Urrutia, M. and Huentes, A. (eds), *Lessons in Development*, Washington, DC: International Center for Economic Growth

Chen, E. (1989b) 'Hong Kong's Role in Asia and Pacific Economic Development', *Asian Development Review*, 7(2): 26–47

Chenery, H. (1960) 'Patterns of Industrial Growth', *American Economic Review*, 50(4): 624–54

Chenery, H.B. (1979) *Structural Change and Development Policy*, London: Oxford University Press

258

Chenery, H. and Bruno, M. (1962) 'Development Alternatives in an Open Economy: The Case of Israel', *Economic Journal*, 72(1): 79–103

Chenery, H. and Syrquin, M. (1975) *Patterns of Development*, New York: Oxford University Press

Chew, S.B. (1986) ' Human Resources and Growth in Singapore', in Lim, Y.C. and Lloyd, P.J. (eds), *Singapore: Resources and Growth*, Singapore: Oxford University Press

Chia, S.Y. (1985a) 'The Role of Foreign Trade and Investment in the Development of Singapore', in Galenson, W. (ed.), *Foreign Trade and Investment: Economic Development in the Newly Industrializing Asian Countries*, Madison: University of Wisconsin Press

Chia, S.Y. (1985b) 'Singapore', in *Patterns and Impact of Foreign Investment in the ESACAP Region*, Bangkok: UN-ESCAP

Chia, S.Y. (1986) 'Direct Foreign Investment and Industrialization Process in Singapore', in Lim, Y. and Lloyd, P. (eds), *Singapore: Resources and Growth*, Singapore: Oxford University Press

Chisholm, A.H. and Tyers, R. (1985) 'Agricultural Protection and Market Insulation Policies: Applications of a Dynamic Multisectoral Policy', in Whalley, J. and Piggot, J. (eds), *New Developments in Applied General Equilibrium Analysis*, Cambridge: Cambridge University Press

Chng, M.K., Low, L., Tay, B.N. and Tyabji, A. (1986) *Technology and Skills in Singapore*, Singapore: Institute of Southeast Asian Studies

Cho, L.J. and Kim,Y.H. (1991) 'Political and Economic Antecedents of the 1960s', in Cho, L.J. and Kim,Y.H. (eds), *Economic Development in the Republic of Korea: A Policy Perspective*, Honolulu: University of Hawaii Press

Choo, H. (1975) 'Some Sources of Relative Equity in Korean Income Income Distribution: A Historical Perspective', in *Income Distribution, Employment and Economic Development in Southeast Asia*, Vols. I and II, Tokyo and Manila: Japan Economic Research Center and Council of Asian Manpower Studies

Choo, Y.J. (1990) 'McKinnon–Shaw versus the Neostructuralists on Financial Liberalization: A Conceptual Note', *World Development*, 18(3): 477–80

Chow, P.C.Y. (1987) 'Causality Between Export Growth and Industrial Development: Empirical Evidence from NICs', *Journal of Development Economics*, 26(1): 55–64

Chowdhury, A. (1992) 'External Shocks and Structural Adjustments in East Asian Newly Industrializing Economies', *Journal of International Development*, 4(5): 1–27

Chowdhury, A. and Kirkpatrick, C. (1987) 'Industrial Restructuring in a Newly Industrializing Country: The Identification of Priority Industries in Singapore', *Applied Economics*, 19(7): 915–26

Chowdhury, A. and Kirkpatrick, C. (1990) 'Human Resources, Factor Intensity and Comparative Advantage of ASEAN', *Journal of Economic Studies*, 17(6): 14–26

Chowdhury, A., Islam, I. and Kirkpatrick, C. (1988) *Structural Adjustment and Human Resources Development in ASEAN*, New Delhi and Geneva: ILO–ARTEP

Christensen, R. (1968) *Taiwan's Agricultural Development: Its Relevance for Developing Countries Today*, ER No. 39, Washington DC: US Department of Agriculture

Chung, B.S. and Lee, G.H. (1980) 'The Choice of Production Techniques by Foreign and Local Firms in Korea', *Economic Development and Cultural Change*, 29(1): 135–40

Cole, D. (1988) 'Financial Development in Asia', *Asia Pacific Economic Literature*, 2(2): 26–47

Cole, D. and Lyman, P. (1971) *Korean Development: The Interplay of Politics and Economics*, Cambridge, MA: Harvard University Press

Cole, D. and Park, Y. (1983) *Financial Development in Korea, 1945–1978*, Cambridge, MA: Harvard University Press

Cole, D. and Patrick, H. (1986) 'Financial Development in the Pacific Basin Market

Economies', in Tan, A. and Kapur, B. (eds), *Pacific Growth and Financial Inter-dependence*, Sydney: Allen & Unwin

Collins, S. and Park, W.A. (1989) 'External Debt and Macroeconomic Performance in South Korea', in Sachs, J. and Collins, S. (eds) *Developing Country Debt and Economic Performance*, Vol. 3, Chicago and London: Chicago University Press

Corbo, V., Krueger, A. and Ossa, F. (eds) (1985) *Export-oriented Development Strategies: The Success of Five Newly Industrializing Countries*, Boulder: Westview Press

Corden, M. (1979) *Inflation Exchange Rates and the World Economy*, London: Oxford University Press

Corden, W. (1984) 'Macroeconomic Targets and Instruments for a Small Open Economy', *Singapore Economic Review*, 24(2): 24–37

Corden, M. (1987) 'Relevance for Developing Countries of Recent Developmnent in Macroeconomic Theory', *World Bank Research Observer*, 2(2): 171–88

Corden, W. (1991) 'Strategic Trade Policy', in Greenaway, M., Bleaney, M. and Stewart, I. (eds) *Companion to Contemporary Economic Thought*, London and New York: Routledge

Cornia, G.A., Jolly, R. and Stewart, F. (1988) *Adjustment with a Human Face*, Oxford: Clarendon Press

Cowell, F. (1977) *Measuring Inequality*, Oxford: Philip Allan

Cromwell, J. (1977) 'The Size Distribution of Income: An International Comparison', *Review of Income and Wealth*, 23(3): 291–308

Cumings, B. (1987) 'The Origins and Development of Northeast Asian Political Economy: Industrial Sectors, Product Life Cycles, and Political Consequences', in Deyo, F. (ed.), *The Political Economy of the New Asian Industrialism*, Ithaca and London: Cornell University Press

Dahlman, C.J. (1989) 'Structural Change and Trade in the East Asian Newly Industrial Economies and Emerging Industrial Economies', in Purcell, R. (ed.), *The Newly Industrializing Countries in the World Economy: Challenges for US Policy*, New Jersey: Lynne Riemer

Darrat, A. (1986) 'Trade and Development: The Asian Experience', *Cato Journal*, 16(2): 695–700

Debeauvais, M. and Psacharopoulos, G. (1985) 'Forecasting the Needs of Qualified Manpower: Towards an Evaluation', in Hinchliffe, K. and Youdi, R. (eds), *Forecasting Skilled Manpower Needs: The Experience of 11 Countries*, Paris: UNESCO

Demery, L. and Addison, T. (1987) *The Alleviation of Poverty Under Structural Adjust-ment*, Washington, DC: World Bank

DeRosa, D. (1988) 'Agricultural Trade and Protection in Asia', *Finance and Development*, 25(4): 50–2

Deyo, F. (ed.) (1987a) *The Political Economy of the New Asian Industrialism*, Ithaca and London: Cornell University Press

Deyo, F. (1987b) 'State and Labour: Modes of Political Exclusion in East Asian Develop-ment' in Deyo, F. (ed.), *The Political Economy of the New Asian Industrialism*, Ithaca and London: Cornell University Press

Deyo, F. (1989) *Beneath the Economic Miracle: Labour Subordination in the New Asian Industrialism*, Berkeley: University of California Press

Deyo, F., Haggard, S. and Koo, H. (1987) 'Labour in the Political Economy of East Asian Industrialisation', *Bulletin of Concerned Asian Scholars*, April–June: 42–53

Dodaro, S. (1991) 'Comaparative Advantage, Trade and Growth: Export-Led Growth Revisited', *World Development*, 19(9): 1153–65

Donges, J.B. (1976) 'A Comparative Survey of Industrialization Policies in Fifteen Semi-Industrialized Countries', *Weltwirtschaftliches Archiv*, 112(4): 626–59

Dore, R. (1986) *Flexible Rigidities: Industrial Policy and Structural Adjustment in the Japanese Economy, 1970–80*, Stanford: Stanford University Press

Dornbusch, R. (1991) 'Policies to Move from Stabilization to Growth', in *Proceedings of the World Bank Annual Conference on Development Economics, 1990*, Washington, DC: World Bank

Dornbusch, R. (1992) 'The Case for Trade Liberalization in Developing Countries', *Journal of Economic Perspectives*, 6(1): 69–86

Dornbusch, R. and Park, Y. (1987) 'Korean Growth Policy', *Brookings Papers on Economic Activity*, 2: 389–454

Dorner, P. (1969) 'Review of Anthony Y.C. Koo, The Role of Land Reform in Economic Development: A Case Study of Taiwan', *American Journal of Agricultural Economics*, 5(3): 710–12

Dorner, P. and Thiesenhusen, W. (1990) 'Selected Land Reforms in East and Southeast Asia', *Asia Pacific Economic Literature*, 4(1): 65–95

Douglass, M. (1983) 'The Korean Saemaul Undong: Accelerated Rural Development in an Open Economy', in Lea, D. and Chaudhri, P. (eds) *Rural Development and State*, New York: Methuen

Easterlin, R.A. (1984) 'Why Isn't the Whole World Developed?' *Journal of Economic History*, 44(1): 1–17

Economist Intelligence Unit (1991) *Taiwan: Country Profile 1991–1992*, London: The Economist Intelligence Unit

Emery, R.F. (1987) 'Monetary Policy in Taiwan, China,' paper prepared for *San Francisco Conference on Challenges to Monetary Policy in Pacific Basin Countries*, September

Enos, J. (1989) 'Transfer of Technology', *Asia Pacific Economic Literature*, 3(1): 3–37

Enos, J. and Park, W. (1987) *The Adoption and Diffusion of Imported Technology in the Case of Korea*, London: Croom Helm

Esfahani, H. (1991) 'Exports, Imports and Economic Growth', *Journal of Development Economics*, 35(1): 1–32

Far Eastern Economic Review (1990) *Asia Year Book*, Hong Kong: Review Publishing Co.

Fei, J., Ranis, G. and Kuo, S. (1979) *Growth with Equity: The Taiwanese*, New York: Oxford University Press

Fields, G. (1979) 'Decomposing LDC Inequality', *Oxford Economic Papers*, 31(3): 437–59

Fields, G. (1984), 'Employment, Income Distribution and Economic Growth in Seven Small Open Economies', *Economic Journal*, 94(1): 74–83

Fields, G. (1985) 'Industrialization and Employment in Hong Kong, Korea, Singapore and Taiwan', in Galenson, W. (ed.), *Foreign Trade and Investment: Economic Development in the Newly Industrializing Asian Countries*, Madison: University of Wisconsin Press

Fischer, B. (1989) 'Savings Mobilization in Developing Countries: Bottlenecks and Reform Proposals', *Savings and Development*, 13(2): 117–31

Findlay, R. (1984) 'Trade and Development: Theory and Asian Experience', *Asian Development Review*, 2(2): 23–42

Fishlow, A. (1990) 'The Latin American State', *Journal of Economic Perspectives*, 4(2): 61–74

Flanders, M. and Razin, A. (eds) (1981) *Development in an Inflationary World*, New York: Academic Press

Frankel, J. (1991) 'The Cost of Capital in Japan: A Survey', *Pacific Basin Working Paper*, San Francisco: Federal Reserve Bank of San Francisco

Friedman, D. (1988) *The Misunderstood Miracle: Industrial Development and Political Change in Japan*, Ithaca: Cornell University Press

Frobel, F., Heinrichs, J. and Kreye, O. (1980) *The New International Division of Labour: Structural Unemployment in Industrialised Countries and Industrialisation in Developing Countries*, Cambridge: Cambridge University Press

Fry, M. (1984) 'Saving, Financial Intermediation and Economic Growth in Asia', *Asian Development Review*, 2(1): 82–102

Fry, M. (1985) 'Financial Structure, Monetary Policy, and Economic Growth in Hong Kong, Singapore, Taiwan and South Korea, 1960–1983', in Corbo, V., Krueger, A. and Ossa, F. (eds), *Export-oriented Development Strategies: The Success of Five Newly Industrializing Countries*, Boulder: Westview Press

Fry, M. (1988) *Money, Interest, and Banking in Economic Development*, Baltimore: Johns Hopkins University Press

Fry, M. (1989) 'Financial Development: Theories and Recent Experience', *Oxford Review of Economic Policy*, 5(4): 13–28

Fry, M. (1990) 'Nine Financial Sector Issues in Eleven Asian Developing Countries', *Working Paper*, IFGWP-90-09

Fry, M. (1991) 'Domestic Resource Mobilization in Developing Asia: Four Policy Issues', *Asian Development Review*, 19(1): 14–39

Galenson, W. (ed.) (1979) *Economic Growth and Structural Change in Taiwan*, Ithaca and London: Cornell University Press

Galenson, W. (1982) 'How to Develop Successfully – The Taiwan Model', in *Experiences and Lessons of Economic Development in Taiwan*, Taipei: Institute of Economics, Academia Sinica

Galenson, W. (ed.) (1985) *Foreign Trade and Investment: Economic Development in the Newly Industrializing Asian Countries*, Madison: University of Wisconsin Press

Gallin, B. and Gallin, R. (1982) 'Socioeconomic Life in Rural Taiwan: Twenty Years of Development and Change, *Modern China*, 8(2): 205–46

Gannicott, K. (1986) 'Women, Wages and Discrimination: Some Evidence from Taiwan', *Economic Development and Cultural Change*, 34(4): 721–30

Gannicott, K. (1990) 'The Economics of Education in Asian Pacific Developing Countries, *Asia Pacific Economic Literature*, 4(1): 40–64

Garnaut, R. (1989) *Australia and Northeast Asian Ascendancy*, Canberra: AGPS

Garnaut, R. (1991) 'Exchange Rate Regimes in the Asian-Pacific Region', *Asia Pacific Economic Literature*, 5(1): 5–26

Gee, S. (1992) 'Emerging Issues of Industrial Relations and Labour Markets in Taiwan', in Lee, C.H. and Park, F.K. (eds), *Emerging Labour Issues in Developing Asia*, Seoul and Hawaii: Korea Development Institute and East–West Centre

Geiger, T. and Geiger, F. (1973) *Tales of Two City-States: The Development Progress of Hong Kong and Singapore*, Washington, DC: National Planning Association

Gereffi, G. and Wyman, D. (eds) (1990) *Manufacturing Miracles: Paths of Industrialization in Latin America and East Asia*, Princeton: Princeton University Press

Giovannini, A. (1985) 'Savings and Real Interest Rate in LDCs', *Journal of Development Economics*, 18(2–3): 195–218

Goh, K.S. (1982) 'Dr. Goh's Press Interview', *Sunday (Straits) Times*, August

Gold, T. (1986) *State and Society in the Taiwan Miracle*, Armonk, NY: M.E. Sharpe

Government of Republic of China (various issues) *Yearbook of the Republic of China*, Taipei

Government of Taiwan Republic (1991), *Taiwan Statistical Data Book*, 1991

Grajdanzev, A.J. (1944) *Modern Korea*, New York: Institute of Pacific Relations

Greenwood, J. (1979) 'The Role of Interest Rates in the Adjustment Mechanism', *Asian Monetary Monitor*, September–October: 11–40

Griffin, K. and Ghose, A.K. (1979) 'Growth and Impoverishment in the Rural Areas of Asia', *World Development*, 7(4/5): 361–83

Griffin, K. and Khan, A. (1978) 'Poverty in the Third World: Ugly Facts and Fancy Models', *World Development*, 6(3): 295–304

Grimwade, N. (1989) *International Trade: New Patterns of Trade, Production and Investment*, London: Routledge

Grossman, G.M. (1986) 'Strategic Trade Promotion: A Critique', in Krugman, P. (ed.), *Strategic Trade Policy and the New International Economics*, Cambridge, MA: MIT Press

Haggard, S. (1986) 'The Newly Industrializing Countries in the International System', *World Politics*, 38 (2): 343–70

Haggard, S. (1988) 'The Politics of Industrialization in the Republic of Korea and Taiwan', in Hughes, H. (ed.), *Achieving Industrialization in Asia*, Cambridge: Cambridge University Press

Haggard, S. (1990) *Pathways from the Periphery: Politics of Growth in the Newly Industrializing Countries*, Ithaca and New York: Cornell University Press

Haggard, S. and Cheng, T. (1987a) *Economic Adjustment in the East Asian Newly Industrializing Countries*, Berkeley: University of California

Haggard, S. and Cheng, T. (1987b) 'State and Foreign Capital in the East Asian NICs', in Deyo, F. (ed.), *The Political Economy of the New Asian Industrialism*, Ithaca and London: Cornell University Press

Haggard, S. and Moon, C. (1990) 'Institutions and Economic Policy: Theory and a Korean Case Study', *World Politics*, 42 (January): 210–37

Harberger, A. (1981) 'In Step and Out of Step with the World Inflation: A Summary History of Countries, 1952–1976', in Flanders, M. and Razin, A. (eds), *Development in an Inflationary World*, New York: Academic Press

Harris, J.R. and Todaro, M. (1970) 'Migration, Unemployment and Unemployment: A Two-sector Analysis', *American Economic Review*, 60 (1): 126–42

Havrylyshyn, O. (1990) 'Trade Policy and Productivity Gains in Developing Countries', *World Bank Research Observer*, 5 (1): 1–24

Helleiner, G.K. (1990) 'Trade Strategy in Medium-Term Adjustment', *World Development*, 18 (6): 879–97

Heller, P. (1988) 'Fund-supported Adjustment Programs and the Poor, *Finance and Development*, 25 (4): 2–5

Hewson, J. (1981) 'The Asian Dollar Market and Monetary Policy', in Monetary Authority of Singapore, *Papers on Monetary Economics*, Singapore: Singapore University Press

Hicks, G. (1989) 'The Four Little Dragons: An Enthusiast's Reading Guide', *Asian Pacific Economic Literature*, 3 (2): 35–49

Hill, C. (1985) 'Oliver Williamson and the M-Form Firm: A Critical Review', *Journal of Economic Issues*, XIX (3): 731–49

Hill, C. (1988) 'Internal Capital Market Controls and Financial Performance in Multi-divisional Firms', *The Journal of Industrial Economics*, XXXVII (1): 72–83

Hill, H. (1990) 'Foreign Investment and East Asian Economic Development', *Asia Pacific Economic Literature*, 4 (2): 21–58

Hill, H. and Johns, B. (1985) 'The Role of Direct Foreign Investment in Developing East Asian Countries', *Weltwirtschaftliches Archiv*, 121 (2): 355–81

Hillerbrand, W. (1990) 'The Newly Industrializing Economies as Models for Establishing Highly Competitive Industrial Base – What Lessons to Learn?', in Kulessa, M. (ed.), *The Newly Industrializing Economies of Asia*, Berlin: Springer-Verlag

Hirsch, S. (1967) *Location of Industry and International Competition*, London: Oxford University Press

Hirschman, A. (1958) *The Strategy of Economic Development*, New Haven: Yale University Press

Ho, S.P.S. (1968) 'Agricultural Transformation under Colonialism: The Case of Taiwan', *Journal of Economic History*, Vol. XXVIII: 315–40

Ho, S.P.S. (1978) *Economic Development of Taiwan*, New Haven and London: Yale University Press

Ho, S.P.S. (1979) 'Decentralised Industrialisation and Rural Development: Evidence from

Taiwan', *Economic Development and Cultural Change*, 28(1): 77–96

Ho, S.P.S. (1984) 'Colonialism and Development: Korea, Taiwan, Kwantung', in Myers, R.H. and Petrie, M.R. (eds), *The Japanese Colonial Empire, 1895–1945*, Princeton: Princeton University Press

Hofheinz, R. and Calder, K.E. (1982) *The Eastasia Edge*, New York: Basic Books

'Hong Kong: Country Profile' *Sunday Mail*, 13 October 1991

Hong, S.F. (1991) 'Advancement of Science and Technology in the Private Sector in the Republic of Korea', in *Institutional Relations in Development, Development Papers*, No. 8, Bangkok: UN-ESCAP

Hughes, H. (1971) 'Singapore', in Asian Development Bank, *Southeast Asia's Economy in the 1970s*, London: Longman

Hughes, H. (ed.) (1988) *Achieving Industrialization in Asia*, Cambridge: Cambridge University Press

Hughes, H. (1989) 'Catching Up: The Asian Newly Industrializing Economies in the 1990s', *Asian Development Review*, 7(2): 128–44

ILO (various issues), *Yearbook of Labour Statistics*, Geneva: ILO

Industry Commission (1990) *Strategic Trade Theory: The East Asian Experience*, Canberra: AGPS

Islam, I. (1983) 'Issues in Inequality and Poverty During Economic Development: The Case of Indonesia', unpublished PhD. Thesis, Cambridge: Cambridge University

Islam, I. (1987) 'Manpower and Education Planning in Singapore', in Amjad, R. (ed.), *Human Resource Development: The Asian Experience*, 4: 114–150

Islam, I. (1990) *Industrial Targeting: Analytical Perspectives and the Experiences of Some Asian Economies*, New Delhi: ILO–ARTEP

Islam, I. (1992a) 'Alternative Approaches to Economic Development and the East Asian NICS' in Mackerras, C. (ed.), *Eastern Asia: An Introductory History*, Melbourne: Longman Cheshire

Islam, I. (1992b) *Between the State and the Market: The Case for Eclectic Neoclassical Political Economy*, in MacIntyre, A.J. (ed.), *Government – Business Relations in Industrialising East Asia*, Sydney: Allen and Unwin, forthcoming

Islam, I. and Kirkpatrick, C. (1986a) 'Export-led Development, Labour Market Conditions and the Distribution of Income: The Case of Singapore', *Cambridge Journal of Economics*, 10(2): 113–27

Islam, I. and Kirkpatrick, C.H. (1986b) 'Wages, Employment and Income Distribution in a Small Open Economy: The Case of Singapore', in *ILO–ARTEP Working Paper*, Bangkok and Geneva: ILO

Jacoby, N. (1966) *US Aid to Taiwan: A Study of Foreign Aid, Self-help and Development*, New York: Praeger

James, W., Naya, S. and Meier, G. (eds) (1989) *Asian Development: Economic Success and Policy Lessons*, Madison: University of Wisconsin Press

Jameson, K. and Wilber, C. (eds) (1979) *Directions in Economic Development*, Notre Dame, Indiana: Notre Dame University Press

Jaspersen, F. (1981) 'Adjustment Experience and Growth Prospects of the Semi-Industrial Economies', *World Bank Staff Working Paper*, No. 477

Jenkins, R. (1991) 'The Political Economy of Industrialization: A Comparison of Latin American and East Asian Newly Industrializing Countries', *Development and Change*, 22(2)

JERS–CAMS (1975) *Income Distribution, Employment and Economic Development in Southeast Asia*, Vols I and II, Tokyo and Manila: Japan Economic Research Center and Council of Asian Manpower Studies

Johnson, C. (1982) *MITI and the Japanese Miracle: The Growth of Industrial Policy, 1925–1975*, Stanford: Stanford University Press

Johnson, C. (1987) 'Political Institutions and Economic Performance: The Government–

Business Relations in Japan, South Korea, and Taiwan', in Deyo (ed.), *The Political Economy of the New Asian Industrialism*, Ithaca and London: Cornell University Press

Johnson, D. (1991) 'Agriculture in the Liberalization Process', in Krause, L. and Kihwan, K. (eds), *Liberalization in the Process of Economic Development*, Berkeley: University of California Press

Johnston, B. and Kilby, P. (1975) *Agriculture and Structural Transformation*, London: Oxford University Press

Johnston, B. and Mellor, J. (1961) 'The Role of Agriculture in Economic Development', *American Economic Review*, 51 (4): 566–93

Jones, L. and Sakong, I. (1980) *Government, Business, and Entrepreneurship in Economic Development: The Korean Case*, Cambridge, MA: Harvard University Press

Jung, W. (1986) 'Financial Development and Economic Growth: International Evidence', *Economic Development and Cultural Change*, 34 (2): 333–46

Jung, W. and Marshall, P. (1985) 'Exports, Growth and Causality in Developing Countries', *Journal of Development Economics*, 18 (1): 1–12

Kahn, H. (1979) *World Economic Development: 1979 and Beyond*, London: Croom Helm

Kapur, B. (1983) 'A Short-term Analytical Model of the Singapore Economy', *Journal of Development Economics*, 12: 355–76

Keesing, D.B. (1967) 'Outward-looking Policies and Economic Development', *Economic Journal*, 77 (2): 303–20

Kim, J. (1986) *Wages, Employment and Income Distribution in South Korea: 1960–83*, Bangkok and Geneva: ILO–ARTEP

Kim, J.G. (1991) 'Rural Industrialization Policy in Korea: Past Performance and Future Direction', *Korean Development Institute Working Paper*, No. 9112

Kim, L. (1988) 'The Acquisition of Technological Capability for the Assimilation of Imported Technology and the Development of Indigenous Technology: The Korean Experience', paper presented to the 17th Pacific Trade and Development Conference, Bali, 20–23 July

Kim, Y. (1987) 'Evaluation of Manpower Policies in the Republic of Korea', in Amjad, R. (ed.), *Human Resource Development: The Asian Experience*, 7: 198–220

King, R. (1977) *Land Reform: A World Survey*, Boulder: Westview Press

Kirkpatrick, C. (1988) 'Real Wages, Profits and Manufacturing Performance in the Small Open Economy: The Case of Singapore', *Mimeo*

Kirkpatrick, C. (1990) 'Export-oriented Industrialisation and Income Distribution in the Asian Newly Industrializing Countries', in van Dijk, M. (ed.), *Industrialization in the Third World: The Need for Alternative Strategies*, Marcussen, HS: Frank Cass

Kirkpatrick, C. (1992) 'Trade Policy Reform and Industrialisation in Developing Countries: The Lessons of Experience,' *Mimeo*, Griffith University

Klenner, W. (ed.) (1989) *Trends of Economic Development in East Asia*, Berlin: Springer-Verlag

Koh, A. (1990) *Booms and Busts in Modern Societies*, Singapore: Longman

Kohli, A. (1986) 'Democracy and Development', in Lewis, J.P. and Kallab,V. (eds), *Development Strategies Reconsidered*, New York and Oxford: Transaction Books

Kohsaka, A. (1987) 'Financial Liberalization in Asian NICs: A Comparative study of Korea and Taiwan in the 1980s', *The Developing Economies*, 25 (4): 325–46

Koike, K. (1988) *Understanding Industrial Relations in Modern Japan*, London: Macmillan Press

Kojima, K. (1977) *Japan and a New World Economic Order*, Boulder: Westview Press

Koo, A.Y.C. (1968) *The Role of Land Reform in Economic Development: A Case Study of Taiwan*, New York: Praeger

Koo, B.Y. (1985) 'The Role of Direct Foreign Investment in Korea's Recent Economic Growth', in Galenson, W. (ed.), *Foreign Trade and Investment: Economic Development in the Newly Industrializing Asian Countries*, Madison: University of Wisconsin Press

Krause, L. (1985) 'Introduction', in Galenson, W. (ed.), *Foreign Trade and Investment: Economic Development in the Newly Industrializing Asian Countries*, Madison: University of Wisconsin Press

Krause, L. and Kihwan, K. (eds) (1991) *Liberalization in the Process of Economic Development*, Berkeley: University of California Press

Krause, L., Koh, A. and Lee, T. (eds) (1987) *The Singapore Economy Revisited*, Singapore: Institute of Southeast Asian Studies

Kravis, I. (1970) 'Trade As The Handmaiden of Growth: Similarities Between The Nineteenth and Twentieth Centuries', *Economic Journal*, 80(320): 850–72

Krueger, A. (1974) 'The Political Economy of the Rent-seeking Society', *American Economic Review*, 64(3): 291–303

Krueger, A. (1978) *Foreign Trade Regimes and Economic Development: Liberalization Attempts and Consequences*, New York: National Bureau of Economic Research

Krueger, A. (1980) 'Trade Policy as an Input to Development', *American Economic Review*, 70(2): 288–92

Krueger, A. (1984) 'Trade Policies in Developing Countries', in Jones, R. and Kinen, P. (eds), *Handbook of International Economics*, New York: North-Holland

Krugman, P. (1984) 'Import Protection as Export Promotion: International Competition in the Presence of Oligopoly and Economies of Scale', in Kierzkowski, H. (ed.), *Monopolistic Competition and International Trade*, Oxford: Oxford University Press

Krugman, P. (1987) 'Is Free Trade Passe?', *Journal of Economic Perspectives*, 1(2): 131–44

Kulessa, M. (ed.) (1991) *The Newly Industrializing Economies of Asia*, Berlin: Springer-Verlag

Kuo, S. (1975) 'Income Distribution by Size in Taiwan: Changes and Causes', in *Income Distribution, Employment and Economic Development in Southeast Asia*, Vols I and II, Tokyo and Manila: Japan Economic Research Center and Council of Asian Manpower Studies

Kuo, S. (1983), *The Taiwan Economy in Transition*, Boulder and London: Westview Press

Kuznets, P.W. (1988) 'An East Asian Model of Economic Development: Japan, Taiwan and South Korea', *Economic Development and Cultural Change*, 36(3): S11–S44

Kuznets, S. (1955) 'Economic Growth and Income Inequality', *American Economic Review*, 45 (1): 1–28

Kwack, S.Y. (1990) 'The Economic Development of the Republic of Korea 1965–1981', in Lau, L. (ed.), *Models of Development: A Comparative Study of Economic Growth in South Korea and Taiwan*, San Francisco: ICS Press

Kwan, T.H., *et al.* (1975) *The Population of Korea*, Seoul National University

Lal, D. (1976) 'Distribution and Development: A Review Article', *World Development*, 5(9): 725–38

Lal, D. (1983) *The Poverty of Development Economics*, Hobart Paperback, No. 16, London: Institute of Economic Affairs

Lal, D. and Rajapatirana, S. (1987) 'Foreign Trade Regime and Economic Growth in Developing Countries', *World Bank Research Observer*, 2(2): 189–218

Lall, S. (1991) 'Explaining Industrial Success in the Developing World', in Balasubramanyam, V. and Lall, S. (eds), *Current Issues in Development Economics*, London: Macmillan

Lansbury, Z. and Zappala, Z. (1990) 'Korean Industrial Relations in Transition ', *Department of Industrial Relations, Working Paper* No. 13, Sydney: University of Sydney

Lau, L. (1990a) 'The Economy of Taiwan 1981–1988: A Time of Passages', in Lau, L. (ed.), *Models of Development: A Comparative Study of Economic Growth in South Korea and Taiwan*, San Francisco: ICS Press

Lau, L. (ed.) (1990b) *Models of Development: A Comparative Study of Economic Growth in South Korea and Taiwan*, San Francisco: ICS Press

Lee, C.H. (1992) 'The Government Financial System, and Large Private Enterprises in the Economic Development of South Korea', *World Development*, 20(2): 187–97

Lee, C. and Naya, S. (1988) 'Trade in East Asian Development with Comparative Reference to Southeast Asian Experience', *Economic Development and Cultural Change*, 38(3): S123–S152

Lee, C.H. and Park, F.K. (eds) (1992) *Emerging Labour Issues in Developing Asia*, Seoul and Hawaii: Korea Development Institute and East–West Centre

Lee, E. (1977) 'Development and Income Distribution – A Case Study of Sri Lanka and Malaysia', *World Development*, 5(4): 279–89

Lee, E. (ed.) (1981) *Export-led Industrialization and Development*, Bangkok and Geneva: ILO–ARTEP

Lee, E. (1984) 'Introduction', in Lee, E. (ed.) *Export Processing Zones and Industrial Employment in Asia*, Bangkok and Geneva: ILO–ARTEP

Lee, J.S. (1989) 'Labour Relations and the Stages of Economic Development', *Industry of Free China*, LXXI(4): 11–29

Lee, K.Y. (1991) 'Press Report', *The Straits Times*, 15 September

Lee, S. (1978) *Public Finance and Public Investment in Singapore*, Singapore: Singapore Institute of Banking and Finance

Lee, S.C. (1991) 'The Heavy and Chemical Industries Plan (1973–1979)', in Cho, L. and Kim, Y.H. (eds), *Economic Development in the Republic of Korea: A Policy Perspective*, Honolulu: University of Hawaii Press

Lee, T.H. (1971) *Intersectoral Capital Flows in the Economic Development of Taiwan, 1985–1960*, Ithaca: Cornell University Press

Lee, W.Y. (1985) 'Republic of Korea', in *Patterns and Impact of Foreign Investment in the ESACAP Region*, Bangkok: UN-ESCAP

Lee, Y. (1987) 'The Government in Macroeconomic Management', in Krause, L., Koh, A. and Lee, Y. (eds), *The Singapore Economy Revisited*, Singapore: Institute of Southeast Asian Studies

Levine, R. (1992) 'Financial Structures and Economic Development', *PRE Working Papers*, WPS 849, World Bank

Levine, R. and Renelt, D. (1991) 'Cross-country Studies of Growth and Policy: Methodological, Conceptual and Statistical Problems', *PRE Working Papers*, WPS 608, World Bank

Lewis, A. (1954) 'Economic Development with Unlimited Supplies of Labour', *The Manchester School*, May: 131–91

Lewis, A. (1965) *Theory of Economic Growth*, Homewood: Irwin

Lewis, A. (1980) 'The Slowing Down of the Engine of Growth', *Economic Journal*, 90(4): 555–64

Lewis, J.P. and Kallab, V. (eds) (1986) *Development Strategies Reconsidered*, New York and Oxford: Transaction Books

Li, K.T. (1988) *The Evolution of Policy Behind Taiwan's Development Success*, New Haven: Yale University Press

Li, K.T. and Yu, T.S. (eds) (1982) *Experiences and Lessons of Economic Development in Taiwan*, Taipei: Academia Sinica

Lim, C. and Lloyd, P. (eds) (1986) *Singapore: Resources and Growth*, Singapore: Oxford University Press

Lim, C., Chowdhury, A., Islam, I., *et al.* (1988) *Policy Options for the Singapore Economy*, Singapore: McGraw-Hill

Lim, L. (1989) 'Labour Standards and Development in Newly Industrializing Countries', in US Department of Labour, *Labour Standards and Development: Theoretical and Empirical Links*, Washington, DC: Bureau of International Affairs

Lim, L.Y.C. and Pang, E.F. (1991) *Foreign Direct Investment and Industrialization in Malaysia, Singapore, Taiwan and Thailand*, Paris: OECD

Lin, C. (1973) *Industrialization in Taiwan, 1946–72*, New York: Praeger

Lin, T.B. (1985), 'Growth, Equity and Income Distribution Policies in Hong Kong', *The Developing Economies*, XXIII(4): 397–411

Lin, T.B. and Ho, Y.P. (1984) *Industrial Restructuring in Hong Kong*, Bangkok and Geneva: ILO–ARTEP

Lin, T.B. and Mok, V. (1985) 'Trade, Foreign Investment and Development in Hong Kong', in Galenson, W. (ed.), *Foreign Trade and Investment: Economic Development in the Newly Industrializing Asian Countries*, Madison: University of Wisconsin Press

Lin, T.B. and Tsui, K.Y. (1991) *Industrial Restructuring: The Case of Hong Kong's Manufacturing Sector*, New Delhi: ILO–ARTEP

Lindauer, D.H. (1984) 'Labour Market Behaviour in the Republic of Korea: An Analysis of Wages and Their Impact on the Economy', *World Bank Staff Working Paper* No. 641, Washington, DC: World Bank

Linneman, H., van Dijck, P. and Verbruggen, H. (1987) *Export-oriented Industrialization in Developing Countries*, Singapore: Singapore University Press

Little, I.M.D. (1979) 'An Economic Reconnaissance', in Galenson, W. (ed.), *Economic Growth and Structural Change in Taiwan*, Ithaca and London: Cornell University Press

Little, I.M.D. (1981) 'The Experiences and Causes of Rapid Labour-intensive Development in Korea, Taiwan Province, Hong Kong and Singapore and The Possibilities of Emulation', in Lee, E. (ed.), *Export-led Industrialization and Development*, Bangkok and Geneva: ILO–ARTEP

Little, I.M.D. (1982) *Economic Development: Theory, Policy and International Relations*, New York: Basic Books

Little, I.M.D., Scitovsky, T. and Scott, M. (1970) *Industry and Trade in Some Developing Countries: A Comparative Study*, London: Oxford University Press

Long, M. and Vittas, D. (1991) 'Financial Regulations: Changing the Rules of the Games', *PRE Working Papers*, WPS 803, World Bank

Low, L. (1985) 'Privatization Policies and Issues in Singapore', *Seminar Paper*, No. 7, Singapore: Department of Economics and Statistics, National University of Singapore

Lundberg, E. (1979) 'Fiscal and Monetary Policies', in Galenson, W. (ed.), *Economic Growth and Structural Change in Taiwan*, Ithaca and London: Cornell University Press

Lutz, I. and Kihl, Y. (1990) 'The NICs, Shifting Comparative Advantage and the Product Life Cycle', *Journal of World Trade*, 24(1): 111–34

Lydall, H. (1977) 'Income Distribution During the Process of Development', *ILO Working Paper*, No. 52, Geneva: ILO

McKinnon, R. (1973) *Money and Capital in Economic Development*, Washington, DC: Brookings Institution

McKinnon, R. (1984) 'Pacific Growth and Financial Interdependence: An Overview of Bank Regulation and Monetary Control', *Pacific Economic Papers*, 117, Research School of Pacific Studies, Australian National University

McKinnon, R. (1986) 'Issues and Perspectives: An Overview of Banking Regulation and Monetary Control', in Tan, A. and Kapur, B. (eds), *Pacific Growth and Financial Interdependence*, Sydney: Allen & Unwin

McKinnon, R. (1988) 'Financial Liberalization in Retrospect: Interest Rate Policies in LDCs', in Ranis, G. and Schultz, P. (eds), *The State of Development Economics*, Oxford: Basil Blackwell

McKinnon, R. (1989) 'Financial Liberalization and Economic Development: A Reassessment of Interest-rate Policies in Asia and Latin America', *Oxford Review of Economic Policy*, 5(4): 29–54

Malkiel, G. and Malkiel, J.A. (1973) 'Male–Female Wage Differentials in Professional Employment, *American Economic Review*, 67(September): 693–705

Manning, C. and Pang, P.E. (1990) 'Labour Market Structures in ASEAN and the East Asian NIEs', *Asian-Pacific Economic Literature*, 4(2): 59–81

Martin, W. and Panoutsopoulos, V. (1991) 'The Changing Composition and Direction of

Trade and The Participation of Developing Countries', paper presented to Economic Prospect for Developing Countries Conference, 22 October

Meier, G.M. (ed.) (1985) *Leading Issues in Economic Development*, 4th edn, New York: Oxford University Press

Mellor, J. (1986) 'Agriculture on the Road to Industrialisation', in Lewis, J.P. and Kallab, V. (eds), *Development Strategies Reconsidered*, New York and Oxford: Transaction Books

Mikesell, R. and Zinser, J. (1973) 'The Nature of Savings Function in Developing Countries: A Survey of Theoretical and Empirical Literature', *Journal of Economic Literature*, 11(1): 1–26

Miners, N.J. (1981) *The Government and Politics of Hong Kong*, 3rd edn, Hong Kong: Oxford University Press

Ministry of Trade and Industry (1986) *The Singapore Economy: New Directions*, Singapore: Ministry of Trade and Industry

Mitchell, T. (1981) 'What Happens to Economic Growth When Neo-Classical Policy Replaces Keynesian? The Case of South Korea', *Institute of Development Studies Bulletin*, 13(1): 60–7

Monetary Authority of Singapore (1982) *Annual Report, 1981–82*, Singapore: Monetary Authority of Singapore

Moon, P.L. (1991) 'A Positive Grain Price Policy (1969) and Agricultural Development', in Cho, L.J. and Kim, Y.H. (eds), *Economic Development in the Republic of Korea: A Policy Perspective*, Honolulu: University of Hawaii Press

Morris, M.D. (1979) *Measuring the Condition of World's Poor: The Physical Quality of Life Index*, London: Oxford University Press

Myers, R.H and Ching, A. (1964) 'Agricultural Development in Taiwan under Japanese Colonial Rule', *Journal of Asian Studies*, 23(23 August): 555–70

Myers, R.H. and Petrie, M.R. (eds) (1984) *The Japanese Colonial Empire, 1895–1945*, Princeton: Princeton University Press

Myint, H. (1969) 'International Trade and Developing Countries', reprinted in *Economic Theory and the Underdeveloped Countries*, London: Oxford University Press, 1971

Myint, H. (1982) 'Comparative Analysis of Taiwan's Economic Development with Other Countries', *Experiences and Lessons of Economic Development in Taiwan*, Taipei: Institute of Economics, Academia Sinica

Nam, S. (1988) 'Alternative Growth and Adjustment Strategies of Newly Industrializing Countries in Southeast Asia', in Streeten, P. (ed.), *Beyond Adjustment: The Asian Experience*, Washington DC: International Monetary Fund

Nam, S.W. (1991) 'The Comprehensive Stabilisation Program (1979)', in Cho, L.J. and Kim, Y.H. (eds), *Economic Development in the Republic of Korea: A Policy Perspective*, Honolulu: Hawaii University Press

Naya, S. (1971) 'The Vietnam War and Some Aspects of Its Economic Impact on Asian Countries', *The Developing Economies*, 9(1): 31–57

Naya, S. (1988) 'The Role of Trade Policies in Industrialization of Rapidly Growing Asian Developing Countries', in Hughes, H. (ed.), *Achieving Industrialization in Asia*, Cambridge: Cambridge University Press

Naya, S. and James, W. (1986) 'External Shocks, Policy Responses and External Debt of Asian Developing Countries', in Tan, A. and Kapur, B. (eds), *Pacific Growth and Financial Interdependence*, Sydney: Allen & Unwin

Naya, S., Urrutia, M. and Huentes, A. (eds) (1989) *Lessons in Development*, Washington, DC: International Center for Economic Growth

Nixson, F. (1990) 'Industrialisation and Structural Change in Developing Countries', *Journal of International Development*, 2(3): 310–33

Norris, K. (1989) *The Economics of Australian Labour Markets*, Melbourne: Longman Cheshire

Nurkse, R. (1953) *Problems of Capital Formation in Underdeveloped Countries*, Oxford: Basil Blackwell

Nurkse, R. (1959) *Patterns of Trade and Development*, Stockholm: Almquist and Wicksell

OECD (1979) *The Impact of the Newly Industrializing Countries on Production and Trade in Manufactures*, Paris: OECD

OECD (1988) *The Newly Industrializing Countries – Challenge and Opportunity for OECD Industries*, Paris: OECD

Okhawa, K. and Rosovsky, H. (1973) *Japanese Economic Growth*, Stanford: Stanford University Press

Okimoto, D. (1989) *Between MITI and the Market: Japanese Industrial Policy for High Technology*, Stanford: Stanford University Press

Olson, M. (1982) *The Rise and Decline of Nations: Economic Growth, Stagflation and Social Rigidities*, New Haven: Yale University Press

O'Malley, W.J. (1988) 'Culture and Industrialisation', in Hughes, H. (ed.) *Achieving Industrialization in Asia*, Cambridge: Cambridge University Press

Onis, Z. (1991) 'The Logic of the Developmental State', *Comparative Politics*, October: 109–26

Osborne, M. (1987) *Southeast Asia: An Illustrated History*, Sydney: Allen & Unwin

Oshima, H.T. (1988) 'Human Resources in East Asia's Secular Growth', *Economic Development and Cultural Change*, 36 (3): S104–S122

Oster, S. (1990) *Modern Competitive Analysis*, New York: Oxford University Press

Oxaca, R. (1973) 'Male–Female Wage Differentials in Urban Labour Markets', *International Economic Review*, 14: 693–709

Pak, K.H. (1983) 'Farmland Tenure in the Republic of Korea', in *Land Tenure and the Small Farmer in Asia*, Food and Fertilizer Technology Center for the Asia Pacific Region, Taipei

Pang, E.F. and Ong, N.P. (1988) 'Labour Absorption in Hong Kong and Singapore since 1970', *Philippine Review of Economics and Business*

Pang, E.F. (1988) 'The Distinctive Features of Two City States' Development: Hong Kong and Singapore' in Berger, P.L. and Hsiao, H.M. (eds), *In Search of an East Asian Development Model*, New Brunswick: Transaction Books

Pang, E.F. (1991) 'Singapore: Market-led Adjustment in an Interventionist State', in Patrick, H. (ed.), *Pacific Basin Industries in Distress*, New York: Columbia University Press

Pang, E.F. (1992) 'Emerging Issues of Labour Markets and Industrial Relations in Singapore' in Lee, C.H. and Park, F.K. (eds), *Emerging Labour Issues in Developing Asia*, Seoul and Hawaii: Korea Development Institute and East–West Centre

Pangestu, M. (1991) 'Macroeconomic Management in the ASEAN Countries', in Ariff, M. (ed.), *The Pacific Economy: Growth and External Stability*, Sydney: Allen & Unwin

Papanek, G. (1988) 'The New Asian Capitalism: An Economic Portrait', in Berger, P.L. and Hsiao, H.M. (eds), *In Search of an East Asian Development Model*, New Brunswick: Transaction Books

Park, F.K. (1992) 'Emerging Issues of Labour Markets and Industrial Relations in Korea', in Lee, C.H. and Park, F.K. (eds), *Emerging Labour Issues in Developing Asia*, Seoul and Hawaii: Korea Development Institute and East–West Centre

Park, S.L. (1988) 'Labour Issues in Korea's Future', *World Development*, 16 (1): 99–119

Park, Y.C. (1983a) *South Korea's Experience with Industrial Adjustment in the 1970s*, Bangkok and Geneva: ILO–ARTEP

Park, Y.C. (1983b) 'Inflation and Stabilization Policies in Korea, 1960–1980', in *Conference on Inflation in East Asian Countries*, Chung-Hua Institution for Economic Research, Taipei

Park, Y.C. (1986) 'Foreign Debt, Balance of Payments, and Growth Prospects: The Case of the Republic of Korea, 1965–88', *World Development*, 14 (8): 1019–58

Park, Y.C. (1987) 'Concentration and Wage Earnings in an Open Economy: A Case Study of Korea', *International Economic Journal*, 1(1): 29–42

Park, Y.C. (1990) 'Growth, Liberalization and Internationalization of Korea's Financial Sector, 1970–89', a paper presented to *Conference on Financial Development in Japan, Korea and Taiwan*, Taipei: Institute of Economics, Academia Sinica

Park, Y.C. (1991a) 'Development Lessons from Asia: The Role of the Government in South Korea and Taiwan, *American Economic Review*, 80(2): 118–21

Park, Y.C. (1991b) 'Financial Repression and Liberalization', in Krause, L. and Kihwan, K. (eds), *Liberalization in the Process of Economic Development*, Berkeley: University of California Press

Park, Y.C. (1991c) 'Macroeconomic Developments and Prospects in East Asia', Ch. 7 in Ariff, M. (ed.), *The Pacific Economy: Growth and External Stability*, Sydney: Allen & Unwin

Parsons, K., *et al.* (1956) 'Land Tenure', in *Proceedings of the International Conference on Land Tenure and Related Problems in World Agriculture*, Madison: University of Wisconsin Press

Patrick, H. (1966) 'Financial Development and Economic Growth in Underdeveloped Countries', *Economic Development and Cultural Change*, 14(2): 174–89

Patrick, H. (1990) 'The Financial Developement of Taiwan, Korea and Japan: A Framework for Consideration of Issues', a paper presented to *Conference on Financial Development in Japan, Korea and Taiwan*, Taipei: Institute of Economics, Academia Sinica

Patrick, H. (ed.) (1991) *Pacific Basin Industries in Distress*, New York: Columbia University Press

Paukert, F. (1973) 'Income distribution at Different Levels of Development – A Survey of Evidence', *International Labour Review*, 108(2/3): 97–125

Peebles, G. (1988) *Hong Kong's Economy: An Introductory Macroeconomic Analysis*, Hong Kong: Oxford University Press

Piore, M. and Sabel, C. (1984) *The Second Industrial Divide*, New York: Basic Books

Porter, M. (1990) *The Competitive Advantage of Nations*, London and New York: Macmillan

Powelson, J. and Stock, R. (1987) *The Peasant Betrayed: Agriculture and Land Reform in the Third World*, Boston: Gunn & Hain

Prebisch, R. (1959) 'Commercial Policy in the Underdeveloped Countries', *American Economic Review*, 49(May): 251–91

Purcell, R. (ed.) (1989) *The Newly Industrializing Countries in the World Economy: Challenges for US Policy*, New Jersey: Lynne Riemer

Pye, L. (1988) 'The New Asian Capitalism: A Political Portrait', in Berger, P.L. and Hsiao, H.M. (ed.), *In Search of an East Asian Development Model*, New Brunswick: Transaction Books

Quah, J., Chee, C.H. and Meow, S.C. (1985) *Government and Politics in Singapore*, Singapore: Oxford University Press

Ragowski, R. (1987) 'Trade and the Variety of Democratic Institutions', *International Organization*, 41(2): 203–23

Ranis, G. (1978) 'Equity with Growth in Taiwan: How "Special" is the "Special Case"?', *World Development*, 6(3): 397–407

Ranis, G. (1979) 'Industrial Development', in Galenson, W. (ed.), *Economic Growth and Structural Change in Taiwan*, Ithaca and London: Cornell University Press

Ranis, G. and Schive, C. (1985) 'Direct Foreign Investment in Taiwan's Development', in Galenson, W. (ed.), *Foreign Trade and Investment: Economic Development in the Newly Industrializing Asian Counties*, Madison: University of Wisconsin Press

Rao, V. (1988) 'Income Distribution in East Asian Developing Countries', *Asian Pacific Economic Literature*, 2(1): 26–45

Rao, V. and Ramakrishnan, M.K. (1980) *Income Inequality in Singapore*, Singapore: Singapore University Press

Riedel, J. (1975) 'The Nature and Determinants of Export-oriented Direct Foreign Investment in a Developing Country: A Case Study of Taiwan', *Weltwirtschaftliches Archiv*, 111(3): 505–28

Riedel, J. (1984) 'Trade as the Engine of Growth in Developing Countries, Revisited', *Economic Journal*, 94(373): 56–73

Riedel, J. (1988) 'Economic Development in East Asia: Doing What Comes Naturally', in Hughes, H. (ed.), *Achieving Industrialization in Asia*, Cambridge: Cambridge University Press

Rieger, H. and Veit, W. (1991) 'State Intervention, State Involvement and Market Forces – Singapore and Korea', in Kulessa, M. (ed.), *The Newly Industrializing Economies of Asia*, Berlin: Springer-Verlag

Robinson, S. (1976) 'A Note on the U-Hypothesis Relating Income Inequality and Economic Development', *American Economic Review*, 66(3): 437–40

Rodan, G. (1989) *The Political Economy of Singapore's Industrialisation: National State and International Capital*, London: Macmillan

Rodrik, D. (1992) 'The Limits of Trade Policy Reforms in Developing Countries', *Journal of Economic Perspectives*, 6(1): 87–106

Rosentein-Rodan, P. (1943) 'Problems of Industrialization in Eastern and South-Eastern Europe', *Economic Journal*, 53(2): 202–11

Sachs, J. (1985) 'External Debt and Economic Performance in Latin America and East Asia', *Brookings Papers on Economic Activity*, 2: 523–64

Sah, R.K. (1991) 'Fallibility in Human Organizations and Political Systems', *Journal of Economic Perspectives*, 5(2): 67–88

Saith, A. (1987) 'Contrasting Experiences in Rural Industrialisation: Are the East Asian Successes Transferable?', in Islam R. (ed.), *Rural Industrialisation and Employment in Asia*, Bangkok and Geneva: ILO–ARTEP

Salome, B. and Charmes, J. (1988) *In-service Training: Five Asian Experiences*, Paris: Development Centre Studies, OECD

Salter, W.E.G. (1959) 'Internal and External Balance: The Role of Price and Expenditure Effects', *Economic Record*, 34(August): 226–38

Samuels, R. (1987) *The Business of the Japanese State: Energy Markets in Comparative and Historical Perspectives*, Ithaca: Cornell University Press

Saxon, E. and Anderson, K. (1982) 'Japanese Agricultural Protection in Historical Perspective', Australia–Japan Research Centre, *Pacific Economic Paper*, No. 92, Australian National University

Schultz, T. (1964) *Transforming Traditional Agriculture*, New Haven: Yale University Press

Scitovsky, T. (1985) 'Economic Development in Taiwan and South Korea: 1965–81', *Food Research Institute Studies*, XIX(3): 215–64

Scitovsky, T. (1990) 'Economic Development in Taiwan and South Korea', in Lau, L.J. (ed.), *Models of Development: A Comparative Study of Economic Growth in South Korea and Taiwan*, San Francisco: ICS Press

Scott, M. (1979) 'Foreign Trade', in Galenson, W. (ed.), *Economic Growth and Structural Change in Taiwan*, Ithaca and London: Cornell University Press

Sen, A.K. (1973) *On Economic Inequality*, Oxford: Clarendon Press

Sen, A.K. (1976) 'Poverty: An Ordinal Approach', *Econometrica*, 44(2): 219–31

Sen, A.K. (1981a) 'Public Action and the Quality of Life in Developing Countries, *Oxford Bulletin of Economics and Statistics*, 43(4): 287–317

Sen, A.K. (1981b) *Poverty and Famines: An Essay on Entitlement and Deprivation*, Oxford: Clarendon Press

Sen, A.K. (1983) 'Development: Which Way Now?', *Economic Journal*, 93(December): 745–62

Sen A.K. (1991) 'Development Strategies: The Roles of the State and Private Sectors', in *Proceedings of the World Bank Annual Conference on Develpment Economics 1990*, Washington, DC: World Bank

Shapiro, H. and Taylor, L. (1990) 'The State and Industrial Strategy', *World Development*, 18(6): 861–78

Shaw, E. (1973) *Financial Deepening in Economic Development*, New York: Oxford University Press

Singapore Science Council (1984/85) *National Survey on R&D Expenditure and Manpower*, Singapore: Singapore Science Council

Singer, H. (1988) 'The World Development Report, 1987 on the Blessing of Outward Orientation: A Necessary Correction', *Journal of Development Studies*, 24(2): 232–36

Song, B.N. (1990) *The Rise of the Korean Economy*, London: Oxford University Press

Srinivasan, T. (1985) 'Neoclassical Political Economy, the State and Economic Development', *Asian Development Review*, 3(2): 38–58

Steers, R.M., Shin, Y.K. and Ungson, G.R. (1989) *The Chaebol: Korea's New Industrial Might*, New York: Harper and Row

Steinberg, D.J. (ed.) (1987) *In Search of Southeast Asia: A Modern History*, Sydney: Allen & Unwin

Stiglitz, J. (1989) 'Financial Markets and Development', *Oxford Review of Economic Policy*, 5(4): 55–68

Stiglitz, J. (1990) *Economic Role of State*, London: Allen & Unwin

Stiglitz, J. (1991) 'Development Strategies: The Role of the State and Private Sectors', in *Proceedings of the World Bank Annual Conference on Develpment Economics 1990*, Washington, DC: World Bank

Stiglitz, J. and Weiss, A. (1981) 'Credit Rationing in Markets with Imperfect Information', *American Economic Review*, 71(3): 393–410

Streeten, P. (1979) 'A Basic Needs Approach to Economic Development', in Jameson, K. and Wilber, C. (eds), *Directions in Economic Development*, Notre Dame, Indiana: Notre Dame University Press

Streeten, P. (ed.) (1988) *Beyond Adjustment: The Asian Experience*, Washington, DC: International Monetary Fund

Streeten, P., *et al.* (1981) *First Things First: Meeting Basic Needs in Developing Countries*, New York: Oxford University Press

Sundararajan, V. and Thakur, S. (1980) 'Public Investment, Crowding-out and Growth: A Dynamic Model Applied to India and Korea', *International Monetary Fund Staff Papers*, 27(4): 814–55

Sundrum, R.M. (1990) *Income Distribution in Less Developed Countries*, London and New York: Routledge

Sung, Y. (1985) 'Economic Growth and Structural Change in the Small Open Economy of Hong Kong', in Corbo, V., Krueger, A. and Ossa, F. (eds), *Export-oriented Development Strategies: The Success of Five Newly Industrializing Countries*, Boulder: Westview Press

Takenaka, H. (1991) 'The Japanese Economy and Pacific Development', in Ariff, M. (ed.) *The Pacific Economy: Growth and External Stability*, Sydney: Allen & Unwin

Tan, A. and Kapur, B. (eds) (1986) *Pacific Growth and Financial Interdependence*, Sydney: Allen & Unwin

Taylor, L. (1979) *Macro-models for Developing Countries*, New York: McGraw-Hill

Taylor, L. (1983) *Structuralist Macroeconomics: Applicable Models for the Third World*, New York: Basic Books

Teece, D. (1986) 'Transactions Cost Economics and the Multinational Enterprise: An Assessment', *Journal of Economic Behaviour and Organization*, 7: 21–45

Timmer, P. (1988) 'Review of Hayami and Anderson', *Asian-Pacific Economic Literature*, 2(2): 66–9

Todaro, M. (1969) 'A Model of Labour Migration and Urban Unemployment in LDCs', *American Economic Review*, 59(1): 138–48

Treadgold, M. (1990) 'Macroeconomic Management in Asia-Pacific Developing Countries', *Asian-Pacific Economic Literature*, 4(1): 3–40

Tsiang, S.C. and Wu, R.I. (1985) 'Foreign Trade and Investment as Boosters for Take-off: The Experiences of the Four Asian Newly Industrializing Countries', in Galenson, W. (ed.), *Foreign Trade and Investment: Economic Development in the Newly Industrializing Asian Countries*, Madison: University of Wisconsin Press

Tullock, G. (1967) 'The Welfare Costs of Tariffs, Monopolies and Theft', *Western Economic Journal*, 5(3): 224–32

Turner, H.A. (1981) *Last Colony: But Whose? A Study of the Labour Movement, Labour Market and Labour Relations in Hong Kong*, Cambridge: Cambridge University Press

Turner, L. and McMullen, N. (eds) (1982) *The Newly Industrializing Countries: Trade and Adjustment*, London: George Allen & Unwin

Tybout, J. (1991) 'Researching Trade-Productivity Link: New Directions', *PRE Working Paper Series*, WPS 638, World Bank

Umemura, M. and Mizoguchi, T. (eds) (1981) *Quantitative Studies on Economic History of Japan Empire, 1890–1940*, Tokyo: Hitotsubashi University

UN (various issues) *Yearbook of International Trade and Statistics*, New York: United Nations

UNCTAD (1989) *Trade and Development Report 1989*, New York: United Nations

UNCTAD (various issues) *Handbook of International Trade and Development*, New York: United Nations

UNCTC (1987) *Transnational Corporations and Technology Transfer: Effects and Policy Issues*, New York

UNDP (1990) *Human Development Report, 1990*, New York

UN-ESCAP (1985) *Patterns and Impact of Foreign Investment in the ESACAP Region*, Bangkok: UN-ESCAP

UN-ESCAP (1991) *Institutional Relations in Development, Development Papers*, No. 8, Bangkok: UN-ESCAP

UNIDO (1979a) *World Industry Since 1960: Progress and Prospects*, New York

UNIDO (1979b) *Industry 2000 – New Perspective*, New York

UNIDO (1982) *Asian Industry in Figures*, New York

UNIDO (1983) *Industry in a Changing World*, New York

UNIDO (1985a) *Industry and Development Global Report, 1985*, New York

UNIDO (1985b) *Industry in the 1980s: Structural Change and Interdependence*, New York

Van Dijk, M. (ed.) (1990) *Industrialization in the Third World: The Need for Alternative Strategies*, Marcussen, HS, Frank Cass

Vernon, R. (1966) 'International Investment and International Trade in the Product Cycle', *Quarterly Journal of Economics*, 80(2): 190–207

Vogel, E. (1979) *Japan as Number One*, Cambridge, MA: Harvard University Press

Wade, R. (1988) 'The Role of Government in Overcoming Market Failure: Taiwan, Republic of Korea and Japan', in Hughes, H. (ed.), *Achieving Industrialization in Asia*, Cambridge: Cambridge University Press

Wade, R. (1990) *Governing the Market: Economic Theory and the Role of Government in East Asian Industrialization*, New Jersey: Princeton University Press

Wang, I.K.I. (1988) 'The Korean Agrarian Reform Experience: The 1949 Land Reform', *Asian Economies*, 65(June): 5–20

Westphal, L. (1990) 'Industrial Policy in an Export-propelled Economy: Lessons from South Korea's Experience', *Journal of Economic Perspectives*, 4(3): 41–59

White, G. (ed.) (1988) *Developmental States in East Asia*, London: Macmillan

Whitehill, A. (1990) *Japanese Management: Tradition and Transition*, London and New York: Routledge

Whitley, R.D. (1990) 'Eastern Asian Enterprise Structures and the Comparative Analysis of Forms of Business Organisations', *Organization Studies*, 11 (1): 47–74

Wijnbergen, S. (1982) 'Stagflationary Effects of Monetary Stabilization Policies', *Journal of Development Economics*, 10 (2): 133–169

Wijnbergen, S. (1985) 'Macroeconomic Effects of Changes in Bank Interest Rates: Simulation Results for South Korea', *Journal of Development Economics*, 18: 541–54

Williamson, O. (1975) *Markets and Hierarchies: Analysis and Antitrust Implications*, New York: Free Press

Williamson, O. (1985) *The Economic Institutions of Capitalism*, New York: Free Press

Wong, K. (1986) 'Saving, Capital Inflow and Capital Formation', in Lim, C. and Lloyd, P. (eds), *Singapore: Resources and Growth*, Singapore: Oxford University Press

Woo, J.E. (1991) *Race to the Swift: State and Finance in Korean Industrialisation*, New York: Columbia University Press

World Bank (1987a) *Korea: Managing the Industrial Transition*, Washington, DC

World Bank (1987b) *World Development Report, 1987*, New York: Oxford University Press

World Bank (1987c) *World Tables, 1987*, Washington, DC: World Bank

World Bank (1989) *World Development Report, 1989*, New York: Oxford University Press

World Bank (1990) *World Development Report, 1990*, New York: Oxford University Press

World Bank, (1991) *World Development Report, 1991*, New York: Oxford University Press

Woronoff, J. (1986) *Asia's 'Miracle Economies': Korea, Japan, Taiwan, Singapore and Hong Kong*, New York: M.E. Sharpe

Wu, P. (1992) 'The Rising Role of Asia-Pacific Countries in the Twenty-first Century', *Industry of Free China*, March: 47–65

Wu, R.I. (1991) 'Taiwan: Adjustment in an Export-oriented Economy', in Patrick, H.(ed.), *Pacific Basin Industries in Distress*, New York: Columbia University Press

Wu, Y. (1985) *Becoming an Industrialized Nation*, New York: Praeger

Yager, J. (1988) *Transforming Agriculture in Taiwan*, Ithaca: Cornell University Press

Yoon, H. (1989) 'Growing Agricultural Protectionism and Its Causes in Korea', in Klenner, W. (ed.), *Trends of Economic Development in East Asia*, Berlin: Springer-Verlag

Youngson, A.J. (1982) *Hong Kong: Economic Growth and Policy*, Hong Kong: Oxford University Press

Yu, T. and Chen T. (1982) 'Fiscal Reforms and Economic Development', in Li, K. and Yu, T. (eds), *Experiences and Lessons of Economic Development*, Taipei: Academia Sinica

Yuan, T. (1986) 'Sources of Growth Accounting for the Singapore Economy', in Lim, Y.C. and Lloyd, P.J. (eds), *Singapore: Resources and Growth*, Singapore: Oxford University Press

Yusuf, S. and Peters, K. (1984) 'Saving Behaviour and Its Implications for Domestic Resource Mobilization: The Case of Korea', *World Bank Staff Working Paper*, No. 628

Zysman, J. (1983) *Government, Markets and Growth: Financial Systems and the Politics of Industrial Change*, Ithaca: Cornell University Press

INDEX